Caribbean Island Hopping
A Handbook for the Independent Traveller
FRANK BELLAMY

SPHERE BOOKS LIMITED
30–32 Gray's Inn Road, London WC1X 8JL

First published in Great Britain by Gentry Books Limited
under the Wilton House Gentry imprint, 1979
Copyright © Frank Bellamy 1979
Published by Sphere Books Ltd,
in association with Gentry Books, 1981

For all those I am fortunate to call my friends,
and especially for those I have loved.

Printed and bound in Great Britain by
Collins, Glasgow

Contents

List of Maps

Introduction
The Eighth Continent
of the World

Some years ago the tourist boards of the various Caribbean countries produced a joint brochure headlined 'The Eighth Continent of The World'. Geographically this is a somewhat far-fetched claim; an infinite number of small islands, even when allied with three or four larger ones, do not constitute a continent. In addition, the total land area of the Caribbean is not great.

Yet the title is very apt. The Caribbean has its own personality and identity. Of course, each country has its own character, one forged principally by history, which itself was largely dictated by topography, climatic conditions, natural catastrophe and other circumstances outside the control of man. Indeed, the traveller is more likely to note the differences rather than the similarities. Perhaps these differences even enhance the Caribbean's claim to be a continent. I only know that there is no easy way to define or describe the Caribbean, so profound and varied is its personality.

As each country's character has been determined largely by its colonial history, the best way to give a background is to divide the Caribbean into language groupings corresponding to the European powers which settled and developed the area: the British, French, Spanish and Dutch. Though this classification is not perfect — it ignores the later, yet very evident, American colonization for example — I think it is the clearest way to give an impression of the Caribbean as a whole.

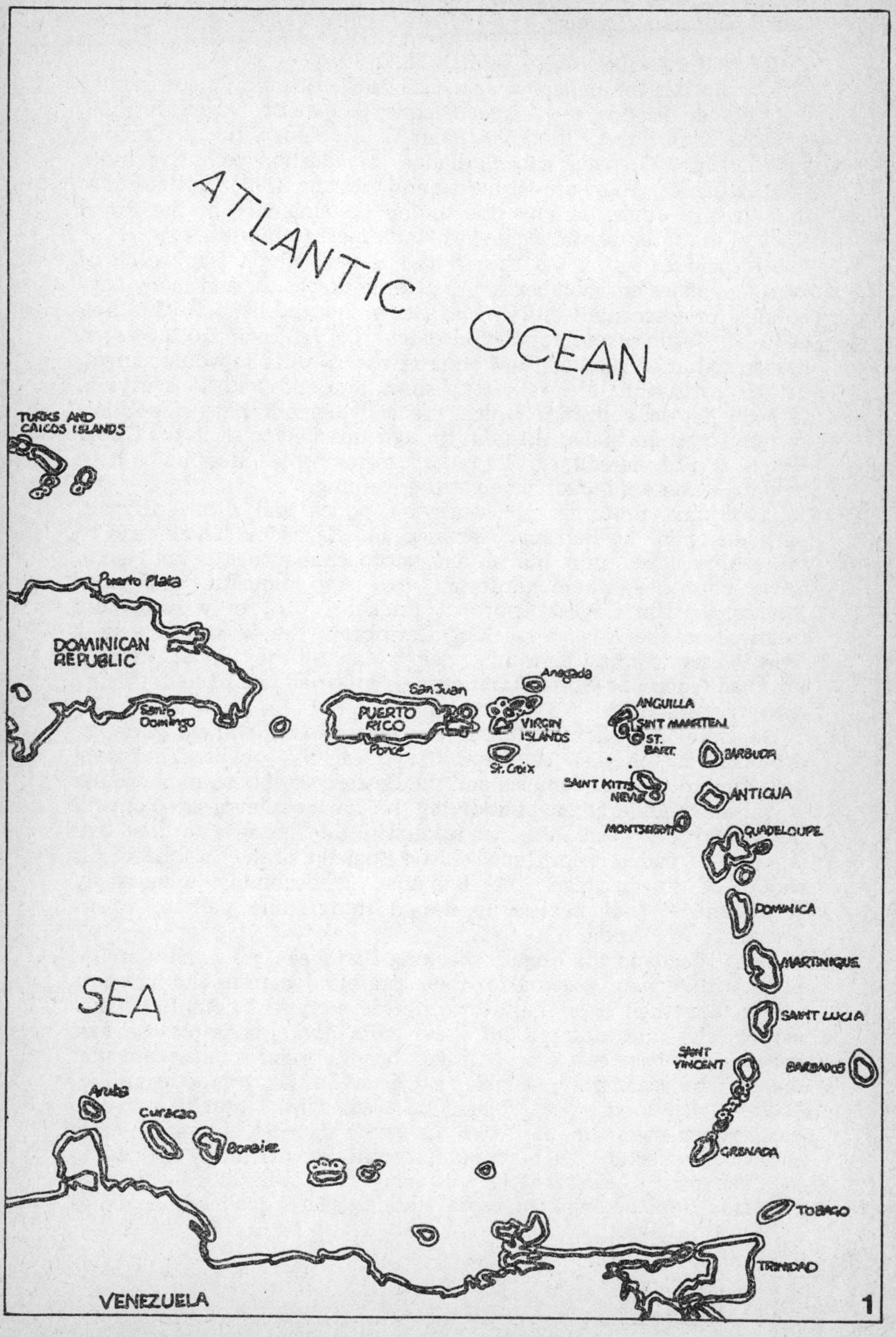

ATLANTIC

OCEAN

TURKS AND
CAICOS ISLANDS

Puerto Plata

DOMINICAN
REPUBLIC

Santo
Domingo

San Juan

PUERTO
RICO

Ponce

St. Croix

Anegada

VIRGIN
ISLANDS

ANGUILLA

SAINT MAARTEN
ST.
BART.

BARBUDA

SAINT KITTS
NEVIS

ANTIGUA

MONTSERRAT

GUADELOUPE

DOMINICA

SEA

MARTINIQUE

SAINT LUCIA

SAINT
VINCENT

BARBADOS

Aruba

Curacao

Bonaire

GRENADA

TOBAGO

TRINIDAD

VENEZUELA

1

THE ENGLISH-SPEAKING CARIBBEAN

This comprises the Bahamas, Jamaica, the Turks and Caicos Islands, the Cayman Islands, the Virgin Islands, Saint Kitts-Nevis, Anguilla, Antigua, Montserrat, Dominica, Saint Lucia, Saint Vincent, Trinidad and Tobago, Grenada and Barbados, in addition to many other smaller islands. There are far more countries and islands in this group than in any other, perhaps due to the pre-eminence of the Royal Navy in the seventeenth, eighteenth and nineteenth centuries.

With the exception of the United States' Virgin Islands, all of these countries are members of the Commonwealth, and many have colonial or associated status with Britain. Queen Elizabeth II is their head of State (except for Trinidad and Tobago, who do, however, recognize her as head of the Commonwealth). As one would expect, British institutions are well established here and traditions held in respect. Those countries which are independent have a political system based on that of Britain, though the right to sit in the Upper House is not hereditary. Those countries which nominally have colonial status are in fact largely self-governing.

Traditional uniforms are worn by police and other officials, particularly in the Bahamas, Jamaica and Barbados. These tend to make officialdom more human and approachable than is the case in those countries where uniforms are less colourful and more functional. The English sport of cricket is not only fanatically followed in the English-speaking Caribbean; the West Indies now field the world's best all-round cricket team (at the time of writing). Football (soccer to North Americans) is followed and played, though less enthusiastically.

Generally there are economic ties with Britain, though these are declining in the area as the dollar is eagerly sought. Yet travel between Britain and Jamaica and the Eastern Caribbean in particular is still much undertaken, considering the distances involved. You will notice however that this traditional influence is not constant; whereas Barbados — christened 'Little England' in the Caribbean — is proud of its heritage, the Bahamas is becoming increasingly Americanized (not necessarily a bad thing), due perhaps to its proximity to Florida.

Most islands in the English-speaking Caribbean are small, perhaps because they were selected for their strategic locations and harbours rather than their agricultural or other development potential. Their lack of size does not prevent them from having some of the best beaches you have ever seen (Antigua has 365) and some spectacular scenery and seascapes — Jamaica and Saint Lucia are good examples. This has led to the development of a substantial tourist industry, particularly over the past two or three decades. In many cases tourism has become the main industry; this is particularly the case in the Bahamas. Unfortunately this has led to what I call 'Tourist Pollution': on the one hand moral standards have declined, insofar as many of the natives prefer to sell worthless articles to the tourists, or beg money, rather than work (to be fair, they don't always have the choice); on the other hand prices have now risen to an alarming extent. Additionally, there has been little encouragement to establish other industries until now. The tourist industry, and the export earnings of those Caribbean countries dependent upon it, was reduced substantially with the onset of world recession, although during 1978 and 1979 it has shown signs of a new resurgence.

Apart from Jamaica, Trinidad/Tobago, Barbados and the US Virgin Islands, all the countries are heavily dependent on imported manufactured goods and foodstuffs. The US Virgins are classed as part of the United States, and the people reap the economic benefits which accrue from this. Jamaica, Trinidad/Tobago and Barbados are just large enough, in terms of population, to support some local manufacturing and food processing industries. The other islands do not have a population large enough to consume manufactured articles or processed foods in the quantity to make production economic. The Bahamas in particular are also faced with sobering transport problems. Thus prices are often high for the native as well as for the visitor (although it is true that in many, if not most countries the difference is substantial).

Apart from the US Virgins, these countries have had a similar history, being settled by British adventurers who introduced indentured labourers and African slaves as cheap labour. To a greater or lesser extent almost all of them were involved in the wars between the European powers which extended to the Caribbean. Independence has been recent, beginning with Jamaica in 1962. Yet the differences between these countries are remarkable. Of course the Caribbean is not a homogenous unit; but neither is the English-speaking group.

THE FRENCH-SPEAKING CARIBBEAN
Again our definition should be handled with care, but in this group I include Haiti, Guadeloupe, Saint Martin, Saint Barthelemy, Marie Galante and Martinique. Straightaway one can argue that Haiti does not belong to this group as it has been independent for a century and a half, thus having developed its own personality, and the people speak Creole (although the official language is French; but then the countryfolk of Saint Lucia speak a kind of Creole which they call 'broken French', yet the official language is English). Following that argument Haiti should have a group to itself; it is unique.

All the other islands are administratively part of France. You can buy the same goods and food you can get in France and at the same price (if you know where to go, but it is not difficult). When you enter you are entering France, and the people have complete freedom of movement between the French Antilles and France. Because they are French. Legally.

This is a two-edged sword. Although both the native and the traveller benefit from the availability of ample French produce, and the natives are provided with modern housing and so on, there is a snag; the French seem to be consciously instilling a French, rather than Caribbean, personality into the country and the people which has tended to reduce the colour and life (I think they call it 'joie de vivre') that is so much part of the Caribbean.

THE SPANISH-SPEAKING CARIBBEAN
In this group are Cuba, the Dominican Republic, Puerto Rico, San Andres and some Venezuelan islands. San Andres and the Venezuelan islands are a long way from the island-hopping route; San Andres is dealt with herein only fleetingly and the Venezuelan territories not at all. Cuba is geographically on the island-hopping route but politics make it difficult and expensive to visit in the way the independent traveller would like. In fact, because I would have obtained a visa only after several months' delay — and not necessarily then — I was unable to go, and thus apologize now to those Canadian readers for whom access is comparatively easy. So for the purposes of this book this grouping really comprises Republica Dominicana and Puerto Rico.

The Dominican Republic shares Hispaniola with Haiti but has little else in common. Independence was won in the nineteenth century, and since then the country has been hard at work trying to develop its own personality and culture in preference to that of Spain. This has largely been successful, the language now being the main link with colonial days. But no significant personality has yet emerged to replace the colonial one, and Santo Domingo in particular is in many ways characterless.

Puerto Rico has been an American Commonwealth since the Spanish-American War, though moves are now afoot to make it the 51st State of the USA. From what I could gather in San Juan this is not an overwhelmingly popular step. Here strong efforts have been made to preserve the cultural heritage, which means Old San Juan features some beautifully restored Spanish-colonial buildings. The first language is very definitely Spanish, though of course much English is spoken (not, I found, among the young, who are becoming very Americanized in other respects).

THE DUTCH-SPEAKING CARIBBEAN
Not really a group at all on an island-hopping trip, this comprises Sint Maarten (the other half of the island shared with France), Curacao, Aruba and Bonaire. Sint Maarten is on the route, but the other islands are likely to interest you only if you are continuing through to South America.

Sint Maarten is a duty-free haven (the airport is in this, the Dutch part of the island) with no customs or immigration controls between it and Saint Martin. Nearby are two other, minute, Dutch islands, Saba and Sint Eustatius.

This introduction is deliberately brief, as it seems pointless to repeat details dealt with in full in the later text. But I hope it gives more substance to the squiggles on the map and begins to give you an inkling of the variety you will discover in the Caribbean.

Part 1
Background Information

PREPARING FOR THE TRIP

Whatever itinerary you choose, this trip is going to be expensive. Proper preparation can help you to get as much as possible from the journey and may save you hundreds of dollars. Thus reading this book in its entirety well before your departure is strongly advised; sections of particular value are this one, Appendix 1, 'How to get there' and Appendix 2 'Some Suggested Itineraries'.

Air fares: These represent the highest cost of the trip, and also the area in which you can save the most money — provided you buy your tickets wisely. The information in this book is correct at the time of writing and the result of thorough research. However, air fares and regulations are notoriously volatile; like all prices, fares generally move in an upward direction (though there are exceptions) and airlines' 'special offers' and conditions are constantly changing. So although this book, and the section on transportation in particular (page 29), will be of great use to you, I suggest you also find a good travel agent — ie one who understands your requirements, which will be different to those of a tourist.

Immigration requirements: With the exception of Cuba, immigration requirements for citizens of the United States, Canada and the United Kingdom are fairly constant throughout the Caribbean. Officials everywhere resent hippies and have framed entry requirements in such a way as to deter them. Normally a visa is not required, only a tourist card which you complete whilst airborne.

But you must be able to show adequate funds to cover your intended stay, *and an onward and return ticket*. This means a continuous chain of tickets from each country you intend to visit to your country of residence. This condition can be particularly onerous for Europeans and Australasians: any traveller who is unable to fulfil it is liable to be refused entry.

My own experience is perhaps the best illustration of how this works in practice. On my first visit to the Caribbean, I was refused entry to Tortola, British Virgin Islands. This was because I had insufficient funds (I had arranged with my bank to collect money in Tortola) and incomplete travel tickets: my Barbados/London ticket could not be accepted, because I did not have a connecting ticket from Tortola to Barbados. Ironically, had I been an American citizen, a ticket covering the short distance from Tortola to Saint Thomas, US Virgin Islands, would have been sufficient.

Full details of immigration requirements are given later in the text, under each country heading. The only country likely to present difficulties is Cuba. Citizens of Canada and a few other countries are allowed entry without a visa. British and American citizens will need a visa — apply well beforehand. See page 142.

Money: Take your money in the form of US dollar Travellers Cheques and enough cash to tide you over the first couple of days. The US dollar is by far the best currency, for citizens of all nationalities; it can be used freely in shops and restaurants in many Caribbean countries. The itineraries listed on pages 23 - 29 give a rough indication of the total costs excluding air travel — which you will have bought beforehand anyway.

You will find a credit card useful — primarily for emergency cash withdrawal when you run out of money! Bank Americard (Barclaycard in the United Kingdom) is the best card for this purpose, and you will find Barclays International to be the best represented bank in the Caribbean. Master Charge is quite good for Americans, but British and Canadian travellers should note that I experienced some difficulty with its British equivalent, Access. The design on the face of this card is quite different to the Master Charge twin circles and I found that it caused a great deal of hesitancy and suspicion. (Bank Americard and Barclaycard share a common design.) First National City Bank will not issue cash against an Access card, or the Canadian equivalent, in many countries — particularly in Jamaica and Barbados.

American Express cards are the best to use when purchasing merchandise, but you will find that cash advances are limited to US$50. (Remember that meals, accommodation and goods are invariably more expensive in those establishments displaying credit card signs.)

In short, I advise Bank Americard/Barclaycard. If you have more than one credit card, take them all.

Insurance: This is very strongly recommended, particularly medical. As you are not travelling on a safari-type tour, you do not require 'expedition' insurance and can insure your baggage against loss or theft.

Vaccinations: The Caribbean is an area to which the worst infection diseases are alien. You need no innoculations to protect you from disease. Trinidad and Tobago require a vaccination against Yellow Fever at the time of writing. You should be able to produce an international certificate of vaccination against smallpox if required.

Don't forget the pills: Generally the Caribbean area can be regarded as being healthy and clean, particularly the eastern part, but there are times when you should be careful. You should not drink the water in Haiti and the Dominican Republic, for instance; in other countries — such as the Bahamas — the water is safe but undrinkable as it is brackish and rust-coloured. Many people travel with a small bottle of chlorine tablets for water purification purposes.

The only place where malaria is possible — though unlikely — is Hispaniola (Northern Haiti). You will encounter mosquitoes throughout however, so it is advisable to take some mosquito coils with you. These are also available locally. As the mosquito menace is not severe these burning coils give adequate protection. You may experience a stomach upset or mild diarrhoea, caused by the change of diet or whatever, so you would be wise to take one of the preparations which rectify this.

Luggage, clothing, etc: Keep this to a minimum — remember that you have to carry it with you when travelling. Temperatures are generally high throughout the Caribbean year-round. The 'coolest' months are January and February, yet even then you may well find daily temperatures over 80°F (27°C). The rainy season is not constant for the area as a whole but is generally in the period August through November. Evenings can be cool, especially in the mountainous areas.

Take at least one sweater, an anorak or jacket and a light plastic raincoat. Additional clothes, sunglasses, etc can be more expensive than in your local store, so make sure you are well-equipped before departure. When packing, I always try to strike an even balance between the requirements of little weight and the need to avoid too frequent washing (laudromats can be very difficult to find in the Caribbean). Sleeping bags are not necessary: I found clean sheets in even the cheapest accommodation.

A cheap watch is a good idea. In many parts of the Caribbean, watches are scarce and regarded as a sign of wealth. There may well be a definite link between being hustled and showing off an expensive-looking timepiece. I am advised that Timex produce a plastic watch which sells at a few dollars and keeps good enough time: this could well be worth investigating.

If you are clean and tidy, with all necessary documentation and adequate funds, you should not find that a backpack is resented — though you may feel that a large holdall is more convenient anyway.

Take a camera and plenty of film.

Experienced travellers should not need, and may perhaps resent, a detailed equipment list. If you have travelled extensively, skip the following paragraph. First-timers may, however, find it useful if I detail what I took with me:

Passport; innoculation certificates; driving licence; insurance certificate.

Travellers Cheques and cash (in US$); separate list of Travellers Cheques' serial numbers; credit cards; air and other travel tickets.

Books and other useful literature; business cards (or cards with your name and home address).

Camera, accessories and film.

Denim suit; two pairs of jeans; pair of shorts; swimming trunks; two pairs of shoes (one pair can be very light: chukka boots, baseball boots or sandals); five shirts; four T-shirts; sweater; socks; handkerchieves; underwear.

Toilet requisites; sunglasses; polythene bags (useful for spare shoes, soiled laundry and leaking bottles).

This I carried in one largish holdall and two shoulder bags (one of which is a small camera bag).

SOME SUGGESTED ITINERARIES

There is so much variety in the Caribbean that the only way to see everything and travel everywhere is to allow several months for the trip. In practice, however, one can see and experience a great deal in a matter of weeks, visiting one part only. You should remember that it is impossible to do anything quickly in the Caribbean, particularly once you have fallen into the rhythm of island living.

Here are a number of itineraries with approximate costs for a single person, travelling during the winter (peak) season. The costs reflect a mixture of living as the natives and as a tourist, and take account of the fact that good meals will occasionally be taken and a drunken night out be sometimes indulged in. There are thus many ways of reducing the costs quoted here: travelling as part of a group or half a couple, making the trip out of season (16 April to 16 December), or 'going native' for the entire duration of the trip. But remember that it is very easy to underestimate exactly how expensive the Caribbean is: don't attempt the trip on radically less than the costs I quote.

Please note that these costs include everything *except air travel*. To work out your total costs, choose your itinerary and then turn to Appendix 1 'How to Get There'. This is divided into three sections — giving information on flights from the USA, Canada and Europe — and provides detailed air travel costings relating to each of the itineraries described below.

Part 1: Background Information

Itinerary One: The Bahamas to Barbados; 60 Days; US$1300 to US$1400.

Day	
1	Arrive Nassau
2	Nassau and New Providence
3	Nassau and New Providence
4	Nassau to South Eleuthera (Rock Sound)
5	South Eleuthera
6	Rock Sound to North Eleuthera
7	North Eleuthera (Current, Spanish Wells, etc)
8	North Eleuthera
9	North Eleuthera
10	The Current to Nassau
11	Nassau
12	Nassau to Andros
13	Andros
14	Andros
15	Andros
16	Andros to Nassau
17	Nassau to Montego Bay
18	Montego Bay
19	Montego Bay
20	Montego Bay to Negril
21	Negril
22	Negril
23	Negril to Mandeville
24	Mandeville
25	Mandeville to Spanish Town
26	Spanish Town to Kingston
27	Kingston
28	Kingston to Port-au-Prince
29	Port-au-Prince
30	Port-au-Prince
31	Port-au-Prince
32	Port-au-Prince to Cap Haitien
33	Cap Haitien
34	Cap Haitien
35	Cap Haitien to Port-au-Prince
36	Port-au-Prince to Santo Domingo
37	Santo Domingo
38	Santo Domingo to San Juan
39	San Juan
40	San Juan
41	San Juan to Saint Thomas
42	Saint Thomas to Tortola (British Virgin Islands)
43	Tortola
44	Tortola
45	Tortola to Saint Thomas and Antigua

46   Antigua
47   Antigua
48   Antigua
49   Antigua to Guadeloupe
50   Guadeloupe
51   Guadeloupe
52   Guadeloupe
53   Guadeloupe to Saint Lucia
54   Saint Lucia
55   Saint Lucia
56   Saint Lucia to Barbados
57   Barbados
58   Barbados
59   Barbados
60   Barbados; return home

Itinerary Two: the Grand Tour, Bahamas to Trinidad; 100 Days; US$2000 to US$2200: Although this is the longest and most exhaustive of the itineraries suggested here, even this does not include every island — or even every country for that matter. Notable exceptions are the Turks and Caicos Islands, the Cayman Islands, Anguilla and Barbuda. Nevertheless anyone hoping to undertake this itinerary should note that it is more likely to take more than 100 days rather than less.

Continue exactly as in Itinerary One up to and including Day 28, Kingston to Port-au-Prince. Then as follows:

Day 29   Port-au-Prince
30   Port-au-Prince
31   Port-au-Prince to Jacmel
32   Jacmel
33   Jacmel to Port-au-Prince
34   Port-au-Prince and Petionville
35   Port-au-Prince
36   Port-au-Prince to Cap Haitien
37   Cap Haitien
38   Cap Haitien
39   Cap Haitien to Tortuga
40   Tortuga
41   Tortuga to Cap Haitien
42   Cap Haitien to Port-au-Prince
43   Port-au-Prince to Santo Domingo
44   Santo Domingo
45   Dominican Republic
46   Dominican Republic
47   Dominican Republic
48   Santo Domingo
49   Santo Domingo to San Juan

97   Tobago
98   Tobago to Trinidad
99   Trinidad
100   Trinidad; return home

Itinerary Three: the Western Islands; Bahamas, Jamaica, Haiti, Turks and Caicos Islands; 44 Days; US$1000 to US$1100: This itinerary is very flexible and can be altered according to which air fare arrangements are most suitable. For example, Nassau may be chosen as the starting and finishing point, and return air fares used on an excursion basis. On the other hand, it may make more economic sense if Port-au-Prince is chosen for the excursion fare, with stopovers at Nassau and Kingston written into the ticket (it is possible to fly direct from Port-au-Prince to Nassau with Bahamasair). Travellers resident in the southern USA could end their holiday in Grand Turk, and fly direct to Miami with Mackey.

British travellers may prefer to use Kingston as the starting and finishing point, so that the very cheap Advance Booking Charter or Earlybird fares can be used for transatlantic travel (but note that Earlybird tickets are not really supposed to be used for this purpose, so you may need to be discreet concerning your intentions).

If you are travelling on an excursion ticket valid for 45 days, be sure to arrive at your turnaround point before it expires. If you have booked on a charter flight or an Earlybird, you will have a specific date and flight written into your ticket: you would be well advised to plan for the time spent in the town named as your turnaround point to be at the end of your trip rather than at the beginning — if you miss your flight, it will cost you a lot of money to get home.

Proceed exactly as in Itinerary One up to and including Day 34; then continue as follows:

Day 35   Cap Haitien to Turks and Caicos Islands
     36   Turks and Caicos Islands
     37   Turks and Caicos Islands
     38   Turks and Caicos Islands
     39   Turks and Caicos to Great Inagua (Bahamas)
     40   Great Inagua
     41
  & 42   Great Inagua to Nassau
     43   Nassau
     44   Nassau; return home

Itinerary Four: The Bahamas to the Virgin Islands; 54 Days; US$1100 to US$1200: This itinerary is really intended for Americans living in the east coast cities. New Yorkers can benefit by using the very cheap air fares from San Juan to New York, whilst residents in Miami can also make cost savings. There are no excursion fares from New York to San Juan, so the time you take over the trip is not of great importance.

The trip includes travel in the Greater and Lesser Antilles in about equal proportions. Thus while there is adequate opportunity for lazing on beaches and sailing in yachts, there is also a fair amount of overland travel in Hispaniola and Puerto Rico.

Proceed as in Itinerary One up to and including Day 16; then continue as follows:

Day 17

& 18	Nassau to Great Inagua
19	Great Inagua
20	Great Inagua to the Turks and Caicos Islands
21	Turks and Caicos Islands
22	Turks and Caicos Islands
23	Turks and Caicos Islands
24	Turks and Caicos Islands
25	Turks and Caicos Islands to Cap Haitien
26	Cap Haitien
27	Cap Haitien
28	Cap Haitien to Port-au-Prince
29	Port-au-Prince
30	Port-au-Prince
31	Port-au-Prince
32	Port-au-Prince to Santo Domingo
33	Santo Domingo
34	Dominican Republic
35	Dominican Republic
36	Dominican Republic
37	Dominican Republic
38	Santo Domingo
39	Santo Domingo to San Juan
40	San Juan
41	San Juan
42	Puerto Rico
43	Puerto Rico
44	Puerto Rico
45	Puerto Rico
46	San Juan to Saint Thomas
47	Virgin Islands (US and British)
48	Virgin Islands
49	Virgin Islands
50	Virgin Islands
51	Virgin Islands
52	Virgin Islands
53	Saint Thomas to San Juan
54	San Juan: return home

Itinerary Five: The Eastern Caribbean; 40 Days;US$800 to US$900:
This is a very flexible itinerary. Islands can be deleted or added as required, and time spent in each altered as it suits you or according to the available yacht transportation, as it is envisaged that much of your travel will be by small boat. I can suggest two ways in which you can book your long distance flights economically: one is to use an exursion fare based on Port of Spain, Trinidad, with a stopover on the outward journey at Antigua, and on the return journey at Barbados. You are not likely to use part of the ticket (the section between Antigua and Port of Spain), but you may find that this works out to your financial benefit in the long term. Another possibility, available to European travellers, is to use the excellent services of International Caribbean Airways, who fly from London and Luxembourg to Barbados. They offer a one way fare from Luxembourg to Barbados for £163 at the time of writing. In addition it is possible to book an Advance Booking Charter (return fares from London start at £241) or Earlybird ticket (though again you should be discreet if you have an Earlybird ticket as it is not meant for this purpose). You would then book a separate ticket Barbados/Antigua and Antigua/Port of Spain/Barbados which would satisfy all immigration requirements; any unused sectors (you would of course have all intended stopovers written into this second ticket) would be refundable.

Day 1 Arrive Antigua
    2   Antigua
    3   Antigua
    4   Antigua
    5   Antigua to Guadeloupe
    6   Guadeloupe
    7   Guadeloupe
    8   Guadeloupe
    9   Guadeloupe to Dominica
    10   Dominica
    11   Dominica
    12   Dominica
    13   Dominica to Martinique
    14   Martinique
    15   Martinique
    16   Martinique to Saint Lucia
    17   Saint Lucia
    18   Saint Lucia
    19   Saint Lucia
    20   Saint Lucia to Saint Vincent
    21   Saint Vincent
    22   Saint Vincent
    23   Saint Vincent to the Grenadines
    24   The Grenadines

All these itineraries should be treated as a guide to help you when planning and travelling, rather than as definite schedules. Very often you will find it impossible to travel on a particular day, so that you will spend a longer or shorter time in a certain place. For instance, mailboat sailings in the Bahamas are not only infrequent but also irregular; if a boat runs once a week (for example The Current to Nassau) there is a 7 to 1 chance that it will not sail on the day it should. Another example is the frequency of scheduled flights from Kingston to Port-au-Prince — two a week. And if you intend to sail by yacht in the eastern Caribbean, you will have to trim your requirements to suit the captain's.

TRANSPORTATION

This section deals solely with your transportation within the Caribbean. Long distance travel information concerning airlines, shipping companies, routes and fares is dealt with in Appendix 1, 'How to Get There.'

Air Travel: Ideally you would want to undertake very little of your travel by this means, even though you will probably embark on this trip with an air ticket covering the whole journey. The romantic conception of Caribbean Island Hopping implies inter-island cruising by private yacht. In practice however you will find that you have to make great use of scheduled air services. The extent of this use will depend on your itinerary and the time at your disposal. So it is as well to be aware of the air travel facilities available.

Private planes: It is of course possible to 'hitch' a lift in a private plane if there is a seat vacant. To do this you should go down to the airstrip or part of the airport which handles this traffic. Depending on the size of the airport, level of activity and facilities available you would then ask around or put up a notice in a prominent place.

Often a small plane may be chartered by a group who find they have one or two seats spare. They are usually very happy to have you along in exchange for a few dollars towards costs. Your success in using this type of travel will of course be mainly dependent on your own initiative, although I give pointers in the later text.

Scheduled flights: the Western Caribbean: Bahamasair operate regular services to the more important Bahamas islands and also international services to Miami, the Turks and Caicos Islands and Port-au-Prince; details are given in the chapter on the Bahamas. Flying is less fun and much more expensive than the mailboats however (particularly if you include taxi fares to and from the airports) so it is unlikely that you will use these services unless stranded on an out island with a schedule to meet.

Between Nassau and Jamaica you will find small boat travel well-nigh impossible and anyway undesirable. The large boats which occasionally make the trip are either cargo ships or cruise liners. You may be lucky and get a cargo boat for a few dollars, but in most cases it is a case of taking a scheduled flight. In practice this means the Air Jamaica flight from Nassau to Montego Bay. Food and service are good, and on a cloudless day you will be treated to splendid aerial views of the Bahamas and Cuba. Flights are daily.

If taking the alternative route to Haiti through the Turks and Caicos Islands (see page 134) you will miss Jamaica. You will probably find it easy to take a boat or private plane, but there are scheduled services if you require them.

I spent two days trying to get a private yacht, cargo/passenger ship, fishing boat or small plane from Kingston to Port-au-Prince. In the end I had to settle for the scheduled flight, which only plys the route four times a week. It seems that Kingston to Port-au-Prince is not a journey commonly undertaken.

Hispaniola, Puerto Rico and the Virgin Islands: You would think that it is easy to travel overland from Port-au-Prince to Santo Domingo, or better still from Cap Haitien along the splendid north coast of Hispaniola to Puerto Plata. It isn't. In fact you should forget the north coast route altogether unless you have boundless patience, stamina and iniative and plenty of time. It is marginally easier to travel by road from Port-au-Prince to Santo Domingo. There is a chance of taking a cargo/passenger ship, but the shape of the island makes it an unnecessarily long trip. So in practice you will have to take the daily Air Florida or Prinair flights.

From Santo Domingo onwards travel becomes much easier. Many airlines fly regular services between Santo Domingo and San Juan, including Aerovias Quisqueyana who make two or three trips in each direction every day. Other airlines include Eastern, but there are financial incentives for taking Quisqueyana, not to mention the fun of travelling in a 25-year-old Lockheed Constellation, an odd-looking yet comfortable aircraft.

You can have even more fun flying from San Juan to the Virgin Islands, and within the Virgin Islands. For these are Antilles Airboat waters with regular short hops, downtown to downtown (thus saving taxi fares and time), by the 'Goose' flying boats. More conventional air travel is also freely available.

The Eastern Caribbean: This is the area in which private yachts abound, so that you will doubtless leave home with the intention of using these as much as possible. However time and other pressures may force you to do some flying, and in any event you will need an air ticket right through to satisfy immigration requirements. Inter-island flights are regular and there are a number of airlines, although only one has a network covering almost all of this area — LIAT (Leeward Islands Air Transport). Although they enjoy a mixed reputation I found the planes (Hawker Siddely 748s and Norman Britten Islanders) comfortable and inflight service pleasant.

Ships and Boats: Cruise and passenger ships are generally much more expensive than flying, largely because they provide sumptuous meals and accommodation and are very expensive to operate. You also have the disadvantage of being among tourists. Some cargo boats take passengers, but these are becoming rarer and may not be as cheap as you expect. To book and ascertain sailings you should visit downtown agents and/or the Harbourmaster's office at the port. Obviously sailings are much more frequent between those countries which trade extensively with each other.

Logically, private yachts are more common in those areas where sailing among the islands is a joy. This means the smaller islands, and principally the Eastern Caribbean and Virgin Islands. It is a good idea to plan beforehand which areas you will visit by this means, if possible, so that you can allow time to make arrangements. Notable areas best visited by cruising yacht are the Exuma Cays in the Bahamas and the Grenadines, between Saint Vincent and Grenada. To get passage on a yacht you should go down to the marina and put up a notice on the noticeboard (where else) stating where you want to go and when. Check back and you will find an offer attached. Many owners often need an extra hand and for a few dollars will be glad to take you. Your personal appearance and articulateness can make a difference here. Alternatively you can seek out the social centre patronised by the yachting fraternity and make a personal approach, but you should note that prices of drinks, etc will be very high.

Land Transportation: Not all countries have a bus service. Only two Bahamas islands, for example, New Providence and Grand Bahama, have buses, and schedules are limited. The British Virgin Islands and some others have no buses at all. Of course regular services exist in the Greater Antilles, and usually at reasonable cost. Jamaica has country buses and minibuses, Haiti the amazing 'tap-taps', Republica Dominicana comfortable and inexpensive coaches and Puerto Rico has city buses (in San Juan) and one cross-island route. Many of the smaller islands — for example Barbados, Saint Lucia, Antigua and Guadeloupe — have various kinds of services at a wide range of prices (Guadeloupe is exceptionally expensive).

Taxis are of course everywhere, but often you can also find public taxis ('publiques' or 'publicos') which are a cheap alternative to taxis or an expensive alternative to buses.

Trains are rarer, as you would expect, yet there is an extensive network in Cuba, two principal routes in Jamaica, a very limited service in the Dominican Republic and a route round most of the coast in Puerto Rico.

This section is only a brief summary as the correct place for detailed information is in the main body of the text. Like all these preliminary sections the intention is to aid your planning for the trip. Full details, often in tabular form, are given when needed in the text.

ACCOMMODATION

What do you require from a hotel? Personally I require only a bed with clean sheets, a shower with water and a washbasin with shaving mirror. A desk and chair are useful extras. I also prefer the hotel to be either centrally located or near arrival and/or departure point(s), on the basis that it is better to walk without luggage than with it.

Although all the countries in the Caribbean are different, I found a fairly consistent pattern of accommodation throughout. This I have divided here into three categories: tourist hotels, guest houses and native lodgings. Note that these generalisations are elastic.

Tourist hotels: Tourist hotels exist to cater for holidaymakers, not travellers. The fact is that most holidaymakers like to have comfortable facilities at least equal to, if not superior to, their own homes. Many tourists nowadays have a preference for large, modern, concrete and glass buildings with swimming pool, restaurant and bars. They often expect these hotels to be standardised to the extent that the hotel they visit in say, Jamaica, is similar to the one in Singapore. I often find that characteristics of these hotels are large size, high prices, range of overpriced additional services (boutiques, casinos etc) and mediocre service. The tourist hotels I stayed in often lacked basic services — for example the Beau Rivage in Port-au-Prince, Haiti usually had no water in the showers during my stay (some guests showered in the fountains outside the hotel). There are of course tourist hotels which offer excellent facilities in an authentic Caribbean style, and many of these are mentioned in the text. As this book is primarily aimed at travellers however, rather than tourists, I do not normally recommend accommodation from this category.

Guest houses and business hotels: This is the accommodation I generally recommend if available. Generally you get what you pay for, a nice clean room, usually but not always with private facilities, all utilities and often meals. Guest houses in Haiti are particularly good value. The trouble is, guest houses are not always listed by the tourist boards, so you need a book like this to help you find them.

Native lodgings: Many natives stay in tourist hotels and guest houses of course. So I use this subtitle as a generic term to encompass the cheapest accommodation I found, from YMCA to whorehouse. I do not usually recommend this type of accommodation because many people would prefer not to use it (standards of cleanliness, hygiene and facilities are generally lower — private bathrooms are unusual for example). On the other hand, to many readers this is the only way to travel. There are two distinct advantages: you are living with the natives, and making cost savings which may add up to hundreds of dollars.

Services provided:
EP: European plan — room only
CP: Continental plan — room and breakfast (breakfast may vary from rolls and coffee to full American or English breakfast).
MAP: Modified American plan — room, breakfast and dinner.
AP: American plan — room and three meals a day
Unless otherwise stated, prices refer to accommodation on European plan.

Room capacity:
S: single room
D: double room
T: triple room
Q: quadruple room
Seasonal variations:
Unless otherwise stated, prices refer to the winter season, 15 December to 15 April. Summer prices will be lower in most cases.

Recommended form of payment: As the Caribbean is traditionally a tourist area, many (if not most) hotels quote prices in US dollars rather than local currency. There is no general rule governing the form of payment for accommodation. Usually, you will find that tourist hotels prefer to be paid in US dollars, while guest houses, business hotels and native lodgings prefer local currency. The main exception to this is Barbados, where even inexpensive guest houses like to be paid in US dollars. The currencies quoted in the accommodation tables are thus not consistent, as they reflect each proprietor's preference.

Part 2
Nassau to Port-au-Prince

THE BAHAMAS

On reaching the Bahamas, Columbus wrote as follows: 'This country excels all others as far as the day surpasses the night in splendour: the natives love their neighbours as themselves; their conservation is the sweetest imaginable; their faces always smiling; and so gentle and affectionate are they that I swear to your Highness there is not a better people in all the World.'

The Spanish soon changed all that. The gentle Arawak Indians were transported as slaves to Cuba and Hispaniola (now Haiti and the Dominican Republic) and officially became extinct in the Bahamas. It is indeed unlikely that any pure-blooded Arawaks remain, but it is pretty certain (though not official) that many Bahamians can claim Arawak forefathers. Today the majority of Bahamians are black, descendants of slaves brought from Africa, with a scattering of whites (many of whom are immigrants, rather than indigenous) and Creoles. There are also some Haitien refugees and Jamaicans. If Columbus returned today to the out islands (or Family Islands, as Bahamians call them) he would be able to write the above quotation again, word for word.

Whilst on the subject of Columbus, let us get him out of the way here and now. It seems that during his travels he discovered just about every Caribbean country with the exception of Barbados and maybe a couple more. That's all right, but the trouble is that most tourist brochures begin with 'Christopher Columbus discovered Buckley Funk on his second voyage, on June 31st 1492........' or

35

similar. And it is not long before one is tired of hearing about him. So apart from almost obligatory references to the supposed site of his first landfall and the supposed site of his burial, there will be no further use of his name in this book.

Some background : Counting every speck of land in the group, the Bahamas comprises some 700 islands. Less than 30 are considered 'important' in terms of population or size.

Around the beginning of the eighteenth century, British interest was strong enough to introduce a governor and drive away the pirates -- this was a haunt of the infamous Blackbeard -- thus giving the islands a more important colonial status (they had previously been administered by British commercial interests). With brief interruptions by a short spell of Spanish occupation, and an even shorter American invasion, the Bahamas remained a Crown Colony until independence in 1973.

Tourism is the main industry. The beginnings of this trade developed between the wars, but it is only since World War 2 that the Bahamas became a very important tourist centre. Tourism is mainly centred around Nassau, the capital, on the island of New Providence, and Freeport on Grand Bahama. The glitter and style of the gaming fraternity is more evident on the latter. Recently the more relaxed principally Bimini, Exuma and the Berry Islands — have proved a great attraction for those tourists who want something out of the ordinary.

Whilst still a British colony the Bahamas attracted foreign business and finance as a tax haven. Many 'offshore' banks, freed from many of the restrictions imposed by the major capitalist countries, are based here. Since independence the government has done nothing to discourage this trend.

Form of government: The political system is based on that of the United Kingdom, with two houses of Parliament, government headed by a Prime Minister and an offical opposition. Queen Elizabeth 2 is the Head of State. For the last 12 years or so the government has been the PLP, headed by Mr Pindling, usually referred to by the people as 'this black government' or 'the coloured government'. Most of the people I spoke to were pleased with the work of this administration, particularly the people of Andros. This island, the largest, had traditionally been one of the most undeveloped. Over the last few years the government has made great strides in development, principally in the areas of greatest need and importance, agriculture, education and transportation. Foreign investment, mainly American, is working with the Bahamians in cultivating crops and livestock by modern means, the frequency of air services has been increased, roads and bridges are being built and repaired and schools built. The opposition has been splintered into factions and is now being reformed into an effective counterforce. This opposition is supported by the Nassau evening paper, the *Tribune*, which is thus hypercritical

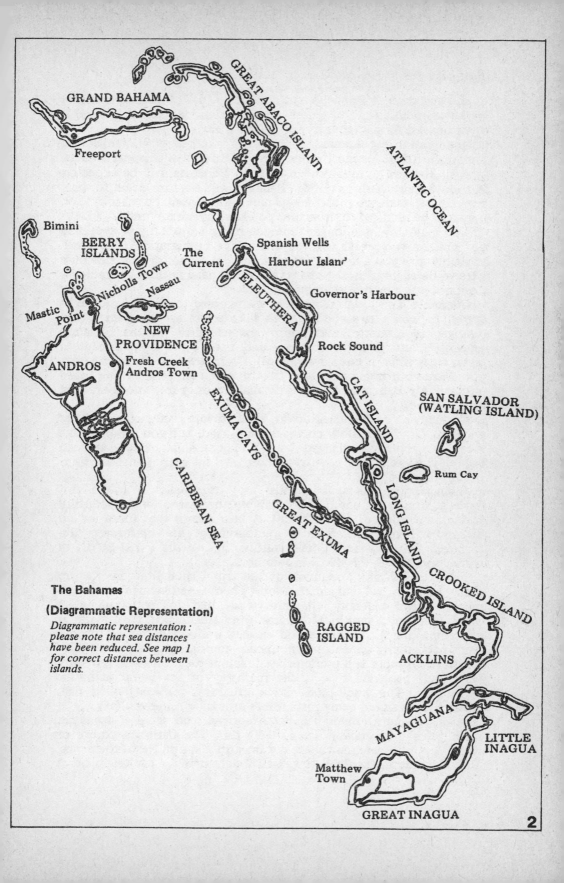

GRAND BAHAMA

Freeport

GREAT ABACO ISLAND

ATLANTIC OCEAN

Bimini

BERRY ISLANDS

The Current

Spanish Wells

Harbour Island

Nicholls Town

Nassau

Mastic Point

ELEUTHERA

Governor's Harbour

NEW PROVIDENCE

Fresh Creek
Andros Town

Rock Sound

ANDROS

CAT ISLAND

SAN SALVADOR
(WATLING ISLAND)

EXUMA CAYS

Rum Cay

CARIBBEAN SEA

GREAT EXUMA

LONG ISLAND

CROOKED ISLAND

The Bahamas

(Diagrammatic Representation)

*Diagrammatic representation :
please note that sea distances
have been reduced. See map 1
for correct distances between
islands.*

RAGGED ISLAND

ACKLINS

MAYAGUANA

LITTLE INAGUA

Matthew
Town

GREAT INAGUA

2

of the government's policies and conduct. Most of its readers (that I spoke to) advised me to ignore the editorial, and indeed I found it described a different country to the one I saw.

Immigration requirements: No visa is required of United States, Canadian, British or most other Western European passport holders. All nationalities, except residents of the Bahamas, will be expected to show an air ticket out of the Bahamas and a return ticket to their country of residence (boat tickets may be accepted, but check). You may also be required to show that you have adequate funds.

You may stay here longer than you had planned: if you expect to be here for two weeks ask for three. The immigration officer will probably give you a few days more than you request in any case. It is wise to be at your most presentable when passing through immigration; not just here, but everywhere.

Customs: The usual allowances with regard to smokes and drink apply. In fact it is a good idea to take advantage of them if you indulge, as cigarettes and liquor are expensive in the Bahamas (cigarettes are 75 cents or more and beer $1 a time, except in restaurants when it costs even more). So buy your duty-frees before you leave your home airport or on the plane (travellers using International Air Bahamas should note that no duty-free goods are sold on the plane).

Currency: The Bahamas dollar, divided into 100 cents, is at par with the US dollar. Both currencies are used, but you should make sure that you have changed your Bahamas dollars into American before you leave the country. There are no currency restrictions which will affect you.

Climate: The Bahama islands are principally — when not entirely — made of coral. This is largely the reason for the beautiful turquoise colour of the sea. But it also means that there are no highlands here. Consequently temperatures are uniformly subtropical. You can expect temperatures in the 70s°F (21-26°C) in winter and 80s°F (27-32°C) in summer.

Food and drink: For much of the trip I thought there was no such thing as bad Bahamian food. Then I had a meal that was mediocre. But generally it is true to say that you will find native dishes to be of a very high standard (and McDonalds, etc are here if you want them). As you would expect, seafood dishes are prominent, particularly conch (prounounced 'conk'), snapper and crayfish (lobster). Grouper is a particularly delicious dish. Chicken, generally fried with peas and rice, is the mainstay of the menu in native restaurants. The traditional native breakfast features boiled fish, although Nassau has many restaurants providing American fare.

Locals prefer German beer to American, and there is usually a small price difference which reflects this. The Caribbean drink of rum is popular here, and there is a Bacardi plant on New Providence. Milk is sometimes difficult to get, although there is a packing plant at

Part 2: Nassau to Port-au-Prince

Hatchet Bay on Eleuthera.

Prices: The Bahamas are very expensive, for natives as well as tourists. In fact the Bahamas are unusual by Caribbean standards insofar as the traveller can live for the same cost as the itinerant native, who suffers the same high prices. The high prices are due mainly to two reasons: firstly the tourist boom which only subsided with the worldwide economic recession and Bahamian independence in 1973; secondly, the Bahamas' dependence on imports, particularly from the United States.

Perhaps as an incentive to increase tourism, there are no excessive prices for visitors (except of course in the obvious tourist traps).

The People: As a generalization it is true to say that the people are very friendly. This is largely natural to them, although there are those who make a special effort. I found friendliness everywhere, but in other respects there are differences in the people on each island you visit, and even in different settlements on the same island.

The population is about 200,000, of which 120,000 live on New Providence. I noticed an abundance of young children, particularly on Andros.

Hustlers: Everywhere people will ask you for a handout. This is an inevitable result of both tourism and poverty (there is high unemployment). In Nassau young people will be offered the opportunity to purchase marihuana or cocaine. I wouldn't (and didn't). Single men will be offered a woman — I understand US$40 is the going rate. I had better things to do with my money. The Tourist Board will advise you not to wander the back streets of Nassau at night. Elsewhere you should certainly be safe.

New Providence: By no means the largest of the islands (it ranks about tenth in size) New Providence nevertheless boasts Nassau, the capital. To many tourists New Providence is Nassau : they come, stay and leave without knowing anything of the island outside Nassau (I even overheard some tourists who thought they were on Grand Bahama!). Only 21 miles long by 7 wide New Providence can be explored in two days (not including Nassau).

Nassau: The city was named after Prince William of Orange Nassau, the man whom many in Northern Ireland seem unable to forget. He, and his wife Mary, were offered the English crown when the reigning monarch James 2 was deposed for his Roman Catholic beliefs in 'The Bloodless Revolution'. Discovered first by the rich and famous, Nassau is now visited mainly by the less rich, but in far greater numbers. Americans are of course the largest group; fairly inexpensive excursions can be made by plane or cruise ship from Miami, and many cruise liners call here.

Bay Street is the centre of downtown Nassau. It is reputed to have more liquor stores in 1 mile than any other place in the world. Interspersed with these are restaurants and shops selling duty-free imported goods.

New Providence (arterial roads and points of interest)

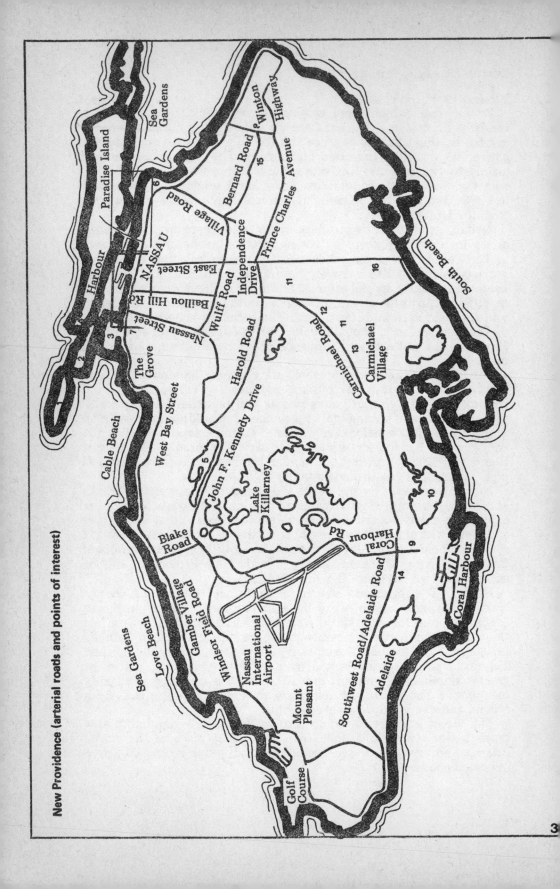

Sea Gardens
Paradise Island
Harbour
NASSAU
Village Road
Bernard Road
Winton Highway
Prince Charles Avenue
East Street
Independence Drive
Baillou Hill Rd
Wulff Road
Nassau Street
The Grove
Harold Road
Carmichael Road
Carmichael Village
South Beach
Cable Beach
West Bay Street
John F. Kennedy Drive
Lake Killarney
Blake Road
Coral Harbour Rd
Sea Gardens
Love Beach
Gamber Village
Windsor Field Road
Nassau International Airport
Mount Pleasant
Golf Course
Southwest Road/Adelaide Road
Adelaide
Coral Harbour

Part 2: Nassau to Port-au-Prince

Arrival in Nassau: There is no bus service to or from the airport and money changing facilities will be closed if you arrive on an evening flight, so you should have a few American dollars in cash with you. Taxis are metered, so if you intend staying at the Mignon Guest House or other downtown accommodation you can expect to pay $6.50 per car.

The above information applies to Nassau International airport. If you have used the services of Chalk's International Airlines you will arrive at Paradise Island. From here you can either take a ferry to downtown Nassau for 50 cents (see map of Paradise Bridge area) or a taxi for perhaps $3. If coming by ship you will arrive in downtown Nassau.

The *Mignon Guest House*, run by Mary and Steve Antonas, parents of the Bahamas tennis champion, is a perfect place to begin a trip of this kind. It is the only cheap accommodation to be centrally located

Accommodation in Nassau

Name	Address	Summer Price per room in US$
Guest Houses		
Mignon Guest House	Market Street (Tel: 24771 or 58662)	EP: *S* $14; *D* $18; *T* $20
Olive's Guest House	Blue Hill Road (Tel: 35298)	EP: *S* $15; *D* $17.
Kentucky Springs Hotel	Fowler Street (Tel: 28302)	EP: *S* $20; *D* $25.
Klonaris Guest House	West Bay Street (Tel: 23888)	EP: *S* $18; *D* $22.
Mitchell's Cottages	West Bay Street (Tel: 24365)	EP: *S* $14/16; *D* $18/20
Pearl Cox Guest House	Augusta Street (Tel: 52627)	EP: *S* $8; *D* $13.
Poinciana Inn	Bernard Road (Tel: 31720)	EP: *S* $19; *D* $23.
Hotels		
El Greco Hotel	West Bay Street/Augusta (Tel: 51121)	EP: *S* $34; *D* $45; Suites $80.
Grand Central Hotel	Charlotte Street (Tel: 28356)	EP: *S* $29; *D* $33
Towne Hotel	George Street (Tel: 28450)	EP: *S* $30/33; *D* $34/42: CP: *S* $39/47; *D* $52/60.
Apartments		
Cable Beach Manor	Cable Beach (Tel: 77784)	EP: 1 bedroom $250 per week; 2 bedroom $340 per week; 3 bedroom $500 per week.
Casurinas Apartment Hotel	Cable Beach (Tel: 77921)	EP: Studio 35; 1 bedroom $50; 2 bedroom $70.

New Providence: Key

1 Long Cay
2 Silver Cay
3 Arawak Cay
4 Lighthouse
5 Lake Cunningham
6 Fort Montagu
7 Fort Charlotte
8 Sandilands (Fox Hill)
9 Coral Heights
10 Millars Sound
11 Golden Gates Estate
12 Sunshine Park
13 Millars Heights
14 Oasis Restaurant
15 St Augustine's Monastery
16 South Beach Estates

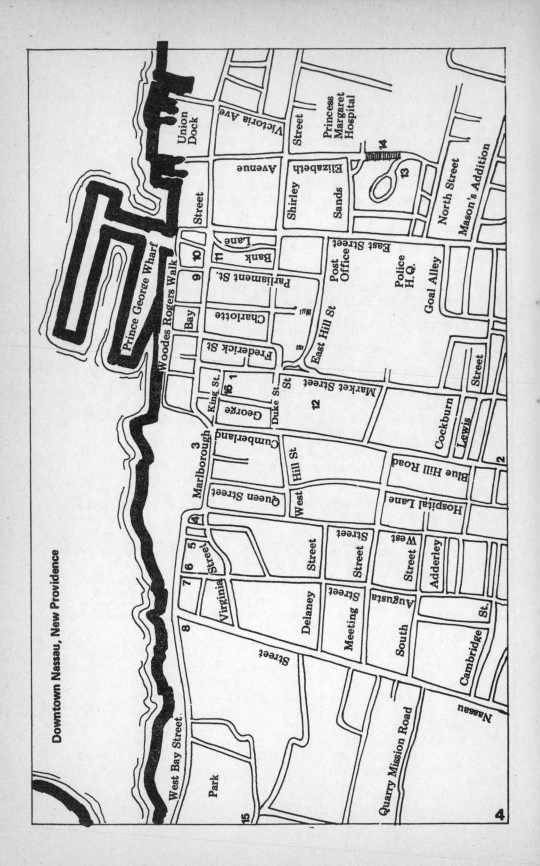

Downtown Nassau, New Providence

Prince George Wharf

Union Dock

Victoria Ave

Street

Avenue

Shirley Street

Elizabeth

Sands

Princess Margaret Hospital

North Street

Mason's Addition

Woodes Rogers Walk

Street

Bank Lane

Post Office

East Street

Police H.Q.

Goal Alley

9 10

11

Bay

Charlotte

Parliament St.

Hill

East Hill St

Frederick St.

Market Street

Street

King St.

16 1

George

Duke St.

12

Cockburn

Lewis

Street

Marlborough

Cumberland

West Hill St

Blue Hill Road

2

3

Queen Street

Hospital Lane

West

Adderley

Cambridge St.

4

5

Virginia Street

Street

Street

Street

West Street

Nassau

6

Delaney Street

Meeting Street

South Street

7

Augusta Street

8

Street

Quarry Mission Road

West Bay Street.

Park

15

4

and has a clientele of youngish travellers and holidaymakers, principally from North America and Europe. There are eight rooms, with
air-conditioning or large fans, and two bathrooms, all on the same
floor. Telephone a reservation from the airport, especially if arriving
on a Sunday when the proprietors have a day off (they do not live on
the premises). Although not the cheapest, this is recommended as a
perfect place to find your feet — and its location is superb.

A cheap alternative to the Mignon is Olive's Guest House. Located
¾ mile from Bay Street on a main road, it has a predominantly West
Indian clientele. There are a considerable number of tourist hotels in
Nassau, on Cable Beach, on Paradise Island and elsewhere in New
Providence, which generally cater for package tourists. One group of
these large hotels, on West Bay Street, surrounds a lovely small hotel,
El Greco, which is certainly quite different to any other hotel on the
island. El Greco is a two-storey building with Spanish-style decor and
furnishings. It boasts what is generally regarded as the best restaurant
in Nassau, Del Prado, a regular (unpackaged) clientele, secluded
freshwater swimming pool, and is just across the road from the
beach.

Of the small number of apartments here, there were two I quite
liked. Cable Beach Manor, though catering to some extent for the
package groups and fairly large, seemed quite well run and good for
families. I preferred the smaller Casuarinas, on the same beach but
further from town, as the atmosphere was more intimate.

Restaurants in Nassau: *McDonalds* is a good and cheap place for a
light breakfast or snack meal. An eating place popular with tourists
and natives is *Skans Cafeteria* on Bay Street, round the corner from
the Mignon Guest House (see map). I couldn't figure out the prices
here: I ordered veal escalope, priced at $2.50. With it I had french
fries, milk and dressing. Yet I was still charged $2.50. Then I went
again and got coffee, which was free. It didn't work out the same at
breakfast, which was slightly more than McDonalds. About the
cheapest place for a meal is *Kentucky Fried Chicken*, which is air-
conditioned into the bargain. Chicken, chips and Coke is $2.15. It
appears to attract an unruly element however, so it can be noisy.

Downtown Nassau: Key

1 Mignon Guest House
2 To Olive's Guest House
3 Sheraton British Colonial
   Hotel
4 Olympia Hotel
5 Ocean Spray Hotel
6 Mayfair Hotel
7 El Greco Hotel
8 Atlantis/Dolphin Hotels
9 Prince George Hotel
10 Rawson Square
11 Parliament Square
12 Government House
13 Water tower
14 Queen's Staircase or 66 steps
15 To Fort Charlotte
16 Cathedral

The American-orientated chemical-food eating places mentioned so far are about the cheapest places to eat in Nassau. But you will want a decent meal occasionally, and the chance to try local food. The *Grand Central Restaurant and Hotel* in Charlotte Street is a Greek-owned establishment specializing in native food and Greek dishes. Prices are much higher than in the cheapie places — beer is $1.50 a time — so it would be advisable to have lunch rather than dinner here. I found the food very good. I tried soup, with warm rolls and butter ($1.50) and conch fritters in sauce ($2.50). Very satisfying and delicious, although only a very light meal. Dinners come in large portions and are superbly prepared, but prices are accordingly higher too.

Some other restaurants in downtown Nassau are the El Toro, Italian Pizza House and Lums. The *El Toro* serves native food at similar prices to the Grand Central; the decor is better but the food

Central Downtown Nassau: Key

1 Mignon Guest House
2 Sheraton British Colonial Hotel
3 Bicycle and scooter hire
4 McDonalds
5 Burger King
6 Kentucky Fried Chicken
7 Italian Pizza House
8 Grand Central Restaurant and Hotel
9 El Toro
10 Skans Cafeteria
11 Air Jamaica/Air Canada
12 International Air Bahamas
13 To tourist office
14 R.H. Curry & Co.
15 Dirty Dicks
16 Cathedral
17 Banks

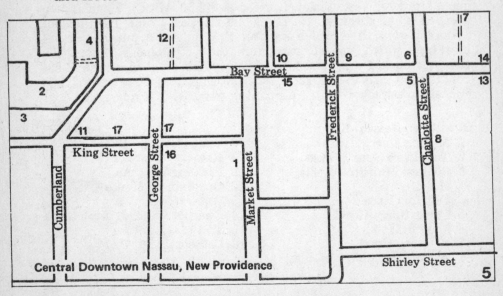

Central Downtown Nassau, New Providence

not quite as good. The *Italian Pizza House* serves mainly Italian dishes, some with Bahamian undertones. A nine-inch pizza costs between $2 and $3. Suitable for a cheapish meal if you are not drinking liquor (which is expensive) but be careful because some prices are high. *Lums* has many native dishes including turtle steak at a cheaper price than in the Grand Central. Native restaurants of varying standards can be found on East Bay Street and at the back of town, usually on or near a main road.

Nightlife: Nightspots in Nassau are not only numerous, but also obvious. A native suggestion was the *King and Knight*, out on West Bay Street. No admission charge, though of course drinks are expensive, and reputably a good floor show. Another suggestion is *Dirty Dick's*, on Bay Street, very close to the Mignon Guest House. The acts include calypso singer Blind Blake, Fire, Shake and Crab Dances, Sapodilla Woman, limbo, steel drums, etc. If you eat a meal here, have a drink and stay all night for the show, you should come out with change from $10 per person.

Transportation: Bicycles can be hired outside the Sheraton British Colonial Hotel. The cost is $4 per day plus a $5 deposit, expensive considering the fact that they are in bad condition, but an enjoyable way to get round the island if you are fit. A couple may prefer to hire a scooter; at $10 a day it works out very little more than a bicycle per person (although gas is extra of course) and allows longer trips to be made. These can be hired from the same place, but you may prefer to shop around. The machines are generally Yamahas and Hondas.

Jitney Bus Services ply the main roads out of Nassau, east, west, north (Paradise Island) and south. The fare is 50 cents, unless you are going to the far west of the island, when it is $1. They do not run to the airport. To take a bus you can either walk out along the road in the direction you wish to travel and find a bus stop (marked on the road or by a stand or post), or go down to Fredericks Street from where many buses leave.

Some of the Jitney bus routes are indirect, zipping through residential areas covering the whole range from wooden cabins to luxury villas. This is particularly true of the Fox Hill Jitney service. If you are not hiring a bicycle or scooter you should thus take the opportunity of seeing something of New Providence and the outskirts of Nassau by Jitney.

Sightseeing in Nassau: A sight to be welcomed by the refugee from the cold northern winter is that of all the beautifully suntanned American girl tourists. Plus Nassau has plenty to offer itself. Paradise Island, which can be reached by ferry from Prince George Wharf (50 cents) or Paradise Bridge (25 cents), features the casino where you can gamble or just walk around. At the end of the bridge, on Paradise Island, is Hurricane Hole, the yacht marina.

Potter's Cay is under the bridge, almost halfway between Nassau and the island. Here is the Produce Exchange, where the incoming boats from the Out Islands bring in cargo, mainly foodstuffs. Along the lower road under the bridge running into Nassau you will see where the small fishing boats tie up. Here you can buy from the wide variety of fish and conch or just watch the fishermen preparing their catch. Here also you can see a small artificial island, made up entirely of discarded conch shells. Potter's Cay dock is where the majority of mail boats to the islands leave from.

The Sea Gardens (at the east end of Paradise Island and opposite Love Beach) are underwater coral reefs of great natural beauty. A glass-bottomed boat can be taken from Nassau (Prince George Wharf) or Paradise Island (ferry point) to view those at the eastern end of the harbour. One of the amazing sights of the Bahamas, even today, is the clarity of the blue-green water. Even in the harbour, where rubbish is continually casually tipped into the sea, the water remains clear.

Horse-drawn surries are more traditional taxis which ply the streets of Nassau. Usually pink or red in colour they generally depart from Rawson Square (opposite Parliament Square). In Rawson Square and along Woodes Rogers Walk (part of which is also known as Market Range, especially in mail boat schedules) is a fine native market. Its goods are largely intended for the tourist nowadays although many stalls, particularly those selling food produce, also serve the indigenous. Most vendors are selling goods made from straw — hats, bags, dolls, etc, but you can also buy wood carvings (and see the carving in progress), beautifully finished pieces of coral in many colours, polished conch shells, necklaces of many types and so on.

Nassau is a fascinating blend of old and new. Near to the Mignon Guest House is Christchurch Cathedral, mock gothic in its architecture. On Paradise Island there are The Cloisters, built in France in the twelfth century, then exported first to the USA and next to the Bahamas. Fort Montagu, the oldest fort in the Bahamas, guards the eastern approaches to Nassau harbour. Old cannons point out to sea along West Bay Street, and colourful artillery pieces guard Parliament and Queen Victoria's statue. Amongst this, and the colourful public

Paradise Bridge: Key

1	Harbourmaster's office	8	Versailles Gardens
2	Produce Exchange	9	Fort Montagu
3	Mail boats	10	Montagu Beach
4	Fishing boats	11	To Holiday Inn
5	Conch Shell Island	12	Yacht Haven
6	Ferry for downtown Nassau and glass-bottomed boats	13	Nassau Harbour Club
7	Casino	14	Nassau Yacht Club
		15	Post office

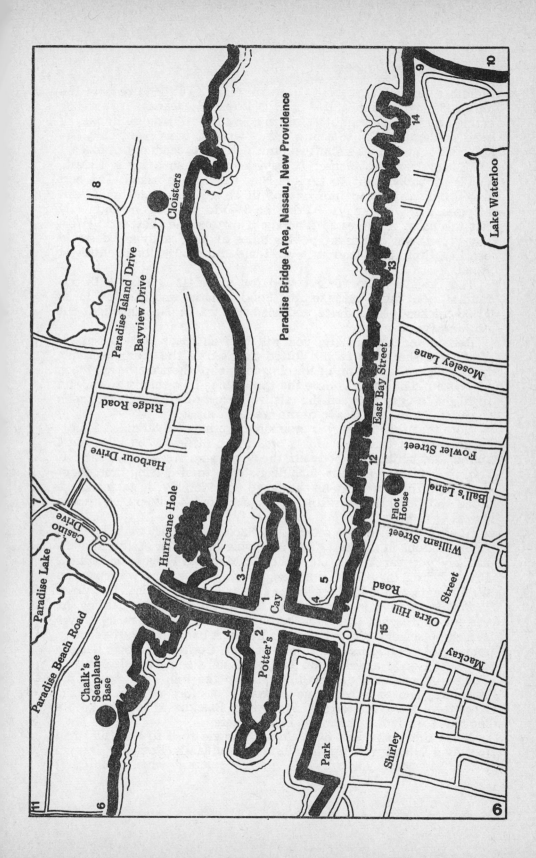

Paradise Bridge Area, Nassau, New Providence

buildings and houses built over the last two centuries, is the mushrooming, Americanized new Nassau. Nuclear-age paper bag eating houses, modern hotels, ocean-going liners, Paradise Bridge, all echo modernity. Yet somehow they blend; it feels right. Only the sight and sound of jet aircraft and the high prices seem out of place.

Visiting New Providence: If staying more than a day in Nassau, you'll probably want to explore New Providence island. The best way to do this is to hire one of those expensive and inefficient bicycles. Allow two days — I did the 30-odd miles in one and really felt the pace. A suggested itinerary is to take the coast road (West Bay Street) out of Nassau, passing miles of fine, sandy and deserted beaches. Cross the island at its west end and return along Southwest Road.

The *Oasis* is a convenient stop for lunch. It is a bar with restaurant, pool table and juke box. Food is native and clientele local. Fried chicken, peas and rice, and salad cost $2.75. Not knockout but not unreasonable either.

Remounted, continuing, you will find all roads lead to Nassau. You'll see shacks or cabins dotted about near the road, whilst an increasing concentration of housing and people heralds the approach of Nassau. The suburbs have the appearance of a shanty town, and highlight the gap between the relative poverty of the Bahamian man in the street and the wealth of the average tourist.

Note that this itinerary is arduous, covering over 30 miles. Simple by scooter, in theory it should present no difficulty by bike, but I found that neither my body nor the cycle were in good condition. It took me nearly 6½ hours, including stops (total cycling time about 4 hours). The route can be shortened considerably by taking Blake Road and Coral Harbour Road past the airport (see map 2). This also passes Lake Killarney.

There's also plenty to see east of Nassau. You can walk, but it is fairly arduous in the heat. You can cycle or scooter easily. Or alternatively you can take a bus either to Montagu Heights or Paradise Bridge. The Jitney Buses run along Shirley Street and will cost you 40/50 cents. These buses generally stop only at recognized bus stops.

Fort Montagu is in a relaxing setting, on the headland guarding the eastern approaches to Nassau harbour, but is in itself really only a gun emplacement with a grandiose name. A handful of rusty cannon remain to remind one of a turbulent past. Continuing down Eastern Road (it's quite a walk) you will eventually come to Blackbeard's Tower. A small sign marks the path up the hill. No longer a tall structure, and in a bad state of repair, it does at least have the advantage of being deserted. From here Blackbeard used to keep a lookout for anyone trespassing in his waters.

From the tower walk back along the main road to Fox Hill Road (see map 7) and walk up the hill into Sandilands (Fox Hill). Here in the main square you will find a bar/restaurant which (naturally)

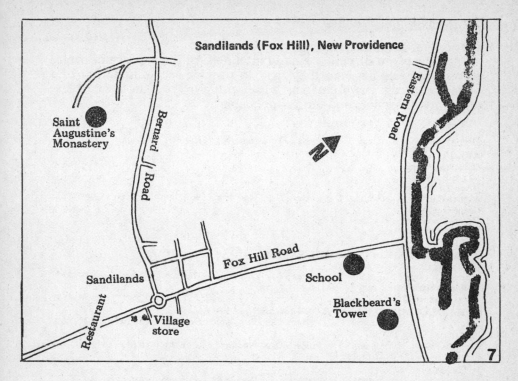

Sandilands (Fox Hill), New Providence

Saint Augustine's Monastery

Bernard Road

Eastern Road

Fox Hill Road

Sandilands

Restaurant

Village store

School

Blackbeard's Tower

7

serves native food. Recommended. They have a pool table, usually occupied. I found the fish dish, fried, with peas and rice and small side salad very good. $2.50. Saint Augustine's Monastery, though of no great antiquity, may be of interest if you are in the area.

Beaches on New Providence: The nearest beach is actually in Nassau. It begins in front of the Sheraton British Colonial Hotel and runs westward to Arawak Cay. Considering it is within the harbour waters it is surprisingly clean. The only problem is that although sandy, it is rocky in places, and steeply shelving at times. Travelling along the north coast in a westerly direction you will see other, fairly empty, beaches: Saunders Beach, Cable Beach, Delaporte Beach, Love Beach and others. More beaches are situated at the west of the island, principally Pleasant Bay, and in the southwest — Adelaide Beach is a stretch some 3 miles long. Elsewhere on the island there is only one other principal beach, South Beach, which is, as its name implies, due south of Nassau.

Travelling to the Out Islands: The chances are you will want to visit the Out Islands by mail boat. The tourist office on Bay Street will be glad to furnish you with schedules and fares on application. Few of these boats run on schedule however. So the best way to find out which boats are leaving and where they are going is to go along to the Harbourmaster's office on Potter's Cay (where most of them leave from) and ask. Please note that the aforementioned office is only open Monday through Friday, and not all day Friday. If it is

Caribbean Island Hopping.

shut on your arrival ask any of the boat crews.

Mail boats are of course mainly intended for the carriage of cargo, so besides being irregular they tend to provide accommodation of a basic standard. The following table will give you an idea of the regularity of services and tariffs applicable:

Destination	Vessel	Leaves From	Departure	Return	Journey Time	Fare One Way
ABACO Cherokee Sound Marsh Harbour Hope Town Man-O-War Cay Great Guana Cay Green Turtle Cay Cooper's Town Red Cay	*Deborah K*	Potter's Cay	Wed 4pm	Sun 6am	7 hrs+	$6
ABACO/BERRY ISLANDS/GRAND BAHAMA Sandy Point Moore's Island Bullock's Harbour Great Harbour Cay	*Captain Dean*	Potter's Cay	Fri 10pm	Wed am	7 hrs+	$10/$12
ACKLINS/CROOKED ISLAND/LONG ISLAND/MAYAGUANA	*Marcella*	Potter's Cay	Tue 7am	Sun 3pm	24 hrs	$25/$30
ANDROS San Andros	*Madam Elizabeth*	Potter's Cay	Wed am	Mon 3pm	5 hrs	$8
ANDROS Staniard Creek Fresh Creek Mastic Point	*Pleasant*	Market Range	Wed 6am	Sun am	4/5 hrs	$7
ANDROS Mastic Point Nicholl's Town Morgan's Bluff	*Miss Beverly*	Potter's Cay	Wed 6am	Sun 4pm	5 hrs	$10
ANDROS Mangrove Cay Driggs Hill	*Captain Johnson*	Potter's Cay	Sat 10pm	Wed pm	6 hrs	$8
ANDROS Mangrove Cay Driggs Hill Long Bay Cays Deep Creek Little Creek Pleasant Bay Mars Bay Smith's Hill Black Point	*Anastasia*	Potter's Cay	Mon pm	Thu	6 hrs	$8
BIMINI AND CAT ISLAND Alice Town	*Goldfinger*	Potter's Cay	Tue 5.30	Thu noon	13 hrs	$12
CAT ISLAND/RUM CAY/SAN SALVADOR Arthur's Town Bennet's Harbour Cove Knowles' New Bight Old Bight Smith's Bay	*Air Pheasant*	Potter's Cay	Tue noon	one week	13 hrs	$10/$15

Part 2: Nassau to Port-au-Prince

Destination	Vessel	Leaves From	Departure	Return	Journey Time	Fare One Way
ELEUTHERA Hatchet Bay Governor's Harbour S. Palmetto Point Rock Sound Savannah Sound	Air Swift	Potter's Cay	Tue 7am	Wed	5 hrs+	$6/$8
ELEUTHERA Current Island Current Bogue	Ego	Market Range	Fri 7am	Tue 2pm	5 hrs	$4
ELEUTHERA Hatchet Bay Alice Town	Offshore	Bahamas Agricultural Corp.	Mon 11am Wed 11am Fri 11am	Sun 9pm Tue 9pm Thu 9pm	5 hrs	$10
ELEUTHERA Rock Sound Davis Harbour	Captain Moxey	Potter's Cay	Tue 4am	Wed/Thu	7/8 hrs	$10
ELEUTHERA Harbour Island	Bahama Daybreak	Market Range	Wed 5am	Sun noon	5 hrs	$5/$6
& Spanish Wells	Liberty D Spanish	Market Range	Thu 6am Thu noon	Tue 6am Tue 6am	4/5 hrs 5 hrs	$7 $7
EXUMA George Town	Jonnett Walker	Potter's Cay	Wed 2pm	Sat 8am	17 hrs	$13
EXUMA Staniel Cay Black Point Farmer's Cay Barrattarre	Captain Moxey	Potter's Cay	Thu noon	Sat	17 hrs	$11/$13
GRAND BAHAMA Freeport	Noel Roberts	City Lumber Yard	Thu 4pm	Sun 7am	14 hrs	$10/$14
LONG ISLAND Simms Salt Pond	Gary Roberts	City Lumber Yard	Fri 7am	Wed 7am	13 hrs	$10/$14
LONG ISLAND/ACKLINS/INAGUA Clarence Town Salina Point Matthew Town	Bahama Land	Potter's Cay	Tue 10am	Sat noon	13 hrs	$15/$30
RAGGED ISLAND	Gleaner	Market Range	Thu 8am	Tue 8am	24 hrs	$16

The above information is taken from a printed sheet published by the Bahamas Ministry of Tourism. Neither they nor I accept responsibility for any changes or inaccuracies therein. In point of fact, I know there are inaccuracies. The towns and harbours named before a vessel's name are not necessarily visited by the boat; for instance, the *Ego* calls at Current Island and anchors at The Current. Cargo transportation between The Current and Bogue is by road. The departure time is subject to weather conditions, particularly in the case of small boats like the *M V Pleasant*, and return time can mean sailing time or docking time in Nassau. Fares are likely to increase of course.

Nevertheless I include this information in the belief that it will be very useful to you and may prove invaluable — after all, the details given here for some vessels (the *Captain Moxey* is one example) are correct in every respect at the time of writing.

As these handbooks exist to give factual information it is not my normal practice to retail anecdotes of my travels. But there are times when this is the best way of getting information across, and so I take the plunge and give details of my experiences on the mail boats so that you will know what to expect.

But first I will point out again that the mail boats exist primarily to transport cargo and mail. They take processed foods, consumer durables, bottled sodas and suchlike supplies to the islands, returning with fresh fruit and vegetables, empty gas cylinders and so on. As most of the islands are surrounded by shallow waters, and one can clearly see the bottom in the harbours, shallow draught vessels specially made for the job must be used. The Out Islanders are very dependent on this service, both for receiving provisions and getting produce to market. Passengers are carried, mainly natives, though an increasing number of tourists are using the service. There is no advance booking, and payment is made on board. As for what to expect, the following narrative should leave you without illusions.

My first voyage was the most comfortable, on the *Captain Moxey* from Nassau to Rock Sound, Eleuthera. I also got the trip for free, or as good as; as the ship leaves at 4 in the morning I had been able to board the previous Monday night, thus saving one night's accommodation — I had been paying $10 a night.

Captain Moxey is the name of the captain, owner, builder and boat. She enjoys a good reputation as a fast and safe ship that sails on schedule. Her captain/owner/builder has something of a reputation too: he built a racing yacht, and the first time he lost a race — that is, he came second — he sold it. He is now building another.

A Ford Mustang, numerous gas cylinders, bags of fertilizer, boxes of processed foods, building materials and countless bottles of Coca Cola comprised the majority of the cargo. It looked as though there were berths to accommodate two dozen passengers, in six four-berth cabins. On this trip I was one of only eight, so only three cabins were in use. There is a galley of some size with seating for maybe six passengers, and two toilets. As is usual on these boats, cargo litters the deck as well as filling the hold, so that one has to clamber over boxes, bags and cylinders in order to reach the upper deck (an unusual feature on these boats).

We left at 4 in the morning, so I'm told. I was asleep at the time. I was awakened by the rolling of the ship or daylight, I don't know which; in any event it was light, and the ship was rolling back and forth. I looked out expecting heavy seas, but it looked calm to me. Of course I now know that the shallow draught of these boats combined with a top-heavy superstructure causes them to wallow at the slightest provocation. However I suffered no discomfort so went straight back to bed, rocked to sleep like a baby by that rolling motion.

One of the crew awakened me for an unappetizing breakfast of grits, sausage (tinned) and fried egg, washed down by coffee. Two Swiss tourists (the only other foreigners aboard) declined all offers of food, and I must admit I gave the matter consideration. But I believe a full stomach helps to prevent and mitigates sea sickness, so somehow I got the cook's culinary efforts inside me. This philosophy proved true, but I'll skip the details.

Eight hours is a long time when you're on a small boat with nothing to see but water. Having exhausted conversation with my fellow passengers the previous night, I went back to bed, maybe sleeping for three hours before being awakened again by the cook. This time he wanted money, the $10 fare. Land was in sight.

My next trip, from The Current to Nassau, was a little more incident-packed. The *Ego,* which putters once a week in each direction from Nassau to Current, was due to leave at 7 am. I hurried down to the landing stage, arriving at 6.58, to find her nowhere near ready for departure. The vessel is smaller than the *Captain Moxey*, with perhaps six berths in total. These are rarely used for sleeping as the ship sails in daylight hours. At 6.58 all cabins were full of people with their luggage, the deck space was about half full with boxes of oranges and tomatoes, whilst more boxes and baskets of fruit were stacked on the roof. Although fully laden, it was obvious more cargo was to be taken as the jetty was covered with full boxes, sacks and baskets, and more were continually arriving.

For over an hour I sat on an orange box and watched the captain slowly winning the struggle of the pier; he was getting the produce aboard slightly faster than it was arriving. Another dozen passengers also joined, making perhaps three dozen in total. The lifeboat and foredeck were stacked high with bananas and the roof groaning with boxes of tomatoes (plus a few passengers who could find nowhere else to go). Jokes were flying. One man muttered something about 'The Wreck of the Hesperus' as he clambered aboard, and several christened our impending trip 'The Last Voyage of the *Ego*'. By the time we left, over an hour later, the gunwhale was two feet lower in the water than when I boarded!

The tide was ebbing, and the captain decided that if we were ever going to leave port, it would have to be now. Gingerly the boat meandered between the sand banks. At one point the propeller touched bottom, and progress slowed as we edged along, the prop churning up sand. Almost out of the harbour, a few minutes later, we came to a complete stop; the propeller was too firmly embedded. After much impassioned exhortation by two seafaring passengers the people in the stern were induced to leave their seats and move forward. The stern lifted, the propeller bit once more into water, and the vessel surged forward. We were out of harbour.

A short stop at Current Island, where a small boat ferried straw baskets to us, then we were away, Nassau-bound. By the grace of God the sea was as flat as the proverbial millpond (ten days previously a boat from Spanish Wells had sunk with loss of life), so that we reached Nassau without further incident — unless I include the remonstrances of an amateur preacher who had found himself a captive audience for 4½ hours.

It was my third trip which was nearly my last. Within 12 hours of my return to Nassau I was aboard the *M V Pleasant*, due to depart for Fresh Creek, Andros, the next morning. I had found the Mignon full (and in any event wanted to slow down the rapid evaporation of my funds) and had therefore arranged with the captain to sleep on board. A little after midnight I went down with my luggage and stepped aboard. The first two cabins I looked into each contained a sleeping body, so I walked round to the other side of the tiny boat. There I found a cabin occupied only by two suitcases and stretched out on the bunk.

Within the hour I heard someone on the quay, footsteps onto the deck and short strides (it didn't take many) to my cabin door. Which was flung open. A short pause, then 'Who dat dere?' I struggled into a semi-recumbent position. 'Oh it you' — this was my captain speaking — 'Dis my cabin, you sleep back there.' I collected my gear and moved a few feet to the last, and only vacant, cabin. Sloop John B stuff.

Our voyage was to take us through a much-documented area in the legend of the Bermuda Triangle, the Tongue of the Ocean. This is one of the few areas in the Bahamas where the sea is very deep, and where many small vessels have been lost. Noting that the *Pleasant* was only some 45 feet in length, and knowing that she cannot run on schedule because of bad weather conditions, I regarded this trip with some trepidation. This area is notorious for sudden squalls which spring up from nowhere.

Soon after dawn we cast off in fair weather, wallowing slightly even within the harbour waters. Past the Sheraton, the lighthouse and as far as Cable Beach. It was then, looking ahead, that I saw the approaching storm. The black clouds with their torrential rain and our puny craft speeded towards each other until suddenly the heavy seas and rain hit us. I was under cover — although on deck — but was immediately soaked to the skin. Twice the boat swung right round and heaved to; twice, after a few minutes, the captain turned the boat back around and continued. Ahead we could see a patch of almost clear sky.

Sure enough, after some twenty minutes the sky was clear and we were in brilliant sunshine. The sea was calmer too, but we were still in sight of land. Once clear of New Providence we ran into very heavy seas, the waves hitting us broadside, rolling the *Pleasant* over to starboard before the swell swung us back over to port. There was nothing to do or see on deck, so I returned to my bunk. The serious-ness of our situation was only driven home to me when I was thrown out of my bunk against the cabin door. So I got on deck to find the boat being unmercifully tossed about by the waves.

But the captain knew his job; every time he spotted a giant wave he turned into it, usually cutting the engine as the seas crashed over our bows. I thought it would smash the glass in the wheelhouse, but it didn't. Thus maintaining a somewhat zigzag course we stayed right way up. At one point, perhaps halfway across, I spotted the mate checking that the lifeboat was ready for use. I thought 'My God, if we sink that thing doesn't stand a chance.'

I had never been seasick before, but there is a first time for every-thing. For perhaps four hours, or it may have been four years, I was wedged at deck level, head over the gunwhale, dying. I won't go into detail; suffice it to say that I was in great danger of being flung overboard, and didn't care. I contemplated jumping, but didn't want to upset the captain.

Due to the seas and the zigzagging our 5 hour journey became 7½ hours of hell. A little after land had been sighted there was a significant calming of the sea — it was still very rough, but less violent, so that I was able to crawl to my bunk and collapse on it from sheer exhaustion. I awoke to find us berthed and unloading at Fresh Creek, the sun sinking in the southwest. Soon I had recovered enough to pay the captain, some $8, and exchange jokes concerning my experience. Like a fool I then asked when he was going back!

These experiences are probably a fair cross-section of what to expect when travelling on the mail boats. Generally the bigger boats are more likely to sail on schedule, are more comfortable but may cost more. Night travel saves you time and money. You may have the opportunity to travel by private yacht quite cheaply. At The Current, Eleuthera, I was offered a free trip to Bimini, the Berry Islands and Miami on a sailing yacht owned by two young French-men. I couldn't accept, but the opportunities are there.

If time is more important to you, and you want to see as many islands as possible in a short time, then you may consider flying between the islands (it is sometimes possible to hop from island to island by plane, but this is not a practical proposition on the mail boats; in practice you have to keep returning to Nassau). I therefore give Bahamasair schedules and fares current at the time of writing. You should add the cost of transportation to and from airports (usually by taxi) to the air fares to give a realistic idea of the cost differential.

Here is an example to show the cost differential between mail boat and air travel, based on a journey from The Current, Eleuthera to Nassau:

Flying: Air fare, North Eleuthera/Nassau, $18. Taxi, Current to North Eleuthera airport, $6 approximately. Taxi, Nassau airport to

Caribbean Island Hopping

Nassau, $6.50. Total $30.50.
   Mail boat : Current to downtown Nassau, $4.
   There is thus a difference in this case of $26.50 for a single person. This may be an extreme example, and of course couples and groups will save on the taxi fares, but the point is valid. Anyway, here are some Bahamasair schedules and fares :

Nassau to:	Depart	Arrive	Frequency	Fare
Andros Town	8.30 am	9.15 am	Daily except Thu	$15
	2.00 pm	2.15 pm	Mon/Fri/Sun	
The Bight (Cat Island)	10.00 am	10.50 am	Fri/Sun	$24
Chub Cay (Berry Islands)	4.00 pm	4.50 pm	Mon/Thu/Fri	$15
Crooked Island	8.15 am	10.00 am	Tue/Sat	$41
Deadman's Cay (Long Island)	10.00 am	11.20 am	Mon/Sat	$32
	3.00 pm	4.20 pm	Thu/Fri/Sun	
Freeport (Grand Bahama)	7.30 am	8.00 am	Daily except Tue	$30
	7.30 am	8.15 am	Tue	
	11.00 am	11.30 am	Daily except Tue	
	11.00 am	11.45 am	Tue	
	4.30 pm	5.00 pm	Daily except Tue	
	4.30 pm	5.15 pm	Tue	
	7.30 pm	8.00 pm	Daily except Tue	
	7.30 pm	8.15 pm	Tue	
Georgetown (Exuma)	10.00 am	10.45 am	Mon/Sat/Sun	$29
	3.00 pm	3.45 pm	Tue/Thu/Fri/Sun	
Governor's Harbour (Eleuthera)	7.45 am	8.10 am	Daily except Tue/Thu	$21
	4.00 pm	4.50 pm	Daily	
Great Harbour Cay (Berry Islands)	8.30 am	9.20 am	Thu	$18
	2.00 pm	2.50 pm	Tue	
	4.00 pm	4.25 pm	Mon/Thu/Fri	
Inagua	11.00 am	12.45 pm	Wed	$51
Mangrove Cay (Andros)	8.00 am	8.25 am	Mon/Thu/Fri/Sun/	$17
	3.00 pm	3.55 pm	Tue/Wed/Sat/Sun	
Marsh Harbour (Abaco)	9.00 am	9.35 am	Tue/Wed/Thu	$27
	10.15 am	11.25 am	Fri/Sun	
	3.15 pm	4.20 pm	Mon/Sat	
Mayaguana	11.00 am	3.45 pm	Wed	$47
Norman's Cay (Exuma)	2.15 pm	2.45 pm	Mon/Fri	$19.50
North Eleuthera	7.45 am	8.40 am	Daily except Tue/Thu	$18
	12.30 pm	12.55 pm	Daily	
	4.00 pm	4.20 pm	Daily	
Rock Sound (Eleuthera)	12.45 pm	1.20 pm	Daily	$22
	6.00 pm	6.35 pm	Daily	
San Andros	8.30 am	8.45 am	Daily	$16
	2.00 pm	2.45 pm	Mon/Fri/Sun	
	2.00 pm	2.15 pm	Tue	
San Salvador	11.30 am	12.30 pm	Thu/Sat	$32
South Andros	8.00 am	8.50 am	Mon/Thu/Fri/Sun	$17
	3.00 pm	3.30 pm	Tue/Wed/Sat/Sun	
Stella Maris (Long Island)	10.00 am	11.15 am	Sun	$32
	11.30 am	1.05 pm	Thu/Sat	
	3.00 pm	4.15 pm	Tue	
Treasure Cay (Abaco)	9.00 am	10.05 am	Tue/Wed/Thu	$27
	10.15 am	10.55 am	Fri/Sun	
	3.15 pm	3.55 pm	Mon/Sat	

Part 2: Nassau to Port-au-Prince

The above details are of course subject to alteration, and do not include all Bahamasair flights. For every flight from Nassau you can work on there being a return flight, and it is sometimes possible to make stops: for example, the Stella Maris flights stop at Georgetown, Exuma.

Another possibility in terms of inter-island travel are cruise ships. Prices are much higher than mail boat fares of course, and also higher than air fares. American Canadian Line operate a 'mini cruise liner' which takes a maximum 64 passengers on a choice of two itineraries around the Bahamas, one tour north of Nassau, and one southbound. Fares start at $230 for a 6-day trip. This and other cruise ship accommodation can be booked at R.H. Curry & Company in Bay Street (see map 5). There is also a company, Windjammer, operating six day cruises (Tuesday morning to Sunday evening — five nights) within the Bahamas by sailing vessels. An itinerary beginning in Freeport and finishing in Nassau alternates with another in the opposite direction. Anyone taking both trips earns a discount and is able to utilise accommodation aboard ship between the trips. Prices range from US$350 to US$500. Details available from Windjammer 'Barefoot' Cruises Ltd, 824 South Miami Avenue, Florida (327 2600) or TransAtlantic Wings Ltd, London (602 4021).

Eleuthera: The name of this island group is derived from the Greek word meaning freedom, so named by dissenters who first left England and then Bermuda in search of somewhere for men to be free from religious persecution. As can be seen from the map, it is a long, thin, awkwardly-shaped island, some 100 miles in length, with a few smaller islands clustered around its northern end. Main industries are agriculture and tourism. The main settlements are Cape Eleuthera, Rock Sound, Tarpum Bay, Governor's Harbour, Hatchet Bay, Harbour Island, Spanish Wells and The Current, but there are other smaller settlements as well. At its narrowest (Glass Window) the island is only as wide as the road.

From the first days agriculture was difficult, because the topsoil, though fertile, was thin, and in many places soon exhausted. Sugar and cotton have been cultivated here in the past, but the crops are no longer economic. Now fruit is grown: tomatoes (many of which are exported direct to the USA), mandarin oranges, mangoes, bananas, custard apples, papya and the best pineapples in the world, so sweet and soft you can eat the core. These crops are mainly produced however for domestic consumption. Rock Sound once had a fishing industry, but this has died and fishing is now conducted only on a small scale. The exception is at Spanish Wells, where fishing and sponging are the main industries.

There are three airports on Eleuthera: North Eleuthera, near Upper Bogue, Governor's Harbour near the US Naval Base (10 miles north of Governor's Harbour settlement) and Rock Sound, a little to the north of Rock Sound.

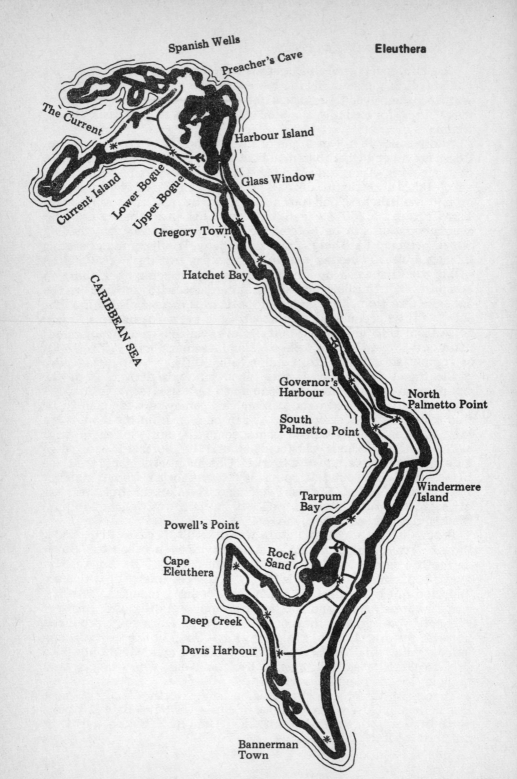

Spanish Wells

Eleuthera

Preacher's Cave

The Current

Harbour Island

Current Island

Lower Bogue

Glass Window

Upper Bogue

Gregory Town

Hatchet Bay

CARIBBEAN SEA

Governor's
Harbour

North
Palmetto Point

South
Palmetto Point

Windermere
Island

Tarpum
Bay

Powell's Point

Rock
Sand

Cape
Eleuthera

Deep Creek

Davis Harbour

Bannerman
Town

8

Transportation on Eleuthera: There is no bus service on Eleuthera, except for children, so that the only means of travelling is taxi, hired car or hitch-hiking. If you are travelling far (remember the island is 100 miles long) a taxi will be out of the question. To hire a car costs $25 a day plus refundable deposit; cars can be hired at airports, the petrol (gas) station in Rock Sound and in other major settlements. A hired car however has to be returned to the place it was hired from, so the only practical way of travelling from one end of the island to the other is by hitch-hiking. As you would expect, there is little traffic, but what there is will be quite likely to stop for you. Thus it is possible to travel to the north of Eleuthera, Spanish Wells or the Current, in a day, if you start early enough.

Rock Sound: I left the *Captain Moxey* at its first stop, Rock Sound, and walking into town found the *Flamingo Lounge Bar and Restaurant.* A single Costs $10 per night in the Guest House above. Note however that this Guest House is managed by the proprietors of Kemp's store, next door to the Flamingo. This Guest House had been omitted from the accommodation leaflet I had picked up from the tourist office, as the previous owner had recently died and presumably no-one had submitted details to the tourist board. I found it good value, and although private facilities were not included I had a room between two bathrooms. If you found it as I did, uncrowded, it could perhaps be accredited five stars for value.

Rock Sound: Key

1	Flamingo Bar/Restaurant	7	Bar
2	Petrol station	8	Mailboat dock
3	Barclays Bank	9	Market place
4	Telecommunications	10	Chase Manhattan Bank
5	Administration building	11	Nu-view Motel
6	Snack Bar	12	Burrows Beach

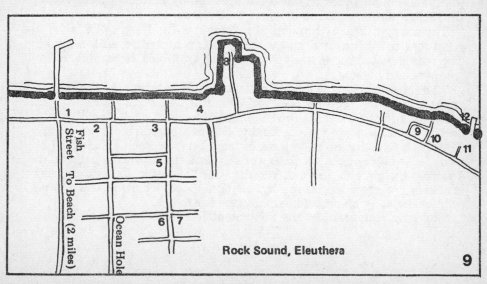

Rock Sound, Eleuthera

Note however that I was around before 16th December, so was probably paying the summer rate.

Food at the Flamingo is mainly native, and by Bahamas standards reasonably priced. Very good too. There are cheaper places such as the snack bar (see map). Accommodation can also be found at the *Nu-View Motel*, $18 single and $23 double (summer rates). The more expensive accommodation is outside the immediate area of Rock Sound.

Rock Sound is one of the nicest places I have been to. The people are almost unbelievably friendly — even the police chief waved to me as I walked up from the quay — and the township enjoys a fine setting. The pastel-painted houses are often adorned or shielded by glorious bushes of flowers. Walking half a mile inland you can look due west and see sea, and, turning round, look due east and see the Atlantic.

The waters of the Sound are shallow and sheltered, but there are no good beaches in the settlement itself. By the Nu-View Motel there is a small, man-made beach, but it is probably better to cross over to the other side of the island, although the water is more likely to be rough here. To reach this beach, walk along Fish Street (by the Flamingo) and after 2 miles you will see it.

Tarpum Bay: This is the first settlement you reach north of Rock Sound. *Ethel's Cottages* (tel: Tarpum Bay 233) now $25 single, $35 double, $40 three to four persons. The *Culmer House & Lodge* has three double apartments at $15 to $40 each, and *Cartwright's Ocean View Cottages* (two cottages) charges $15 for a single and $35 for a double. All summer prices.

Governor's Harbour: This is the major settlement on Eleuthera. However, the only accommodation I know of for anything like a sensible price is *Scriven's Villas;* $25 (summer rate) for a single or double. The *Blue Room Bar and Restaurant* in Pinder's Lane serves good and cheap snacks. It also features Happy Hour, 7 pm to 10 pm on Friday nights, when all drinks are 50 cents.

Travelling north, if hitching, be prepared for long waits. It is a good idea to pick a nice spot where you can sunbathe while waiting. The roads get progressively worse, the potholes becoming more frequent and bigger.

The Current: This is a small village largely catering for the tourist trade. *The Rock*, run by Mrs Sue Williams, is a small establishment with just four apartments (efficiencies). The cost is $8 single (****) and $16 double (***) — actually $8 per person — year round. There is a bar, but no restaurant or maid service. Each efficiency has two beds (convertible to sofas for daytime use), private bathroom, cooking equipment and refrigerator. Cooking utensils, cutlery and crockery are provided, as are towels, linen, etc. There is also a table with chairs, easy chairs and ample space for living.

The only restaurant in the settlement is at the *Current Yacht and*

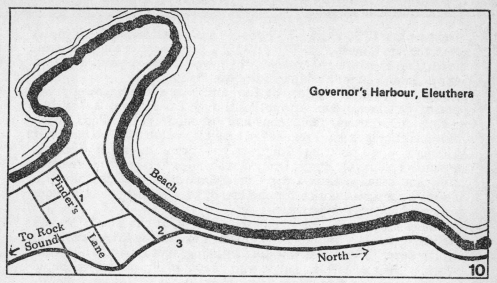

Governor's Harbour, Eleuthera

Governor's Harbour: Key
1 Blue Room
2 Police

3 Petrol (gas) station/store

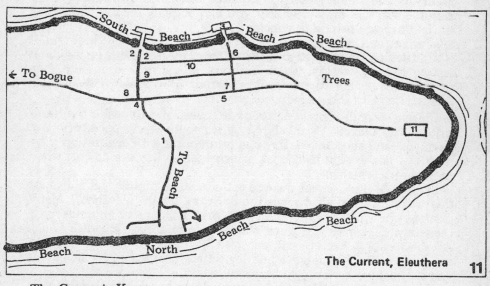

The Current, Eleuthera

The Current: Key
1 The Rock
2 Current Club
3 Mailboat jetty
4 Arthur's Store
5 Durham's Store
6 Church

7 Library and telephone
8 Dolly's
9 Monica's Spot
10 Bicycle and car hire
11 Reservoir

Diving Club ($63 single, $85 double a day, American Plan, winter rates) where a meal costs $10 to $12. The only other tourist accommodation is at the *Sea Raider*, which you pass on your way into town (from $30 for a double, European Plan, winter).

Of the two stores in Current, Durham's seems to have lower prices and a wider range than Arthur's. Although frozen meat is available, mainly frankfurters, hamburgers and bacon, fresh or indeed frozen fish is difficult to get. Fresh-baked bread is available in two places; at Monica's Spot or from Dolly, in the turquoise house opposite Arthur's (see map). Burge, Dolly's husband, often goes out to catch fish, but usually needs a day's or several days' notice. Dolly also needs to be given notice for the bread, so it is best to put in your orders when you first arrive.

There are beaches all round the Current, situated as it is on a headland, but the best by far is the one nearest The Rock (known as North Beach). For those who like to plunge in it is best at high tide, when it shelves steeply. Those who prefer shallower waters should pop down at low tide, when they can walk out for 25 yards before being immersed. Trees behind the beach provide shelter when the sun gets too hot. During my stay the water was placid, but this is not of course always the case. This beach also provides the best spot for observing the sunset. Near the Equator the sun drops quite quickly into the sea, and on a clear day you can actually see the orange ball of fire dropping behind the horizon.

Bicycles and cars can be hired at the Current, but not scooters. It is a difficult place to get to or leave from by land, and its mailboat service is only weekly. Even if flying into North Eleuthera, you would need a taxi to get to the Current. But these difficulties in themselves make it a perfect get-away-from-it-all spot.

Current Island: This isle, about 6 miles long opposite the headland at the Current, is inhabited by a people, fairly poor, who live from the land and the sea. Its usual intercourse with civilization is by means of the weekly mail boat, which means they are cut off when the weather is inclement.

Spanish Wells: Nassau was the main base for pirates, yet a little of this business was also carried out from north Eleuthera. Many pirates, when offered the choice of the hangman or an amnesty if they turned to peaceful ways, settled in and around Spanish Wells. As these shores were — and can still be — hazardous to shipping, wrecking became a popular and legitimate profession. In inclement weather men with storm lanterns would guide ships onto the reefs.

Nowadays the community is very industrious — and also the only segregationalist settlement in the Bahamas. Until recently blacks were not allowed to sleep on the island unless involved in a special project. This attitude is now being relaxed, through, I was told, the intervention of the Queen.

The people work very hard, their main industries being fishing and diving for sponges. Traditionally they intermarry so that there are few family names here and the people tend to look alike — no wonder that they are clannish.

Although usually referred to as an island, Spanish Wells is actually a picturesque town with narrow winding streets, good harbour facilities and effective Hurricane Holes (safe refuges for the small boats when hurricanes hit the island) cut into the mangrove swamps. The island itself, reached from the mainland by a ferry, is called Saint George's Cay.

The cheapest accommodation is *Saint George's Hotel*, $6 single and $12 double. There is other accommodation available, but at higher prices (from $24 for a double).

The Other Settlements in Eleuthera: Hatchet Bay was originally a salt water lake separated from the sea by a narrow strip of land. A man-made cut has dissected this, providing ideal harbour conditions. There is now a marina and yacht club. There is also a regular mail boat service which means Hatchet Bay has many imported goods available for sale. It is also a centre for packing milk, orange juice, ice cream and other foods. This makes Hatchet Bay perhaps the foremost shopping centre on Eleuthera.

Gregory Town is known for its surfing facilities. One spot here is said to be one of the finest places for surfing in the world.

Harbour Island is one of the oldest resorts in the Bahamas; its tourist life began at the end of the nineteenth century. Most accommodation is expensive here however; the cheapest listed is the *Sunset Inn*, $14 single and $22 double.

Shortly before Harbour Island the road crosses Glass Window. This is the narrowest part of Eleuthera, little wider than the road, where Atlantic meets Caribbean. When I passed through there was a strong easterly wind, making the Atlantic very rough and throwing huge foaming breakers against the rock and over the road. Meanwhile, in contrast to the choppy royal blue Atlantic, the turquoise Caribbean was as smooth as a mirror.

San Salvador: This is the supposed site of Columbus' first landfall in the Bahamas, though there is some doubt in the matter. I have even seen a map on which the nearby, much larger, Cat Island is named San Salvador — presumably in error! The British renamed San Salvador Watling Island, but in 1926 officially gave it the title of San Salvador, presumably in deference to the great explorer. The island, which is about the same size as New Providence and the nearest of the Bahamas to Europe, now boasts a monument to Columbus and an important airfield.

Long Island: Along with Abaco, to a limited extent Eleuthera, and one or two other islands, Long Island has an economy with the accent on agriculture. Like so many of the Bahamas, it is a narrow strip of land, hence the name. The main settlement is Dead Man's Cay, so named after a rotting skeleton discovered there, whilst the township of Stella Maris is growing in size and importance. Other settlements, such as Simms, Seymours, Dunmores and Glentons, carry the names of the families who lived there in the early days of post-Columbian settlement.

Columbus definitely came to this island, populated at the time by Lucayans, and it was here that he first saw the hammock, later to be adopted by all European seamen. This was also the first place that Europeans saw tobacco being smoked. As already stated in the section on Spanish Wells, many pirates accepted the amnesty offered by Governor Woodes Rogers, and quite a few of their number decided to settle on Long Island.

One of the first crops to be grown here with success was sea island cotton. Crops today are corn, bananas, mangoes, peas and other vegetables and fruit. Long Island leads the Bahamas in stock rearing; sheep, hogs, goats and horses are raised here. The total population is only a few thousand.

I do not know of any cheap accommodation here, though you could try the *Thompson Bay Apartments* near Stella Maris, Otherwise go native.

Andros: This is the largest Bahama island, 104 miles long by 40 wide, yet very sparsely populated. The interior, which is unexplored, is inhabited mainly by the Chickcharnies, little people who may be related to the Irish leprechauns. They are little red-eyed pixies with three fingers and three toes. They have been known to hang by their tails from cottonwood trees.

In the middle of the nineteenth century a group of about 50 Seminole Indians, fearing enslavement, left the Florida Everglades and canoed to the northwest coast of Andros. Their descendants still live at Red Bay Village with their own administration and traditions.

The west coast of Andros shelves gradually into shallow water. There are 80 miles of mud flats in all shades of sand, brown and green. The east coast is paralled by the world's third largest underwater reef, some 120 miles long. Inside it is 12 feet deep; outside — the Tongue of the Ocean — it is 6,000 feet deep. Nearby are the Andros Blue Holes (seemingly bottomless holes in the ocean floor).

The main settlements are on the east coast, Congo Town, Drigg's Hill, Mangrove Cay, Fresh Creek (Andros Town), Staniard Creek, Mastic Point and Nicholls Town.

Accommodation in Andros: The following summary of economic accommodation in Andros contains one interesting fact; the only guest house named above but not listed by the tourist board, Fowlers, is of poor value. This highlights my opinion that the tourist board do a good job here, listing all accommodation (when the proprietors supply them with details), and not just the expensive stuff, as many Caribbean countries (notably Jamaica and Haiti) do. So get the official brochure.

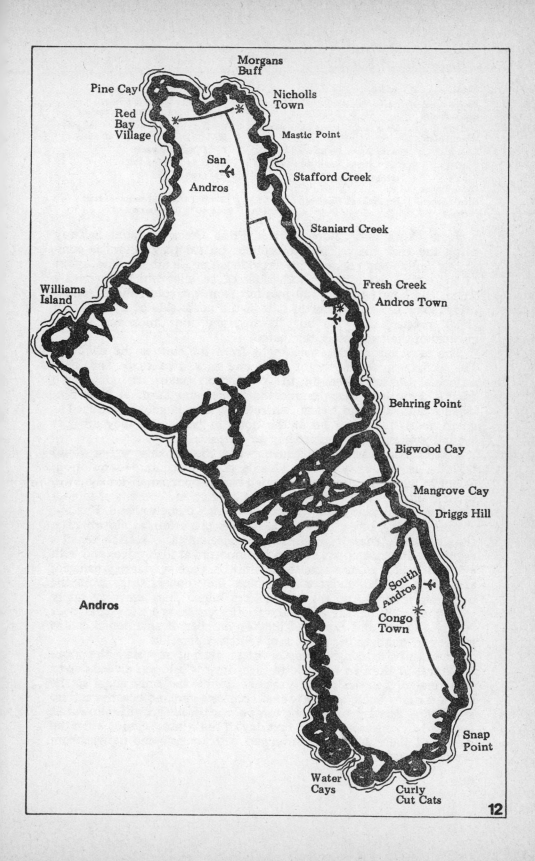

Morgans
Buff

Pine Cay

Nicholls
Town

Red
Bay
Village

Mastic Point

San

Stafford Creek

Andros

Staniard Creek

Williams
Island

Fresh Creek
Andros Town

Behring Point

Bigwood Cay

Mangrove Cay
Driggs Hill

Andros

South
Andros

Congo
Town

Snap
Point

Water
Cays

Curly
Cut Cats

12

Name	Address	Price per Room
Congo Beach Guest House	Congo Town	EP: *S* $12; *D* $14 (all year). MAP: *S* $20; *D* $30 (all year).
Oliver's Guest House	Main Street, South Mastic Point	EP: *S* $10***; *D* $14**** (all year) MAP: *S* $16.50; *D* $27 (all year).
Tinker's	Main Street, South Mastic Point	EP: *D* $12 (all year).
Fowler's	Main Street, South Mastic Point	EP: *S* $12**; *D* $24*.
King's Guest House	Mangrove Cay	EP: *D* $10.
Chickcharnie Hotel	Fresh Creek (see map)	EP: *S* $ 32.80*; (summer rates) *D* $ 40** (summer rates)

Fresh Creek and Andros Town: Fresh Creek is about halfway along the east coast. The atmosphere on stepping ashore is completely unlike any part of New Providence or Eleuthera. The layout of the settlement is along both sides of an inlet which serves as a natural harbour. A causeway juts out from the south shore , and a bridge joins this to the north. It is in the north side of town, Fresh Creek proper, that the boat berths, and the Chickcharnie, the cheaper of the two hotels, is situated.

The most noticeable aspect right from the start is the children. They come in a variety of sizes and ages, two sexes and large numbers. Chasing them in the population stakes are our canine friends. I noticed dogs around the homes and farms in New Providence and suburban Nassau where they were largely introduced as guard dogs. But here, and at the hotel in particular, they are just around, sometimes in packs. They are harmless.

Fresh Creek is a small settlement which the romantic writer would describe as a shanty town. This is not an accurate description, although many buildings are wooden and the people obviously poor, for a shanty town is usually part of a big city and consists of temporary dwellings made from whatever materials come to hand. Rusting, stripped bodies of car wrecks are here in profusion, as elsewhere in the Bahamas. There is a shortage of mechanics to service vehicles regularly, and spare parts have to be imported at high prices and with great difficulty from Nassau or Miami. Cars are very rarely garaged, and often parked under trees, where they collect drips from the overhead foliage. And the salt air is a killer. They are very rarely waxed. In addition, there are no wrecking yards, as are found all over North America and Europe. Thus the number of abandoned cars is disproportionate to the number of vehicles operating.

Tourism is a fringe industry here. During my stay the more expensive of the two hotels, the Lighthouse Club, was closed due to 'electrical difficulties', and I seemed to be the only guest at the Chickcharnie. There are no tourist comforts here, no beaches and no swimming. Boating and fishing can be worthwhile activities however. I arrived from Nassau on the first day of the winter season, when the streets of the capital were thronged with tourists and natives from the Out Islands.

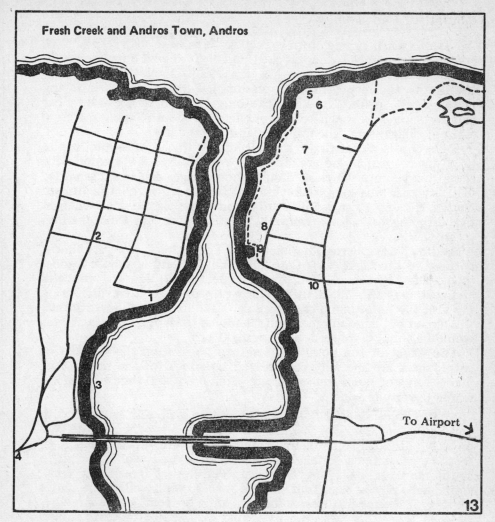

Fresh Creek and Andros Town, Andros

To Airport →

13

Fresh Creek and Andros Town: Key
1 Chickcharnie Hotel
2 Square Deal Restaurant
3 Mailboats dock here
4 Bridge Inn
5 Cannon
6 Lighthouse
7 Lighthouse Club
8 Andros Yacht Club
9 Liquor store
10 Bank

The Chickcharnie Hotel was my first disappointment in terms of accommodation. The price for a double room is $40.00 and up, but a single person has to pay almost the same. This price does not include bathroom, but as that was next door to my room it caused no discomfort. There also appeared to be some problem with the water supply (to be fair, this can be experienced almost anywhere in the

Bahamas). When I came down at 8.10 for breakfast, using the outside staircase, I found all doors locked and had to wait for perhaps 30 minutes. Just little hangups like that, caused by the novelty of tourism to the management (I presume). Perhaps they add to the charm of the place. The hotel can only keep going because its bar and restaurant are open to the public, and it also features a well-stocked village store. The food here is not too good.

Everyone in Fresh Creek was friendly, with the exception of the hotel management who are, however, courteous. I was treated with some reserve on my arrival, though the manager can be forgiven for this. My hair was long, unkempt and knotted from that nightmare voyage and my clothes filthy from sprawling on the deck amongst the cargo (most of it, ironically, destined for the Chickcharnie) trying to die.

Andros Town, across the inlet from Fresh Creek, consists almost entirely of the *Lighthouse Club* and facilities, and is almost a ghost town. The Lighthouse Club, Andros Yacht Club, liquor store, bank and customs office make up the main part of the settlement. During my visit the hotel complex, which can take up to a hundred guests, was closed but in good repair and scheduled to re-open shortly. Rates would be about $45 per double room, MAP.

The effect of the hotel's closure can be seen on the way out of town; there are specially constructed buildings for the hotel staff, many now obviously unoccupied. Some do still house families, whose poverty is evident.

Mastic Point: Mastic Point comprises two main settlements, north and south, separated by a road junction. This is officially the case anyway, although some of the natives are unsure which is which. In fact the inhabitants populate both sides of a road winding north to south more or less along the coast. The houses bunch into small settlements in perhaps four or five places, whilst elsewhere single houses, or groups of three or four, straddle the road. Other stretches of road are either bordered by mangrove swamps or thick undergrowth, with no habitation. At one point in the south end of town the road runs by a small cemetery. Here small, simply carved tombstones alternate with the crudest of wooden crosses. This contrast of moderate wealth with abject poverty is echoed throughout, and seen to best advantage by just walking up the road.

In the south part of town there are three stores, Noah's Family Fare, Tinker's and Fowler's. The houses here are predominantly

Mastic Point: Key

1 Bahama Harbour	5 Oliver's Guest House
2 Boatbuilding	6 Tinker's Guest House
3 Store	7 Cemetery
4 Desert Inn Bar/Restaurant	8 Fowler's Guest House

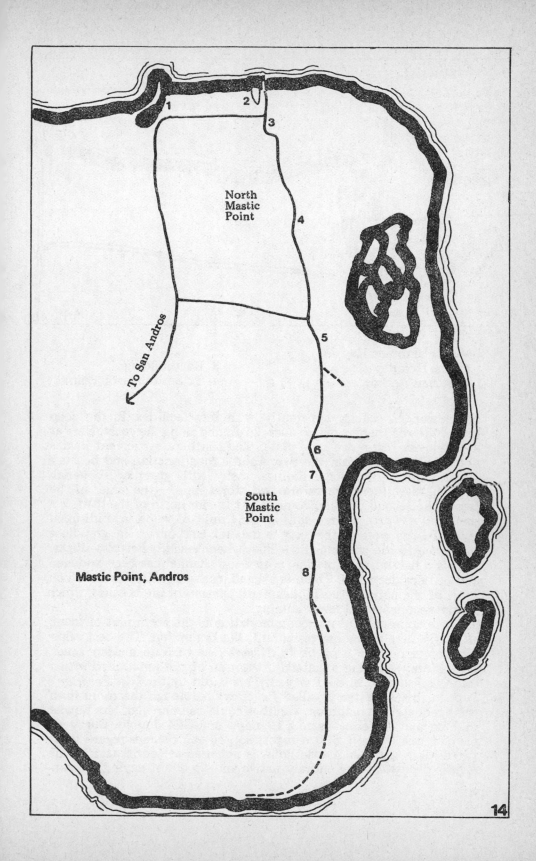

North
Mastic
Point

To San Andros

South
Mastic
Point

Mastic Point, Andros

14

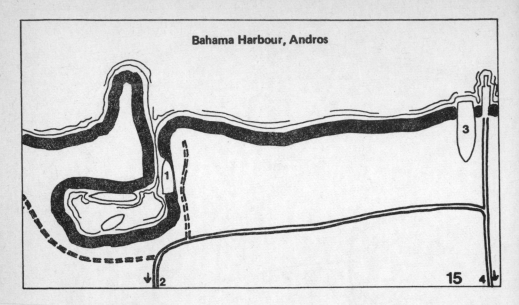

Bahama Harbour, Andros

15

Bahama Harbour: Key
1 Miss Beverley
2 To San Andros
3 Boatbuilding
4 To South Mastic Point

crude wooden shacks, apparently with few facilities. In the deep south, the road tapers out to a track running along the coast. Here at low tide are extensive mud flats. The northern settlement begins about half a mile from the San Andros road junction and boasts a larger number of stone buildings, many with gigantic TV aerials towering over them. There are two stores here — the larger of the two is the second one you come to. At the far north of the town is a small jetty, where a large ship is being built of wood in traditional style. To the west of the jetty is Bahama Harbour — the grandiose title given to the charming little inlet where the *Miss Beverley* docks. This is a natural baby marina, where the channel has been widened and perhaps deepened. There is a small, rocky headland from which some of the natives fish. Flotsam and jetsam dot the beaches, which are not recommended for swimming.

There appears to be no accommodation in the north part of town, although there is one bar/restaurant, the *Desert Inn*. The best value for accommodation is probably *Oliver's Guest House*, a clean, small, single-storey building situated just south of the junction. Further south is *Fowler's*, where I stayed. This is run by the *Miss Beverley's* Captain (his daughter is called Beverley). Although the room itself was adequate, the bathroom facilities could be improved. Mrs Fowler told me that her prices were $12 single and $24 double (European plan). I was charged $10 a night, so you can perhaps regard these figures as negotiable. Mastic Point is not used to tourist traffic, the regular clientele being entirely native and no doubt paying substantially less. If Oliver's is full, try *Tinker's* (near the cemetery).

Walking up the road I felt like Dr Livingstone. People would stop and stare, though often only after I had passed them. Silence would fall upon the children as if I was a Martian, although some of the braver (or ruder) ones would call out 'Hey white man, give me a dollar.' I would turn round and say 'My name is Frank.' Some would then reply 'Hey Frank, give me a dollar,' but the majority were stopped in their tracks.

The other settlements in Andros: Travelling between the settlements is difficult, as again there is no bus service. Hitching a ride is the only possible means of travel, but this is harder than on Eleuthera, with less traffic going shorter distances. All the settlements, such as Blanket Sound, Love Hill, Stafford Creek, are small and it may be impossible to find accommodation — or a cooked meal. One place that does serve food, very good too, is Emily's, a little yellow shack on the way into Stafford Creek. If you get a chance to eat here, and you are not in a hurry, do.

The road from Mastic Point northwards is in poor condition and metalled for only a short part of the way. But it is an interesting ride, as the road is bordered on both sides by young pine trees. Farms can be seen, both for crop-growing and for cattle rearing. There is an increasing incidence of joint Bahamian-American agricultural development here. As elsewhere in the Bahamas, the soil can be shallow, but where it is deep it is rich and fertile. This entire area was once the property of Neville Chamberlain, before he was summoned to the United Kingdom by his family to enter British political life. The natives in these parts (though few, if any, can have known him) all speak highly of him.

The Exumas: Originally I had Great Exuma on my schedule, largely because of the prospect of sailing down the Exuma Cays, part of which are a national park. However I was reliably advised that this journey was something of a waste of time by mail boat, and should be undertaken by private yacht; one can then set a course with the accent on scenic beauty and take time over it.

Great Exuma is now being developed as the newest place for expatriate Americans and others to buy their island homes in the sun. A one-day inspection tour, flying both ways, is available for $29. This includes transfers from your hotel to the airport and return, a tour of the island and lunch at the Bahama Sound Beach Club. This tour is organized by an outfit wishing to sell luxury homes (or it may be sites) so there are two points to note: it may be a good idea to give the impression that you are considering buying a luxury home, or looking them over for a relative, employer, etc; if you sign up on the dotted line you get your $29 back. Contact Bahama Acres Ltd, Beaumont Arcade, Bay Street (very close to the Mignon Guest House), Naussau. Telephone 28015.

If you travel by more plebian means you will require accommodation, which is generally expensive here. You could try *John Marshall's Guest House* in George Town. European Plan rates are: single $14, double $22. MAP: single $21, double $36. Groups of four could try *Regatta Point Apartments* where a two-bedroom apartment costs $36 ($9 per head).

Grand Bahama: This is one island I had no inclination to visit. Formerly one of the least developed of the islands, it became important sometime after Dr Castro's successful revolution in Cuba terminated Havana's position as the rich Americans' playground in the Caribbean. Chosen partly because of its proximity to Miami, Freeport was built speculatively as a tourist and gaming centre. Thus you have seven 18-hole golf courses, the International Bazaar stocked with goods from all over the world, red London buses, all tourist paraphernalia and very high prices to boot (in fact, although there is very much accommodation available, the cheapest room is $19 to $25 — the *El Conquistador Hotel*).

Sometime during my trip in the Caribbean — I forget where — I was talking to an American girl when the subject of the Bahamas cropped up. 'I didn't like the Bahamas,' she said. This amazed me, as the girl was obviously not stupid. 'Where did you go?' I asked. 'Freeport.'

Nevertheless, we try to please all tastes in this book, so I include this short section and maps. The tourist board (addresses in

Freeport/Lucaya: Key

1 International Bazaar
2 El Casino
3 Golf courses
4 Williams Town
5 Rand Memorial Nature Centre
6 Shopping centre
7 Columbus Theatre
8 Castaways Resort
9 Indies House
10 Holiday Inn

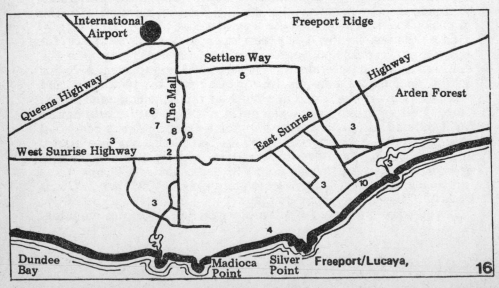

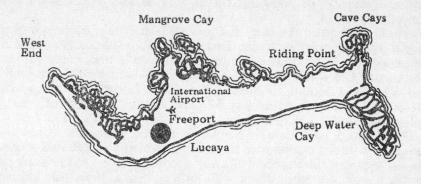

West
End

Mangrove Cay

Cave Cays

Riding Point

International
Airport

Freeport

Deep Water
Cay

Lucaya

Grand Bahama

Appendix 2) produce a good brochure on the island which, with their accommodation brochure, should supply all the information you need if you are that way inclined.

Great Inagua: You will almost certainly visit this island if you intend to reach Haiti by way of the Turks and Caicos Islands, whether travelling by sea or air. Here are two sights of interest. Firstly there is the salt lake, a contributor to the Bahamas export balance sheet, and the pink flamingoes, for which the island is a sanctuary. The pink flamingo is the national bird of the Bahamas, and there is also a colony of them on Paradise Island. Much of Inagua is a national park.

Inexpensive accommodation is available in the island's main settlement, Matthew Town, at *Ford's Inagua Inn*. The year round price is $11 for a double, European Plan. There is another hotel, *The Main House*, in the main settlement again, offering American plan rates (room and three meals) as follows: single $17.50 and double $32.50. Of this, you can assume that at least $10 per person is for food. You won't see many tourists here.

Bimini: An island becoming increasingly popular as a tourist centre. The Bahamas Tourist Board claims that the Biminis are 'The Game Fishing capital of the World'. In addition, the discovery of ruins of unknown antiquity and associated with the Atlantis legend has been well publicised locally. Accommodation can be found at *Brown's Hotel* in North Bimini. Rates are: EP, single $20, double $25; (summer). The Compleat Angler, once Ernest Hemingway's home is very popular. It charges $30 single and $50 double.

Chalk's Airlines, who fly seaplanes from Miami to Paradise Island, Nassau, have two flights each day which make a stop in Bimini. For an extra fee ($20) you can stop over as long as you wish in Bimini before flying on to Nassau. This facility is also available in the opposite direction.

Crooked Island: Like Inagua, Crooked Island may become a stop over if you are travelling to the Turks and Caicos Islands. So you will be pleased to know that accommodation here is reasonably priced. *The Sunny Lea Guest House* at Colonel Hill charges $8 for a single and $12 for a double, EP. *The T & S Guest House* at Cabbage Hill offers singles at $10, doubles at $14 and two bedroomed cottages at $24, all EP. MAP is available also, at $17 single and $27 double.

The Legend of Atlantis: No book on the Bahamas would be complete without a reference to Atlantis, which was situated somewhere between Gibraltar and Florida according to legends dating as far back as Plato, who, along with other Greeks, heard the stories from the Egyptians. Most of the evidence has been based on written and verbal accounts up to now, but recently underwater remains of what appear to be man-made buildings have been discovered. Andros and the Tongue of the Ocean feature strongly in the Atlantis legend, and also in the so-called Bermuda Triangle Mystery.

Personally I give very little credence to the Bermuda Triangle Mystery. Too many explainable happenings have been given an air of mystery, and disappearances outside the area have been included in the legend to bolster the romance and sell more books. Additionally, conditions in the Bahamas area are notoriously fickle, as I know from experience, and the history of the Bahamas is saturated with shipwrecks, few of which, if any, appear in the Bermuda Triangle stories.

The legend of Atlantis appears to me more feasible. Troy was discovered by an archaeologist following the tales of Homer, and digging where those stories indicated the city would be; Bible stories have been proved true by excavation. It is significant that the Atlantis legend originated in Egypt, a country with a style of architecture — the pyramids — only found elsewhere in Mexico and Central America.

Now remains of structures which can only be man-made have been discovered in the Bahamas. Off Bimini a pavement or wall has been discovered of such length that it can only be photographed from the air or in sections. Off north Andros photographs have been taken of the foundations of what appears to be a two-roomed building. As the bottom of the ocean pushes upwards in part, more may be discovered in the future.

Anyone interested in these legends should read a specialist book before leaving for the Bahamas.

Leaving the Bahamas: It may be possible to get a seagoing cargo ship from Nassau to Jamaica (Kingston, Ocho Rios, Port Antonio or Montego Bay), but it will be difficult and not necessarily cheap. I think this is a case where it is best to fly. This is one of the air tickets that you will have bought in your home country.

Part 2: Nassau to Port-au-Prince

I recommend Air Jamaica. First, there are pecuniary advantages. Although they charge the same fares as anyone else, the fare Nassau/Montego Bay/Kingston is very little more than the Nassau/Montego Bay fare. This means that you could fly into Montego Bay, make a complete circuit of the island by road, then fly from Montego Bay to Kingston a day or two before you intend leaving the country. Additionally they have a flight originating in Chicago which stops in Nassau, so you could save money on sector fares if you are coming from Chicago (a good travel agent can explain this to you). Full details of this and other ways of travelling from North America are dealt with in Appendix 1 'How to Get There'.

Try to make your reservation for the flight from Nassau as far in advance as possible, especially if travelling at Christmas or at any other peak period.

There is no Jitney bus to the airport so a taxi is the only practical means of getting there. At $6.50 that is expensive for one, so if alone try to team up with someone going to the airport at the same time. One suggestion is to make your way to the Sheraton British Colonial where you have a good chance of finding someone wanting to split the cost of a taxi.

There is a $3 departure tax from Nassau. Air Jamaica check-in will require all your documentation to be in order. That means normally that they will insist on a ticket from Jamaica elsewhere and a ticket to your home country. I showed them my ticket from Barbados to London which they accepted only grudgingly.

The flight itself was enjoyable. Service was good, as was the food (a cold snack meal), though bar service is not free. The complimentary rum bamboozle is. Air Jamaica also produce an excellent inflight magazine. But the greatest pleasure of the trip for me was the view. It is worthwhile getting a window seat, as on a clear day the vista below is beautiful. We were hardly in the air before New Providence slipped away behind us, its submarine coastline of coral, rock and sand clearly visible through the turquoise sea. The clarity of the water in the Bahamas is remarkable when seen from a boat, but viewed from the air it is stunning.

I had hardly disposed of my rum bamboozle before we were over Andros; and it is that part of Andros which must be the most spectacular when seen from the air, the island's midriff between Behring Point and Mangrove Cay. Muted greens, browns, beige and sand colours produce a picture more exhilarating then one can imagine by just studying a map. And the water is so clear I could never be sure which was land and which sea.

You will probably be enjoying your meal when Cuba approaches, surrounded by that same turquoise window. This is a more familiar sight, a plan of cultivated, neat fields, frequently scored by roads, in turn straddled by towns rather than settlements, rather like a spider in its web. A second cup of coffee or a drink later and the plane is dipping steeply towards Sir Donald Sangster International Airport, Montego Bay, Jamaica.

JAMAICA

Until C.C. arrived Arawak Indians were quite hapilly living in Xaymaca, 'Land of Wood and Water'. He renamed it Saint Jago, presumably for the usual religious reasons. The island remained under Spanish control until 1655 when a force of Cromwell's soldiers, who should have gone to Haiti instead, landed and despatched the Spaniards. It was some time after this that the island was rechristened Jamaica.

The island is 144 miles long and 49 miles wide and a complete contrast to the Bahamas. It is very mountainous, the highest peak, Blue Mountain Peak in the eastern parish of Saint Thomas, rising to 7,402 feet. Roughly speaking, the mountains run along the spine of the country, with other hilly areas too. The largish town of Mandeville is 2,000 feet above sea level. There is a hilly area with few roads between Falmouth and Mandeville which is known as the Cockpit Country. This is the home of the first independent Jamaicans, the Maroons, runaway slaves who established independent villages during the Spanish and British colonial periods. Their name is an anglicised version of the Spanish word 'Cimarrones'. They harassed the planters to such an extent that various treaties were signed granting them extensive rights of self-government. I am given to understand that even today the Maroons have almost complete control over their own affairs.

The rest of the country is politically divided up into three counties, from left to right Cornwall, Middlesex and Surrey. These are subdivided into parishes. Government of the country is based on the British system with a two-chambered legislature, Prime Minister and Cabinet and official opposition. At the time of writing the head of state is Queen Elizabeth 2, but the prime minister has stated that he hopes to persuade the people to change this. There are two main political parties, the Jamaica Labour Party which is nationalist, and the People's National Party, which is labour, or socialist. The PNP forms the present government, having been recently re-elected with a landslide majority. The Prime Minister is Michael Manley; his father, Norman Manley, led Jamaica to independence in 1962, making it the first British Caribbean colony to become independent.

Immigration Requirements: Broadly the same as the Bahamas, with no visa required of most nationalities. Technically, Canadian and US citizens do not even need a passport (this also applies in many other countries) but I can't imagine any reader of this book travelling without a passport. You should have a certificate to show you have been vaccinated against smallpox and those air tickets I keep stressing the need for. Again ask for a week more than you think you'll need, as you will probably stay longer than you planned.

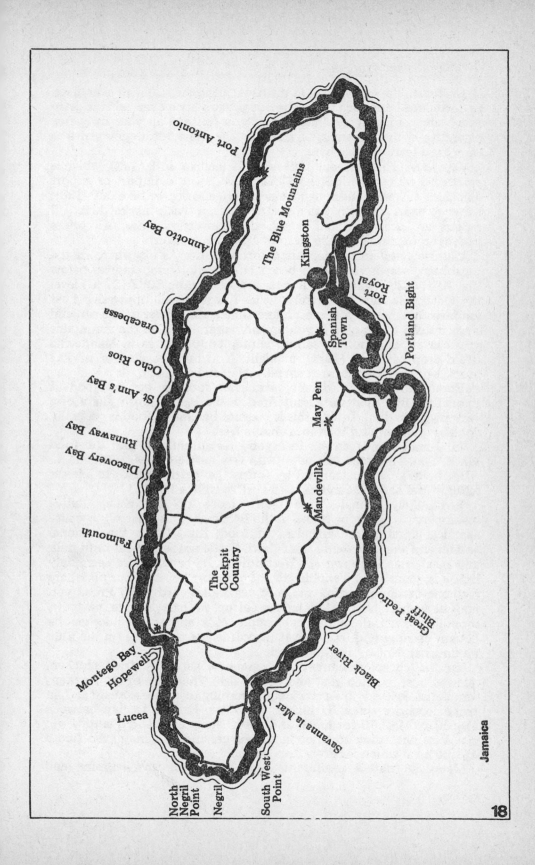

Port Antonio

Annotto Bay

The Blue Mountains

Kingston

Oracabessa

Port Royal

Ocho Rios

Portland Bight

St Ann's Bay

Spanish Town

Runaway Bay

May Pen

Discovery Bay

Mandeville

Falmouth

The Cockpit Country

Great Pedro Bluff

Montego Bay

Black River

Hopewell

Lucea

Savanna la Mar

North Negril Point

Negril

South West Point

Jamaica

18

Customs: You may bring in the usual allowances. There is no need to introduce liquor as this can be bought at a little over half the price you were paying in the Bahamas. If you finished all your duty-free cigarettes in the Bahamas, buy 200 on the plane before you arrive as they are a terrible price here.

Currency: The currency unit is the Jamaican dollar (J$), which is worth US 58 cents. US$1 = J$1.70. It is illegal to import or export Jamaican currency (although residents are allowed to take out J$20); these controls mean that there is, at times, a black market here. US dollars are accepted, but watch the conversion rates. All prices except accommodation are given in J$ in this section.

Climate: very much dependent on altitude. As elsewhere in the Caribbean, sea breezes keep beach and coastal temperatures below the 90°F (32°C) mark in summer and around the 80°F (27°C) level in winter. So there is rarely what I would call oppressive heat (though this means you can underestimate the power of the sun and burn instead of tanning if you are not careful). Up in the mountains you can expect cooler weather; winter temperatures in Mandeville often drop to 50°F (10°C) at night. You may be glad of it. The months of heaviest rain are generally May and October.

Food and Drink: For me, Jamaican food is not as good as Bahamian. But then restaurant food in the Bahamas is usually of a very high standard. I think this is because Bahamian food is generally cooked to order, and therefore always fresh

In Jamaica one can eat in a good restaurant yet find the food bland — international cuisine — with few native dishes on the menu. Also, because it is patronised by tourists, expatriates and (to a lesser extent) the native bourgeoisie, the prices will be high.

Fortunately Jamaica has many more of the cheap native restaurants than can be found in the Bahamas. This is largely because Jamaica is fairly self-sufficient in food; the goat is the national animal and the hen the national bird. Cattle are reared for both milk and meat, rice is grown (in Westmoreland), bananas are seemingly limitless, yams (not dissimilar to the potato when on your plate) are just one of the incredible range of vegetables cultivated. Fruits you may never have heard of include sweetsop, soursop, mango, pawpaw, sapodilla, ortanique and otaheiti apple. Milk and orange juice can be bought cheaply and even excellent coffee is grown here (in the Blue Mountains). Not to mention sugar.

In the cheap restaurants the menu is generally fried chicken, stewed beef, curried goat and boiled fish. There are of course many variations. Prices will vary widely according to where you are and, in some localities, may be higher in winter. Expect to pay between J$1.60 and J$2.50 for lunch or dinner. The quality and quantity will not vary according to price in this range, and you may even find a J$1.60 meal which is better than a J$2.50 one.

Jamaican native restaurants and bars seem unwelcoming and

hazardous to the wary tourist. They are usually shabby outside, dark within and often feature locals framing the doorway. They can sometimes be difficult to find too — round the back of a house or up some stairs. But all are safe for the traveller, with the possible exception of those in some parts of Kingston.

The standard accompaniment to the meat/fish/fowl dishes mentioned above is peas 'n' rice, or boiled rice, with tomato and possibly lettuce or banana. In better restaurants you should be served a wide variety of Jamaican vegetables. Often the rice is served in a separate bowl.

Saving money by economizing on food is more easily done here. A good breakfast can cost between J$1 and J$2, depending on whether you use a native restaurant or your hotel for the purpose. Lunch can easily consist of a spiced bun (12 cents from snack bars and grocery stores) or beef patty, and soft drink, fruit juice or milk. This leaves you free, appetitewise and budgetwise, for a humble or good, but anyway filling, dinner in the evening. Local dishes include ackee and salt fish, suckling pig, jerk pork, stamp-and-go mackerel, pepperpot soup, and curried goat (which I sometimes found hard to get).

The local beer, Red Stripe, is very good and available everywhere. Prices start at 40 cents, then increase — 45, 50, 60, 70 — depending on where you are. The most I paid was 70 cents in the Dome restaurant (Montego Bay) but you can pay a lot more in the tourist places, usually over J$1. The Jamaican white rum is very fine. Expect to pay 20 to 40 cents a time in a native bar, or 80 cents for 'Half a Q'; a 'Q' — a bottle the size of a hip-flask — generally costs about J$1.50. Superb mixed with a little ginger. Appleton's, the leading distillery, makes various types of white and red rum.

Accommodation in Jamaica: Unlike the Bahamas the tourist board here does not list much of the available accommodation. This means that what they call cheap I call expensive. The prices I paid therefore ranged between US$5 and US$15 per night (the listed places charge tax and service charge on top of the listed price). The unlisted places are pretty basic and generally, with the exception of Negril, patronised by natives only.

The economy and cost of living: Jamaica's main exports are bauxite (for aluminium), tourism and agricultural produce, chiefly bananas and sugar, in that order. Unfortunately, in recent years all have declined. Many tourists have been kept away by the tales of violence, the bauxite mining has run into difficulties (particularly around Mandeville), and overseas markets are less receptive to Jamaican agricultural produce (most bananas were exported to Britain, but the collapse of the pound sterling over the last few years has made Jamaican bananas very expensive for the British housewife).

In addition to this, social changes within Jamaica intended to improve the lot of the 'Sufferers' (as Jamaica's poor describe themselves) have disturbed the smooth flow of commerce, discouraged investment and added a burden to the public purse. These same results have also been caused by the hysterical attitude of much of 'The Free World' towards Jamaica's socialist policies and friendship with Cuba. It was suggested to me in Jamaica, and I believe there to be an element of truth in this, that much of this unfavourable publicity — mainly the exaggeration of Jamaica's reputation as a violent society and the threat of imminent communism — has been generated to foster dissatisfaction with the government. The people had their own answer to that one. Anyone who knows the Jamaicans will realize that they are perhaps the least likely of all the people on earth to accept the restrictions of a communist society, as we know it.

Jamaicans in the towns seem to live better than their Bahamian counterparts, largely because Jamaica is self-sufficient to a great degree. But there is a great difference here between what the native pays and what the visitor is expected to pay.

So the average tourist can expect to find Jamaica more expensive than almost all other Caribbean countries. Prices of accommodation rise every year. Tourist haunts are very expensive; uptown in Mo'Bay the visitor can pay J$1.50 for a beer in a nightclub featuring international music and other tourists for company. Downtown clubs/bars provide excellent local music, dancing facilities and company, and the same beer at 45 cents. So whilst the tourist can find Jamaica pricey, the traveller will find the opposite — that it is far cheaper than the Bahamas. Although I don't recommend it, it is possible to live here on US$10 a day. I spent US$22 a day, yet this was largely because I was forced to use expensive accommodation until I found the cheap places. Using this book a couple can expect to pay from US$28 to US$36 a day between them without economizing too much.

The people: 'Out of many, one people.' This is the national motto, which is printed on some of the banknotes. It is certainly true. Jamaica has been a melting pot for all the world's races, and although the negro strain predominates there is a wide variety of physiognomy. Among Jamaicans themselves there is no racialism; a man may hate another illogically because of his politics, but not because of his colour. What little racialism there is has been introduced by the tourists, and is mainly due to a lack of understanding on both sides.

The Jamaicans are outgoing, colourful, cheerful, excitable, loving, gentle if shown respect and vicious when upset. One of the unique points about Jamaicans is that a gentle man can become violent if he thinks he, or Jamaica, is being insulted, whilst a potentially dangerous hustler will be kind and helpful if shown respect.

Jamaicans are colourful in their dress, mannerisms, music and most of all speech, their unique patois. Perhaps vibrant is a better word. When spoken fast, as it usually is, and with strong accentuation, this patois sounds like a foreign language. This is one of the strengths of the reggae music, where a good vocalist can add excitement to what would otherwise be mundane lyrics.

The total population of Jamaica is around the two million mark. There are lots of pretty girls, and many beautiful women.

Transportation: You can get almost anywhere in Jamaica by bus or minibus. Country buses are very old and crowded, slow and cheap. You can learn much about the country by travelling on them. I understand that they theoretically run to schedules, but nobody knows what these schedules are. Minibuses run when they feel like it, provide a very fast and efficient service at a slightly higher price than country buses and are very dangerous. Jamaican drivers must be high in the Top Ten of the World's Worst Drivers, and the more reckless become minibus drivers. Shared taxis are also available, though at a high price and without any advantage to be gained from using them. As far as normal taxis are concerned, you should note that by no means all are metered and you should therefore always confirm the fare before jumping aboard.

There are two cross-country railway routes, both of which start in Kingston. The longer of the two runs through Spanish Town, May Pen, Mandeville and such places as Balaclava, Kendal, Ipswich and Cambridge to Montego Bay. The second major route skirts the Blue Mountains then passes along the coast to Port Antonio. Both routes afford splendid views of Jamaica's spectacular scenery.

There is also a domestic airline, Trans-Jamaican, serving five airfields. This is only really of interest if you are short of time, as you will miss too much by flying. The airports served are Kingston (Tinson Pen, downtown), Montego Bay, Ocho Rios, Port Antonio and Mandeville. Jamaica Air Taxi will fly just about anywhere you can land a plane, but this is charter of course and therefore only suitable for groups unless you can get an empty seat. Bookings with both these lines can be made with Air Jamaica offices in North America or Europe.

There are city buses in Kingston and Montego Bay.

Banks: Be very careful about changing money in Jamaica. When you exchange cash or travellers cheques be sure to get a receipt from the bank. You will need it to change your Jamaican dollars back into US dollars when you leave the country. No bank gave me one of these slips, although I changed in excess of US$200, so that when I tried to change a paltry J$12 back into real money on leaving, the clerk in the airport bank refused. For $12!! This I believe was deliberate, as Jamaican currency was worth only half its face value outside the country. A Jamaican lady in the queue before me was forced to take J$100 out of the country illegally for the same reason.

I found Jamaican banks amongst the World's Worst, particularly First National City Bank (although I found this bank pretty bad throughout the Caribbean). Service is uniformly poor for Jamaicans and visitors.

The Music: This is where it comes from. Reggae, the best modern dance music. Now firmly established worldwide as one of the principal forms of rock music, it is based on a hypnotic, eminently danceable beat with lyrics telling of everyday life in Jamaica, particularly in the shanty towns, love songs and many numbers with strong sexual undertones or overtones. If you are a puritan don't worry — only a Jamaican can understand the words!

Its beginnings were in the early sixties, a development from North American rhythm & blues and jazz blended with Caribbean calypso. At this stage it was known as bluebeat. Later progressions took it through ska and rock steady to reggae, the beat which has made Jamaican musicians internationally famous.

The music has always enjoyed some popularity in England (largely because the sizeable Jamaican community there ensures a large market), from the early days of Prince Buster's 'Al Capone'. Desmond Dekker and others enjoyed much success in the sixties, and the mid-seventies saw the music mushroom in popularity in the United States, principally through Bob Marley and the Wailers. British and American big-name artists now regularly record reggae music.

Bob Marley's songs are centred principally upon the Rastafarian cult. His success has led to Rastafarian philosophy and references becoming perhaps the most important theme of late-seventies reggae, with artists like Tapper Zukie building almost all their material around the religion, in itself the strongest rallying point of West Indian youth.

Although almost everywhere you will hear reggae throbbing from bar-room juke boxes, it is a strange fact that the rather insipid Jamaican 'Radio One' rarely plays reggae, preferring international 'pop'.

The Rastafarians: This cult is becoming better known all the time as its adherents grow in number throughout the world. Rastafarians are easily recognised by their beards and braided hair. The terms 'Rastaman' and 'Natty Dread' (the hair style is often referred to as 'dread locks') are used to describe sect members of differing outlook. A Rastaman is usually a reserved, peace-loving hippy, whilst the Natty Dread convey heavy political and violent overtones, As far as I can tell there is no visual difference between the two.

The beliefs of the cult are both religious and political. Rastafarians draw a parallel between their own history and that of the Jews in the Old Testament. They regard Ethiopia both as their home and their promised land; the New World to which their ancestors were transported they believe to be Babylon. Jamaicans are more itinerant than most Caribbean peoples, and have spread throughout the world in large numbers. Many Rastafarians in other parts of the world (eg England) regard their current country of residence as Babylon.

Although the cult originated in Jamaica, it has spread to the extent that many young people in other Caribbean countries — the Bahamas and Saint Lucia are two examples — have adopted the dread locks and subculture. One of the chief vehicles for the dissemination of the cult is the very excellent reggae music produced by Bob Marley and others.

How Safe is Jamaica?: A great deal has been written about violence in Jamaica, and there is some truth in it: as the English proverb says, 'no smoke without fire'. There are two types of violence, the first directed against tourists, and the second of a political nature. The most common motive for the first is robbery, and it is usually confined to the beaches and resort areas. In recent years, Montego Bay was the centre of this activity but it is now sparsley populated with tourists, who stay away through fear and because other places have become more fashionable. This reduction in the numbers of tourists and extensive operations by the security forces have cleared away the criminal element. As mentioned later, I found it perfectly safe to walk about in downtown Mo'Bay at any hour of the day or night. The tourists, and with them part of the criminal element, have now departed for Ochos Rios and Negril. Thus these areas can be dicey unless you are careful.

Violence of a political nature is normally centred on Kingston, where certain areas are more dangerous than others. The tourist is usually safer than the native. At the time of writing, the two warring political factions, supporters of the JLP and the PNP, have declared a truce, and stated that they want to work together to rebuild the nation's prosperity. However, the ingredients for a volatile mix are still there. My advice is to check the latest situation at home - with your country's Foreign Office or Department for Foreign Affairs. You can't trust the newspapers.

If I mention the violence, I should also mention the steps being taken to prevent it. The government and the press are actively promoting reconciliation between different groups of political supporters. You will see many people with the words 'peace' and 'love' embellished on their clothing. Most arguments now seem to end with an apology and a drink — I even saw one man jump off his bicycle to break up a fight between two complete strangers. Many people offered me their services as guides purely out of a concern for my safety and well-being.

As a general rule, your attitude to the Jamaicans will determine the way they treat you. If you think that you will feel fear or animosity for any reason, then don't come!

Some Important Notes: Smoking or trading in ganga — grass — is illegal and carries severe penalties.

Be careful but not paranoid with your baggage.

When venturing out at night leave your valuables safely locked away and carry no more money than you will need (mainly because you may otherwise spend it; the chances of being robbed are very slight).

Arrival in Jamaica (Montego Bay): The Jamaican Tourist Board stress the friendliness and hospitality of the Jamaican people. However they are now so concerned about the exaggerated reputation Jamaica has for crimes of violence, and the effect of this on tourism, that an over-protective attitude and excess of officialdom make one feel anything but welcome on arrival.

Immigration was not the trial I expected it to be, but then the official was well aware of both my professions. If you have the correct documentation, it should present no problem. However, the facilities of customs, immigration and tourist information share one open-plan building, not air-conditioned. An Air Canada flight arrived shortly before mine and the airport officials were unable to cope adequately. So expect a lot of waiting, for immigration, then baggage claim, then customs, all in the heat. To be fair, I learned that the airport is being reorganised, so it may well have improved sufficiently by the time of your arrival. Just inside the building is a long rank of porters with trolleys who do not pester you and provide a very good service for very little money. Few people seem to use the tourist information booth, who are very helpful.

Not like the bank. Incredibly, for a country that outlaws the import and export of its currency, there is only a small bank with one cashier (turn left as you go out). It is however possible to use US dollars in Jamaica, so you may prefer to wait before getting Jamaican money (perhaps the next day). But what I found obnoxious was the so-called 'Courtesy Corps'. They stopped me on the way out to ask my destination and grudgingly pointed out the bank. My announced intention of walking to the hotel (literally just outside the airport on the main road) was dismissed. I might lose something on the way (very reassuring for a new visitor) and it was too hot for walking. Leaving the bank I was approached by a friendly taxi driver who told me the fare would be J$3. I was not convinced, but before I could be on my way I was pounced on by two more of the 'Courtesy Corps' who more or less hustled me into that taxi. Not my idea of courtesy.

Another, last observation, enough to instil insecurity into the most intrepid traveller, was the sheer number of uniforms about; inside, immigration officers, customs officials, porters (which I'm not

Montego Bay: Key

1	Ocean View Hotel	6	Coral Theatre
2	Pelican Grill	7	Park and library
3	Verney House Hotel	8	The Parade
4	Harmony House Hotel	9	YMCA
5	Duty free shopping	10	YWCA

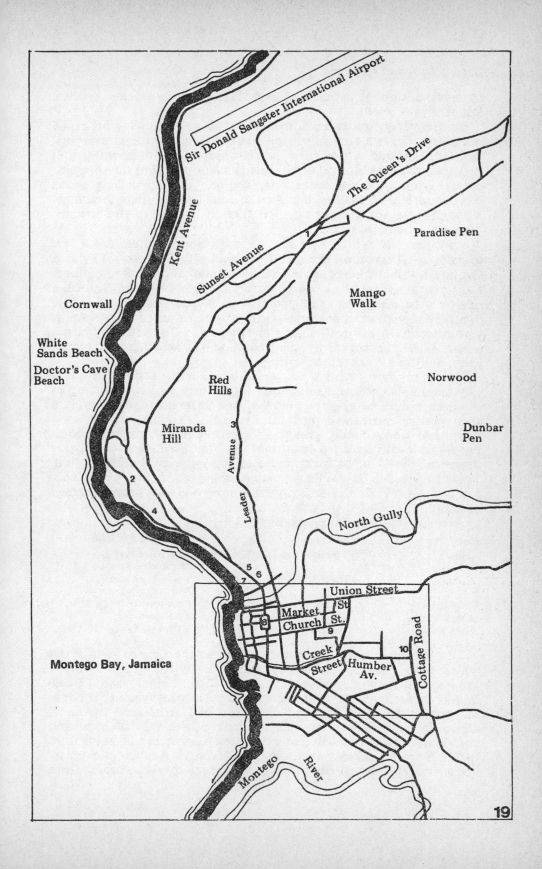

Sir Donald Sangster International Airport

The Queen's Drive

Kent Avenue

Sunset Avenue

Paradise Pen

Cornwall

Mango Walk

White Sands Beach

Doctor's Cave Beach

Red Hills

Norwood

Miranda Hill

Leader Avenue

Dunbar Pen

3

2

4

North Gully

5 6
7

Union Street

Market
Church

St
St.

St.

9

Creek

10

Cottage Road

Street

Humber Av.

Montego Bay, Jamaica

Montego River

19

complaining about); outside, the 'Courtesy Corps' and police, loitering with intent.

Montego Bay: uptown or down?: The main, big hotels start at the north end of town and follow the coast, roughly, up to the airport, with the odd one or two (like the Half Moon and Intercontinental) scattered as far as Rose Hall. So this is where you find the shopping arcades, tourist trade restaurants, wayside vendors selling wood carvings, etc. And the beaches. And of course the tourists. And most (though there are few anyway, less than in Nassau) of the hustlers. This is not Jamaica for me.

Downtown is full of real life. During the day there are a few tourists, but I saw none at night. Uptown it is difficult to walk down the street without being spoken to by people who want something. Here you are ignored as people go about their business. But ask a question, or directions, and you will be helped most courteously. Similarly if you extend a greeting it will be returned with warmth and interest. Downtown's narrow streets pulse with hustle and bustle occasionally punctuated by the pounding of reggae from a record shop. But it is at night that it swings.

One of my best evenings out on the whole trip was here, with free Christmas celebrations, Jamaican-style. A stage had been set up in the main square outside the town hall and different reggae musicians and vocalists performed most of the night. Young and old were there, and whole family groups with little children running about. People danced. I watched two-foot-long lengths of sugar cane being shaved of the skin, or bark, and sold for immediate consumption. There were small boys selling peanuts, oranges and corn on the cob. I was the only tourist enjoying the show and the people seemed pleasantly surprised that I was there.

Accommodation in Montego Bay

Name	Address	Price per room in US$
YMCA	Humber Avenue	$5 per person per day ****. $18 per person per week *****.
YWCA	Church Street	$4 per person per day. $14 per person per week.
The Walpole	Union Street	$8 per room; S***, D ****.
MaComba Club	Church Lane	$6 per room.
Ocean View	Sunset Avenue	S $17**; D $26**.

You can walk easily from the airport to *the Ocean View Hotel* which is the cheapest accommodation listed by the tourist board in Montego Bay. Winter rates are about US$17 single and US$26 double including 5 per cent tax and 10 per cent service. It is clean, the rooms are well furnished and have two entrances, and maid service is good. The price also includes a breakfast of toast and coffee, with extras available at extra cost. Dinner has to be ordered before 2 pm on the day you require it, as this is a small hotel (guest house really) and can only afford to prepare meals to order. I was served a three-course meal, the main course being T Bone steak supplied with too many different kinds of vegetables to count and a separate bowl of rice which I couldn't even touch. There was certainly no stinting on quantity, and at J$4.50 it was good value by hotel and tourist restaurant standards. A beer here is 50 cents. If the comfort and standard of accommodation is more important to you than its cost, then you should ignore the star rating given above and stay here.

The location of this hotel is an important factor in its acceptability. If you intend to have several days in Mo'Bay and while away many happy hours downtown, then the situation of the Ocean View is inconvenient, which is one of the reasons why I moved out. It is also a little over half a mile to the beaches and main hotel area. But if you intend only to overnight in Mo'Bay you may find it convenient, as there are no transport costs to and from the airport. It is situated on a bus route, and you can stop buses outside the door either in the direction of Rose Hall (J35 cents) or downtown (J5 cents).

Downtown you could try the *YMCA* on Humber Avenue, which costs US$5 per person per day or US$18 per week; thus extremely good value for stays of four nights to a week. This is also available for couples, as there are some double rooms. Spartan washing facilities are of the communal variety, and the rooms starkly furnished, but then what do you expect? Millie, who runs the place, is very friendly, and has some tourist guests, though the majority are natives. Staying here also solves another problem, that of laundry. There are no laundromats in Mo'Bay, and the only way you can get washing done — apart from doing it yourself – is using the laundry downtown or that at the Intercontinental Rose Hall. Both take time and cost money, the Intercontinental being the more expensive of the two. Prices at the town laundry are about J50 cents for a shirt and J80 cents for a pair of trousers. The YMCA has some stone age washing facilities however, and for the price of a packet of washing powder (J41 cents) you can do it yourself. The YMCA is also conveniently situated for the bus to Negril.

Ladies could try the *YWCA* in Church Street. The building is not labelled so ask for directions when you get near to it. In the heart of the downtown area are some guest houses, usually situated over a bar or restaurant. *The Walpole* in Union Street could be a good bet for couples at US$8 per room daily. Very centrally located, it provides a better standard of furnishing than the YMCA, and two adequate bathrooms. Another place is at the *MaComba Club* (principally a bar and discotheque) on Church Lane. The price here is US$6 per room. These last two places are for those who want to hear the non-stop rhythm of reggae when at the hotel.

Eating in Mo'Bay: A patty and soft drink can be bought for J60 cents for lunch at any of the little snack bars (look out for them, as they are so small and dimly lit you could easily walk straight past) and I found that J$1 bought me breakfast of spice cake, orange juice and a pack of cigarettes. Of course you cannot live on this fare, and you will want a proper meal at least once a day. If you want native food the downtown restaurants are best. The standard of cuisine is not as high as in the Bahamas, but besides being the cheapest way of trying native dishes (lunch is usually J$3 or less) you will find that the choice of native dishes offered in the uptown restaurants is small (whatever they tell the folks back home, the tourists seem to prefer the food they are used to). I tried the *Dome House*, where I had ackee with cod fish, and the *Little Delicious*, where I had fried chicken in sauce with salad, peas 'n' rice and yams. Both were J$3; beer was J70 cents at Dome House and a huge glass of orange juice (not pure) US 20 cents at Little D.

For a fairly good meal in pleasant surroundings you could try the *Town House* in Church Street. The extensive menu includes some native dishes with French, American and 'International' cuisine. It is in the basement of an old house, cool with brick walls, thoughtful decor and a slightly rustic atmosphere. It is fairly expensive, though you would only need one meal the day you eat here, and they take credit cards. I paid J$9 for a three-course meal with beer, but you could pay half or twice as much and anything in between. It claims to be Montego Bay's first and most popular restaurant.

The nearest cheapish food place to the Ocean View is the *Pelican Grill*, a walk of a little over a mile. Food is mainly American type with a few local dishes such as curried goat (about J$4). A hamburger meal will cost you about J$3, including french fries, etc. The *Front Porch*, next to the Pelican Grill, was also recommended to me.

Back downtown, *Uncle Vic's* was suggested by a knowledgeable native as being good and cheap. The *Walpole* also has a restaurant.

Bus Services: The number one bus runs between downtown Mo'Bay and Rose Hall every 40 minutes and every 30 minutes at

Downtown Montego Bay: Key

 1 The cage (tourist information)
 2 YMCA
 3 YWCA
 4 Little Delicious Restaurant
 5 Laundry
 6 Pemco Hotel (expensive)
 7 First National City Bank
 8 Dome House Restaurant
 9 Walpole Hotel, restaurant/bar
10 Ma Comba bar/discotheque
11 Uncle Vic's Restaurant
12 The Dome
13 No 1 bus to Rose Hall
14 Snack-it Snack Bar
15 Bus stop for Negril
16 Bus terminals all directions
17 Town House Restaurant
18 The Parade
19 Post office

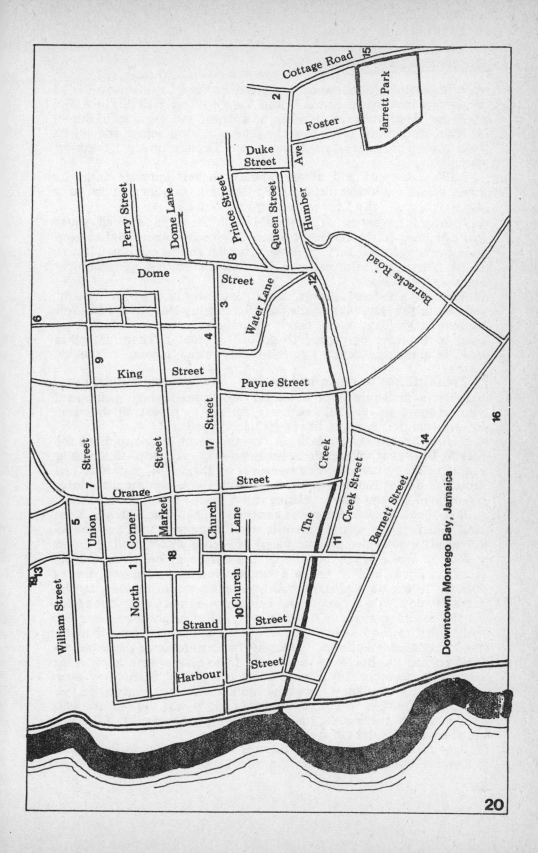

Downtown Montego Bay, Jamaica

20

rush hour times. The fare from the Ocean View to downtown is 15 cents, and from town or the Ocean View to Rose Hall 35 cents. Bus stops are clearly marked between downtown and the start of Sunset Avenue, and from there on the bus will stop when and where requested. There are other services too. These municipal buses are green.

Hall's Transport and others operate ancient country buses for lower prices and longer distances. For less than a dollar you can go to Falmouth, and Ocho Rios will cost you about J$2.

Tourist Information: You should visit the Cage, a small, squat brick building in the centre of town. Originally constructed to keep runaway slaves until they could be returned and/or punished, it now houses the tourist information office which is staffed by a charming and very helpful lady.

Beaches: The best known beach, and the one which brought tourism to Mo'Bay, is Doctor's Cave. During my stay there I saw few tourists in Mo'Bay, so the beach was relatively uncrowded. But get used to the idea of paying to go on (50 cents). There are other beaches along the coast, but these very often belong to the big hotels.

Tourist things to do around Mo'Bay: The Jamaican Tourist Board provides a multiplicity of colourful brochures to help you spend your money, so it would be crazy for me to repeat all the same information. But here is a brief selection anyway.

Rafting on the Martha Brae: A one-and-a-half hour trip down the Martha Brae near Falmouth. A boatman takes you down the river at a cost of J$12 per raft. For transport to Falmouth, expect to pay around a dollar, round trip, on the country bus, and maybe double by minibus. If you take a bathing suit you can swim from the raft.

Rose Hall: Annie Palmer was known as "The White Witch of Rose Hall". In fact she was not a white witch (one who uses her powers for good, usually healing, purposes) or even a witch at all. She was called the White Witch because of the colour of her skin, and the story, as I was told it (in the Bahamas, would you believe) runs as follows: In the days of slavery Annie Palmer would be seen, by the servants and slaves, at first on her balcony and then a short time later on the beach (perhaps 500 yards away). But nobody ever saw her walk down to the beach. So she was presumed to have gone there by the exercise of evil powers. In fact she had a number of slaves build a tunnel from the house to the beach; these slaves were kept in leg irons and dungeons until the job was completed, when they were killed. So only she knew about the tunnel. When not engaged on this she found the time to murder six husbands; it was the seventh who found out what was going on. This is the story I was told. If it is not true please write and tell me.

Rose Hall can be seen from the main road. It is between 300 and 500 yards from the beach, on the right-hand side as you travel from town to the Intercontinental Hotel. Guided tours are available from 9.30 until 5.30 at a cost of J$2.

South of Mo'Bay, past Reading, is *The Rocklands Feeding Station*, a bird sanctuary. It is open from 3.30 until dusk and admission is J$2.

The Governor's Coach Tour leaves Mo'Bay railway station at 10 am every Tuesday, Thursday and Friday, returning at 4 pm. The cost is J$16 per person, including snack lunch. It will take you 40 miles inland, features a calypso band and a visit to Appleton's rum distillery (free samples?) and is full of tourists. Book (two days in advance if possible) with Jamaica Tours (telephone 952 2887).

The Maroons are best visited from Montego Bay or Mandeville. Descended from runaway slaves who formed guerrilla bands and harassed the planters, they still live under military order and it is recommended that you have a guide if you wish to visit them. They form an almost separate state within Jamaica, as they have a constitution affording them a large measure of self-government. They charge for photographs, so check the price before shooting.

Montego Bay to Negril: You can go by taxi, minibus or country bus. The country buses are slow, noisy, old, uncomfortable and cheap. They are also probably the safest way to go — if you hit anything, then God Bless the anything! I was told by the tourist office that buses leave at 9.30, 12 noon and 2.30, but they seem to be more frequent than that. They leave from south of town, but drive right through it — because of the one-way system — before commencing their journey proper. This means that if staying at the YMCA you have a short walk to the bus stop, on Cottage Road (see map). It is a large tin hoarding halfway along. The fare to Negril is J$1, and there are two routes: along the coast road to Hopewell, then south through Chigwell, Chichester, etc to Savanna-La-Mar, then west to Negril; or along the coast road for the whole trip.

My bus (Hall's Transport) took the inland route. The beginning and end of the trip was along roads recognizable as such, although potholed, particularly in the latter stages. But for the majority of the journey (timewise) we bounced along unsurfaced roads which petered out into little better than cart tracks, and at one point was a cart track. The thought of a big bus thundering along a cart track no wider than the vehicle, cut between sugar cane fields (growing right up to the road) sounds incredible, but I was in it. Progress was slow on these sections due to the inadequate roads, uphill gradients (we sometimes climbed uphill at less than 2 miles an hour) and frequent stops. We would often stop between sugar cane fields with no sign of habitation. Someone would get off, and disappear heavily laden, or someone would emerge from the crop and climb aboard. Our progress was further slowed by a puncture and arguments with passengers complaining about broken items in their baggage. You will have plenty of time to observe village life. My bus left at 1.45 and got to Negril at about 7.30.

Minibuses are more frequent, more expensive and more dangerous. They buzz along at high speed slamming on the brakes to pick up or drop passengers. Expect to pay J$2 to J$2.50 but negotiate this before entering. Taxis are more expensive again and the fare should definitely be agreed before acceptance.

Negril: Negril is usually described as 'unspoilt' (though I found it very much spoilt) and according to the tourist board 'will remain unspoilt'. By this they mean an absence of high rise hotels, flashy boutiques and restaurants, and ersatz discotheques. But there are too many tourists already, of the trendy type who tell the folks back home that they go to an away-from-it-all place. Prior to my visit a new 250 room hotel (yes 250!) had just been opened. In this 'away-from-it-all' place I saw more tourists than I had seen in the Bahamas and Montego Bay combined!

The 7-mile beach is in itself superb. Protected by a reef, the bottom barely shelves at all and you can walk out a fair way and still be only waist deep. When the sea is calm it is perfect for poor swimmers (like me) and children. The sea is warm and there are plenty of shady spots on the beach.

The older generation tend to stay on the beach itself, or at the west end of Negril where the coastline is rocky and more suitable for strong swimmers and diving. The centre of Negril is the new Mecca for the young, mainly American (Jamaicans were constantly asking me which State I came from). All these tourists go down to the beach regularly, so that it is, in my opinion, crowded. This means that vendors ply up and down selling arts and crafts, and heavy dudes stroll by, eyes popping out of their heads at the sight of expensive-looking cameras. I was told in Mo'Bay that the hustlers and thieves had been run out of town; this is where many of them have come to.

Negril seems to have been hippified for some time. This means that I wasn't offered 'grass', marijuana or 'ganga' but more precisely 'lambsbread', apparently the name of a popular variety. Its vendors seemed genuinely surprised that they had to explain this to me.

To summarize: the beach is beautiful but crowded, so come out of season. It is more dangerous here than in Mo'Bay, but if you are careful you should be all right. I made a point of speaking to anyone who spoke to me, but it is what you say and how you say it that matters.

Accommodation

Name	Address	Price per room in US$
Rocky Edge	Main road, Negril centre	$6 per room: S****, D****.
Tigress Cottages	Main road, Central Negril	$9, 12 and 17 per room: S***, D****. $60, 70 and 110 per week.
Tensing Pen	West Negril	$12 per person per night: S***, D***.
Various	Red Ground	From $6 to 12 per person (or per room).

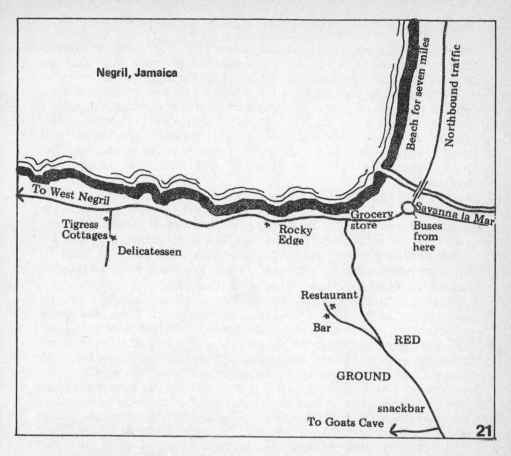

Negril, Jamaica

Beach for seven miles

Northbound traffic

To West Negril

Tigress
Cottages

Delicatessen

Rocky
Edge

Grocery
store

Savanna la Mar

Buses
from
here

Restaurant

Bar

RED

GROUND

snackbar

To Goats Cave

21

I wouldn't particularly recommend where I stayed. The bus dropped me off at a roundabout, where a small boy offered to take me to his mother's house. 'It is very clean with two bathrooms' (which wasn't strictly true). It was dark, I didn't know the place, so I thought, what the hell, why not. I was taken to Red Ground at the back of town. Marion was the proprietor. The cost is US$6 per bed (the original figure I was quoted by the boy, which Marion tried to hike to $8 and was only reduced again by hard bargaining). It would be OK for a couple, but the facilities are inferior to those at the YMCA in Mo'Bay. I did find that staying there afforded me a large measure of protection for some reason.

There is in fact a large number of houses in Red Ground taking in guests, at prices between US$6 and US$12 per bed (or per room). They usually have no identification. The best advice I can give if you want to stay up here is to arrive in daylight and take one of the more expensive places, where towels, soap and toilet paper, etc are normally provided.

If you want to stay nearer the beach and action, try *The Rocky Edge*, which is centrally situated. This is primarily a restaurant and bar with reasonable meals at fair prices (J$2 for a fish or chicken dinner) and drinks at about Mo'Bay non-tourist levels. Mary also has a small number of presentable rooms, with two bathrooms.

Further along the same road you will come to a minor junction, and a sign advertising *The Delicatessen*. It is embellished with a picture of a cat. On the left is Papa Lawrence's establishment, *The Tigress Cottages*. This comprises a large number of cottages and apartments set in spacious grounds. There is a restaurant near the road, and self-catering facilities up the hill. The clientele is exclusively tourist.

Out west there is no beach but also no shortage of rocky coves. If you prefer diving and snorkelling you could try *Tensing Pen*. It is built in very attractive rustic style with thatched rooves and very well laid out with winding paths and flowering shrubs. It is about 3 miles from the Negril roundabout however, so you will need to organize some form of transport. Over the road is a Rastafarian vegetarian restaurant from which good vibes issue.

Eating, drinking and making merry: All these activities can be undertaken at the Rocky Edge. The food and drink are quite reasonable, as described earlier, and there is the perennial juke box. The company, mainly native, is good too. Up in Red Ground there are restaurants and snack bars, again with reasonable prices for what you get, not to mention the Delicatessen and Papa Lawrence's.

Leaving Negril: The difficult part is getting to Savanna-la-Mar, from where services to Mandeville and straight through to Kingston are readily available. A bus leaves Negril, from the roundabout, at about 9.30 am bound for Kingston. The fare to Mandeville is about J$2. Minibuses leave at intervals, at a higher fare, although most will be going as far as Savanna-la-Mar only. Hitchhiking is possible but not recommended; it is far more difficult than in the Bahamas, and here there are regular cheap bus services. The wisest thing to do is to make an early start and be prepared to change at Sav. A minibus from Sav to Mandeville should cost you J$3, but agree the fares first.

Mandeville: I'm not one to welcome cool weather generally, but I was glad of the relief from the heat. In the colonial days, Mandeville was where the administrator's families escaped for the summer; it was also Jamaica's main tourist centre, as it was believed in those days that a sub-tropical climate caused degeneracy.

The town is larger than I imagined, and somewhat spread out. One always seems to be walking up or down a hill, and the roads are rarely straight. The old colonial atmosphere is prevalent in the architecture and the way the town is laid out. The parish church looks very English, the small courthouse has Georgian overtones, whilst many buildings feature sash windows rather than those designed for a sub-tropical climate. Jamaicans in Montego Bay and Negril told me that Mandeville is a wealthy town, but all the people

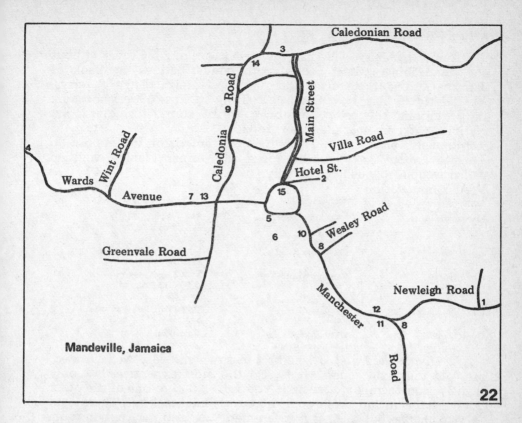

Mandeville, Jamaica

22

Mandeville: Key

1 Mayfair Guest House
2 Mandeville Hotel
3 Hotel Belair
4 To Hotel Astra
5 Bus/minibus terminal
6 Manchester Parish Church
7 Tudor Theatre
8 Texaco petrol (gas) station
9 Esso petrol (gas) station
10 Post office
11 Restaurant/bar
12 Grocery store
13 Esquire Restaurant
14 First National City Bank
15 Court house

I spoke to complained of poverty. The town looks well off, with many neat, well-kept houses, so perhaps the people have fallen on hard times recently. Mandeville is cool in all senses of the word; besides the weather the people are extremely pleasant and together. There are no tourists here which perhaps explains it.

Manchester is the most recent of Jamaica's fourteen parishes. It was formed in 1814 with Mandeville as the administrative centre. More recently the discovery of bauxite in the hills around brought prosperity and expatriates. There is an Alcan plant just north of the town. Staff members, largely American, live in Mandeville and are provided with a Kentucky Fried Chicken restaurant.

I found that Mandeville had the advantages of a big town without the disadvantages. It is packed with banks; besides the Bank of Jamaica and Workers' Bank there are the foreign banks, Barclays, First National City, Nova Scotia, etc. They are in two areas; most are in or around the centre of town, whilst some, including First National City, are near the Belair Hotel.

Ironically, although in 1976 the town voted for the opposition Jamaica Labour Party, the birthplace of Norman Manley, who led Jamaica to independence, is nearby.

Accommodation

Name	Address	Price per room in US$
Mandeville Hotel	Near Main Square	CP: *S* $15 to $23 *D* $26 to $42. Plus 5% tax.
Belair Hotel	Caledonia Road	*S* $15**; *D* $20***. Plus 5% tax.
Astra Hotel	Far end Wards Avenue	*S* $12 to $14***; *D* $16 to $23***. Plus 5% tax; 10% service.
Mayfair Guest House	Newleigh Road	US$9 to US$12 per room: *S***, *D***.
Guest Houses	Wards Avenue and Caledonia Road	Unknown

The Mandeville Hotel is the best in town and very well situated, just off the main square. It is also the most expensive, but only slightly, and there is no saving if you take a taxi to one of the other hotels. Rates include bathroom of course, and breakfast. There is no service charge, but there is a government tax of 5 per cent on room rate. They will only take cash or travellers cheques and prefer foreign currency. The hotel's main drawback is its size — it has 66 rooms.

The Belair is further from the centre of town and could be expensive for a single person, at US$15 plus 5 per cent tax. I ate at the Belair and found it acceptable, but I suspect that what you choose is important. I had pepper steak at J$4.50. There is no native food on the menu, although the clientele appeared to be native bourgeoisie and businessmen. Credit cards are accepted. Both the Belair and the Mandeville have swimming pools.

The Astra is a long way out of town and you will definitely need a taxi. The higher priced rooms have carpets on the floor. All rooms have private facilities, telephone, etc. Credit cards are accepted. All these hotels are of a higher standard of comfort than those generally recommended in this book.

I stayed at *The Mayfair Guest House*, about three-quarters of a mile from the town centre on Newleigh Road. The rooms costing US$12 include a private bathroom. Cash, Jamaican dollars, is preferred for payment. The management is very suspicious of travellers' cheques. I would say US$12 is a good price for a double, but steep for a single. I have been told that the Mayfair was almost a whorehouse catering for expatriates when the bauxite industry was booming, but you wouldn't know it now (that's why a single costs the same as a double).

There is cheaper guest house accommodation available. One is apparently located on Caledonia Road, past the Belair, and others on Wards Avenue, above restaurants there. Wards Avenue is your best bet as there is more of it and it is centrally located. Enquire at the police station.

Restaurants and Bars: Native restaurants, bars and betting shops abound here. Food is cheaper than in Mo'Bay and Negril. A pork chop dinner with peas 'n' rice, yams, tomato, lettuce and chicken soup costs J$1·80 at the bar/restaurant at the junction of Manchester and Newleigh, and this seems to be the standard price. Chicken dinners cost the same.

Manchester Road has a number of restaurants, but the main area is Wards Avenue, just across from the traffic lights. Soft drinks sell for J20 cents and a shot of rum is the same price. I found the *Esquire* restaurant/bar upstairs on Wards Avenue (before you get to the Tudor Theatre) good and cheap. The only trouble is there was no reggae; they were playing old American rock 'n' roll (unless it was misguidedly for my benefit).

Mandeville to Spanish Town: Spanish Town was the capital of Jamaica until 1872, although Kingston had been the commercial capital, chief port of entry and most important centre for some time. The square is said to be one of the finest examples of Georgian architecture in the western hemisphere. There is a memorial to the British Admiral Rodney and a cathedral — to Saint Jago de la Vega — which is supposed to be the oldest in the West Indies. There is also a folk museum. In the short time I was there I found the people amongst the most friendly in Jamaica. Unfortunately although everyone was helpful, no-one knew of any accommodation in town (there are hotels outside the town). So I did not stay very long.

My recommendation is as follows: leave Mandeville early. Walk or taxi down to the bus terminal in the centre of town. You will soon be hustled into a bus or minibus bound for Kingston. Ask to be put out at Spanish Town (I was charged J$1.50, but I was told later that this is on the cheap side). If you are there before 12 you will have plenty of time to look around before taking a regular bus into Kingston (fare 20 or 30 cents).

Kingston: Kingston was founded at the end of the seventeenth century as a planned city subsequent to the sinking of Port Royal. Downtown is laid out in blocks, with Victoria Park five blocks from the waterfront and George 6 Memorial Park further north.

You are strongly recommended to arrive in Kingston before dark. I think the best place to stay is mid-town, closer than uptown to the action and probably cheaper, and safer than downtown. Many accounts have been given concerning the risks to personal safety in Kingston, but the bars on the windows tell their own story.

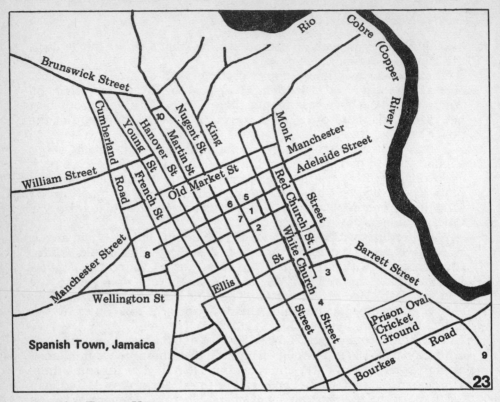

Spanish Town, Jamaica

23

Spanish Town: Key

1 The Park
2 Court house
3 St Jago's Cathedral
4 Prison
5 Rodney Memorial
6 Post office
7 Folk Museum
8 Market
9 Hospital
10 Trinity Chapel

Accommodation in Kingston

Name	Address	Price per room in US$
Green Gables Guest House	Cargill (Road or Avenue	S from $9 ****; D from $16 ****.
Indies Hotel	Holborn Road	S $14 **; D $18 ***.
Green Lantern	5½ Ripon Road (Cross Roads area)	$8 per room; S ***, D ****.
Peters Motel	7 Richmond Avenue	$9 per room (no bath); S **, D ***. $14 per room (bath): S **, D **.
Retreat Guest House	19 Seaview Avenue	CP: S $10; D $16.
Duke's	Corner Duke and Queen Streets	$6 per room: S ***, D ***.

Kingston: Key

1 Victoria Park
2 George VI Memorial Park
3 Sabina Park

98

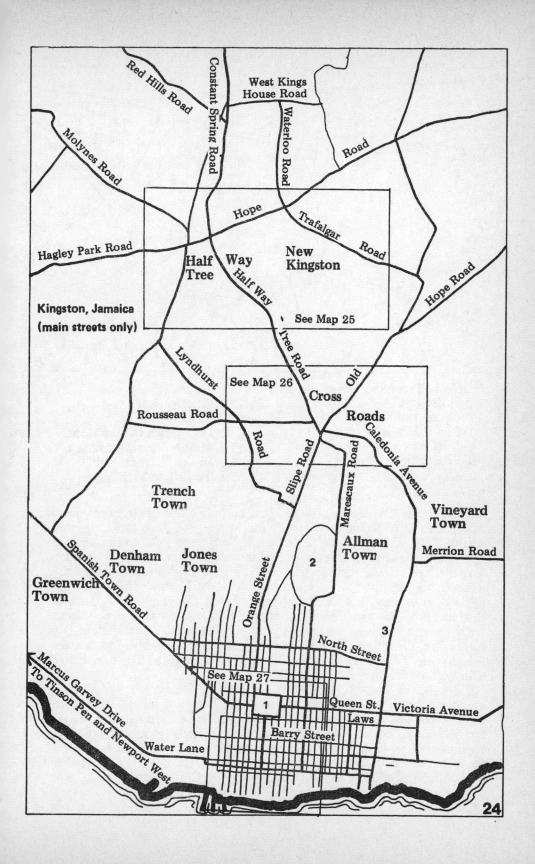

Kingston, Jamaica
(main streets only)

Red Hills Road

West Kings House Road

Constant Spring Road

Waterloo Road

Road

Molynes Road

Hope

Trafalgar Road

Hagley Park Road

Half Way Tree

New Kingston

Half Way

Hope Road

See Map 25

Lyndhurst

Tree Road

See Map 26

Cross

Old

Rousseau Road

Roads

Caledonia Avenue

Road

Slipe Road

Mareseaux Road

Trench Town

Vineyard Town

Spanish Town Road

Denham Town

Jones Town

Allman Town

Merrion Road

Greenwich Town

2

3

Orange Street

North Street

Marcus Garvey Drive

See Map 27

To Tinson Pen and Newport West

1

Queen St.

Victoria Avenue

Laws

Water Lane

Barry Street

24

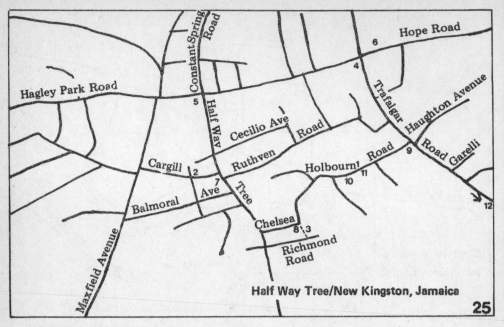

Half Way Tree/New Kingston, Jamaica

25

Half Way Tree/New Kingston: Key

1 Hotel Indies
2 Green Gables
3 Peters Motel
4 YMCA
5 Post office
6 Devon House
7 MacDonalds
8 Take 5 Club
9 Courtleigh Manor Hotel
10 Middle East Restaurant
11 Indies Pub and Grill
12 To Cuban Embassy

The Green Gables, run by a Scottish lady, represents fairly good value and may be your best bet on arrival in Kingston. It is well situated for conveniences in the Half Way Tree area and is located just off a bus route. Depending which road your bus from Spanish Town takes into Kingston, you may be able to dismount before the downtown terminus, very close to the Guest House — keep half an eye on your Esso map and half an eye on the road. Occupants of the cheapest rooms share a bathroom with one other room. Rooms with private facilities are available at slightly higher cost. There is a restaurant, cheap by hotel standards but more expensive than native restaurants (about US$3 for a chicken dinner) and a bar, called The London Tavern.

I stayed at *The Indies Hotel*, not having discovered the cheaper accommodation at the time. The rooms here are all standard with twin beds, good wardrobe facilities, plenty of drawer space, air conditioning, hot water in the shower, glasses — and everything worked. After difficulties elsewhere with the plumbing, it was good to have superior accommodation which, besides having essentials like toilet paper, also had nice little touches like book matches and

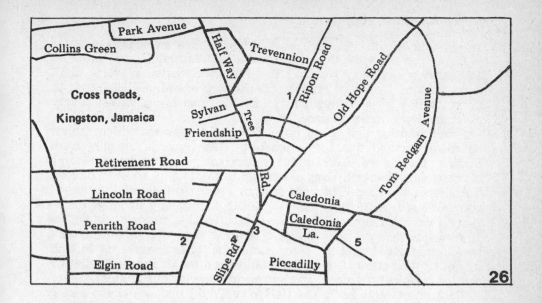

Cross Roads, Kingston: Key
1 Green Lantern
2 Haitian Embassy
3 Post office
4 Carib Theatre
5 YWCA

tourist newspapers. The hotel seems to cater for natives and business-men, rather than tourists (of whom there are few in Kingston anyway).

Guests at the Indies Hotel are able to use, free of charge, the swimming pool at the nearby Courtleigh Manor Hotel. There is also a laundry service — allow two days for items to be returned. If you don't expect food to be cheap here, at least it's good. Breakfast ranges from US $1 (juice, toast, coffee) to US$2.50 for the works. six choices in all. The lunch and dinner menu includes fillet steak at US$6, chicken at US$3, pizzas from US$2.50, hamburger US$1. A very wide choice in all, at reasonable prices, but with no native food. The breakfasts include a pot of coffee, not just a cup.

If you are looking for cheap accommodation and find the Green Gables full, try *Peters Motel* at 7 Richmond Avenue. Note, however, that the facilities are quite basic, and in value for money terms both the above are better.

The Green Lantern at 5½ Ripon Road charges US$8 per room, whether occupied by one or two persons. This is nearer to downtown than the other suggested accommodation, and is thus more con-venient during the day but may inhibit your night-time walking. This establishment is run and patronized by natives and has about eight rooms. Bathroom facilities are shared. Very loud reggae pounds from the juke box. The building is single storey, and I was impressed by the cleanliness of the rooms, most of which have washbasins.

I was able to visit but not inspect *The Retreat Guest House* at 19 Seaview Avenue, run by Mrs Miller. Security is very tight; entrance was barred (literally) and no way was Mrs Miller going to open up if I wasn't staying there. So all I can say is that it is very quiet and lives up to its name.

I will mention one cheap hotel situated downtown which cannot be recommended due to its location. The hotel is upstairs from *Duke's*, mentioned later under restaurants, and under the same management. I actually stayed here on my last night, so as to be near the airport bus stop. The very spartan shower/toilet facilities are of course shared. Although there is nothing intrinsically wrong with the place I cannot recommend it. I was treated as a curiosity, being the first white man to stay there. I suspect that if hordes of young travellers started using the place some resentment would set in, and of course the criminal element would soon be attracted. Definitely not for couples or women, and you should not go out at night.

Restaurants and Bars: On Half Way Tree Road is a cheap eating place, *MacDonalds*. It has no relationship with the American chain of similar name. Curried goat is J$2 here — the cheapest I had ever seen it — and all meals are cheap by Kingston standards (Kingston prices are a little higher than Mandeville's). The quality was very poor, but you are unlikely to get food poisoning.

Beer seems to be a standard US80 cents at the Indies, Green Gables and *Take 5 Club*. This latter is next to Peters Motel, and is a nightclub with native entertainment and clientele. Over the road from the Indies Hotel is *The Pub and Grill*, under the same management as the Indies. I was impressed with neither the food nor service, which was very slow. And it was too much like an English pub. It is frequented by expatriates, businessmen staying at the Indies, and the native bourgeoisie.

Downtown you could try *Duke's* restaurant at the corner of Duke and Queen Streets. Chicken is J$2, stew beef J$2.10, curried goat J$2.10. I tried the chicken, with pepper strips, tomato, peas and rice, and found it very good.

Two restaurants in New Kingston were recommended to me for their cleanliness and economy. Both are in Knutsford Boulevard, opposite the British High Commission (which is appropriately on Trafalgar Road). One is the *Victoria Grill*, next to the Citibank building, the other is the pharmacy attached to the Imperial Life over the road. Both are patronized at lunchtime by the local office staffs.

Transport: Buses run downtown along Half Way Tree Road, Trafalgar Road (number 14) and Old Hope Road. Most of them (the exception is number 14) terminate in King Street (see downtown map). Fares will be between J 15 and 35 cents. Buses to Port Antonio and other parts of Jamaica go from the corner of Pechon

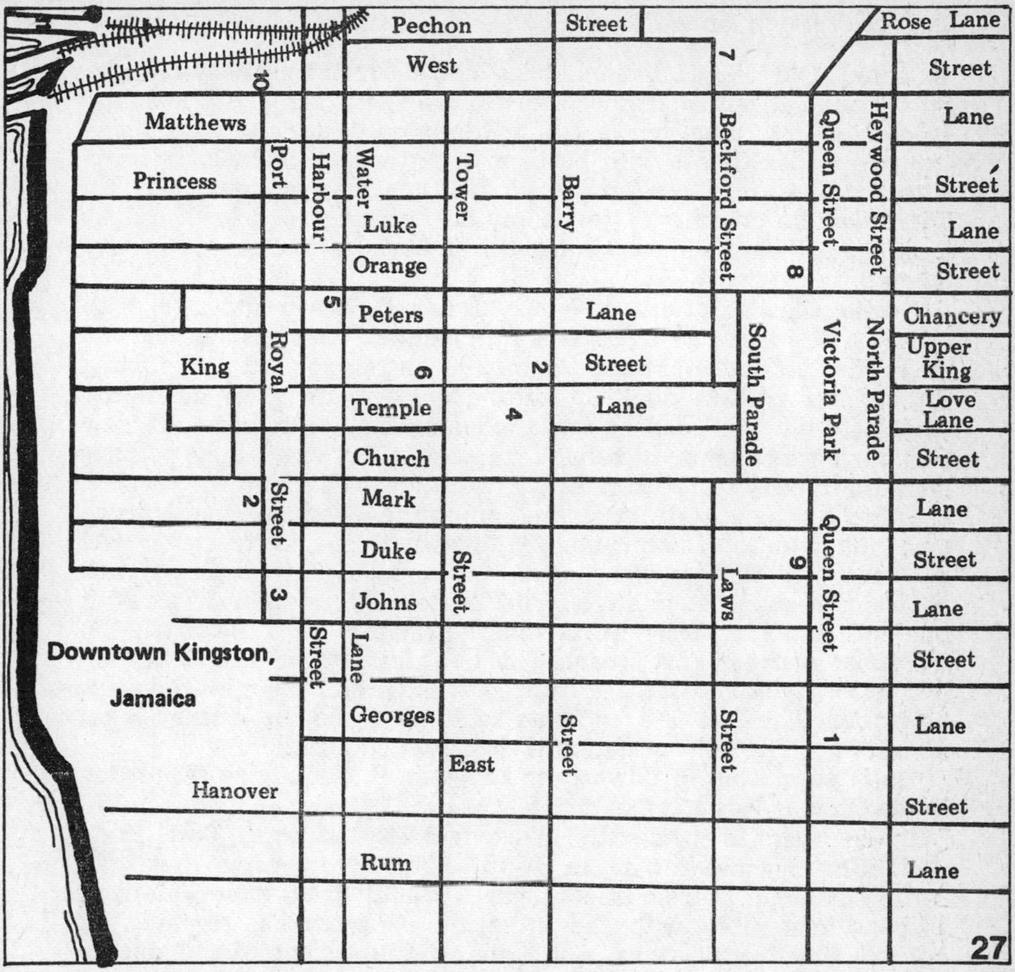

Map labels (Downtown Kingston, Jamaica):

Pechon Street · West · Rose Lane · Street · Matthews · Lane · Princess · Port · Harbour · Water · Tower · Barry · Beckford Street · Queen Street · Heywood Street · Street · Luke · Lane · Orange · Street · Peters · Lane · Chancery · King · Royal · 6 · 2 · Street · South Parade · Victoria Park · North Parade · Upper King · Temple · 4 · Lane · Love Lane · Church · Street · Mark · Lane · Duke · Street · Queen Street · 9 · Street · Johns · Laws · Lane · Street · Downtown Kingston, Jamaica · Street · Lane · Street · Georges · Street · Street · Lane · Hanover · East · Street · Rum · Lane · 27

Downtown Kingston: Key

1 Police headquarters
2 Post office
3 Tourist bureau
4 Public buildings
5 Lloyds Shipping Agency
6 Terminus for most city buses
7 Buses to provinces
8 Airport bus
9 Dukes Hotel/bar/restaurant
10 Crafts market
11 Ferry for Port Royal

Street and Beckford Street. Note that after dark, buses at the King Street terminus are parked higher up the street.

Downtown: Downtown Kingston is pleasant in the daytime. A bus ride into town provides interesting sights — try to get a window seat — and I found the town and people more cordial than I expected. Old dilapidated buildings alternate with new skyscrapers, but I found the streets wider and less crowded than a glance at the Esso map and casual conversation intimated. Sidewalk vendors dot the pavements. Those with business to attend to hurry past those with nothing to do. I was not hassled, either for a handout or to buy dope. On the contrary, I found myself either ignored or, if caught looking at a map, helped. I think this is because tourists are a rarity down here.

During the late afternoon you will see the heavy dudes begin to arrive. After dusk decent citizens hurry about their business and the buses turn around in a more brightly lit and populated part of King Street (nearer the Parade). But during the day downtown has all the facilities you will need — banks, cheap restaurants, bars, the new harbour development, supermarkets — and a day in the area, perhaps including a ferry trip to Port Royal, would be well spent.

Down by the waterfront redevelopment has produced an attractive area, aimed at tourists but not yet filled with them. The area is well laid out with flowers and bushes, and shopping/office plazas with apartments above at intervals. The Tourist Information Office is at one end, and the Victoria Crafts Market at the other. Nearby is the ferryboat pier for Port Royal. The boat leaves here at 8, 9, 10 am and 1 to 7 pm and returns from Port Royal on the corresponding half hour. The fare is J 15 cents each way, and the journey takes 20 minutes. The railway station is also situated near here.

Half-day closing in downtown Kingston is Wednesday (Thursday in the Cross Roads area).

Port Royal: In its day the Wickedest City on Earth, Port Royal was built by the English in 1655, immediately after they had captured Jamaica from the Spanish. Brandy was imported from England ostensibly with the intention of providing revenue for constructing fortifications — though no doubt some of the income derived from its sale found its way into the royal purse. It didn't take long before the Caribbean pirates made this their base. Here they unloaded their loot captured from Spanish galleons and settlements; merchants came from Europe to bargain for the goods and gold. With an economy based on brandy and piracy it is not surprising that public morality was reputedly lower than anywhere else. Whorehouses alternated with warehouses. Perhaps a third of the population were pirates (or buccaneers as their apologists prefer to call them). Others were tradesmen and artisans who, although often mediocre in their standard of work at home, were able to make a good living here.

The most famous pirate was Henry Morgan. Accounts differ as to whether he was merely greedy for loot and action, or whether he had any patriotic motive. His operations, including the famous sacking of Panama, were carried out against the Spaniards, he was knighted, and did become Governor of Jamaica. But then intelligent and cunning men with great wealth at their disposal have a way of finding favour with the authorities.

In 1962, four years after Henry Morgan had passed away, Port Royal was hit by an earthquake. About a quarter of the population were killed and most of the town fell into the sea, leaving only Fort Charles and a few houses standing. Lewis Galdy was a celebrated survivor of the disaster. First swallowed up by the land, he was then, in a succeeding spasm, flung into the sea and survived by swimming until picked up. Half of the remaining residents died through disease in the following weeks, most of the survivors eventually moving over to the mainland to found Kingston.

Nowadays there is little to see in Port Royal. There is the Quarterdeck in Fort Charles — upon which Nelson is said to have impatiently paced, the police training academy, a small museum with excavated submarine remains, and Lewis Galdy's tombstone — upon which his experience is engraved. But it is worth the trip for the atmosphere. Now a small fishing settlement of humble dwellings, a disused Anglers' Club building (starkly magnificent when seen from the pier), and a hotel with something about Henry Morgan in the title, it is worth a visit in the late afternoon. On a clear, or slightly cloudy day the views of Kingston and the mountains behind can be beautiful. As it sinks the sun casts a pink glow over the capital, whilst even more dramatic views can be observed by turning west. There is a small fishermens' bar near the pier where the beer is 40 cents and the reggae continuous.

Tourist Things to do Around Kingston: Quite a lot. The cheapest is free — the superb views of the mountains and coast. As stated before, these can be seen to best advantage from Port Royal and its ferry in the late afternoon. The new downtown harbour development is also free until you start buying things, and it has been constructed largely with the visitor in mind. Time spent there can be rewarding. Devon House, near Half Way Tree, is always quoted as one of Jamaica's great houses still maintained in colonial splendour. Its restaurant employs waiters dressed up as pirates and serving wenches, but cleaner, and you can bet that all tourists to Kingston go there. At the eastern end of Old Hope Road is a botanical garden and small zoo. A trip to the Blue Mountains by whatever means you choose could be rewarding.

Port Antonio: Port Antonio has perhaps the most beautiful scenery in Jamaica. Wide river valleys flanked by thick, lush vegetation meander down from the towering Blue Mountains to a sleepy, friendly town. Although it is being promoted as a tourist spot, I would be very surprised if you find many tourists there.

Trade is largely based on the export of bananas. But there is some fishing, for sport as well as food. There are fine views over the town and bay from the hills, and nearby is the famous Blue Hole, an almost land-locked lagoon so deep that the water is cobalt blue,

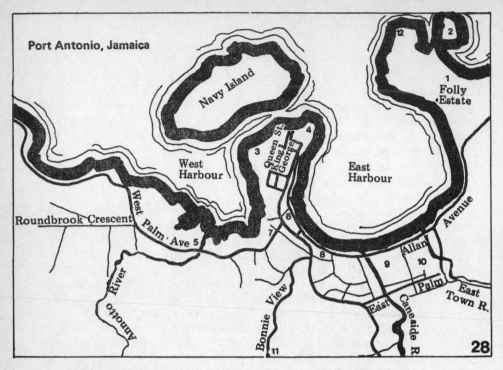

Port Antonio, Jamaica

Navy Island

West Harbour

East Harbour

Folly Estate

Roundbrook Crescent

Queen St. King George

West Palm Ave 5

River Annotto

Bonnie View

East

Caneside R.

Allan Avenue

Palm

East Town R.

28

Port Antonio: Key
1 Mitchell's Folly
2 Woods Island
3 Ferry to Navy Island
4 Fort George
5 Railway station
6 Court house

7 Market
8 Parish church
9 Olivier Carder Park
10 Evelight Park
11 To Bonnie View
12 Lighthouse

surrounded by lush green vegetation. Rafting down the Rio Grande is also available — similar to the Martha Brae experience. The site of Mitchell's Folly is in Port Antonio. This was a stately mansion, built on classical Roman lines in 1905, by a rich New Yorker for his bride. However, on their arrival, it collapsed: sea water had been mixed in with the concrete used for its construction.

Port Antonio's easterly position makes it a possible departure point for Haiti, though this may be more difficult than you imagine.

Arrive early in the day if you want to find cheaper accommodation than that advertised by the tourist board. One good tip is to try the police station: all places offering rooms for rent have to register, so the police generally know about the cheap ones.

On the shores of the Blue Hole is a new restaurant, the Blue Lagoon, which features vegetarian and native seafood dishes. The proprietor is Horatio Spencer, whom you should ask to speak to. Expect to pay around US$4.50 for a meal.

106

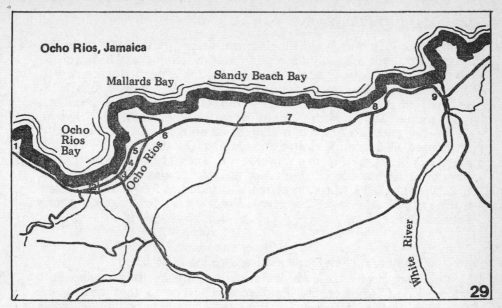

Ocho Rios: Key
1 Bauxite plant
2 Club Maracca
3 Market
4 Post office
5 Cove Theatre

6 Buckfield
7 Carib Ochos Rio Hotel
8 Jamaica Inn
9 White River (settlement)

Ocho Rios: Literally, from the Spanish, 'Eight Rivers'. This is the new tourist Mecca. Unlike Negril however, which has a centre from which the tourist areas spread, the hotels are ranged over some 40 miles of coastline. These hotels are mainly of the villa or cottage variety, though I am advised that guest house accommodation does exist. Dunns River Falls, one of Jamaica's foremost tourist attractions, are about 4 miles west of Ocho Rios' centre and Fern Gully. You can climb to the top in your swimming gear assisted by a surefooted local guide.

Ian Fleming lived around here, in its unspoilt days, and drew much inspiration for his James Bond novels. The bauxite plant at Ocho Rios was used in the movie 'Dr No', although it had a more sinister purpose and was ostensibly blown up. 'Boonoonoonoos', a patois word meaning something like 'groovy baby', is the title the local tourist board have given to their events programme.

Travelling west you arrive at Runaway Bay and Falmouth. Again, very touristy, although Discovery Bay, the site of C.C.'s landing, may be of historical interest. To the non-tourist this area's greatest attraction probably lies in the splendid views the coastal road affords.

From Jamaica to Haiti: You can get to Haiti from Kingston or

Port Antonio but it is a difficult proposition, particularly from the latter. You will probably have purchased a ticket from Kingston to Port-au-Prince in your home country, as this is needed for entry to Jamaica. The problem is that you will not be allowed into Haiti without an onward or return ticket. If you do not have these tickets, you should buy a return ticket Kingston/Port-au-Prince/Kingston (a 17-day excursion fare is available) or an onward ticket to Santo Domingto (Kingston/Port-au-Prince/Santo Domingo). ALM (Dutch Antillean Airlines) Fly one a week, on Tuesdays, and Air Jamaica have four flights a week (on Tuesdays, Wednesdays, Thursdays and Saturdays). ALM's Kingston office is situated at The Mall, Constant Spring Road (Halfway Tree area). Fares are as follows: Kingston/Port-au-Prince:

one way US$ 91

return US$182

17-day excursion US$132

Kingston/Port-au-Prince/Santo Domingo: US$120

You may prefer to leave Jamaica by more exciting means, as I tried to do. However my field research showed that trade, and therefore traffic, between Jamaica and Haiti is very limited (as is shown by there being only four scheduled flights per week, and most of the passengers on these seem to be going on to Curacao). The scarcity of cargo boats or private planes ruled out my original plan to leave from Port Antonio and I therefore explored all avenues of departure from Kingston.

Ship: It appears that most cargo or passenger vessels only stop at Haiti on the way to Jamaica, and then rarely. I tried the harbour at downtown Kingston and found nothing Haiti-bound. There are two agents here; La Ocean in Kingston Mall, and Lloyds (who are agents for Booth Line and other passenger-carrying cargo lines) in Harbour Street. Private yachts sometimes leave from the Port Royal area, though very rarely, and you could try the Royal Yacht Club near Palisadoes Park. Most cargo boats leave from Newport West. You can take a number 5 bus from either King Street or Port Royal Street (see downtown map) but make sure you are standing at a bus stop. Ask. When boarding ask to be put off at Grace Kennedy. Here you will find Grace Kennedy Travel and Grace Kennedy Shipping. Try the shipping company first. Again your chances of finding something are slim, but you might just get lucky. The fare could vary from nothing to, say, US$50/US$60. If you are desperate, and really want to go by sea, you could try the fishing boats by the ferry pier.

Private Plane: From what I was told, it is more likely that you will get a plane for Haiti from Port Antonio than from Kingston. It is possible to phone Jamaica Air Taxi from town to ask if they have a chartered aircraft for Haiti with spare seats (be sure they understand that you don't want to charter one yourself). Do this as soon as possible; they will keep your number and phone you if anything becomes available (they have to check with Montego Bay). Or you can go down to the airstrip at Tinson Pen (opposite Grace Kennedy) and ask around.

Scheduled flight: If condemned to the scheduled flight at least console yourself that it could be worse. Express buses, route number X97, leave from Victoria Park regularly (Orange Street). Sometimes minibuses pick up from the same point and go through to departures at the airport. The fare is J 50 cents.

I found the airport check-in service better than average, and the airport itself better than Montego Bay. Like Mo'Bay, it too is being renovated, but there is far less inconvenience — and no 'Courtesy Corps', but courtesy instead. Remember that when changing your Jamaican currency back into US dollars you must show your original receipt.

The flight is pleasant, comfortable, and short. ALM serve a very light snack, but coffee and drinks are available on request. They also give away free American cigarettes.

HAITI

My travelling has taken me the throughout Europe and Asia, to the Indian subcontinent, North Africa, the United States and Mexico, yet I have never been anywhere like Haiti. Haiti has been described as 'West Africa in the Caribbean', but in truth I feel it must be unique. The history of this country and its people is one of hardship, strife, independence and forced insularity. Haiti's achievement in attaining and keeping independence has been so unusual and contrary to prevailing political philosophy that the people have suffered from misrepresentation ever since.

Hayti, populated at the time by Arawak Indians, was discovered by you-know-who in 1492. The name was promptly changed from Hayti — meaning High Land — to Hispaniola, Little Spain. At this time Haiti and Santo Domingo were one, the division of the island into two countries occurring later. As usual, the Arawaks welcomed their European visitors but soon found themselves exploited, being press-ganged into mining for precious metals. Repression, disease and massacres soon wiped out the natives so that, as elsewhere in the Caribbean, blacks were imported from West Africa in shockingly vast numbers (estimates range as high as 50 million) to continue the exploitation of the country.

In 1969 the part of Hispaniola which is now Haiti was ceded to France. The French continued the exploitation of the land and people, increased the rate of human imports from Africa (mortality rates were so high among the slaves that replacement was continually necessary just to maintain the workforce). But they were more successful than the Spanish would probably have been — the Spanish Empire was in decline — so that Sainte-Dominique (as they called it) became the richest jewel in the French Imperial crown.

Like Jamaica, Haiti is a mountainous country, but to a far greater extent. Thus nature provided a haven for those free souls able to escape the drudgery and deprivations of slavery and, as has been seen throughout the world in the past and the present, these same hills provided the perfect base for guerrilla bands, known as 'Marrons', who would institute raids on the colonizers. So the ingredients were there for subsequent events when the French Revolution shocked Europe in 1789.

When the oppressed of France cast off their chains and equality for all was proclaimed, there was thus a nucleus in Haiti which could take this right. The conditions and times were conducive to an event which has never been repeated before or since: a successful revolt of slaves. That this revolt was ultimately successful was due largely to perhaps the vital ingredient, a great leader. This was Toussaint L'Ouverture, a former slave who had educated himself and worked himself into a position of great power in the colonial infrastructure. He persuaded the guerrilla bands that it would eventually be necessary to work in concert, but that success would only be attained by astute planning, stealth and ruthless action when the time came to strike.

In the summer of 1791 the slaves rose. They massacred most of the whites, burned the farms and committed the atrocities usual when an oppressed people at last has an outlet for its hate. This is when the maturity and wisdom of Toussaint made the crucial difference between eventual success or failure. Rather than relaxing, or trying to accumulate wealth and power for himself, he spent five years travelling the country to educate the people. He taught them that it was necessary to work, and not to hate. He offered their original lands back to those settlers who wished to cultivate it with free labour. He built up an army capable of defending the new-found freedom.

In 1801 Toussaint proclaimed the independence of Haiti with himself as Governor. But Napoleon was at the height of his glory, having conquered most of Europe, where now only England stood against him. He could not tolerate the legalization of a situation which had been de facto for some years, and consequently sent an army of 40,000 which included his brother-in-law, Jerome. Toussaint was captured by treachery and imprisoned in France where he was to die less than two years later. But he had able lieutenants, including General Christophe, Dessalines and Petion. So it was that a scorched earth policy, ruthless warfare and yellow fever caused the unconditional surrender of the French army on 18 November 1803. On 1 January 1804 Haiti became the first independent black state, and was to remain the only one for 150 years.

A long period of domestic squabbling and insulation from the rest of the world kept Haiti from developing economically. There was no great leader of the stature of Toussaint, which led Haiti to periods of fragmentation. The country was divided at one time with Henri

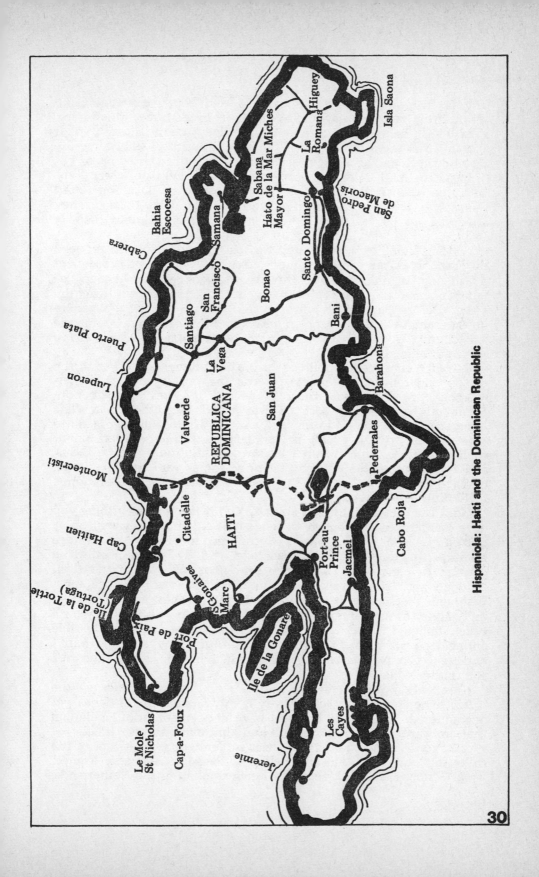

Hispaniola: Haiti and the Dominican Republic

30

Christophe holding sway in the north and Petion controlling the south (from where he gave aid to Simon Bolivar's forces which were, with British help, to liberate South America from the Spanish yoke) and in 1844 the eastern part of the island separated to become the Dominican Republic. The political vacuum was filled with chaos.

In 1915 this led to American intervention. US troops were sent with the ostensible purpose of maintaining order, but soon found themselves victims of the guerrilla bands which quickly formed. They remained for 19 years, until President Roosevelt withdrew them in 1934.

Political stability is fairly novel to Haiti, having been introduced by Francois Duvalier — Papa Doc — after his election and subsequent presidency beginning in 1957. Duvalier re-introduced the concepts of independence and black power which had slipped away over the years. Before Papa Doc power rested with a mulatto oligarchy unrepresentative of the people and backed by the army, bourgeosie and church. Customs and the system of government were in many respects colonial.

Duvalier organized a political revolution, returning power to the blacks and remaining defiant towards the pressures of the international power blocks. Haiti pioneered the principle of non-alignment with either east or west, and paid the price. The bourgeosie who had fled principally to the United States organized an economic boycott which further accentuated the impoverishment of Haiti. But Duvalier secured his own position in domestic terms, and Haiti's internationally, so that now, some years after his death, his son is able to pursue the task of organizing an economic revolution.

Haiti is a dictatorship. But apart from this, almost everything you have learnt from newspapers or hearsay is either an exaggeration or untrue. It is not a country I would recommend for an average holiday, for there is nothing average here. It is a schizophrenic country, a contrast between rich and poor, cleanliness and filth, kindness and acquisitiveness, joie de vivre and low life expectancy. Although the tourist literature claims fine beaches, you have to go out of the towns to find unpolluted ones: it is not the country for a beach holiday. But it is a must for the traveller who is adaptable enought to assimilate a new lifestyle. During my stay in Haiti I experienced more than at any other time in my life. And I thought I was unshockable!

Immigration Requirements: There is no fear of hippies by the officials here, probably because it is not a problem Haiti has yet encountered. You should however have all documentation, including that onward or return ticket and international certificate of vaccination against smallpox. No visa is required from citizens of the following countries: Austria, Belgium, Canada, Denmark, France, West Germany, Israel, Liechtenstein, Luxembourg, the Netherlands,

Switzerland, the United Kingdom of Great Britain and Northern Ireland (British passport holders from the Commonwealth or British colonies should check with their nearest Haitian Consulate) and the USA. Australian and New Zealand passport holders will need a visa. A tourist card is issued on arrival in Haiti.

Customs: One quart of liquor and one carton of cigarettes (200) may be brought into Haiti by the tourist. Inspection is thorough, and drug laws are strictly and fairly enforced.

Currency: The currency unit is the gourde. One gourde equals 20 cents US currency. There is no charge for changing US dollars into gourdes, and no restriction on changing any gourdes you are left with back to dollars (but try to do this before you get to the airport in case the bank there is unmanned). US dollars are accepted everywhere at the official rate. Note that prices are quoted in both gourdes and US dollars, so be sure you know which is which when purchasing anything.

Credit cards can be used in many hotels and restaurants, but not in travel agents (except Southerlands Tours, which is the American Express agent and will therefore take Amex — and advance you up to US$50 on receipt of a cheque if necessary). If you want to make a cash withdrawal on your BankAmericard or MasterCharge you should go to the Banque Nationale de Republique d'Haiti which is the only authorized agent.

Climate: Very much dependent on altitude. The average annual temperature is 80°F (27°C) in the coastal areas (where the towns are situated) and 76°F (24°C) in the hills and mountains. It is at night when the cool of the hills is most likely to be experienced. Rain is most likely in the hills, and the driest months generally are from December through March, the tourist season.

Average Temperatures

Month	January	February	March	April
Average Low	68°F 20°C	68°F 20°C	69°F 21°C	71°F 22°C
Average High	87°F 31°C	88°F 31°C	89°F 32°C	89°F 32°C

Month	May	June	July	August
Average Low	72°F 22°C	73°F 23°C	74°F 23°C	73°F 23°C
Average High	90°F 32°C	93°F 34°C	94°F 34°C	93°F 34°C

Month	September	October	November	December
Average Low	72°F 22°C	72°F 22°C	71°F 22°C	69°F 21°C
Average High	91°F 33°C	90°F 32°C	88°F 31°C	87°F 31°C

The People: the vast majority are black, with a minority of mulattoes. Power and wealth seem to be held by the few but without racial bias. I was told that until recently there was some racialism here, and that Papa Doc rose to power on a racialist ticket. I have no corroboration of this, and I found no prejudice because of my colour. In fact I found Haiti to be the first completely racially tolerant country I have ever visited.

Haiti has been independent so long, and under slavery for such a relatively short time, that European traditions have scarcely invaded the African way of life. In all my dealings with the people I found them genuinely helpful and loving. It is true that the poor in particular always wanted something from me, usually money, and if all I had was the shirt on my back they would take that. A trait which can be annoying. But even when I had no money people were anxious to help, and one guide, Jacques (he calls himself Jack for English-speaking tourists), even offered to lend me some.

Before arriving in Haiti, I had been told (in Jamaica) two things about the Haitian people: that they are very cultured and live in fear. I found more truth in the former than in the latter. In general I found the people uncowed by authority. I even witnessed occasions when the police were jeered for overzealousness in the execution of formality. And the police provide food and shelter to the needy on occasion. It should be noted that although visitors need a permit to travel around the country, the native is free to go where he pleases.

Sometimes I found the friendliness of the people a handicap. It means the solo traveller need never be alone, but for me it caused difficulties in working. Plenty to write about Haiti, and no time to write it!

The Arts: Painting is the most noticeable of the Haitian arts. There are a few painters of real talent, in the primitive style, and many others who have more enthusiasm than ability. But the real volume is in the field of commercial art, whether it be the exuberant decoration of the tap-taps or the hurried daubings produced in vast quantities for the tourist market. That money is the motive is proved by the repetition of popular lines. One can see the same painting in half a dozen different locations around town and up at Boutilliers. This means that the vast majority of visible Haitian painting is really of the 'paint-by-numbers' class, a craft rather than an art. I was more impressed with the mahogany carvings. Here a far greater level of skill is evident, the fine finish of the woodwork proving a strong contrast to the crude work executed in Jamaica. Much of this is also functional, and often a strong inventiveness of design is evident. Had I been returning home from Haiti I would surely have bought something.

Music and dance are surprisingly undeveloped in Haiti. The only real style of music I could perceive as indigenous is that based on the Voodoo ceremonies; during the day, in restaurants and so on, you are more likely to hear recorded American, French or British music (I heard many instrumental interpretations of Beatles' tunes). And dance routines, whilst at least in rhythm to the music, are fairly basic and lack inventiveness. But the Haitians are able to appreciate good dancing. In Cap Haitian I saw three men dancing well on a raised platform to a small orchestra; a huge crowd were strongly appreciative of the fine display they were given. And when I gave an impromptu performance to the accompaniment of Voodoo drums in 'Le Cap' a strong crowd, shrieking with delight, soon formed.

Guides: These come in two categories, official and unofficial. As far as I am aware I never encountered an official one. Guides can cost you a lot of money, or save you a lot. It depends on the guide.

Wherever you go you will be found by someone wishing to help you. If you want a guide he will assure you that he is the best and can help you save money. If you don't want a guide then he 'understands' and isn't one.

The independent traveller is classed as a tourist, and few Haitians comprehend that you are not in a mad rush to see all the tourist sights, watch a Voodoo ceremony, buy paintings, souvenirs or a woman. But if you are persistent without being offensive you will be all right. A guide can cost you money by taking you to tourist functions, restaurants and travelling. A cheap restaurant will be expensive if you pay for two people, and all travel costs will be doubled. Because of the discrepancy between native living costs and tourist prices a guide can save the tourist a lot of money, and will think he is saving *you* money. Yet if you speak Creole or French you can easily find these cheap places yourself and live at perhaps just double native costs.

You may find a guide useful if you can remain in control and perhaps use his services for just the first day or two, until you know your way around. Jacques, who can be found outside the Hotel Beau Rivage, has useful contacts, and will keep a low profile if you prefer just to wander rather than be taken anywhere specific.

Language: Officially French, but only a minority speak it. Everybody speaks Creole. Creole is more than a patois, it is as different to French as Italian is to Spanish. Thus if you speak to the poor people, especially in rural areas, in French they will be unable to understand you. At the airport some English is spoken, but to a far lesser extent in Port-au-Prince — even our recommended hotel is Creole and French speaking only. I found English spoken more in 'Le Cap' than in the capital. There is some Spanish spoken, largely because of the Dominicans here.

Food and Drink: Haitian food is good but piquant and tough on the teeth. Everything seems to be prepared to be as tough as possible -- you even need a hacksaw for the bananas. Maybe the Haitians like a good chew. If your teeth are less than perfect be careful what you eat and particularly avoid Tassot Creole (almost all Haitians have perfect teeth).

The other characteristic of the food is the piquant sauces. Although French and 'International' cuisine of a high standard is available, the food is generally Haitian with the uniqueness that suggests — Caribbean ingredients yet prepared in a style to be found nowhere else.

Local dishes are lambi (conch), lobster, steak-au-poivre, chicken Creole, riz 'djon djon' (rice with black mushrooms) and the inevitable riz et pois -- peas 'n' rice (really rice and beans).

The national drink is Barbancourt rum; the industry was established a little over 100 years ago. Rum punch is a popular drink and easily available in hotels and tourist places. There is a local beer, named 'Prestige', and imported varieties.

Shopping, Banking and Office Hours: Life begins at dawn in Haiti, and, for many, before that. From 4.30 am the streets become increasingly populated and by 7.30 am they are a hive of activity. Although shops catering for the tourists will be open late, you should note that business hours are generally 8 am to 4 pm; the Tourist Office is open from 8 am to 2 pm and banks from 9 am to 1 pm. So try to get your business done in the morning.

Transportation: Varies from colourful to comfortable but is never mundane. The transport which epitomizes Haiti is the *tap-tap*, and I can think of no better description than that given in a book compiled for travel agents and given me by the Director of Promotion in the Tourist Office:

'A tap-tap is the ultimate in adventurous transportation. It is a prayerful thing, an inter-city gaudily painted truck with such expressions as 'God is my Savior' and 'Pray for Me' across the front. The name 'tap-tap' is derived from the sound of the vintage engines which emit a tapping sound as they labor over the hills.'

The name tap-tap is also colloquially given to the public transportation within and around Port-au-Prince. Actually called *camionettes*, these are Japanese pick-up trucks with wooden, brightly painted bodies and bench seats. They generally carry eight or ten passengers and ply up and down along the main roads in the same way as a bus service. They are far more regular than a bus service, however and stop to pick up or drop passengers on request. The fare is usually 20 cents or 1 gourde.

Publiques are cheap taxis which collect passengers going to different places around town and drop them off in an order which is convenient to, and decided by, the driver. They can be great for sightseeing but not so good for someone in a hurry. Usually older vehicles than normal taxis, they are identifiable by a letter 'P' prefixing the licence number and a red ribbon tied to the rear view mirror. The fare anywhere in town is supposed to be 20 cents, but I was charged US$2 to the airport from the tap-tap terminus.

Normal taxis with English-speaking drivers carry the prefix 'L' on their licence plates and are of course much more expensive. The official charge from the airport to any downtown destination is US$5 per car, and 50 cents for a journey around town.

Haiti now has a domestic airline — Haiti Air Inter — with regular services to Cap Haitien, Jacmel, Jeremie and Les Cayes from Port-au-Prince. Details current at the time of writing follow:

Part 2: Nassau to Port-au-Prince

Depart From	At	Arrive	At	Frequency	Fare in US$
Port-au-Prince	0700	Cap Haitien	0735	Daily except Sun.	$17 one way
	0800		0835	Daily except Sun.	$34 return
	1015		1130	Mon/Thu/Sat	
	1400		1435	Daily except Sun.	
	1500		1535	Daily except Sun.	
Cap Haitien	0745	Port-au-Prince	0820	Daily except Sun.	
	0845		0920	Daily except Sun.	
	1140		1215	Mon/Thu/Sat	
	1445		1520	Daily except Sun.	
	1545		1620	Daily except Sun.	
Port-au-Prince	0700	Jacmel	0715	Daily except Sun.	$8 one way
	1430		1445	Daily except Sun.	$12 return
Jacmel	0725	Port-au-Prince	0740	Daily except Sun.	
	1455		1510	Daily except Sun.	
Port-au-Prince	1000	Jeremie	1050	Daily except Sun.	$22 one way
Jeremie	1100	Port-au-Prince	1150	Daily except Sun.	£40 return
Port-au-Prince	0800	Les Cayes	0845	Daily except Sun.	$21 one way
Les Cayes	0855	Port-au-Prince	0940	Daily except Sun.	$40 return
Port-au-Prince	not known	Port de Paix	not known	3 a week	$19 one way
Port de Paix		Port-au-Prince		3 a week	$34 return

Voodoo: In Haiti there is complete religious toleration, although Roman Catholicism is the official religion. There are some Protestant churches founded by missionary types from North America. Voodoo is an African religion no more sinister than Christianity, which it exists alongside. Most Haitians attend both Roman Catholic and Voodoo services, particularly in the rural areas. I visited only a tourist Voodoo ceremony, and thus know insufficient about it to be able to give an accurate account. Therefore I quote below an extract from an official explanation of the cult:

'A knowledge, even elementary, of Africa and its peoples is essential if we want to understand and study Voodooism. Haitian Voodooism, according to many ethnologists, cannot claim kinships with all the regions of Black Africa. It has its origins rather in religions practised in Dahomey and Nigeria, and to a somewhat lesser extent in ritual practices in the Congo, Angola, Senegal and Guinea. We find the same organization of the clergy, the same supernatural world, and the same ritual. The priest is a 'houngan' or 'mambo', and the servants of the divinity are 'hounsis'.

'Under the supreme God, called the Grand Master and without whose permission nothing can happen, there are groups of spirits, some of them hierarchized, called Loas. They are appointed by God to supervise man and the universe. But in popular Haitian imagination they become personalities endowed with will, intelligence and passions. Hence their anthropomorphism. In Haitian belief, the Loas remain powers to whom they appeal to lavish their benefits on human beings. These divinities are honoured in ceremonies of service, obligation or duty.

'The dance is intimately associated with the Voodoo religion and occupies such an essential place in it that we could almost define

Voodooism as a religion expressed through the dance. The drum which beats the rhythm of these dances has become the very symbol of Voodooism. Its songs are hymns composed in honour of the divinities. These songs are powerful and original, sometimes slow and nostalgic, sometimes rousing. During the ceremonies, singing is always accompanied by dancing; the actual dances vary from one rite to another. The principal musical instruments played at these ceremonies are drums; they are made of oak, mahogany or pine and covered with ox-hide.

'The main symbols employed in Voodoo ceremonies are called veve. They are drawn by hand on the ground with ashes, flour or oatmeal.

'The Voodoo temple is called a Houmfort. It contains flags in the national colours, drums, a few pictures of Catholic saints, and certain veve symbols.

'It is certain that Voodooism played a large part in the genesis and development of the War of Independence. There is no doubt that certain leaders, Macandal, Boukman, Biassou or Romaine the prophetess, were high priests of Voodooism. All Haitian history books consider the famous ceremony of the Caiman wood as one of the events which originally contributed to the War of Independence. It was one of a number of pacts under which 'Dahomians engaged in a perilous enterprise bound themselves with their partners' thereby creating a spirit of solidarity and unlimited confidence between the partners concerned, and absolute discretion. There is no doubt that these African leaders used Voodooism to instill dynamism into the masses under their orders and imbue them with the mystique that is essential to the accomplishment of great tasks.

'But just as the Christianity of the Middle Ages is not the Christianity of today, so Voodooism is increasingly losing ground. It is a religion of the night, and the spread of electricity and literacy in country districts is causing it to decline.

'President Francois Duvalier said: 'I remain convinced that Voodooism, an extremely interesting religious phenomenon, is condemned to disappear sooner or later, and that in the more or less near future it will belong uniquely to our folklore.' '

Some Hints: Get plenty of small change. Taxis, tap-taps and others may not have change and will try to get away without giving you any if you thrust a dollar bill at them. Mosquito coils are essential in Cap Haitian. They can be bought locally, but it is a good idea to take some with you.

Arrival in Haiti: An immediate contrast to Jamaica. You are met by the recorded rhythm of Voodoo drums, which is a welcome change from the insipid muzak of other international airports. Although customs and immigration are thorough, they are speedy, courteous and helpful. There is a tourist information desk which will give you any advice you may need. Be sure to ask them for their guide to Haiti and map of Port-au-Prince.

I was surprised to find almost everybody spoke good English thus making passage extremely easy. There are local buses downtown, very cheap, and taxis; the latter are a minimum US$5 per car or US$2.50 per person But you may prefer to wait around in the airport terminal for a few minutes, acclimatizing yourself, reading the tourist information and getting your bearings.

Port-au-Prince: There can be no place like it; it has echoes of the east, undercurrents of West Africa, a little French chic, a Caribbean climate and friendliness. Whatever opinions one may have of life here, it must be admitted that Port-au-Prince is unique. In what other French-speaking country, for example, can one see, on television, a German football match with commentary in English? Little is known about Haiti throughout the world, yet Haiti remains in touch with the world.

Leaving the recorded Voodoo drums and disciplined bustle of the airport behind you, head downtown by taxi or 'tap-tap'. A tap-tap is fine for any centrally located hotel, but you may prefer a taxi or publique until you get your bearings. If you are staying at the Santos Pacot Guest House, which is recommended, you will need a taxi in any case.

Port-au-Prince is located in the Plain of the Cul-de-Sac, guarded by towering mountains. Looking inland from the waterfront, Le Perchoir is reminiscent of the Blue Mountains behind Kingston. But here the resemblance ends, as you will see when you drive into town.

First you are faced with an impossibility: the driving is worse than in Jamaica. There is a word to describe it — crazy. Haitians either drive on the right or down the middle of the road, depending on how much traffic is about. Careering down into the city you are struck by a bustling activity, apparent chaos and a variety in the people which is reflected in the humble architecture. Standing proud above it you will see the new cathedral. Through the haze. For Port-au-Prince is the first polluted city you will meet. Nassau was clean enough, as the aquamarine harbour waters proved; downtown Montego Bay was scruffy but hygienic, whilst downtown Kingston, although dirty, was being tidied up. But here you will notice a light smog, particularly in the early evening, open sewers along many of the streets, people openly urinating, brown water in the harbour and all-pervading smells and aromas. Outside a few of the hotels or a good restaurant you will not drink the water; if the locals don't, why should you?

It is a photographer's delight. As everywhere in the Caribbean there are people who will not be photographed and others who insist on it (if your camera is not a Polaroid be sure to advise them it is 'ne pas automatique'). And when you have finished with the people there is the architecture. The amazing Iron Market (more about *that* later), decrepit, unpainted or peeling buildings held together by their neighbours, imposing public buildings such as the cathedral and

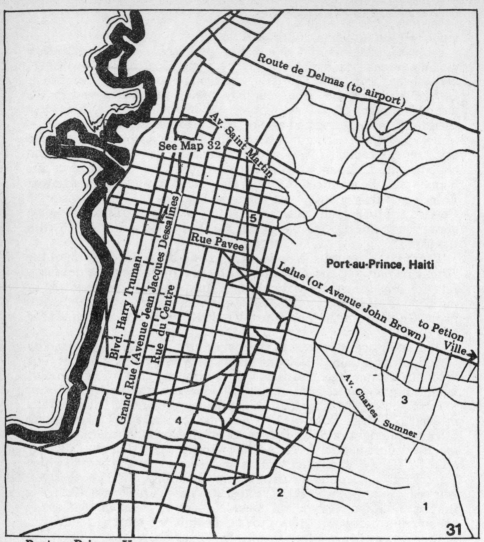

Port-au-Prince, Haiti

See Map 32

Route de Delmas (to airport)

Av. Saint Martin

Rue Pavee

Lalue (or Avenue John Brown)

to Petion Ville

Av. Charles Sumner

Blvd. Harry Truman

Grand Rue (Avenue Jean Jacques Dessalines)

Rue du Centre

5

4

3

2

1

31

Port-au-Prince: Key

1 Santos Pacot Guest House
2 Hotel Prince
3 Canadian Embassy

4 Cemetery
5 Cathedral

Presidential Palace (best seen from the east in the late afternoon when the misty mountains behind imbue it with a regal presence). There is the *Negre Marron* (or *Le Marron Inconnu*, the unknown slave) — one of those rare statues which is a work of art, when most are merely memorials. The sculptor, Albert Mangones, has his subject resting in mid-fight or mid-flight, legs outstretched, a broken chain strung from the left ankle and a massive sword resting in his right hand on the ground. His head is thrown back as he sounds a call to arms through a conch shell.

Going up towards the mountains the squalor is gradually left behind as you pass among modern villas and old maisons which are truly '*très jolie*'.

And things happen. I was photographing *Le Marron Inconnu* when I heard behind me, from the Place, the sound of a bugle. My guide insisted I freeze. I looked up to see that the city had come to a complete standstill.. Pedestrians had stopped in their tracks. Motorists had ground to a halt and had left their vehicles to stand at attention. The whole effect was of a three-dimensional mural. The national flag was being lowered. This done, the silence was shattered again and the bustle resumed.

And the very next day was a national holiday — 2 January, Heroes' Day. On such occasions the President drives among the people distributing money to the poor. Again I saw it happen, twice. Returning from Boutilliers by car we were forced to wait by the roadside. A few minutes later we heard the wail of police sirens and saw the motorcade with police motorcycle escort. Towards the rear of the convoy was the President's official car, and as he swept past and I snapped a photograph money was flung out of the vehicle to those willing to scramble for it. Two points were noticeable: firstly, that spontaneous applause erupted amongst the excited crowd as the convoy hove into sight; and secondly, it was only a minority that made any attempt to gather the money. The successful ones were happy, yet the unsuccessful ones were not disappointed.

Then maybe fifteen minutes later we had stopped in a gas station when we heard approaching sirens again. Quickly I grabbed my camera and ran to the roadside. This time it was the President's mother, Papa Doc's widow. A young-looking woman, she leaned out of the car window and showered notes and coins as she passed me. My guide was a lucky recipient.

But enough of all that. You will have your own experiences.

Accommodation In Port-au-Prince

Name	Address	Price per room in US$
Guest Houses		
Santos Pacot Guest House	20 Rue Garoute -northwest of Rue Turgeau (Tel: 5-4417)	MAP: *S* with bath $12, shared bath $10; *D* with bath $18, shared bath $15; *T* with bath $24, shared bath $21.
Prince Hotel	30, Rue 3 (Tel: 2-2765)	Summer, EP: *S* $22/$30; *D* $27/$35; *T* $35/$40.
Sendral's Guest House	Ruelle Sendral, Bourdon 14 (Tel: 2-0614)	MAP: *S* $19; *D* $31; *T* $50
Hillside Guest House	147 Martin L King (Tel: 5-5419)	CP: *S* $8/$10; *D* $18/$15; *T* $21/$21/$24.
USA	Rue du Centre	EP: $5 per room
Lys Guest House	77 Rue du Centre	EP: $5 per room
Central Hotel	Rue du Centre	EP: $5 per room
Embajadour	Rue du Peuple	EP: $5 per room

I strongly recommend the *Santos Pacot Guest House*. The only fault I could find with it was its location, at least 15 minutes' walk from the hub of the downtown activity. But even that can be an advantage as its lofty situation affords fine views from the balconies. The prices quoted above include full breakfast and evening meal, so that the cost of accommodation alone is really US$5 per person. There is no air-conditioning but all rooms have a fan. There is a small swimming pool.

If you deserve, or merely want, a touch of luxury, then you will not better the *Prince Hotel*. This 20-room hotel is a converted Grand House with the intimate atmosphere that suggests, and the manager, Claude, takes the trouble to make each guest his friend. It has a swimming pool of course, situated over the bar and all rooms have private facilities (and constant water -- drinkable — which is a problem in Port-au-Prince from which many of the more expensive hotels are not exempt). The conversion has been undertaken to preserve a family atmosphere and human scale.

The *Beau Rivage* is a must to avoid. I stayed here through force of circumstances and regretted it almost immediately. The single price of US$23 (before tax and service) includes only a scanty breakfast served reluctantly and inefficiently by scruffy waiters. English is a language heard only on television and spoken brokenly by most of the staff (there are about three, including the manager, who speak good English) who do not go out of their way to be courteous. Rooms would be good for a US$12 hotel. In fact, if it was a US$12 hotel I wouldn't be complaining so vociferously about it. In $5 hotels in Haiti I was always able to get a shower when I wanted one, but here I was able to get only about three in four days. I saw some clients showering in the ornamental fountains outside the entrance to the hotel (there was water in those). For a single room it rates equal worst with the Chickcharnie in Fresh Creek, Andros, Bahamas. The only good thing about it is its location, on the harbour front, handy

Downtown Port-au-Prince: Key

1 Hotel Embajadour	12 Banque National de la Republique d'Haiti
2 Lys Guest House	
3 Hotel Central	13 ITT
4 Hotel USA	14 Presidential Palace
5 Hotel Beau Rivage	15 Port administration building
6 Le Tiffany Restaurant	16 Cathedral
7 Restaurants	17 Iron Market
8 Gare du Nord (bus station for Cap Haitien)	18 Negre Marron
	19 Market
9 US Embassy	20 Tourist office
10 British Vice-Consul	21 Post office
11 Pan American Airways	

Av. Saint Martin

8   19

Quai

Rue

Macajou

17   3 2
Rue   des

Aubry

Cesars

15 du

Peuple

1

Rue

4

Dr

21 20

des

16

13

Rue

Rue
du

Miracles

10 12

Rue

Rue

Rue

Pavee

Av. Marie-Jeanne

Americaine

Centre

du

9
11

de

(Main

du

Revolution

Guilloux

7

l'Arsenal

Street)

Rue

18

Boulevard Harry Truman

6

Dessalines

Rue Monseigneux

14

7

Boulevard JJ

la

Reunion

5

de

Rue de la

Downtown
Port-au-Prince, Haiti

Rue

32

for downtown and the Tiffany Restaurant.

Cheap accommodation can be found among the squalor and bustle in the centre of town. There are many hotels on Rue du Centre. I inspected three of them. I found the *USA* at US$5 per room poor value. It is very seedy and the restaurant prices downstairs are high, although the owners are very pleasant. *Lys Guest House* at 77 Rue du Centre is quite acceptable. The bedrooms are clean and decorated, although toilet facilities are shared and not too good. Over the road is the *Central Hotel*, somewhat bigger. From what I could make out all rooms have a private bathroom (although the water is not always connected) but toilet facilities and bedrooms are of a spartan nature. What do you expect for US$5? This hotel is possibly a whorehouse. I stayed one night here and spent some time trying to persuade a half-naked Spanish-speaking prostitute (Dominican) that I was not a potential customer. It was only when I put some clothes on that she got up off my bed and left.

The Embajadour is also centrally located. Shower and toilet facilities are shared, but there is a lounge, a small kitchen and a helpful honest manager. Both the staff and the clientele are very pleasant.

Other guest houses offer much the same facilities as my first choice, the Santos Pacot, and some of these are better situated. *Sendral's Guest House* is air-conditioned, with a swimming pool and good views. According to the Tourist Board's guide for travel agents it has excellent French and Haitian cuisine. In the same price range as Sendral's are: the *Paulema Hotel*, situated on Route Delmas in the residential sector, telephone 70430; *Thor Auberge Inn*, Thor-le Volant, telephone 20465; *Villa Bel Soleil*, a six-roomed guest house at 94 Rue 5, Haut Lafleur Duchene, telephone 23147; *Hillside Guest House*, 53 Alix Roy, telephone 25419. All of these guest houses have a swimming pool. The *Pension La Guite's* main claim to fame is its (and I quote) suitability 'for the extremely budget-minded'. As it is included in the glossy book for travel agents you can expect it to be clean, and I would anticipate prices similar to the Santos Pacot's. The purple prose continues, 'With its clientele of Haitians from the provincial cities coming to Port-au-Prince and visitors in town from the islands surrounding Haiti, this centrally located guest house has a most Caribbean character.' It is located on Avenue Ducoste No. 5, and the telephone number is 24423. There is no swimming pool.

Eating in Port-au-Prince: Three restaurants spring to mind. Almost opposite the Beau Rivage is a small snack bar intended, I think, for members of the Association of Chauffeurs and Guides. They do allow visitors to eat there. A dinner (example, barbecued chicken with rice, bananas and avocado pear) will cost 7½ gourde or US$1.50 (always check whether prices are in gourdes or dollars). A Coca Cola is one gourde (20 cents) and local 'Cola Champagne' ½ gourde or 10 cents. Liquor prices are listed in US dollars.

On the corner of Boulevard Harry Truman and Rue Paul VI is a large restaurant with modern fittings. For a restaurant that takes credit cards the prices are reasonable, about 1½ times the snack bar mentioned above. They do a three-course lunch (up to 4 pm) for US$2.95. The clientele is almost entirely tourist. The food is good but service bad.

The Tiffany is expensive by Haitian standards — your guide will catch his breath when you mention it. The prices are about the same as you would expect in a 'good' Jamaican restaurant: US$1 for soup, US$4 for Tassot Creole, US$4.75 for a steak. The food is largely native and genuinely so. Therefore if unused to piquant sauces, or if your teeth are not perfect, avoid Creole dishes. The service is excellent and the food is very good indeed. The clientele is predominantly tourist with a sprinkling of rich Haitians. I have no hesitation in strongly recommending it for a good meal, but it will cost you.

There are many cheap snack bars around town with differing standards of hygiene and price ranges. The menus are usually prominently displayed (frequently painted on the wall) but think twice (at least) before drinking the water.

Sights in Port-au-Prince: The Iron Market is one of the stand-out sights of Port-au-Prince, along with the Cathedral, Palace, Le Marron Inconnu and the mountains behind the town. They stand out because of colour, size, strength and majesty. Standing proud among or behind Port-au-Prince's teeming, squalid, noisy streets, all these have 'presence'. And in all cases a presence felt most in the late afternoon.

Downtown is dominated by the Iron Market, both in its role as the nucleus of business dealings, and visually. Painted a flamboyant red and green and with a tin roof that gleams in the sun, it can stop you in your tracks at first sight. It boasts minaret-cupolas that could be straight from Agra or Fatehpur Sikri in India! According to legend a Moslem city in India ordered an iron market to be manufactured in France; at the same time Port-au-Prince required an enclosed market. The French are supposed to have sent the wrong market to the right place. I was advised by the Tourist Office however that this story is unlikely to be true (sorry to spoil your fun). Whatever the case, the Moslem influence is strongly represented with an accuracy which suggests that the designer had at least been to Agra. The colour scheme just has to be Haitian. (This colour combination, incidentally, is often used for shop signs and other graphic art throughout Port-au-Prince, consciously or unconsciously derived from the town's centrepiece.)

Inside the market you can buy almost anything you are never likely to need, a wide variety of items you would only dream about, and who knows how many things you don't know the use of. Oh, and you may get something you want.

Outside the market, for an area of perhaps half a square mile, the streets have become a large market area. Here more mundane goods, such as foodstuffs, clothes, cigarettes, and shoe repairs can be purchased. The vendors have long since occupied the sidewalk, and on busy days now take up most of the street as well. This forces pedestrians to walk down the middle of the road, cramming to the side every time an impatient klaxon heralds the approach of a vehicle.

There is another market, dealing principally in food stuffs, near the oddly named Gare du Nord (!) -- the bus station. This is merely an area of muck with a Texaco gas station where the inter-city tap-taps terminate. This market is very dirty and smelly. On the other side of the port administration buildings is a good spot to buy native carvings. Workshops line the road and you can see the carvers at work. Nearby, paintings are displayed, many showing by their repetition that they are mass-produced.

Petionville: Going up into the hills from Port-au-Prince you progressively leave the squalor behind. Over the years the rich have done this, and now many of them live in the town of Petionville, 1100 feet up and 4 miles from Port-au-Prince. Many of the plush hotels are here, as are the most expensive restaurants and night clubs.

Boutilliers: The mountain you see towering over Port-au-Prince is Le Perchoir. Boutilliers, at the top, can be reached in two ways: shared station wagon to Petionville and on up, or the hard way — walking directly up the side of the mountain. I took the hard way, but this is only recommended if you are fit and used to fell-walking. If you doubt your ability don't try it -- the sun is very hot and you could choose far better places in which to get sunstroke. The path itself is fairly easy to find and even easier to negotiate — it has been formed by girls walking up all day, every day, carrying several gallons of water on their heads.

This method of progress has its advantages. It obviously affords far better views of the plain, town and bay below, and allows you to take photographs when and where you want to. Also it gives you the opportunity of studying the lifestyle of the poor people in the hills. Although they are faced daily with long walks uphill carrying heavy loads, they have the benefits of peace, serenity, and less squalor and crowds than in the town. They appear to be very industrious.

Kenscoff: Kenscoff is a little further from Port-au-Prince (12 miles) and in the same direction. At an altitude of 4,000 feet, the climate is considerably cooler than on the coast. Rich Haitians come here in the summer months.

Port-au-Prince to Cap Haitien and onward: Assuming you will visit Cap Haitien, here are three suggested means of travelling between Port-au-Prince and Santo Domingo:

1 Tap-tap to Cap Haitien, returning to Port-au-Prince by the same means. Fly from Port-au-Prince to Santo Domingo.
2 Tap-tap to Cape Haitien, fly back to Port-au-Prince, spend

about two hours in the airport then fly Port-au-Prince to Santo Domingo.

3 Tap-tap to Cap Haitien. Bus across the north of Hispaniola turning south around around Santiago for Santo Domingo. A variation is to go back to Port-au-Prince anyway, and take a bus from there to Dominicana (this is probably easier).

If you are taking option 1 or 2, it is a good idea to make a reservation on your intended flight to Santo Domingo before you leave Port-au-Prince for the north, as the Pan American agent in Cap Haitien will not phone for you if you already have a ticket.

Route option 1: First you will need a permit to take the bus to the north. I was told by some people that it was not essential, but mine was inspected on both northbound and southbound trips. To obtain one you should go to the Tourist Office with your passport and Tourist Card: the permit will be typed out and stamped while you wait. If you ask they will also give you a very good Texaco map of Haiti.

It is strongly advised that you make a reservation on a bus the day before you wish to travel, at about 4 to 5 pm, so that you can be sure of getting a seat (and possibly a good one). To reserve, you simply go down to the bus terminal (Gare du Nord — see map) and find a truck or bus bound for 'Le Cap'. I paid US$4 fare each way. Northbound, I suspect I was overcharged by perhaps a dollar. I know that the return trip, in a far better vehicle, was genuinely US$4.

Both north- and southbound buses leave at about 6 am, arriving at their destination between 1 and 3 pm. They all make three trips per week in each direction.

Most of the vehicles comprise a truck chassis with handbuilt wooden superstructure custom-made to the owner's requirements. This means that each row of seats is meant to accommodate at least six and more usually seven persons. In terms of discomfort this may well be the worst journey of your life — remember that a truck has very rudimentary suspension. This discomfort can be alleviated however. As these tap-taps have no aisle as such, entry and exit is made by scrambling over the passengers sitting in the centre of the bus. When booking, you should request a window seat. This will leave you relatively undisturbed, although pushed against the woodwork and covered in dust (but you get the benefit of the breeze — glazed windows are a rarity). For the best views (north Haiti) get a seat on the right-hand side of the bus going up, or better, on the left-hand side coming down. You have to keep to the seat number allocated to you (it will be marked on your ticket). The numbers are crudely painted on the *back* of the seat.

As well as the trucks there are some old buses, also gaily painted. But I found that the best transport was an unromantic, red and white bus called Ebenezer. This was actually built for the purpose of carrying passengers so that the only discomfort is the overcrowding

(39 passengers instead of the 27 it was designed to carry). It even has fans to circulate the air! Ask for seat 39 northbound or 34 southbound.

If the bus leaves with any empty seats it will stop to pick up until the driver thinks he has enough passengers. He is not always in agreement with his original passengers on this question. Two crewmen travel up on the luggage rack.

The journey itself is visually spectacular at times, if you can stay awake. The route begins and ends on good roads, but in between there are stretches with gravel surface or no surface at all and road repairs and construction may well be in operation. At these points the bus lurches off the road and trundles along until it can rejoin the straight and narrow. At one point an iron girder bridge spans a wide river bed; Ebenezer can buzz across this, whilst the trucks roar and bump over the riverbed, fording the rivulets with no reduction in speed.

All along the route small settlements can be seen: thatched mud and wattle huts, the occasional wooden building, usually gaily painted in pastel colours, Caribbean-style. Vendors surround the bus every time it stops, selling cold drinks, fruit, bread, biscuits, nuts, cigarettes. There are more children about than in Port-au-Prince. Most of the population of Haiti is rural, and this is perhaps the best way to observe them. There are also two towns of some size, Saint Marc and Gonaives. Throughout the journey frequent stops are made at police checkpoints, although your permit will probably be asked for only on entry to Cap Haitien.

One of the greatest pleasures for me was the scenery, which is spectacular in the north. Returning to the capital, we left a little after dawn, at 6.45, with me sitting at the back of the bus on the left-hand side. The mountains as seen from Cap Haitien are an inspiring sight anyway, but when seen from a mountain road in early morning, they are incomparable.

It had rained in the night, so that the lush foliage and trees on the mountainsides glistened in the rays of sunlight which filtered through gaps in the clouds. The dust had been turned to a fine mud, rich red in parts, creamy beige in others. With the alternating patches of light and shade the full range of greens speckled the mountainsides, from emerald to turquoise. The mountains themselves were most spectacular, plunging into each other in seemingly endless rows with no real valleys in between. The road was simply a snake, carved into the mountainside and winding up or down at a rate which reduced the bus to a speed of 10 mph. At times it would double back on itself, and other vehicles could be seen far away tackling the ascent or descent in bottom gear.

The bus station in Cap Haitien is at the south end of town, which necessitates a taxi ride into the town centre. Taxis are usually shared, and the fare should be 2 gourde (40 cents). Agree this first and do not pay more. When you make your return reservation you will be without baggage, so it is easy to take a quiet stroll down to the bus station. The next morning you will be up before dawn and with baggage, so you may prefer to order a car in advance. I just walked, and pretty soon a taxi found me.

Back in Port-au-Prince 'publiques' meet the incoming buses. The fare into town is 2 gourde, but you will be charged more if going direct to the airport. Again agree this first.

It is possible to take a tap-tap to the airport from Grand Rue (Avenue Jean Jacques Dessalines) at the corner of Rue Macajou. The fare is 1 gourde per person.

Route option 2: As above to Cap Haitien. The advantage of this option is that the tiring overland trip is halved. You also save taxi fare, time and trouble between Port-au-Prince and the airport, as you can arrange your schedules so that you have only a 2-hour wait between planes. You will still need to get to the airport in Cap Haitien of course.

It is best to make your air reservations Cap Haitien/Port-au-Prince and Port-au-Prince/Santo Domingo before you leave Port-au-Prince. Allow at least three days for the journey. I would recommend four — i.e. a day travelling to Le Cap, a day for a visit to the citadelle and Sans Souci, a spare day, and a day for your return. Three days can be enough if you take an afternoon flight back to the capital, as this will give you two half days and two nights in Cap Haitien itself (not counting the excursion). When planning, remember that although the PanAm flight to Santo Domingo is daily, there are no Sunday domestic flights at the time of writing. It is possible to book with a travel agent or separately with Haiti Air Inter and Pan American. This will cost you perhaps an extra $13 but you do save time and energy. Book as soon as possible.

Route option 3: This is the most time-consuming and frustrating of the three suggestions listed here, and is not necessarily any cheaper. Whether you go to 'Le Cap' and try to cross the border up north, or instead return to Port-au-Prince to take the overland route from there, you will find yourself faced with a tough proposition. In either case, for travel to Cape Haitien see Option 1.

Go to the Ministry of the Interior for a permit to leave Haiti by this means. When you have obtained it, telephone or visit the Dominican consulate to check with them (it should be OK for US, Canadian and British citizens).

There is no surfaced road between Cape Haitien and the border, and next to no traffic taking that route. Your best chance, and that a minute one, is to find a ship leaving Cap Haitien and bound for a north-coast Dominican port.

It is more likely that you will be forced to return to Port-au-Prince. Here you will find occasional, but very rare, buses to Santo Domingo. But don't get excited — they are usually arranged months

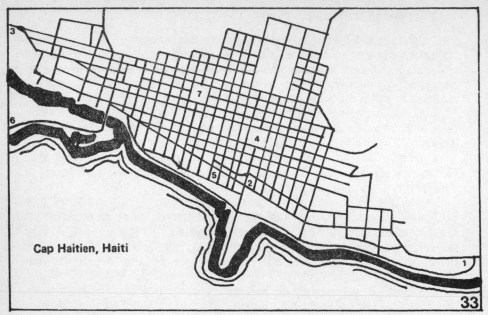

Cap Haitien, Haiti

33

Cap Haitien: Key

1 Brise de Mer Guest House
2 Pension Colon
3 Bus station
4 Cathedral

5 Banque National
6 To airport
7 Market

in advance. There is a more regular service of big trucks that make the journey, but to take advantage of this you will need to speak Creole or at least French. Some Spanish would help too. Try down by the harbour. This is also the place for your last alternative to flying. You could try the port authorities who will advise you if any ships are likely to be leaving for Santo Domingo.

Cap Haitien: In itself this is a more charming town than Port-au-Prince with less evident squalor. The streets are cleaner, quieter, the buildings less humble, more picturesque, painted in different pastel colours à la mode Caribbean. There is a cathedral in the town and a chateau on the hill, but apart from this no outstanding sights in the town itself. But a charming, peaceful atmosphere. The poor part of town, at times unbelievable in its squalor, is south, not far from the bus station.

Accommodation: I would recommend the *Brise de Mer* guest house 'the best according to the guest', situated in the north of 'Le Cap' (see map). The telephone number is (693) 2-0821. Rates are US$18 single, US$30 double, US$42 triple, 5 percent tax additional. These rates include private bathroom, some rooms with balcony, and two meals per day. American Express, BankAmericard and MasterCharge are accepted.

Of the cheap pensions I would suggest you try the *Columb*. There is only one bathroom (albeit a satisfactory one), no fan and no protection against mosquitos. But then I was charged a mere US$3 per night. Expect to pay about US$5-6 for a double. I ate only once in the cafe downstairs because they tried to rip me off (some Haitian hadn't paid all their bill and they were trying to get me to make up the difference — without my knowledge — as I found out later). A good cheap place to eat is a snack bar nearby. Turn right when leaving the Colomb, then right at the corner and left at the Air Haiti office. The snack bar is about two blocks along on the right.

The Citadelle and the Palace of Sans Souci: The massive Citadelle was built shortly after independence — it took ten years to complete — by King Henri Christophe to repulse a possible French invasion. On top of a mountain, it can be seen with the naked eye from Cap Haitien, although it is some considerable distance from the town. It could accommodate 10,000 people within its 12-foot thick walls — the Royal Family were allocated 40 rooms. Cannons in various states of disrepair are everywhere and there is a magazine that holds 45,000 cannon balls. Henri Christophe's tomb is in the centre with the inscription 'Here lies Henri Christophe, King of Haiti. I am reborn from my ashes.'

The Citadelle is reached by way of the town of Milot. Take a tap-tap or publique to Milot and register at the police station. Here you organize your entry and transport (which is by horse, as you ascend by means of a mountain track) to the Citadelle. Expect to pay US$1.50 for a ticket, US$1.50 for a horse and the same again for a guide. Allowing for meals (and including something for the guide) you can expect to pay about US$8 for the excursion.

On the way back down you can visit the ruins of the Palais de Sans Souci, which was designed to rival Versailles in France. It would have been splendid in its day, but it was devasted by an earthquake and now remains only as a reminder.

Jacmel: Jacmel is a quiet town on the Caribbean coast, important for the coffee, orange and tangerine industries. Coffee is Haiti's main export, and you can visit a coffee sorting plant in Jacmel.

There are many houses with New Orleans-style wrought iron balconies. These were brought from France and Belgium as ballast for the ships, which were to return laden with coffee and fruit. There are two nearby beaches: Black Sand Beach, in the town itself, and Raymond Des Bains, twenty minutes away.

Tortuga: This island off Haiti's north coast was discovered first by C.C. and then by the pirates. It is claimed that Henry Morgan, Jean Laffite, Blackbeard and Captain Kidd used to rendezvous here until the Spanish asked them to move along. That is when they made Port Royal their home base.

The topography of the island is fairly mountainous with numerous caves and coves and white coral sand beaches. Scuba diving is said to be superb here, both in terms of natural wonders, and also because the area abounds in old wrecks. This island alone is bigger than some Caribbean countries.

THE TURKS AND CAICOS ISLANDS
Geographically these islands are part of the Bahamas group, and at times in their history they have also been so politically. Control of the islands has been fought over by Bahamian interests, the French, Spanish and British. At the end of the eighteenth century the islands became part of the Bahamas, separating in 1848. In 1874 they became a dependency of Jamaica from whom they finally separated on Jamaican independence in 1962. The Turks and Caicos Islands are a crown colony.

Nowadays there is a strong American influence. There is a US Navy missile base and an increasing amount of American investment in the colony, and of course tourists. The facilities of deep sea fishing, scuba diving, yachting and just lying on white coral sand beaches are those principally available to the visitor. The total indigenous population is merely 6000.

Immigration: No visas are required. You do need an ongoing and return ticket and a valid smallpox vaccination certificate.

Customs: You may introduce the usual tobacoo or cigarette allowance and all reasonable private effects.

Currency: The US dollar and Turks and Caicos crown are both legal tender. US$ Travellers Cheques are widely accepted, but there are very few places which honour credit cards.

Climate: The temperature range is between 77°F and 83°F (25-28°C), and the climate generally is very similar to the Bahamas. There is little rainfall in the most easterly islands.

Travelling Through and Within the Islands: There are regular services from the United States (Miami and Fort Lauderdale) and the Bahamas (Nassau, Mayaguana and Great Inagua). There used to be connections also with Haiti (Cap Haitien and Port-au-Prince) as the local airline, Turks and Caicos Airways, provided domestic services in Haiti. As these latter services have recently been taken over by Haiti Air Inter, the current situation is very vague. Check with your travel agent. Some details of international air connections follow:

Depart from	At	Arrive	At	Frequency	Airline	One-way Fare in US$
Miami	0750	Providenciales	1115	Tue/Thu/Sat	Mackey	$71
Miami	0750	Grand Turk	1205	Tue/Thu/Sat	Mackey	$71
Fort Lauderdale	0650	Providenciales	1115	Tue/Thu/Sat	Mackey	$71
Fort Lauderdale	0650	Grand Turk	1205	Tue/Thu/Sat	Mackey	$71
Providenciales	1135	Miami	1550	Tue/Thu/Sat	Mackey	$71
Providenciales	1135	Fort Lauderdale	1635	Tue/Thu/Sat	Mackey	$71
Grand Turk	1245	Miami	1550	Tue/Thu/Sat	Mackey	$71
Grand Turk	1245	Fort Lauderdale	1635	Tue/Thu/Sat	Mackey	$71

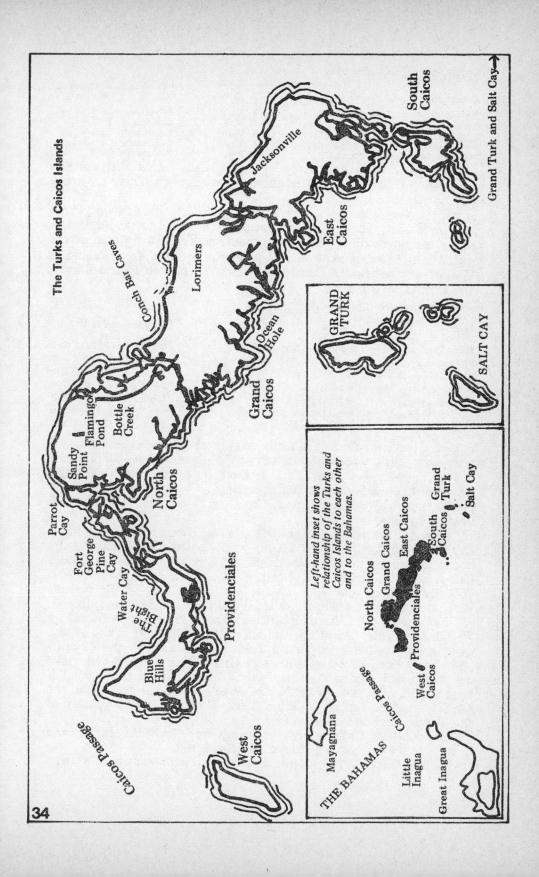

The Turks and Caicos Islands

Conch Bar Caves

Jacksonville

Lorimers

East
Caicos

South
Caicos

Grand Turk and Salt Cay →

Ocean
Hole

Grand
Caicos

Parrot
Cay

Sandy
Point

Flamingo
Pond

Bottle
Creek

North
Caicos

Fort
George
Pine
Cay

Water Cay

The Bight

Blue
Hills

Providenciales

West
Caicos

Caicos Passage

GRAND
TURK

SALT CAY

Left-hand inset shows
relationship of the Turks and
Caicos Islands to each other
and to the Bahamas.

North Caicos

Grand Caicos

East Caicos

Grand
Turk

South
Caicos

Salt Cay

Providenciales

West
Caicos

Caicos Passage

Mayagnana

Little
Inagua

THE BAHAMAS

Great Inagua

34

Caribbean Island Hopping

Depart from	At	Arrive	At	Frequency	Airline	One-way Fare in US$
Nassau	1100	South Caicos	1345	Wed.	Bahamasair	$77
Inagua	1300	South Caicos	1345	Wed.	Bahamasair	unlisted
South Caicos	1400	Inagua	1445	Wed.	Bahamasair	unlisted
South Caicos	1400	Mayaguana	1545	Wed.	Bahamasair	unlisted
South Caicos	1400	Nassau	1745	Wed.	Bahamasair	$73

Turks and Caicos Airways provide daily scheduled services between the islands, so getting about is easy enough. There are many private planes too.

An inter-island service is provided by sailing sloops, a few of which are motorized. There are also various motorized-barge services — some are operated by the government, and others by commercial outfits. Air Florida now operates regular services from Miami to Grand Turk and South Caicos, with a connection to Puerto Plata in the Dominican Republic.

Accommodation

Name	Address	Summer rates in US$
Turks Head Inn	Grand Turk (Tel: 2466)	EP: *S* $22; *D* $35; *T* $45.
Salt Raker Inn	Grand Turk (Tel: 2260)	EP: *S* $32, *D* $40; *T* $48.
Balfour Beach Cottages	Salt Cay	EP: *S* $20; *D* $20; *T* $30.
Brown House	Salt Cay	AP: *S* $38; *D* $60; *T* $90.
Corean's Cottages	South Caicos	EP: *S* $20; *D* $20; *T* $30.
Bassett Apartments	Airport Road, South Caicos	EP: *S* $20; *D* $30; *T* $40.
Village Inn	South Caicos	EP: *S* $15; *D* $20; *T* $30.

Don't bank on finding a ready supply of native guest houses — remember that the total population of the islands is only 6000.

The People: You will find a mixture of islanders: English, Americans, Canadians and Haitians. English is the language of the people but many islanders speak Creole, a by-product of their many years of trading with Haiti.

There are townships in the Salt Islands (Grand Turk 2,500; Salt Cay 370 and South Caicos 1,100) while in the Caicos Islands the population lives in small scattered settlements. Middle or Grand Caicos has 400 inhabitants, North Caicos 1,100 and Providenciales 700. East Caicos and West Caicos are uninhabited at the present time, though they once had industrial and plantation settlements.

The Islands: The Caicos Islands, separated from the Bahamas by 30 miles of water, comprise the majority of the land in the group. They are separated from Grand Turk and Salt Cay by the 22-mile-wide Turks Island Passage. Although Grand Turk and Salt Cay make up only a tiny part of the land area (Grand Turk is about 9 miles long and Salt Cay nearly 5) they provide a home for about half the population. The capital is Grand Turk. Here is a brief summary of the islands, starting in the west:

West Caicos: Uninhabited, a sanctuary for wild birds, and bordered by a fine fishing ground. Rarely visited.

Providenciales: At present, this is the main centre of tourist development. There has been substantial American investment here, with most facilities being provided around the narrow middle of the island, at Turtle Cove. Also on this island are the ruins of a great house, Stubbs Hall.

The Cays: Linking Providenciales with the main Caicos Island group are a number of small cays, of which Pine Cay, Fort George Cay and Parrot Cay are notable. Pine Cay is one of the few islands in the group with no fresh-water problem. Its main claim to fame is its superb beach but it also offers the visitor some of the best diving to be experienced in the Caribbean. Fort George Cay, logically, has a fort, established in 1798. Now in ruins, it is nevertheless an interesting sight, surrounded by a National Park.

North, *Grand* (or *Middle*) *and East Caicos:* These three chunks of the Caicos Islands' biggest land mass are largely uninhabited and undeveloped. Plans are afoot for the exploitation of North Caicos, principally at its north end, and work is already well advanced. East Caicos is entirely uninhabited. The beaches of all three of these islands are mainly situated on the north, Atlantic, coasts.

South Caicos: The main port here — which is probably the most important port in the entire island group — is Cockburn Harbour. Salt used to be exported from here, whilst today it is important insofar as trade with Haiti is concerned. You may well be able to get an empty fruit boat returning to Cap Haitien from here.

Grand Turk: This is the seat of administration and main centre of commerce. You should be able to find native accommodation on or near Front Street. *Salt Cay* is about 10 miles south.

THE CAYMAN ISLANDS
There is some argument for not including this island group in this book at all, as it does not fit conveniently into most island-hopping schedules. Nevertheless, readers intending to spend several months in the Caribbean may get the opportunity to make a visit, whilst those undertaking a route roughly based on Itinerary Three may be able to include the Cayman Islands as a stopover (example: Miami/Grand Cayman/Jamaica/Haiti/Turks and Caicos Islands/Bahamas/Miami).

The Cayman Islands group consists of three islands — Grand Cayman, Cayman Brac and Little Cayman — and lies 480 miles south of Miami. Cayman Brac and Little Cayman are about 80 miles east-northeast of Grand Cayman, on which is located the capital, Georgetown. This is also the commercial centre.

Tourism is a flourishing industry and is very important to the island's economy. Facilities provided are of an up-market standard and are inevitably centred around the beaches, excellent diving and yachting and, of course, fishing. Informality is nevertheless the keynote. Both the standard and the cost of living are high (the latter due to the fact that most food and other necessities have to be imported).

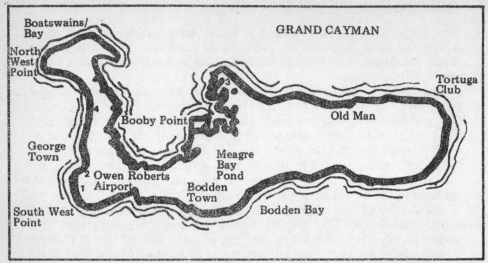

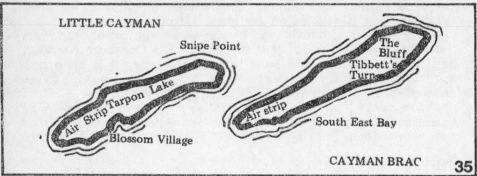

35

Grand Cayman: Key
1 Casa Bertmar
2 Sea View
3 Rum Point
4 Holiday Inn

In 1670 the islands were ceded to the British crown (from Spain) and the first natives included 'mixed groups of shipwrecked sailors, marooned mariners (which I would have thought were the same thing), debtors, buccaneers and beachcombers. The group is a British colony and the head of government a Governor appointed by Queen Elizabeth 2. He is assisted by an Executive Council made up of three appointed and four elected members. There is also a Legislative Assembly, most of whose members are elected.

Immigration: Again, as seems to be the rule everywhere in the Caribbean, no passports are necessary for US and Canadian citizens. Although of course you will take yours. British and Commonwealth citizens do not need visas. The authorities stress the need for a return ticket.

Customs: You need expect no trouble introducing your personal effects and reasonable quantities of cigarettes and liquor.

Currency: Legal tender here is the Cayman Islands dollar (CI$) which currently equals US$1.25 approximately. US$1 = CI 80 cents. US, Canadian and (it is claimed) British currency are accepted in the islands.

Climate: Similar to that of other small Caribbean islands: average 80°F (27°C) in summer and 75°F (24°C) in winter.

Language: English, liberally spattered with nautical terms and pronunciation, which in itself shows Cornish, Welsh, Irish, Scottish and English regional variations, not to mention echoes of the American south.

Food: Local specialities are of course based on seafood. Try the following: turtle steak, turtle soup, codfish and ackee, conch stew and seafood newburg. The island chefs also prepare an excellent Steak Diane.

Transportation to, through and within the islands: If you have planned a visit here and included it in your itinerary, the flight cost will be included in your long-distance round-trip ticket. At the other extreme you may never have intended to come here at all, but just have happened to meet the captain of a yacht who was headed this way. Whichever way you come, you will still need some idea of flight schedules which are detailed below:

Depart From	At	Arrive	At	Frequency	Airline	One-way Fare in US$
Miami	0800	Grand Cayman	0910	Fri/Sun	Cayman Air	$ 88
Miami	1330	Grand Cayman	1440	Daily	Cayman Air	$ 88
Miami	1345	Grand Cayman	1501	Daily	Southern	$ 85
Miami	2030	Grand Cayman	2150	Mon/Tue/Fri/Sun	Lacsa	$ 88
Grand Cayman	0940	Miami	1100	Mon/Fri/Sat/Sun	Cayman Air	$ 88
Grand Cayman	1505	Miami	1625	Mon/Tue/Thu/Sat	Cayman Air	$ 88
Grand Cayman	1530	Miami	1642	Daily	Southern	$ 85
Grand Cayman	1600	Miami	1720	Thu/Fri/Sat/Sun	Lacsa	$ 88
Grand Cayman	1800	Miami	1920	Wed.	Cayman Air	$ 88
Grand Cayman	1505	Kingston	1605	Wed/Fri/Sun	Caymn Air	$ 42
Kingston	1635	Grand Cayman	1735	Wed/Fri/Sun	Cayman Air	$ 42
Grand Cayman	2210	San Jose	2250	Mon/Tue/Fri/Sun	Lacsa	$ 89
San Jose	1300	Grand Cayman	1540	Thu/Fri/Sat/Sun	Lacsa	$ 89
Grand Cayman	1030	Cayman Brac	1115	Sat	Cayman Air	$ 24
Grand Cayman	1545	Cayman Brac	1630	Mon/Wed	Cayman Air	$ 24
Grand Cayman	1730	Cayman Brac	1815	Fri/Sat/Sun	Cayman Air	$ 24
Cayman Brac	1130	Grand Cayman	1215	Sat.	Cayman Air	$ 24
Cayman Brac	1645	Grand Cayman	1730	Mon/Wed	Cayman Air	$ 24
Cayman Brac	1830	Grand Cayman	1915	Fri/Sat/Sun	Cayman Air	$ 24

Please note that these schedules are included to give you an indication of frequency, and that both they and the fares are subject to revision.

The natives of the Cayman Islands are very much a sea-faring people, whether it be via luxury yacht or humble fishing boat. You thus stand a good chance of visiting the two smaller islands or leaving the country by sea.

There is a bus service on Grand Cayman from George Town to West Bay. Buses leave George Town hourly on the hour, but check. The fare from George Town to Holiday Inn is 50 CI cents. and from

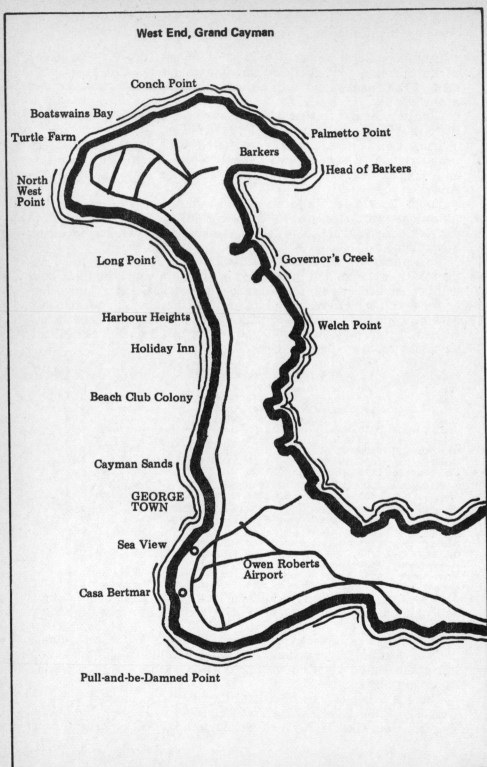

West End, Grand Cayman

Conch Point

Boatswains Bay

Turtle Farm

Palmetto Point

Barkers

Head of Barkers

North West Point

Long Point

Governor's Creek

Harbour Heights

Holiday Inn

Welch Point

Beach Club Colony

Cayman Sands

GEORGE TOWN

Sea View

Owen Roberts Airport

Casa Bertmar

Pull-and-be-Damned Point

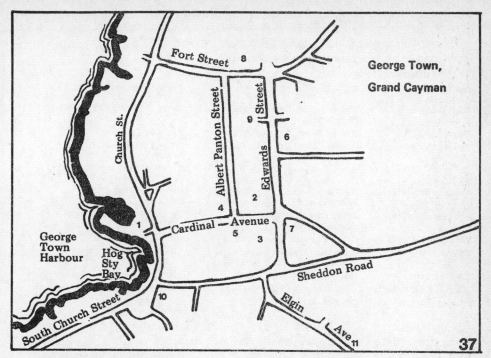

George Town, Grand Cayman

George Town: Key

1 Tourist information
2 Bank of Nova Scotia
3 Bank of Montreal
4 Royal Bank of Canada
5 Barclays Bank
6 Canadian Imperial Bank of Commerce
7 Post office
8 Legislative assembly
9 Courts building
10 Old Court House
11 Police

Holiday Inn to West Bay Town Hall 50 CI cents. Some official taxi fares (per car) are as follows: airport to George Town CI$3, to Sea View Hotel CI$3.60, to Casa Bertmar CI$4.40, to Rum Point CI$18, to Bodden Town CI$9.

Car hire rates begin at US$15 a day for a Fiat 124 or other small car (Cico-Avis and National Car Rentals). Honda 50s are available from Caribbean Motors at US$9.50 per day or US$26 for three days. Bicycles can be hired from Green Thumb in George Town (US$2 per day or US$12 per week), Eldemire's Rent-a-Bicycle at the Casa Bertmar (US$2.50 per day) and Buccaneer's Inn on Cayman Brac (US$3 per day). In length, Grand Cayman is comparable with New Providence in the Bahamas, and in area somewhat smaller, so a bicycle would seem to be an ideal way of getting around. You should remember that public transport is located only in the western part of the island and take this into account when choosing your accommodation.

139

Horse riding can be undertaken at about US$6.50 per hour. Excursions by sea or air are also available.

Accommodation:

Name	Address	Winter rates in US$
Casa Bertmar	Winter Haven, Grand Cayman (Tel: 9-2514)	MAP: *S* $38; *D* $72; *T* $92.
Sea View	George Town, Grand Cayman	EP: *S* $30; *D* $40; *T* $50.
Sunset House	George Town, Grand Cayman (Tel: 9-2511)	MAP: *S* $38/$50/$69; *D* $63/$69/$80; *T* $80/$86/$97. Efficiencies EP: *D* $52; *T* $60.
Galleon Beach Hotel	West Bay Beach, Grand Cayman (9-2692)	EP: *D* $50/$65/$75.
Ambassadors	South Sound, Grand Cayman (Tel: 9-5515)	EP: *S* $30; *D* $40; *T* $46. 1 Bedroom Apt: *D* $55; *T* $63.
Eldemire Guest House	Grand Cayman (Tel: 9-5387)	CP: *S* $28; *D* $42; *T* $52.
Glasshouse	Pease Bay, Bodden Town Grand Cayman (Tel: 7-2362)	EP: Efficiency: *D* $35.
Dillon Cottage	Little Cayman	EP: $200 per week double.
Kingston Bight Lodge	Little Cayman (Tel: 8-3244)	AP: *S* $54; *D* $79.
Buccaneers Inn	Cayman Brac	AP: *S* $45/$55/$60; *D* $75/$80/$90.

Casa Bertmar and Sunset House specialise in catering for divers. Both are situated south and within walking distance of George Town. The coastline is rocky and both have boats and equipment to take parties diving. Accommodation at Casa Bertmar has a rustic ambiance (although air-conditioned) and there is a bar, restaurant and sandy sunbathing area by the sea. Sunset House was being improved and extended during my visit.

CUBA

The chances of more than a handful of this book's readers visiting Cuba at any time is very slight. Only Canadians and the citizens of a few Scandinavian countries (and citizens of countries in the Soviet-aligned bloc) are able to visit Cuba without a visa.

Geographically, Cuba is conveniently situated for incorporation into a Caribbean island-hopping itinerary. But politics make this a much more difficult proposition. It is easier to fly to Havana from Moscow or Rabat than from Miami or Nassau, and in addition there are no international services from the eastern end of the island to Jamaica or Hispaniola. So in practice one has to fly to Havana from Kingston and return to Kingston from Havana (fare US$82 each way.

One might think it is also possible to fly (or get a ship) from Kingston to Havana, travel through the island and hop on to Haiti by some means. This is what I had intended to do. Accordingly I applied for my visa in good time (about a month before departure). I went along to the Cuban Embassy in London, explained in detail what my intended visit to Cuba would entail, and was given three copies of a visa application form which had to be completed and returned with passport-sized photographs. This I did. On subsequent enquiry I was told to expect my visa in about two weeks. I went back after three weeks expecting to collect it and was disappointed. I spoke to an official who said a mistake had been made, and that my application had been incorrectly processed. There were basically two categories of visa, those granted for cultural visits and exchanges, and tourist visas. If I intended to write a book of this type, then I would need to be interviewed by the Cultural Attache. OK, I thought, I'm not proud; I have about a week left, I'll see the Cultural Attache.

It was not as easy as that. First I would need an appointment for an interview, perhaps in a week's time. Then my application would be sent to Havana with the Cultural Attache's recommendations and be returned in about four months' time.

'Four months? How can it take four months?'

'Well, it takes two months to get to Havana and two months to come back. So it may take more than four months if they need time to study it in Havana.'

Now I would have thought it could get to Havana in two days, travelling via Kingston. But then maybe I'm just appallingly ignorant.

So I thought I would enquire about a tourist visa. Could they change my application to one for a tourist visa? 'We don't issue tourist visas. If you want to visit Cuba as a tourist you should contact one of the travel agencies who organize tours to Cuba.' Patiently I explained that a charter flight from London — or anywhere else for that matter - · to Havana and a tour featuring tourist hotels, visits to factories, sugar cane plantations and industrial estates would not serve the purpose of my visit to the country. Patiently, I again explained that I would have to travel alone (all their schemes involved my movements in daylight hours being under supervision), finding out about cheaper accommodation, local transportation, restaurants — the sort of information contained herein. Consternation for a moment.

'Do you mean you would want to travel through the Provinces?'

'Well yes; I would enter at Havana and leave Cuba in the east. I would probably get a boat or something to Haiti.'

'I don't think....... well I can arrange an interview for you with the Cultural Attache.'

I was beginning to feel.I was not wanted. Whether my abrasive and critical style of writing made them lack confidence in seeing glowing reports of the Workers' Paradise in print, or whether my one-year membership, a few years ago, of a British non-Communist political party worked against me, I don't know. Anyway, I was able to ascertain that if I could wait at least four months I had the chance of a visa being granted on a cultural basis. This would involve meetings being fixed up with Cuban writers and that sort of thing. Also, if I went along to a travel agency which specialized in tours to socialist countries, I could book a holiday to Cuba. Tourist visas were normally processed by the travel agency for the group as a whole and were then 'rubber-stamped' by the Embassy. Since the idea of being professionally castrated did not appeal to me, Cuba had to be dropped from my schedule. And so the largest island in the Caribbean has to be relegated to a minor place in a book on the Caribbean.

Since my experiences, Cuban visas have become easier to obtain and in fact I have very recently sent a number of independent travellers to the island, through my work as a travel consultant at TransAtlantic Wings. Although accommodation has to be booked and paid for before a visa can be granted, the procedures are now much more straightforward. Even US citizens are now being granted visas, although these are usually confined to participants of package tours (contact Amigo Tours, Miami).

History: Cuba was a Spanish colony up until the Spanish-American war, although there were many attempts at independence. This war began after the US warship *Maine* blew up in Havana harbour and resulted in Spain's loss of both Cuba and Puerto Rico. Cuba became politically independent but was dominated economically by the United States, which had strong interests in the sugar and tourism industries. It was in 1933 that the Batista regime, now a byword for corruption and cruelty, came to power. The successful revolution of 1959 established a socialist form of government and economy headed by Fidel Castro. Despite the economic blockade organized by the United States, Castro has been successful in improving the lot of the common people and enjoys great popularity.

Immigration: Canadians may visit Cuba armed only with a passport. US citizens will need a visa, and also require permission from the US State Department. British passport holders should note my experiences, given in detail above, although obtaining a visa is not quite so difficult now.

Currency: The currency unit is the Cuban peso, which is exchanged (in Cuba) at a rate of US$1.20 = 1 peso. All money has to be changed into pesos on arrival, any unspent pesos being changed back into the original currency on departure.

Climate: Average winter temperature in the coastal and lowland areas is about 75°F (24°C) rising to around 80°F (27°C) in the summer. You can expect some slightly cooler weather, especially at night, in Cuba's beautiful (so I'm told) mountains.

Food and Drink: People of African descent make up only 25 per cent of Cuba's total population — less than in almost any other Caribbean country. The remaining 75 per cent are of Spanish, Amerindian or other descent and various mixtures. Thus I would expect the food to show a strong bias towards Spanish dishes. I am told that the rum is very good, and that there is a good local 'coca cola' (maybe they left the recipe behind). I am led to believe that they make good cigars here.

Accommodation: Cuba is a fairly well developed country, with

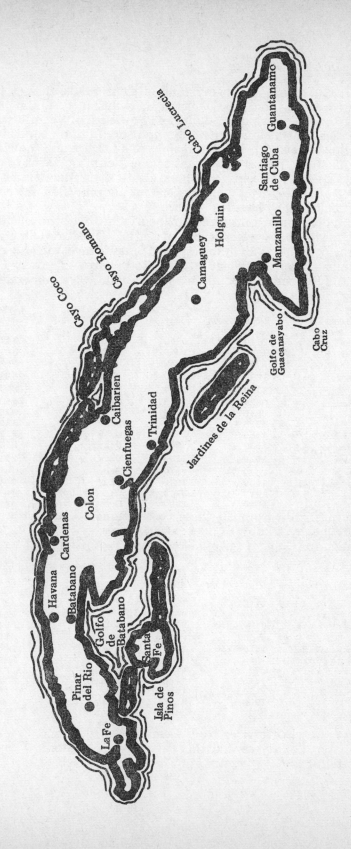

Cuba

Cabo Lucrecia

Cayo Romano

Cayo Coco

Guantanamo

Santiago
de Cuba

Holguin

Manzanillo

Camaguey

Cabo
Cruz

Golfo de
Guacanayabo

Caibarien

Trinidad

Jardines de la Reina

Cienfuegas

Colon

Cardenas

Havana

Batabano

Golfo
de
Batabano

Santa
Fe

Pinar
del Rio

Isla de
Pinos

La Fe

38

some large towns and many long straight roads, dissecting great cultivated areas. You should have a fair chance of finding suitable lodgings of the native type, though a knowledge of Spanish will help. If you decide to visit Havana only, you should find abundant hotels of varying sizes and prices but mainly of a fair age and showing signs of dilapidation. This is not meant as a criticism; it seems to me that the government has achieved a great deal just in maintaining Cuba's solvency and integrity as an independent nation, when one considers the difficulties they have had to face.

Transportation within Cuba: When I flew over the island, those same straight roads were devoid of traffic. Thus 'travelling through the provinces', as the official put it, may prove to be a difficult undertaking. You should expect buses to be few and crowded. Flying is probably a better way to get about, and I give below details of Cubana's domestic services:

From Havana To	Depart From	Arrive At	Frequency	One-way Fare in US$
Camaguey	0740	0850	Daily	$41.30
Camaguey	1940	2040	Daily	$41.30
Camaguey	2010	2210	Daily	$41.30
Cienfuegos	1040	1130	Fri./Sun.	$21.80
Holguin	1140	1310	Daily	$47.80
Nueva Gerona	0630	0700	Daily	$13.10
Nueva Gerona	0840	0915	Daily	$13.10
Nueva Gerona	1230	1305	Daily	$13.10
Nueva Gerona	1430	1505	Daily	$13.10
Nueva Gerona	1630	1705	Daily	$13.10
Santa Clara	1015	1105	Daily	$21.80
Santiago	0640	0810	Daily	$54.30
Santiago	1500	1630	Daily	$54.30
Santiago	1915	2115	Wed./Thu./Sun.	$54.30
Santiago	2010	2350	Daily	$54.30

Return flights from all these destinations to Havana are at the same frequency. I know of no excursion fares.

Flights to Cuba: I give below details of Cubana's services to Havana.

To Havana	Depart From	Arrive At	Frequency	One-way Fare in US$
Madrid	1410	1810	Thu.	$479
Berlin/Madrid	0045/0430	0830	Wed., fortnightly	$543
Prague/Madrid	0100/0430	0830	Sun.	$543
Barbados	0130	0530	Wed.	$218
Port of Spain/Barbados	1310/1450	1950	Wed.	$218
Georgetown (Guyana)	1215	1950	Wed.	$234
Kingston	1820	1950	Wed.	$82
Mexico City	1345	1745	Mon./Fri.	$156
Panama City	1130	1500	Sat.	$168
Lima	1000	1530	Thu., fortnightly	$325
Montreal	0800	1400	Fri./Sat./Sun.	$180

There are also services from Luanda, Conakry and Freetown in Africa. Aeroflot fly several times a week from Moscow to Havana (en route for Lima) with stops in Frankfurt and Rabat.

Part 3
Port-au-Prince to
the Virgin Islands

LA REPUBLICANA DOMINICANA
(THE DOMINICAN REPUBLIC)
I love Haiti, and I shall return, but it is always a relief to get back to
civilization. The most incredible feature of the two countries which
share Hispaniola is the difficulty one has in travelling between them.
Almost equally incredible is the difference.

Chalk and cheese are far more similar. Haiti seems out of place
because it is West Africa transplanted. Dominicana is the opposite
extreme -- Latin America in the Caribbean. It has echoes of Mexico,
but is cleaner and more prosperous. When I was walking through
Santo Domingo unidentifiable chords were struck in my memory
bank. But although far more international, it remains first and
foremost Dominicana.

The Airport of the Americas itself contrasts strongly with Port-au-
Prince: big, modern, efficient with all the facilities you would expect
in such a place. Formalities are straightforward enough, but transport
to town could present a problem as the airport is a long way out. The
taxi fare is 8 to 10 pesos (US$8/10) per car. I was told by everyone
that there is no bus service, but in fact there is (at least from the
town to the airport). Ask. The company is Expressos Dominicanos
and the fare US$2 per person. Their town terminal is centrally
situated, near the recommended accommodation.

Some History: Discovered like most of the islands by our friend
C.C. and rapidly exploited by Spanish imperial interests, Hispaniola

was, for much of the sixteenth century, the centre of Spain's American interests. Santo Domingo was the headquarters of same. In 1795 Spain was forced to cede its two-thirds of the island to France. As this event coincided with the revolution in Haiti, Toussaint was forced to pacify Dominicana too, a problem from which the Haitians were freed when this country reverted to the Spanish crown following the downfall of Napoleon. Independence was first declared in 1821 and lasted a full four months before a Haitian army put the country back under its wing. So it is from 1844 that independence is usually dated, although there was a four-year period when Dominicana returned — voluntarily — to Spanish control.

Domestic rule has been turbulent with very many revolutions, presidents and constitutions. The most famous dictator, General Trujillo, ruled from 1930 until his assassination in 1961. Anarchy could well have been the order of the day in the sixties, but the intervention of the CIA and US marines helped to establish a stable government which continues today.

Immigration: Citizens of the United States, Canada, Jamaica, Mexico, Puerto Rico and Venezuela need proof of identity, not necessarily a passport. Those without a passport must purchase a tourist card for US$2. British passport holders, citizens of many western European countries (and some other countries) need a passport but no visa or prepaid tourist card and are allowed to stay up to three months. All visitors are required to show return tickets. As in almost all countries, there is a departure tax (3 pesos here). For some reason, the government insists that 'Passengers belonging to the religious group *Hare Krishna* are not permitted to enter the Dominican Republic.'

Customs: You may introduce the usual quantities of liquor and cigarettes and any personal effects you are likely to be carrying.

Currency: The Dominican peso is officially at par with the US dollar. In fact it is only worth US 82 to 85 cents. By strict currency control the 'parity' is, however, maintained. This is how it works:

If you change US dollar Travellers Cheques or cash in a bank you get a rate of 1:1. However, if you try to change pesos back into dollars you will find it impossible! The only official exchange point for this purpose is at the airport, and that is shut most of the time. Even if you can find it open, you can only change back up to half of what you originally changed, and then only by showing your first receipt. So of course there is a flourishing black market, conducted quite openly on the streets (El Conde seems to be the main one for this). Rates may change, but at the time of writing US$10 will buy you 11 pesos, US$20 23 pesos and US$100 buys 115 to 118 pesos. You can also change back the other way: for example to buy US$20 you would pay 25 pesos. This is the first country I have visited where the activities of banking were carried out on the streets — the banks I visited were empty! So my advice is to change as many Travellers

Cheques as you think you will need into US dollars *before* you leave Haiti. Then change the dollars into pesos, all at once or a bit at a time, on El Conde.

You should note that US dollars are not only accepted but eagerly sought everywhere — in shops, restaurants, hotels, etc — but only at a rate of 1:1, and that change will be given in pesos. All costs in this section are given in pesos.

Cost of living: Higher for the natives than in Haiti, but the discrepancy between what the natives pay and what you pay is much less. Of course, unscrupulous traders will try to take you for a few cents or dollars, but if you buy from listed prices you should have no problem. In fact, for me Dominicana worked out cheaper than Haiti.

A standard hotel charging 5 pesos a night will offer much the same value for money as its equivalent in Haiti. But for 8 pesos a night you will get far better value — equivalent to paying US$10 or 12 in Haiti or Jamaica. A meal in an economical native restaurant will cost the same as in Jamaica or Haiti, about US$1.50. But remember that if you are paying with pesos changed on the street, it is actually costing you slightly less. Also note that El Conde is the main shopping street; if you go north, towards the poorer part of town, the same goods will be cheaper.

Climate: Much the same as Haiti's. During my visit it was substantially cooler, dropping to about 60°F (16°C) at night in Santo Domingo. But then these were freak conditions — it was snowing at the time in Nassau!

The people: In ethnic terms, the full range from sickly white to ebony black, with the vast majority in between. There are a lot of fat girls and women in Santo Domingo, but also a lot of pretty and beautiful ones. I was told that sex is as natural to them as it is elsewhere in the Caribbean, but don't be fooled — many are in it for the money. The incidence of male tourists being led to prostitutes, particularly in the old part of town, is so high that even the official tourist guide makes an oblique reference to it. So, if after nocturnal· company, accept no offers of help in finding it and keep your money and valuables locked out of harm's way.

Language: Spanish. And except at the airport, little English is spoken. In general, the people seem to find it difficult to understand the average traveller's pidgin Spanish. They particularly do not understand the meaning of 'No dinero'.

Food and drink: A strong Spanish and Italian influence. The Spanish accent is weaker here than in Puerto Rico, partly, I guess, because Dominicana became independent before Puerto Rico changed hands, and partly because Dominicana wishes to play down its colonial past whilst Puerto Rico is proud of its cultural heritage.

The Dominican national dish is sancocho, a concoction also found in parts of South America. Having no set recipe, it is based on many different meats and vegetables cooked in a broth. You will find the

Caribbean favourite of fried chicken with rice (pollo con arroz) and many dishes that travellers to Spain will know. Almost every restaurant in central Santo Domingo seems to sell pizza, lasagne is freely available, and there are a number of Italian restaurants of differing standards and prices.

Rum (you guessed it) is the national drink. It seems that every Caribbean country claims the best rum, but for me the white Jamaican is still tops.

Transportation: There are speedy and regular bus services throughout the Dominican Republic at reasonable cost. The terminals are conveniently clustered around Puerta del Conde in Santo Domingo (see central downtown map). Some of the main bus companies (with telephone numbers in Santo Domingo) are:

Estrella Blanca (EBL; telephone 682 0523)
Compania Nacioñal de Autobuses (CNA; telephone 565 6681)
Metro (MET; 566 3919)
Expresos Dominicanos (EXP; 682 6610 and 687 6313)
La Experiencia (LAE; 689 3576 and 689 9242)

Here are some details of bus services from Santo Domingo:

From Santo Domingo To	Departure Times	Bus Company	Price
Airport	6.30 am to 4.30 pm	Expresos Dominicanos	$2.00
Bonao	7 am/1.45 pm/3.30 pm	Expresos Dominicanos	$1.00
Bonao	6 am to 6 pm (2 hourly)	Compania Nacional	$0.70
Jarabacoa	8 am/5 pm (3 a week)	Expresos Dominicanos	$2.00
La Vega/Santiago	7/8/10.30 am/1.45/5 pm	Expresos Dominicanos	$2.00
Santiago/Puerto Plata	7.30/10 am/4 pm	Metro	$3.25
Puerto Plata	8 am/5 pm	Expresos Dominicanos	$3.00
San Pedro de Macoris	6.30 am to 4.30 pm	Expresos Dominicanos	$0.75
San Pedro de Macoris	5.40 am to 7.40 pm	La Experiencia	$0.60
San Pedro/La Romana	2 pm	Metro	$1.50
La Romana	7 am	Metro	$1.50
Pedernales	6.30 am	Estrella Blanca	$9.00
Bani/Azua	6.30 am/1 pm/1.30 pm	Estrella Blanca	$3.00
Bani/Azua/San Juan	6.30 am/1,30 pm	Estrella Blanca	$6.00
Bani/Azua/San Juan	1.30 pm	La Experiencia	$2.75
Barahona	2.30 pm	La Experiencia	$2.75
Barahona	2.30 pm	Estrella Blanca	$6.00
Hato/Mayor/Seibo/Higuey	7 am/1 pm/4 pm	La Experiencia	$2.50
Hato Mayor/Sabana/Miches	6.30 am/3 pm	La Experiencia	$2.50
Higuey	7 am/1 pm/4 pm	La Experiencia	$2.50

If you want to do some flying you will be pleased to learn that the domestic airline, Alas del Caribe, operates regular services at reasonable fares. Remember that you will have to add taxi fares between town and airport in most cases, and also that this airline operates from Herrera airport in Santo Domingo (more convenient than the Airport of the Americas). Here are some sample one-way fares (return fares are sometimes D$1 less than double):

Santo Domingo (Herrera) to: Barahona D$11   Puerto Plata D$12.50
                            Santiago D$11   Cabo Rojo (Pedernales) D$16.50
                            San Juan D$12   Constanza D$11
                            Sabana D$8   Samana D$9

Taxis are called 'carros de concho' and operate on a sort of

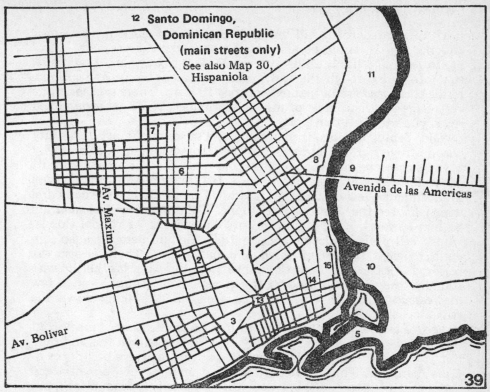

12 **Santo Domingo,**
Dominican Republic
(main streets only)
See also Map 30,
Hispaniola

11

8

9

Avenida de las Americas

Av. Maximo

7

6

16

1

15

10

2

14

13

3

5

Av. Bolivar

4

39

Santo Domingo: Key
Areas
1 'Old Town'
2 San Carlos
3 Ensanche Lugo
4 Indepencia
5 Sans Souci
6 Villa Consullo
7 El Ensanchito
8 Le Fuente

9 El Ancon
10 La Francia
11 Agna Duke
12 Capotilla
Buildings
13 Puerto del Conde
14 Hotel Commercial
15 Post office
16 Alcazar Columbus

publique system; they cruise regular routes picking up and dropping passengers on the way. The fare is 20 or 25 cents. For your own taxi on a specific route or for a specific destination, ask the driver for a 'carrera': the fare will vary between $1 and 2 within Santo Domingo, but agree this first. Taxis are painted either blue and white or red and blue. It is possible to telephone for a taxi and be collected anywhere; the number is 565 1313.

There are buses within Santo Domingo, called 'guaguas', with a fare of 10 cents.

Santo Domingo: Although the drive into town from the airport is long, it is also pleasant. You will immediately notice a very good, fast, uncrowded road, and thoughtfully laid out gardens between it and the sea. It would be nice to stop and take a short walk. 'New' Santo Domingo has little of interest. Wide highways and boulevards run into and through the town, and apartment blocks and spacious residential areas are in marked contrast to Haiti. There is at least one very large park and most of the big, flashy hotels. To get around and see it you will need transport.

'Old' Santo Domingo is something of a misnomer; most of the city was destroyed in the hurricane of 1930, which perhaps explains why it lacks character and soul. The real old part of any interest lies south of Calle Mercedes; here there are a few buildings of architectural interest, and a few of historical interest. One of them is the cathedral which houses the tomb of Christopher Columbus (the last mention of him I swear). Also, at the end of El Conde, is Puerta del Conde, whose bell pealed independence in 1844. Behind here a mausoleum contains giant statues of three national heroes. There is also the restored Alcazar, or Casa Columbus (not him, his brother — who founded the city, the first in the Americas, in 1498). And a few interesting buildings which can be seen when walking down the street.

People talk of the 'old Town' as if it has some kind of magic, but don't be taken in. You may find yourself being shown this and that, but if you are being guided at night be wary of travelling north of Calle Mercedes. This is not the old town, merely the poor part and the red light district. I think you will be quite safe from attack, but anyone who takes you there is hustling, and those boys are pros.

Accommodation: Accommodation is better value for money than in many parts of the Caribbean. In Santo Domingo I would suggest you get somewhere centrally located, near Puerta del Conde. There you will find restaurants of all prices, bus terminals, moneychanging facilities, airline offices, with the old town near at hand.

Name	Address	Price per room in pesos
Anacaona Hotel	Palo Hincado 303 Santo Domingo Tel: 689 0622	S $8.05****: D $13.80****· T $18.40****.
Hotel Aida	Espaillat/El Conde, Santo Domingo	S $8.05***: D $13.80***.
Dominicana	El Conde, Santo Domingo	S from $5**; D $7**.
Comercial	El Conde/Hostos, Santo Domingo	S $11.50; D $13.

You will find it difficult to find better value than at the *Anacaona Hotel* (slogan 'the best in the heart of Santo Domingo'). The rates quoted above are year round and include tax. If you are paying in pesos changed on the street (possible even if arriving at night as pre-payment is not necessary) remember that these equal US$7, US$12.20 and US$16 respectively. All rooms have good private bathroom, no water shortage, constant hot water (I'd forgotten what that felt like), telephone and air-conditioning. A very well run hotel.

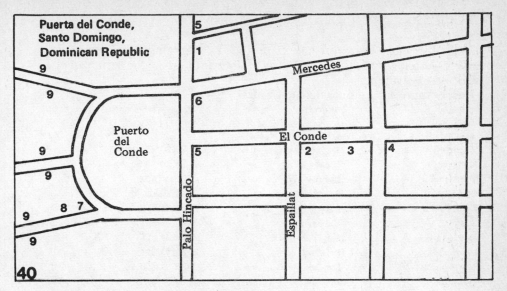

Puerta del Conde, Santo Domingo, Dominican Republic

Puerto del Conde

Mercedes

El Conde

Palo Hincado

Espaillat

Puerta del Conde, Santo Domingo: Key

1 Hotel Anacona
2 Hotel Aida
3 Hotel Dominicano
4 Aerovias Quisqueyana
5 Snack bars/restaurants
6 Travel agency
7 Petrol (gas) station
8 Expressos Dominicanos (airport bus)
9 Other long distance buses

Try to telephone a reservation from the airport if you speak Spanish.

If the Anacaona is full, which is quite possible, you could try the *Hotel Aida* at the corner of El Conde and Espaillat. Prices are the same, as are facilities, superficially, but the appearance is more dingy.

If saving money is of prime importance you could try the *Dominicana Hotel* on El Conde, not that I'm recommending it. I was charged $5, but you should treat all quoted prices as negotiable. I got a bed with clean sheets, soap, towel and toilet paper. However the other four beds in the room were covered in dust, as was the washbasin which had not been cleaned — or indeed used — for some time. The bathroom ('bano') down the hall had a peculiar water supply system; the only running water came from a spout on the bath and was transferred somehow to two oil drums. The door was not lockable or even properly shuttable, but then I had left all notions of privacy behind in Haiti. My room had a balcony, but there was nothing worth looking at.

Alternatively you could try the *Comercial Hotel*, a large well known establishment further down El Conde, or any of the small pensions which can be found with a little searching in the streets running off El Conde.

Restaurants in Santo Domingo: There are plenty of restaurants but none that I would specifically recommend or advise you to avoid. I suggest that you just walk about, observing the prices, food and clientele. Prices in expensive restaurants are higher than in the Haitian equivalent.

Accommodation outside the Capital

Name	Address	Price per room in pesos
Villas del Mar	Juan Dolio, San Pedro de Macoris	S $14; D $17.
Macorix	San Pedro de Macoris	S $9.20; D $13.80.
El Naranjo	Higuey	S $4.20; D $9.20.
Montemar	Cabañas, Puerto Plata	S $10: D $20.
Cofresi	Puerto Plata	S $10; D $15.
Long Beach	Puerto Plata	S $9; D $12.
Caoba	Valverde, Mao	S $7, D $11.
Maguana	San Juan	S $8; D $11.
Ugarocuya	Barahona	S $9; D $11.
San Cristobal	San Cristobal	S $8; D $10.50.
Montana	Jarabacoa	S $6;D $10.
Nueva Suiza	Constanza	S $5; D $8.
Mi Cabana	Constanza	S $5: D $8.
Mercedes	Santiago	S $6; D $10.
Arienm	Santiago Rodriguez	S $4; D $5.

Leaving the Dominican Republic: Communications with Puerto Rico are very good so you should be able to find a ship. There are at least four airlines flying the route, Dominicana, Eastern, Prinair and Aerovias Quisqueyana. There seems to be an open-rate situation on fares: whilst Eastern charges D$69 for the round trip, Quisqueyana charges only D$54. A one-way flight will cost you D$27 (or US$24 if you changed your money on the street). Quisqueyana operate a fleet of two 25-year-old Lockheed Constellations with two or three flights a day in each direction. The Quisqueyana office is on El Conde, a stone's roll from the Dominicana Hotel. Check schedules and make your reservation there — they fly pretty full. You should note that none of the sales office clerks, airport check-in staff or stewardesses speaks English. *If you are not a citizen of the USA or Canada make sure you have your US visa which is needed for Puerto Rico and the US Virgin Islands.* You should also have an onward or return ticket.

The bus terminal for the airport is on Puerto del Conde. The Company is Expresos Dominicanos and the fare D$2. Usually the bus is travelling much further than the airport, perhaps to Santiago, so you may be the only person dismounting there. You buy a ticket before boarding the bus.

On boarding the aeroplane you should be given two forms required by the US authorities; one for immigration (unless you are a US citizen) and one for customs. I had expected a somewhat hairy flight, expectations seemingly confirmed by the crude design of the plane's interior and the struggle with which the four engines started one by one. From the outside, too, the plane is a weird sight: four propeller engines, a streamlined body with small circular windows and three fins at the back. With most passengers braced for take-off, this veteran staggered into the air. But in fact it was a superb flight: less noisy than I expected, though I was sitting between the engines; less bumpy, though flying at a lower altitude than a jet. The seats were more comfortable with greater leg room than is normally the case with modern jets. The passengers were very friendly and talkative. Catering was provided and free rum and coke. Why is it that the cheap airlines seem to give better service?

PUERTO RICO

At 100 miles long by 35 wide, Puerto Rico is about the same size as the Bahamian island of Andros, though with a personality at the opposite end of the spectrum. With the US Virgin Islands, it must be the richest part of the Caribbean, both US Commonwealths benefitting from their association with the world's richest nation. The population is around 3 million — again a strong contrast with Andros — with a long life expectancy the norm.

Gold was first sought by the Spanish after their arrival in the first years of the sixteenth century, but as this was not available in substantial quantities they turned to the growing of sugar and coffee. As with the rest of the Caribbean, these crops were initially lucrative but became less so in the course of time, so that by the early years of this century Puerto Rico's poverty was a byword in the Caribbean. Steps were taken to correct this in the 1940s with an intensive industrialization programme and the initiation of the tourist industry.

In the meantime Puerto Rico had changed hands. Following the Spanish-American war Spain ceded Puerto Rico to the United States in 1898. Puerto Ricans became US citizens in 1917, elected their governor for the first time in 1948 and became a Commonwealth associated with the United States in 1952. During my stay the US administration was making moves to appoint Puerto Rico as the 51st State of America (thus ousting Pan American from the position), not necessarily with the approval of the Puerto Ricans. Or so I was told.

Immigration and Arrival: All except US and Canadian citizens will need a USA visa. Multi-entry is recommended in case you retrace your steps (eg. San Juan/Saint Thomas/Tortola/Saint Thomas). It is always best to apply for a United States visa in your home country; in particular, Australian and New Zealand citizens resident in the United Kingdom can expect difficulties if they apply in London. Onward and homeward tickets should be available for presentation, and a certificate proving immunisation against smallpox.

On arrival US and Canadians should have few problems, but the rest of us get the usual US immigration hassle: long queues and being sent back if their forms are not filled out perfectly (when filling

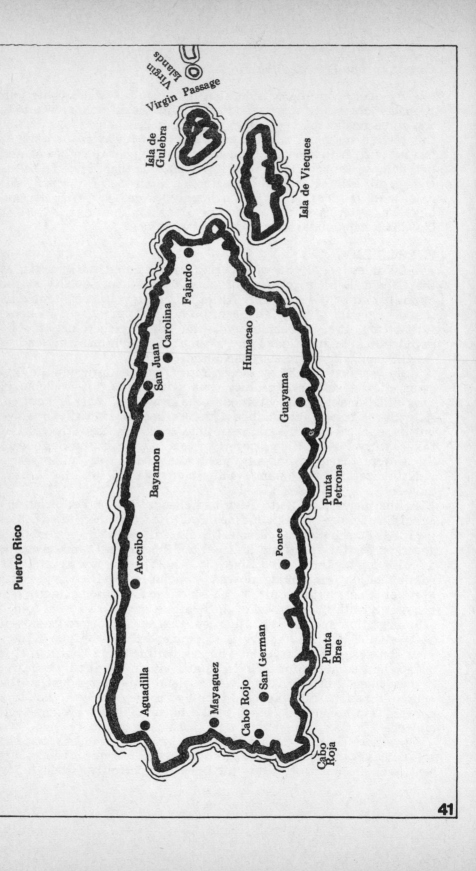

Puerto Rico

Virgin Islands

Virgin Passage

Isla de Gulebra

Isla de Vieques

Fajardo

Carolina

San Juan

Humacao

Guayama

Bayamon

Punta Petrona

Arecibo

Ponce

Punta Brae

Aguadilla

Mayaguez

Cabo Rojo

San German

Cabo Roja

41

them out press hard). But these guys are only doing their jobs, and it is the law of the USA that scrutiny should be strict. The same with customs.

Once outside you have a choice of transport, but it is advisable to decide on your hotel first and perhaps see the tourist information people. Taxis and limousines stop immediately outside the terminal. A taxi should cost about US$4 per car, and a limousine about US$1.50 per person. For publicos and the bus you walk up the ramp towards the car park; you will take a publico if you are going to another town, but if you are staying in San Juan there is little point. The bus stop is easily found, but beware; it is adorned with a large sign which says 'No baggage or large packets allowed'. I ignored this, as is my wont, and in fact was allowed on the bus when it eventually came. The fare is 25 cents, but you must have a quarter as entry is through a coin-operated turnstile as in Miami and other American cities.

Note that there are two airports in San Juan: Isla Verde International, at which you almost certainly arrived, and Isla Grande in town, from which you will probably leave.

Currency: The US dollar is the only legal tender. Travellers Cheques and credit cards are widely accepted.

Climate: Similar to Hispaniola, with an average 80°F (27°C) in summer and 75°F (24°C) in winter on the coast. Mountain areas can be cooler. The island benefits from the easterly trade winds, but rainfall is higher here than in Hispaniola. That shouldn't trouble you — you may welcome it.

The People: Predominantly Caucasian of Spanish descent with all that implies. This was the first Caribbean country in which I found the people offensive; but then it isn't really a Caribbean country at all. Culturally and ethnically its soul is from the Mediterranean, economically and politically it is part of the United States. Thus the values and morals of western 'civilization' govern the attitudes and personality of the people.

Nobody will stop you here in the street to ask 'Que pasa hombre' ('What's happening, man'). No spontaneous handshakes, or any bodily contact except perhaps pushing. Certainly no free love.

One good point: at least those very few people who ask you for money are genuinely poor, maimed or both, the casualties of society. But the majority are 'Poor no more'.

Language: Spanish. Preserved (rightly in my view) along with other cultural ties. A great deal of English is spoken, particularly of course in tourist areas (although during my stay most tourists seemed to be Spanish-speaking too), but surprisingly little by the younger generation.

The Cultural Heritage: This is seen to best effect in the architecture. Not the tower blocks and urban sprawl of new San Juan of course, but the preserved and restored buildings to be seen in and around the old town. Because the town was attacked so often down the centuries most of the buildings are actually comparatively recent. But with a large budget being available for restoration, and a great civic and national pride in its heritage being evident, San Juan manages to combine cultural authenticity with well-kept and clean streets. Many new buildings (including the outstandingly beautiful Casa de Espagna on Ponce de Leon Avenue) have been constructed in the colonial style.

All this, with the fort that surrounds it, gives San Juan a Spanish flavour far stronger than that of Santo Domingo, and even than that of Madrid. The Old Town, though admittedly touristified, is very charming, particularly during the day.

Transportation: Good roads and modern vehicles make getting about the island less of a trial than in many other countries on this trip. Throughout Puerto Rico, distances are expressed in kilometers but speed in miles per hour.

Bus: Buses ply the main streets of San Juan on regular schedules. The majority terminate in Plaza de Colon (Columbus Square) in the old town, near the entrance of Fort San Cristobal. Travelling eastwards these buses take Avenida Munoz Rivera, whilst on the return trip to Old San Juan they use Avenida Ponce de Leon. Both these roads are one-way streets, and in both cases the buses proceed *against* the traffic flow. Special bus lanes, identified by a yellow line, exist for this purpose, which is a feature of San Juan. Thus it is important that you look both ways when crossing any street.

Bus stops are identified by yellow posts bearing the legend 'Parada de Guaguas' with shelters often provided. The fare is one quarter on almost all buses, and you must have the exact change as you enter through a coin-operated turnstile. If taking a bus from the old town to the Miramar area note that you can take any except numbers 10 and 41 (although I was told the exact opposite by the tourist information people, whose literature is similarly misleading). If staying on the Atlantic coast (Condado, Ocean Park) you should use number 10. Number 41 serves the Isla Verde hotels. To and from the airport you can take number 17, which also serves Los Angeles.

At the time of writing the only long-distance bus is one which goes to Mayaguez; The company is Puerto Rico Motor Coach, address 327 Recinto Sur, Old San Juan, and fare US$3.50. It departs from Rio Piedras.

Publicos: Inter-city transportation is usually undertaken by public cars displaying 'P' or 'PA' after the numbers on their licence plates. They generally terminate in the main plaza of a town; in the capital they leave from Plaza de Armas, Old San Juan, Stop 15, Santurce, and the airport (Isla Verde). The fare to Mayaguez is about US$4.50/$5, and to Ponce maybe US$3.50.

Taxis are metered. Rates are 40 cents to start and 10 cents every 1/5 mile. Check that the flag is up when boarding. They also charge

25 cents per suitcase.

Boats: San Juan Bay can be crossed by ferry. These leave the old town (from the pier near the tourist information centre) every 15 minutes and the fare is 10 cents. A daily launch also leaves the east coast town of Fajardo bound for the islands of Vieques and Culebra. Departure from Fajardo is at 9.15 am and 4.30 pm, arriving in Vieques 1 hour 20 minutes later. The earlier boat continues to Culebra arriving at about 11.30 am. Return times are: from Vieques 7.30 am and 3 pm, and from Culebra 1.30 pm. Fares one way: Vieques US$2, Culebra US$2.25.

San Juan: The capital is an almost schizophrenic contrast between the charming old town and a modern city as up-to-date and hectic as you are likely to find anywhere. I am tempted to dismiss the new city as a featureless concrete jungle of skyscrapers, wide roads and overpriced tourist entertainments built on a naturally beautiful coastline. So I will succumb to temptation.

The old town of San Juan was enclosed within a strong city wall and defended by the forts of El Morro and San Cristobal. The building of these fortifications was a continuous process justified by repeated attacks (mainly by the English) but in the end unable to prevent history taking its course. The fort of San Cristobal itself seems to have been designed mainly with aesthetics in mind, leaving it vulnerable to an attack from its landward side.

Accommodation in San Juan

Name	Address	Price per room in US$ (Summer)
The Old Town		
San Cristobal Hotel	450 Norzagaray, Old San Juan	S $9; D $16.
YMCA	Stop 1, Avenida Ponce de Leon	S $9***.
Various small hotels	Near Calle Luna, Old San Juan	From $5 per room; expect low levels of hygiene and security
Condado/Miramar Area		
Miramar Guest House	Olimpo 609 Miramar (Tel: 724 9610)	S from $5****; from $30 weekly D from $8****; from $48 weekly
Hotel Toro	605 Miramar Avenue, Miramar. (Tel: 725 5150/2647)	S $10-$12***; D $12-$14****; T $15-$18*****.
Miramar Laguna (ex- Iberia)	604 Ponce de Leon, Miramar. (Tel: 723 0100)	S $13.60***; D $20*** (rates recently increased)
Hotel Miramar	606 Ponce de Leon, Miramar. (Tel: 724 6239)	S $12.40-$16.80; D $14.60-$18.90.
Olimpo Court Hotel	603 Miramar, Miramar (Tel: 724 0600)	S $14-$24; D $15-$26.
Ocean Side Hotel	54 Munoz Rivera, near Hilton. (Tel: 722 2410)	S $14.70***; D $16.80-$25.20***.
Borinquen Hotel	Fernandez Juncos, Miramar	S $18-$22*; D $28-$32**.

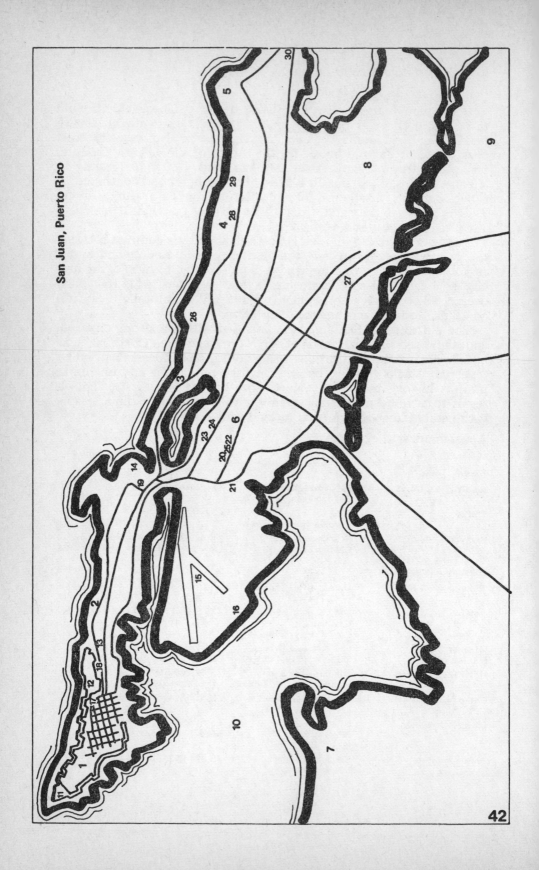

San Juan, Puerto Rico

42

Part 3: Port-au-Prince to the Virgin Islands

Accommodation in San Juan

Name	Address	Price per room in US$
The Coastal and Easterly Hotels		
Casa Mariana	5 Cervantes Street, Condado. (Tel: 724 3046)	S $10-$14; D $14-$18 (near the sea; 7 air-conditioned rooms).
Bolivar Hotel	609 Bolivar, Santurce (Tel: 724 5023)	S $9.95; D $12.55.
Ocean Breeze Guest House	8 Tapia, Ocean Park (Tel: 727 4002)	S $8-$12; D $15-$18 (9 rooms and efficiencies).
Lily's Guest House	2064 España, Ocean Park (Tel: 725 8964 & 727 0548)	S $10-$14; D $14-$20.
Interline Guest House	20 Uno Este, Villamar (Tel: 726 5546)	S $10-$12; D $16-$18. (nearish to airport)

There is a government tax of 5 per cent on room rates. As a general rule, those prices listed above which include cents are inclusive of tax, whilst it should be added to those prices quoted in round figures. There is no compulsory service charge, so you should tip according to the standard of service.

Accommodation in San Juan is spread out from Old San Juan to the Isla Verde airport area, a distance of perhaps some 6 to 10 miles. There are three principal locations (for the purposes of this book): in the Old Town, in the Miramar/Condado area, and along the coast from Condado to Isla Verde.

Old San Juan: The *Hotel San Cristobal* is opposite the entrance to the fort of the same name. It is an old hotel, about eight stories high and with signs of decay. It is quite well known, and many youngish people stay here. Service was, from my observations, slow in coming and curt on arrival. The rooms have fine views, but I thought that the

San Juan: Key
Areas
1 Old San Juan
2 Puerta de Tierra
3 Condado
4 Ocean Park
5 Punta Las Marias
6 Miramar
7 Catano
8 Santurce
9 Hato Rey
10 San Juan Bay
Points of Interest
11 Fort El Morro
12 Fort San Cristobal
13 El Capitolio
14 Fort San Jeronimo
15 Isla Grande Airport
16 Antilles Airboat Base
Hotels
17 San Cristobal
18 YMCA
19 Ocean Side
20 Miramar Guest House
21 Borinquen
22 Toro
23 Miramar Hotel
24 Miramar Laguna
25 Olimpo Court
26 Casa Mariana
27 Bolivar
28 Ocean Breeze
29 Lily's
30 To Interline Hotel and Isla Verde Airport

159

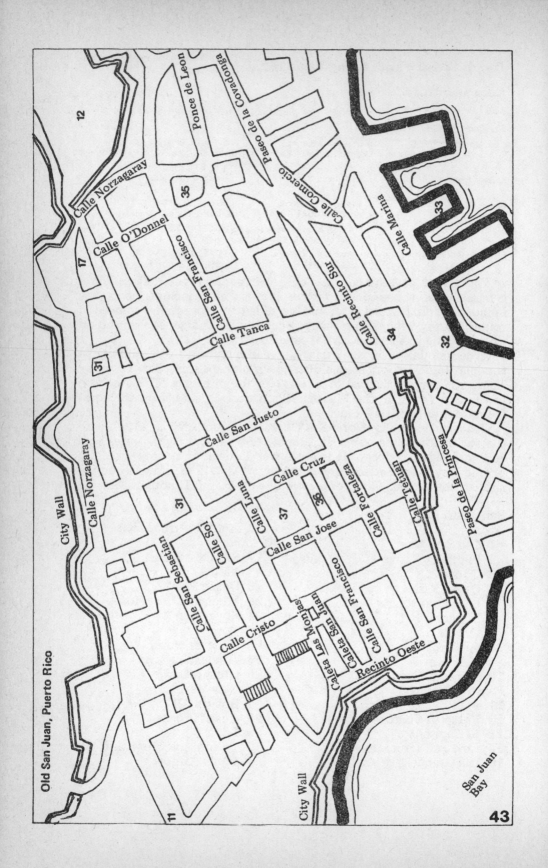

Old San Juan, Puerto Rico

hotel was only average, or below, in terms of value. The *YMCA* is expensive by Y standards at US$9 for a single. But it is also good by Y standards. Although furnishings and decor have that institutional flavour Ys love (I think they believe it is good for you) it is comfortable enough with good bathroom and toilet facilities. Cheap accommodation is located on or near Calle Luna, the poorest part of town (yes, there are some poor here). This accommodation is regarded with some humour locally. Expect to pay US$5 or less and regard all quoted prices as negotiable. To find it, use the Spanish method. Find a bar (finding a doorway that isn't a bar is more difficult), go in and ask for 'habitacione'. They will usually answer 'Aqui non' but direct you to the nearest. Good luck.

Miramar/Condado: There are a large number of hotels in this vicinity, mainly very touristified and overpriced. Most are set along the coast at Condado and will be of little interest to you. The ones you may prefer are in Miramar, further from the beach but on or near the main bus route between Old San Juan and Isla Verde airport. With frequent bus services (the fare is only 25 cents) you will find most of what you want quite accessible. In fact I used to walk into the Old Town and take the bus back.

The *Miramar Guest House* offers the cheapest rates at US$5 single without air-conditioning and US$6 with. Weekly rates are US$30 and US$35 respectively. Double rooms are US$8 and US$10 with appropriate rates for a week-long stay. The rooms are comfortable yet tatty. No rooms have private facilities, but bathrooms are frequent. The manager is a Liverpudlian and has retained his scouse sense of humour. This must be the best value around for a single and worth considering for a double too. However, the *Hotel Toro* represents the best value for two or more people travelling together. It is a smallish, owner-managed hotel designed in Spanish style with a restaurant next door (details are given in the Restaurants section below). Besides the normal rooms, some two-bedroom suites are available, comprising one bedroom with two twin beds, the other with a double. All rooms have private facilities, air-conditioning and ice box or refrigerator. The hotel also has a laundromat. This is my recommended accommodation for couples and groups.

The *Borinquen Hotel* is a moderate hotel at luxury prices with a casino, cocktail lounges, boutiques, and all that sort of thing. I would

Old San Juan: Key
(see also map 42: San Juan)

11 To Fort El Morro	33 Catano ferry terminal
12 Fort San Cristobal	34 Post office
17 San Cristobal Hotel	35 Plaza de Colon
31 Laundromats	36 Plaza de Armas
32 Tourist information	37 City hall

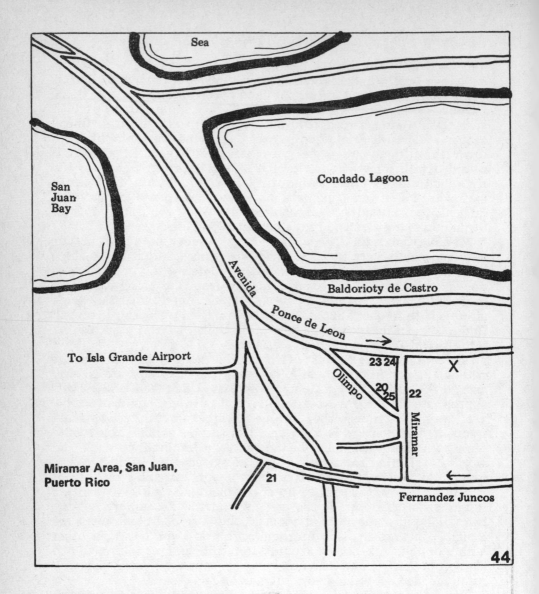

Sea

Condado Lagoon

San
Juan
Bay

Avenida

Ponce de Leon

Baldorioty de Castro

To Isla Grande Airport

Olimpo

23 24

X

20
25

22

Miramar

Miramar Area, San Juan,
Puerto Rico

21

Fernandez Juncos

44

Miramar Area, San Juan: Key
20 Miramar Guest House
21 Hotel Borinquen
22 Hotel Toro
23 Hotel Miramar

24 Hotel Miramar Laguna
    (formerly Hotel Iberia)
25 Hotel Olimpo Court
 X Bus stop (no 17 for airport)
Arrows show direction of buses

like to be very critical of it (for a start, service was bad) but that
would not be fair. I think it is probably typical of the big hotels (it is
one of the biggest, its Cloud Room giving magnificent views of San
Juan) and reasonable when judged by those standards. For the

traveller, however, it represents poor value.

There are three moderately priced hotels in this area (and one slightly outside). At the time of my visit the *Iberia Hotel* was about to change its name to the *Miramar Laguna.* All rooms have private facilities, including a lounge and kitchenette. American Express cards are accepted. The *Hotel Miramar,* not to be confused with the guest house of the same name, and the *Olimpo Court* are the two other reasonably priced hotels in this area. Outside the Miramar area proper, towards old San Juan, is another small hotel, the *Ocean Side*, close to the towering Caribe Hilton. It is well sited for buses and beaches. Rooms and facilities are very slightly better than those of the Toro, but then prices are significantly higher. This is probably because they accept all major credit cards.

Most hotels in the *coastal and easterly* group are in the expensive to very expensive bracket, and it is unlikely that you would want to stay in this part of San Juan anyway. Nevertheless I have given details of the cheapest of them.

Restaurants in San Juan: Generally I found prices high (Bahamas levels and over), food good and service bad. Cuisine is generally Puerto Rican, American and Spanish, but ethnic restaurants abound — for example Chinese, French, Argentinian, Italian. Food is generally well cooked from the widest range of meats, fish and vegetables. Service is of the lowest standard in the Caribbean, due I think to a combination of the Spanish influence, the country's recent rise to prosperity, and an uncomplaining tourist clientele. Service is abrupt and intimidatory, dishes being served at a frequency to suit the waiter rather than the diner.

The *D'Arco Restaurant* is on the ground floor of the Hotel Toro, 605 Miramar Avenue. It is open all day and takes BankAmericard and MasterCharge. This is one of the best restaurants I found and by local standards gives very good value for money. I ate there twice. The first time was for dinner when I was impressed by the quality of the food (Puerto Rican and American menu). Service was merely inefficient, not rude. My second visit, for breakfast the next morning, was less successful. The food itself was OK — orange juice, coffee and pancakes for US $1.50 — but the waiter truly dreadful. Staring with hate-filled eyes, he attempted to intimidate me (and the other guests too) by word and action,changing his tone completely when it was time to pay. He even asked for a tip (which he didn't get). I was about to advise the management (which is very competent) of this bad advertisement for them, when the thought occurred to me that this chappie was probably working out his notice anyway. (An aside: I was bemused by the reaction of many tourists to this behaviour. They squirm while they eat, are ingratiating towards the waiter and overtip when paying. Intimidation works!)

El Mediterraneo, 254 San Justo in Old San Juan, is open all day and accepts most credit cards. It serves international cuisine with the accent on Spanish. I tried Paella Valenciana which was very good indeed. Again service was bad. The waiter brought the paella dish to my table then shovelled it out on to my plate as if it was Kat-o-meat. When the dessert — flan — arrived it hit the table so hard that the creme wobbled as though sinking in a tidal wave of caramel. But when it was time to pay the waiter took time to point out a Spanish print on the wall, helped himself to one of my Haitian cigarettes and suddenly remembered that I was his long-lost brother. I had to laugh: ten minutes after my arrival a group of four tourists entered and seated themselves at the table next to mine. This waiter then intimidated them all into having exactly the same as I had ordered!

Palm Beach (or some similar name) is located on a corner somewhere in the old town. Distinguished by modern featureless furnishings, a long counter at the back and credit cards in the window, this is a must to avoid. Dreadful food at credit card prices. Service OK.

Fornos in the Hotel Iberia (now Hotel Miramar Laguna), 604 Ponce de Leon, serves dinner and cocktails only. The food is predominantly Spanish with Puerto Rican and international dishes. They accept American Express, BankAmericard, and MasterCharge. Although the à la carte menu is expensive they also offer a daily menu with 6 or 7 choices — a three-course meal (four including coffee) for anything from US$4 to $6.50. I chose the most expensive: superb Spanish soup, delicious sirloin steak with french fries and salad, flan and coffee. As they charged me only 50 cents for the Cuba Libre this was the cheapest full meal that I had sampled on the trip so far — and also the best. Very strongly recommended, especially if you choose from the set menu. Don't go in jeans. Service tended towards the abrupt, but was certainly not rude or overbearing.

Puerto Rican snackbars, bar/restaurants and cafeterias are to be found all over town, but are particularly thick on the ground in the old part. Prices vary, but are generally at about Bahamian levels. Liquor is reasonably priced, 50 cents for local beer, 55 cents for Cuba Libre, but beware of the Puerto Rican coffee! This concoction — which I hope is unique — is a brew made with milk as an intrinsic element, the result being a sort of coffee-flavoured hot milk. Fortunately they have Expresso coffee, and if you want something that approximates to real coffee you ask for American Express — expresso with hot water added.

Some Sights of Interest in San Juan: You should visit one of the tourist centres who will give you glossy brochures full of very useful information and advertisements, They can be found at:

Isla Verda Airport (Tel: 791 1014/3443/1853/5365)

Banco de Ponce building, Hato Rey (headquarters) (Tel: 764 2390)

La Casita, Old San Juan (behind the post office and near pier one) (Tel: 722 1709)

Foyer of City Hall, Calle San Francisco, Old San Juan

I intend to list here just the outstanding sights in San Juan.

I liked Casa de Espana best, although I could not find it listed in any of the tourist guides. A magnificent building, apparently recently built, it specializes in social functions (wedding receptions, etc.) for the wealthy.

San Juan's fortifications, El Morro and San Cristobal, although occupied on occasion, seem to have done the job they were designed for most of the time. The Earl of Cumberland led the only invading force to occupy El Morro. He was driven out by dysentry. This was in 1598, three years after Sir Francis Drake was unable to secure the harbour. The Dutch also met with failure. San Cristobal, the fort at the other end of the old town, was built in the eighteenth century to prevent the town and El Morro being attacked from the landward side. Both forts are open from 8 am to 5 pm. There are many other beautiful and historical buildings in the old town which is well worth at least one long visit.

Metropolitan San Juan also has sights for the architectural buff. El Capitolio on Avenida Ponce de Leon near Casa de Espana is the home of the Legislature of Puerto Rico. The parallel road of Avenida Munoz Rivera runs along a coastline that can be dramatic at times, past a statue of John the Baptist, until it arrives at a largish park. A little further on, near the Caribe Hilton, is the small Fort San Jeronimo which the British unsportingly battered in 1797. It was rebuilt two years later. Puerto Rico is the world's largest producer of rum, and you can visit the Bacardi plant near Catano (free samples). Most beaches involve travel as you would expect, but there is a small one in the Miramar/Condado area (see Miramar map). It is crowded and not much good for swimming, but OK for half a day's sunbathing and getting wet.

Out on the island: If you have time to make a visit outside the capital, or perhaps a trip round the island, you are unlikely to be disappointed. The mountains run almost the length of the island, through the centre. Whilst the northern side is green and fertile, the southern side is dry. These mountains, named the Cordillera Central, carry a spectacularly scenic road, the Ruta Panoramica. You are likely to see sugar cane plantations in the lowlands and coffee at higher altitudes. There are many rivers and 23 man-made lakes (no natural ones).

Accommodation outside San Juan: Details of the cheaper accommodation intended for tourists follow. You can also expect native accommodation to be available, particularly in the larger towns.

Name	Address	Price per room in US$
Punta Borinquen	Aguadilla (at former Air Force Base) (Tel: 891 1510 ext 6128)	$30-$35 per villa (2 & 3 bedroom villas)
Hotel Delicias	Facing wharf, Fajardo (Tel: 863 1818 & 863 1577)	S $15.75; D $21.
Ranchos Guayama	Bo. Cimarrona, Guayama; Rte. 713 & Rte. 712	S $15.75; D $15.75-$30.75.
Hacienda Gripinas	Rte. 527, Jayuya (Tel: 763 8855)	S $14-$17; D $18-$21.
Hotel El Sol	El Sol St., Mayaguez (Tel: 833 0303)	S $14.70-$19.95; D $21-$26.25.
Hotel La Palma	Mayaguez (Tel: 832 0230)	S $8.40-$12.60; D $18.90-$21.
Posada Porlamar	Ocean Front, Rte 304, Parguera	S $12-$14; D $14-$18.
Hotel Villa Parguera	Ocean Front, Rte. 304, Parguera (Tel: 892 9588)	S $8-$22; D $8-$22.
Hotel El Coche	La Rambla, Ponce (Tel: 842 9607)	S $12.60; D $15.75-$18.90.
San Jose Guest House	47 Cristina St, two blocks from plaza (Tel: 842 0281)	S $14.70; D $18.90-$25.20.
Villa Antonio	On beach, Rte 115, Rincon (Tel: 823 2645)	S $12-$15; D $17.20; T $25; Cabins $35-$40.
Hacienda Roses	On coffee plantation, Rte. 140, Utuado (Tel: 894 2374)	MAP: S $13-$14; D $16-$20.
Hotel Vivi	Rte. 111, Utuado (Tel; 894 2376)	S $8.40-$12.60; D $12.60-$18.90.
La Casa Roig Guest House	10 Betances, Yauco	S $4-$10; D $6-$10.
Parador El Verde	Edge of rain forest, Rte. 186, El Verde (Tel: 786 5325)	S $12-$15; D $17-$20.

Leaving Puerto Rico: This is quite a simple undertaking by air, whether you are bound for the Virgin Islands or back to the States.

Finding an alternative means to scheduled air is not so simple. There was once a regular boat service between San Juan and the Virgins, but I was told emphatically that this is no longer in operation. Cruise ships ply regularly between San Juan and Saint Thomas, and vice versa, but the chances of one having accommodation vacant for this part of its voyage are slim. Also, of course, this would be the most expensive way to make the crossing. If you want a brief taste of life on a cruise ship, you could try it. Rather than running after the shipping lines, try a travel agent: they usually know the schedules and can always ring round for you. Alternatively, you could try a private yacht: there is a small marina between Miramar and Puerto de Tierra. A private plane, or an empty seat on a charter, might possibly be available from Isla Grande airport — check in the terminal building.

If you decide to opt for scheduled air, remember that there are two airports. All intercontinental and most international flights use

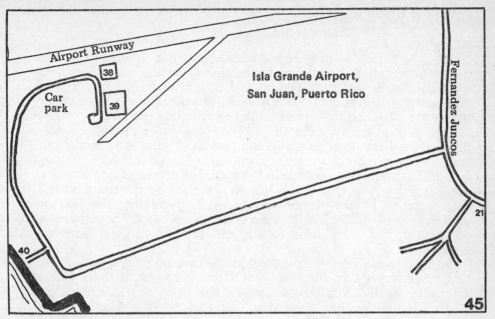

Airport Runway

38

Car park

39

Isla Grande Airport,
San Juan, Puerto Rico

Fernandez Juncos

21

40

45

Isla Grande Airport: Key
21 Hotel Borinquen
38 Airport control tower
39 Airport terminal building
40 Antilles Airboat Base

Isla Verda, 'the airport'. Whilst this is more convenient than international airports in many other countries, due to the cheap bus service, you may find Isla Grande more suited to your requirements.

Air Caribbean, Dorada Wings, Prinair and Saint Thomas Taxair all operate regularly from Isla Verde airport, with Prinair having the most frequent schedules. All will get you to the US Virgins, while Dorado Wings and Prinair also service the British Virgin Islands. Booking with a travel agent will save you an unnecessary trip to the airport.

But *Antilles Airboat* must be the best way to go. This company has taken out the formality and put back the fun into flying. It operates 'Goose' flying boats (reputedly 40 years old) which take off and land on water yet taxi up a ramp so that you are able to board on dry land. If you have never flown this way before, you should try it just for the experience. Its San Juan base is near Island Grande airport, on San Juan Bay (see map). The ramp is within walking distance of the Miramar hotels (about ¾ mile).

On checking in, the first thing you will notice is that after your baggage is weighed, so are you. Then you just lounge around in the sunshine with your nine fellow passengers until the plane comes in. There is none of that usual international airport rubbish here — barely audible announcements punctuating dreary muzak, crowds, bustle, officials and supercilious airline staff. Just a few minutes sitting in the sun.

The plane itself is quite small, with a passenger cabin described to me as being 'about as big as a water closet' seating nine passengers, with the tenth alongside the pilot. I found all the seats good for photography, and none uncomfortable, but obviously it is best to sit beside the pilot and watch him work the primitive controls.

Besides the fun of take off and landing, the airboats probably provide the best views of the Virgin Islands. Flying at a low altitude and a slow speed gives a truly birds' eye view of this island group. Antilles Airboats also score from the angles of price and convenience. Most major settlements in the Virgins are built by the sea, a normal happenstance in the Caribbean but here inevitable, due to the physical nature of the islands. Thus the airboats can fly downtown to downtown, and long trips to airports and bus or taxi fares are avoided.

Here are some schedules, correct at the time of writing but subject to change, from San Juan to Saint Thomas and Saint Croix (other schedules are listed in the section on the US Virgin Islands, pages 170 - 1). Note that the latest check-in is 15 minutes before departure, although 30 minutes is recommended.

San Juan To	Depart	Arrive	Frequency	Fare in US$
Saint Thomas	7.00 am	7.45 am	Daily except Sun	$18
Saint Thomas	8.25 am	9.05 am	Daily except Sun	
Saint Thomas	10.00 am	10.45 am	Daily excep Sun	
Saint Thomas	11.00 am	11.45 am	Daily except Sun	
Saint Thomas	1.15 pm	2.00 pm	Daily	$18
Saint Thomas	3.00 pm	3.45 pm	Daily	
Saint Thomas	4.30 pm	5.15 pm	Daily	
Saint Croix*	7.00 am	8.15 am	Daily except Sun	$21
Saint Croix	9.25 am	10.10 am	Daily except Sun	
Saint Croix*	11.00 am	12.15 pm	Daily except Sun	
Saint Croix*	1.15 pm	2.30 pm	Daily	
Saint Croix*	3.00 pm	4.15 pm	Daily	
Saint Croix*	4.30 pm	5.40 pm	Daily	

*Saint Croix flights marked thus are via Saint Thomas

Fajardo To	Depart	Arrive	Frequency	Fare in US $
Saint Thomas	9.30 am	10.00 am	Daily except Sun	$14.50
Saint Thomas	9.55 am	10.20 am	Daily except Sun	
Saint Thomas	3.45 pm	4.10 pm	Daily except Sun	
Saint Thomas	3.55 pm	4.20 pm	Daily except Sun	
Saint Croix	10.45 am	11.25 am	Daily except Sun	$17.50

THE US VIRGIN ISLANDS

Although if we include every piece of land in the group there are some 50 islands, the name 'US Virgin Islands' usually means the main three — Saint Thomas, Saint Croix and Saint John. Saint Croix was the first of the islands to be settled, by the British and French early in the seventeenth century. There was the usual squabbling between the British, French and Spanish before the island was eventually purchased by Denmark in 1733. The Danes had already

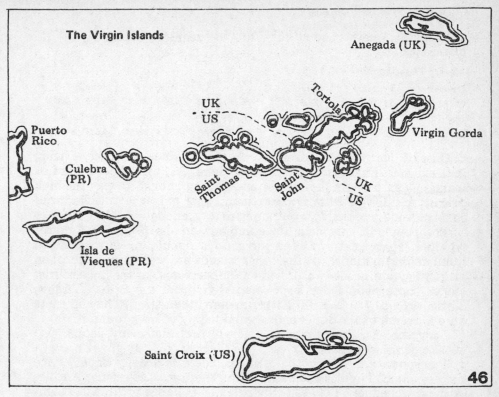

The Virgin Islands

Anegada (UK)

Tortola

UK
US

Puerto
Rico

Virgin Gorda

Culebra
(PR)

Saint
Thomas

Saint
John

UK
US

Isla de
Vieques (PR)

Saint Croix (US)

46

settled Saint Thomas and Saint John in the second half of the
seventeenth century, using the island — and Saint Croix in particular,
mainly for agricultural purposes. With the decline in importance of
sugar the Danes began to lose interest and in 1917 were happy to sell
the islands to the United States for $25 million.

The US Virgins are an unincorporated Territory under the Department of the Interior with a non-voting Delegate in the House of
Representatives. The Governor is elected every four years. There are
15 Senators.

One of the greatest attractions of the US Virgins is their position
as a free port. US citizens are allowed a duty-free quota of US$200.
If you've ever wanted to buy a very good and usually expensive
camera this may be the place to get it. But I suggest you check the
prices before you leave home so that you have an idea of how much
you are actually saving. Liquor by the bottle is almost unbelievably
cheap.

Immigration: There are no formalities for US citizens except a
return ticket and evidence of sufficient funds. Others require a US
visa of course. If you have just arrived from Puerto Rico there are no
formalities at all.

Currency: The US dollar. Credit cards are accepted more widely
here than anywhere else I can think of.

Climate: Weather conditions are as near perfect as makes no difference.

Average Temperatures

January	February	March	April	May	June
77°F 25°C	77°F 25°C	78°F 26°C	78°F 26°C	79°F 26°C	81°F 27°C

July	August	September	October	November	December
82°F 28°C	82°F 28°C	81°F 27°C	80°F 27°C	78°F 26°C	76°F 24°C

Cost of living: Apart from duty-free attractions, the cost of living is the highest I have encountered anywhere. But then, the standard of living is high too. As the natives are earning enough to pay the high prices, and the tourists expect them, it is only the traveller who suffers. And he probably won't be here long enough to mind.

The people: I can make no comment on the people as I doubt whether I have met any. The indigenous population is so small in number that nationals of the other islands are welcomed with open arms: they are needed to provide a labour force for the huge tourist trade. Those people that I spoke to were from the British Virgins, Antigua, Saint Lucia, Saint Kitts or some other island. They all came here in search of the dollar and seemed happy to have found it.

Language: English, although you will find that many people also speak Spanish, French or Creole.

Transportation within the islands: There is a daily boat service between Saint Thomas and Saint John. There are also regular Antilles Airboat schedules between the islands (Charlotte Amalie, Saint Thomas is their home base). Details of these services between Charlotte Amalie, Saint Thomas; Christiansted, Saint Croix; and Cruz Bay, Saint John, follow.

Saint Croix To	Depart	Arrive	Frequency	Fare in US$
Cruz Bay, Saint John	8.45 am	9.10 am	Daily except Sun	$14
	9.00 am	9.25 am	Sun only	
	3.45 pm	4.10 pm	Daily	

Saint John To	Depart	Arrive	Frequency	Fare in US$
Saint Croix	9.15 am	9.40 am	Daily except Sun	$14
	9.30 am	9.55 am	Sun only	
	4.15 pm	4.40 pm	Daily	

Saint Thomas: Key
Accommodation
1 Hotel 1829
2 Michele Motel
3 Tropic Isle
4 Villa Santana
5 Danish Chalet
6 Estate Thomas
7 Maison Greaux
8 Midtown
9 Miller Manor
10 New Holiday Isles
11 Ramsey's
12 Villa Fairview
13 West Indian Manner

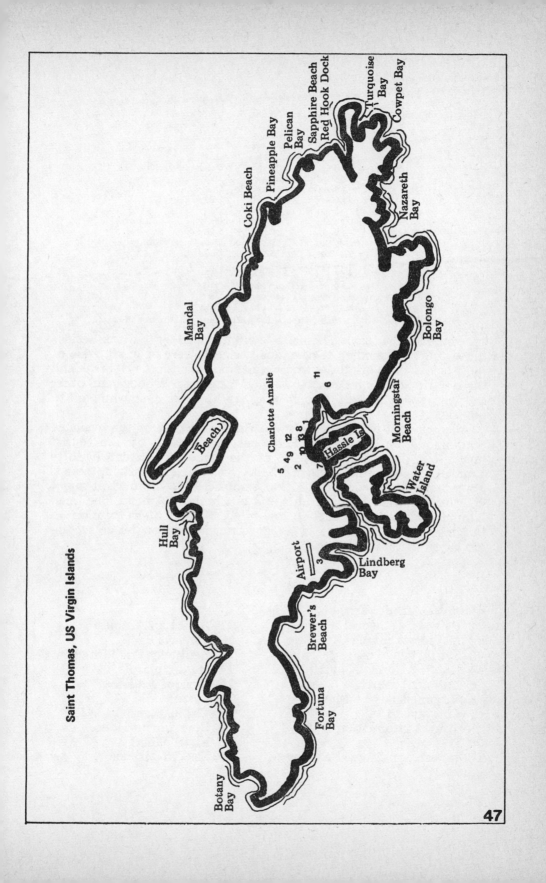

Saint Thomas, US Virgin Islands

Botany Bay

Fortuna Bay

Brewer's Beach

Hull Bay

Mandal Bay

Beach

Airport

Charlotte Amalie

Coki Beach

Pineapple Bay

Pelican Bay

Sapphire Beach

Red Hook Dock

Turquoise Bay

Cowpet Bay

Nazareth Bay

Bolongo Bay

Morningstar Beach

Hassle Is.

Water Island

Lindberg Bay

Caribbean Island Hopping

Saint Thomas To	Depart	Arrive	Frequency	Fare in US$
Christiansted,Saint Croix	7.05 am	7.30 am	Daily except Sun	$12.50
	7.45 am	8.10 am	Daily except Sun	
	8.00 am	8.25 am	Daily	
	8.30 am	8.55 am	Daily	
	9.00 am	9.25 am	Daily	
	9.40 am	10.05 am	Daily except Sun	
	10.05 am	10.30 am	Daily	
	10.30 am	10.55 am	Daily	
	10.50 am	11.10 am	Daily except Sun	
	11.30 am	11.55 am	Daily	
	12.45 am	1.10 pm	Daily	
	1.35 pm	2.00 pm	Daily	
	2.35 pm	3.00 pm	Daily except Sun	
	3.10 pm	3.35 pm	Daily	
	4.20 pm	4.45 pm	Daily	
	4.30 pm	4.55 pm	Daily	
	4.40 pm	5.05 pm	Daily	
	5.15 pm	5.40 pm	Daily	
	5.30 pm	5.55 pm	Daily	

Services from Saint Croix to Saint Thomas are as frequent, and the fare the same.

Saint Thomas: Saint Thomas is a virgin raped by tourism. Besides those tourists spending their annual vacation here or in all three of the islands, there are those who have come for a few days' break and the daytrippers from San Juan headed for duty-free booze and other shopping treats. But the people who live here like it, so who am I to quibble?

Accommodation: I list below a small selection of the available accommodation. There are 51 places in all listed by the tourist board, but those on other parts of the island (ie outside Charlotte Amalie) are much more expensive. As far as I can ascertain, there is no really cheap accommodation in Saint Thomas, although it might be worth checking out the outskirts of Charlotte Amalie. The 'map numbers' given in the table below refer to each hotel's location on the map opposite. There is no government tax on hotel accommodation in the US Virgins.

Charlotte Amalie: Key
1 Catholic Cathedral
2 Methodist church
3 Synagogue
4 Dutch Reformed church
5 Lutheran church
6 Virgin Islands Legislature
7 Coast guard
8 Tourist information
9 Post office
10 International Travel Agency Inc.
11 American Airlines
12 Barclays Bank
13 Kentucky Fried Chicken
14 Market place
15 Bank of America
16 Library
17 The 99 steps
18 Government House
19 King's Wharf
20 Eastern Airlines

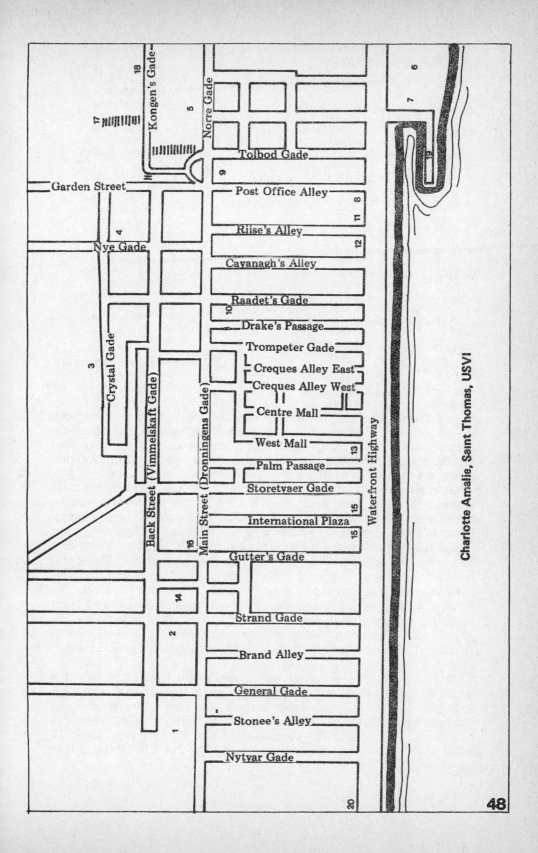

Charlotte Amalie, Saint Thomas, USVI

Kongen's Gade
18
Norre Gade
17
5
9
Garden Street
Tolbod Gade
Post Office Alley
4
8
Nye Gade
11
Riise's Alley
12
Cavanagh's Alley
Raadet's Gade
3
10
Crystal Gade
Drake's Passage
Trompeter Gade
Creques Alley East
Creques Alley West
Back Street (Vimmelskaft Gade)
Centre Mall
West Mall
13
Main Street (Dronningens Gade)
Palm Passage
Storetvaer Gade
15
International Plaza
Waterfront Highway
16
15
Gutter's Gade
14
Strand Gade
2
Brand Alley
General Gade
Stonee's Alley
1
Nytvar Gade
20

6
7
19

48

Name	Address and map number		Price per room in US$ and service charge
Hotel 1829	Central Charlotte Amalie (Tel: 774 1829)	(1)	S $36, D $44; T $56; 10% s.c.
Michele Motel	Contant 61, Charlotte Amalie (Tel: 774 2650)	(2)	S $20; D $50; T $66; no s.c.
Tropic Isle Hotel	Near the airport, Lindberg Bay (Tel: 774 1980)	(3)	S $40; D $50; T $64; no s.c.
Villa Santana	Denmark Hill, Charlotte Amalie (Tel: 774 1311)	(4)	S $30; D $60; T $70; 10% s.c.
Danish Chalet	About 1 mile from Charlotte Amalie (Tel: 774 5764)	(5)	CP: S $20-$24; D $30-$36; T $42-$48; no s.c.
Estate Thomas	East of Charlotte Amalie (Tel: 774 2542)	(6)	CP: S $31; D $41; T $51; no s.c.
Maison Greaux	West of Charlotte Amalie (Tel: 774 0063)	(7)	CP: S $32-$36; D $44-$48; T $54-$58; no s.c.
Midtown	Central Charlotte Amalie (Tel: 774 9157)	(8)	S $30-$46; D $40-$50; T $60-$70; no s.c.
Miller Manor	On hill above Charlotte Amalie (Tel: 774 1535)	(9)	CP: S $38; D $44-$54; T $58-$68; no s.c.
New Holiday Isles	In Charlotte Amalie (Tel: 774 9873)	(10)	S $32; D $44; T $56. no s.c.
Ramsey's	East of Charlotte Amalie (Tel: 774 6521)	(11)	S $28; D $40; T $52; no s.c.
Villa Fairview	On hill about 1 mile from Charlotte Amalie (Tel: 774 2661)	(12)	CP: S $20-$22; D $32-$36; T $44-$48; no s.c.
West Indian Manner	In Charlotte Amalie (Tel: 774 2975)	(13)	S $32; D $44; T $56; no s.c.

The *Tropic Isle* is conveniently situated, being very near to both the airport and Lindberg Beach. It is on the bus route into Charlotte Amalie. I found the rooms satisfactory and service good. They have no restaurant, however, and the only restaurants within walking distance are those in nearby expensive hotels.

Charlotte Amalie: This is the capital of the US Virgin Islands. Its harbour is interesting, host as it is to all kinds of private yachts, cruise ships and some cargo vessels. Not to mention the seaplanes. Pastel-painted and white houses dot the hillsides behind the town, whilst between hills and water is that shopper's paradise. There is a bus service within the Charlotte Amalie area and to Red Hook and Bordeaux; you may like to use this to see some of the island.

In the last week of April Saint Thomas celebrates Carnival. The ceremony derives originally from Voodoo but in its present form bears no relationship with same. For a start, it is a party in the streets, not a religion. Many of the participants are costumed as followers of Satan, but whether they triumph or are routed I cannot say.

Saint Croix: This is the largest of the Virgin Islands; in fact it is larger than the other two put together. Which is what they are — put together; for while Saint John is only about 3 miles from Saint Thomas, Saint Croix lies 35 miles south of both of them. There are two towns on Saint Croix, Christiansted and Frederiksted, some 12 miles apart. Christiansted, founded in 1734, was the capital of the

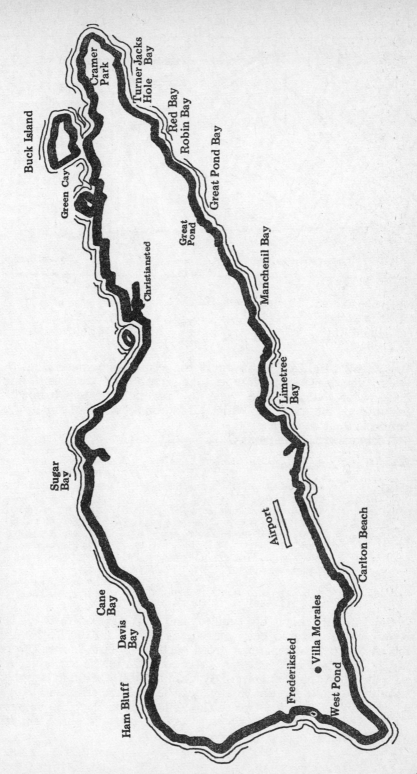

Saint Croix, US Virgin Islands

Buck Island

Green Cay

Cramer Park

Turner Jacks Hole Bay

Red Bay

Robin Bay

Great Pond Bay

Christiansted

Great Pond

Manchenil Bay

Limetree Bay

Sugar Bay

Airport

Carlton Beach

Cane Bay

Davis Bay

Ham Bluff

Frederiksted

• Villa Morales

West Pond

49

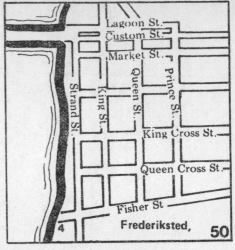

Christiansted

Frederiksted, 50

Christiansted and Frederiksted: Key

1 The Lodge
2 Island Inn

3 Royal Scotia
4 Smithfield

Danish West Indies. This is where the seaplanes come in, and this is where you leave from if you take a trip to Buck Island and its underwater National Park. Near to Fredericksted is a tropical rain forest and the restored Whim Greathouse. A regular bus service connects the two towns.

Accommodation in Saint Croix

Name	Address and Map Number		Price per room in US$ and service charge
The Lodge	43A Queen Cross Street, Christiansted (Tel: 773 1535)	(1)	CP: S $44; D $52; T $68; no s.c.
Island Inn	29 Prince Street, Christiansted (Tel: 773 2418)	(2)	S $36-$40; D $50-$60; T $70-$80; no s.c.
Royal Scotia	43 King Street, Christiansted (Tel: 773 2138)	(3)	S $30-$40; D $44-$60; T $54-$70; no s.c.
Smithfield	Near Fisher & Strand St. junction Fredericksted (Tel: 773 0510)	(4)	S $30; D $36; T $46; 5% s.c. MAP $13 per person.
Villa Morales	Near Whim Great House, Frederick St. (Tel: 772 0556)	(5)	S $24; D $30-$36; T $42-$48; no s.c.

Saint John: This is the smallest and least developed of the island group and is situated between Saint Thomas and the British Virgin Island of Tortola, separated from each by about 3 miles of water. Much of it is a National Park. Accommodation is available in the park itself, at the Cinnamon Bay Camp, but unfortunately bookings have to be made months in advance. Beach huts, tents and bare sites are available. There are two settlements — Cruz Bay, the larger, and Coral Harbour. There is no bus service, travel around the island generally being by jeep.

176

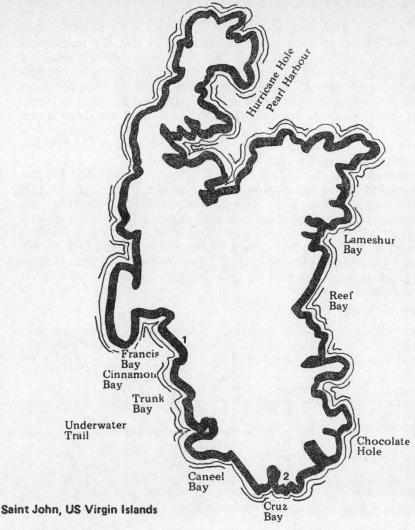

Saint John, US Virgin Islands

51

Saint John: Key
1 Cinnamon Bay campsite   2 Sewer's Guest House

Accommodation in Saint John

Name	Address and Map number		Price per room in US$ and service charge
Cinnamon Bay	Cinnamon Bay, northwest St. John (Tel: 776 6330)	(1)	Beach Huts $31; Tents $18; Bare sites $6; no s.c.
Sewer's Guest House	Near Ferry Dock, Cruz Bay (Tel: 776 6814)	(2)	S $30; D $40; T $50; no s.c.

Leaving the US Virgin Islands: If homeward bound you will find Saint Thomas almost as busy an airport as San Juan. There are direct flights to New York and Washington, DC from both Saint Thomas and Saint Croix with American Airlines, who also fly to Boston, Buffalo and Providence. Eastern fly to Miami, besides having a comprehensive network of services in the area and serving many parts of the United States from San Juan. Delta and American also have services from the USA to San Juan. Prinair serve the British Virgin Islands and Saint Maarten, whilst LIAT — Leeward Islands Air Transport -- have extensive services from both Saint Thomas and Saint Croix throughout the eastern Caribbean; details of LIAT flights are given in Part 4 (page 187).

If proceeding to the British Virgin Islands you may like to take a launch called either the *Bomba Charger* or the *Bomba Cruiser* (for reservations, telephone 774 7920 or 774 3389). Schedules of this and Antilles Airboats are given below. If you need help from a travel agent you will be pleased to learn that there is an agency which knows what it is doing (something I was unable to find in Tortola). This is International Travel Agency Incorporated, 32 Dronningens Gade (near Raadets Gade), Charlotte Amalie. Telephone 774 8700. Ask for Julie Olive.

Bomba Charger/Cruiser Schedule

From Saint Thomas To	Depart	Arrive	Frequency	One-way fare in US$
West End, Tortola	8.30 am	9.30 am	Sat/Sun	$ 6 Mon to Sat;
	9.30 am	10.30 am	Mon/Fri	$6.50 Sun.
	10.30 am	11.30 am	Tue/Wed/Thu	
	11.30 am	12.30 am	Sat	
	12.30 am	1.30 pm	Fri	
	1.30 pm	2.30 pm	Mon	
	3.45 pm	4.45 pm	Sat	
	5.00 pm	6.00.pm	Mon/Tue/Wed/Thu	
	5.30 pm	6.30 pm	Fri	
Road Town, Tortola (via West End)	11.30 am	1.10 pm	Sat	As above
	12.30 pm	2.15 pm	Fri	
Spanish Town, Virgin Gorda (via West End)	8.30 am	10.45 am	Sun	$7.50.
	10.30 am	1.00 pm	Tue/Thu	

Antilles Airboat Schedules: US Virgins to British Virgins

From	To	Depart	Arrive	Frequency	One-way fare in US$
Saint Thomas	Roadtown Tortola	8.04 a.m.	8.25 am	Daily except Sun	$13
		1.04 pm	1.25 pm	Daily except Sun	
		3.44 pm	4.00 pm	Daily except Sun	
Saint Croix	Roadtown Tortola	7.36 am	8.25 am	Daily except Sun	$16.50
		12.36 pm	1.25 pm	Daily except Sun	
		3.16 pm	4.00 pm	Daily except Sun	
Saint Croix	West End Tortola	11.30 am	11.55 am	Tue/Thu/Sat	$14.50

THE BRITISH VIRGIN ISLANDS

Officially I have never been here. I arrived without an onward air ticket (except for my Barbados/London ticket) because I hadn't intended flying — I was going to cruise the rest of the way by private yacht. I also arrived without funds (to be exact I had US$3) because I had written to my bank from Port-au-Prince, Haiti, and expected to collect US$300 in Tortola. So Mrs Smith made short work of me (officialdom at the seaplane base consists of two persons — one for immigration and one for customs). It was made clear to me that unless I produced adequate funds and an air ticket from the BVI to Barbados I would not be allowed to enter.

The two travel agencies I tried here told me different tales concerning a LIAT island-hopping ticket to Barbados, and they were both wrong (the true story is detailed in Part 3, page 00). So I decided to collect my money and go back to Saint Thomas. Although I was never officially allowed in, the authorities were wise enough to allow me time to conduct my research.

Geographically the BVI are part of the same island group as the USVI, with two exceptions — Saint Croix which lies a long way to the south, and Anegada BVI which is a coral island and not volcanic like the others. So in the BVI you will find the same spectacular seascapes, with myriad islands whose superb coastlines rise steeply into the green hills (though they are not always sparkling green, as rain can be scarce). But although nature has provided the same basic materials, I found the BVI greatly preferable to the USVI. The differences between the two groups is entirely man made.

Tourism, its extent and type, has to be the chief difference. The British Virgins have little of it, but what they do have is very up-market. No daytrippers or two-nighters mainly seeking cheap booze, but the very rich who have come for two weeks away from it all or who are just passing through in their luxury yachts. As per capita expenditure is so much more, the islands' ecomomy has benefited substantially from a far smaller number of tourists. There are more marinas here than banks, and whole industries have grown up to service the sailing clientele — out-of-the-way luxury resorts, yacht clubs, ships' stores and so on. I loved the names of many of these places: The Bitter End, The Last Resort (situated would you believe on Bellamy Cay — no relation) and Past and Presents being just three. I don't expect the type of tourism to change, as the BVI does not have an airport capable of handling intercontinental jets.

But the type of tourism is not the only difference, although it is this which gives Roadtown, the capital, its character. Whereas Charlotte Amalie seems to exist mainly as a huge shopping centre, one gets the impression that Roadtown's facilities are primarily meant to serve the needs of the community. Buildings and services in the capital are geared towards local consumers, whilst the expensive hotels and clubs are either out of town, on another part of Tortola, or, as is becoming increasingly usual, on the other islands. All this makes Roadtown a humble — though reserved rather than friendly — settlement, sleeping in the sun.

Immigration: US, Canadian and British citizens may enter

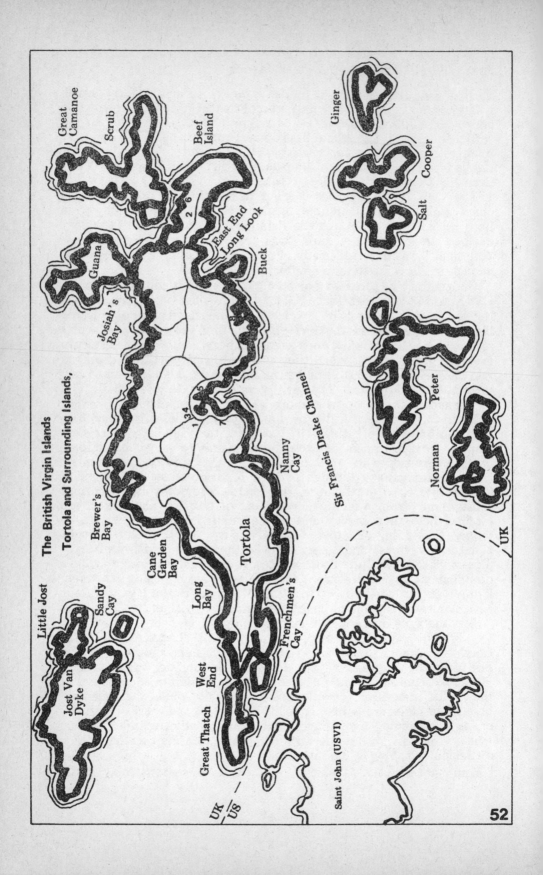

The British Virgin Islands

Tortola and Surrounding Islands,

Little Jost

Jost Van Dyke

Sandy Cay

Great Thatch

West End

Long Bay

Cane Garden Bay

Brewer's Bay

Frenchmen's Cay

Tortola

Nanny Cay

Josiah's Bay

Guana

Great Camanoe

Scrub

Beef Island

East End

Long Look

Buck

Sir Francis Drake Channel

Ginger

Cooper

Salt

Peter

Norman

Saint John (USVI)

UK
US

UK

52

without passports if they can produce other identification. Few other nationalities require a visa. You must have sufficient funds and *a continuous chain of tickets* to your home country. For US citizens that can mean Saint Thomas or Puerto Rico. You are also supposed to have arranged accommodation in advance. There is a $2.50 departure tax.

Customs: There is no restriction on the amount of liquor you may introduce into the BVI provided it is for your own consumption. Liquor by the bottle is cheap here however -- very little more than in the US Virgins.

Currency: The US dollar is the official currency. There are few places which accept credit cards, American Express being the only one to have established a foothold.

Climate: Temperatures are of the same range as we have found elsewhere, between 77°F (25°C) and 85°F (29°C) through the year. It is little cooler at night, with beneficial effects from the Trade Winds. There is an annual rainfall of 45 inches.

The cost of living: The islands' dependence on imports and the financial status of most visitors means that prices are usually high, especially in those businesses which cater for the tourist trade. However, it is possible to live cheaply if you wish to do so.

The people: I found the people very much more reserved than in most of the Caribbean. This is partly because they all seem to have achieved something, or built something, and have a pride in their work and themselves. I think it is also partly because the small indigenous population has been used to expatriates for so long. You will never be asked for a handout here.

Transportation: There are no buses. Any resident who travels frequently has a car (all number plates are pre-fixed 'VI' and numbered sequentially, so you can get an idea of the age of a vehicle from its number — an old Landrover may be VI 200 and a new Mercedes VI 2000). Thus transport for the visitor is by shanks' pony or taxi. Taxi rates are controlled by the government and have one peculiarity: there are two types of fare, 'single' and 'charter'. A single passenger will be charged the charter fare, while two or more people travelling in the same taxi will be charged the single fare on a per person basis. As the charter fare is three times the single fare, one person will pay more for a taxi than two people travelling together. For example, the single fare to Beef Island from Roadtown is US$2; thus a couple will pay US$4, whilst a single person has to pay the

The British Virgin Islands: Key

1	Roadtown, Tortola	5	Village Cay Marina
2	Airport	6	The Last Resort
3	Central Guest House	7	Sea View Guest House
4	Wayside Inn	8	Maya Cove Yacht Club

charter fare of US$6. Here are some official fares:

From Roadtown To	Fare in US$ Single	Charter	From Roadtown To	Fare in US$ Single	Charter
Fort Hill	$0.75	$2.25	Cane Garden Bay	$1.75	$ 5.25
Long Look	$1.75	$5.25	West End	$2.00	$6.00
Brewers Bay	$2.00	$6.00	East End	$2.00	$6.00
Long Bay	$2.00	$6.00			

Between the islands there are some boat services, such as the *Bomba Charger/Cruiser*, the schedules of which are given below:

Depart From	At	Arrive	At	Frequency	Fare US$6.50 return
West End	9.45 a.m.	Spanish Town	10.45 a.m.	Sun	
Tortola	12.00 p.m.	Virgin Gorda	1.00 p.m.	Tue/Thur	
Spanish Town	1.00 p.m.	West End	2.00 p.m.	Tue/Thur	
Virgin Gorda	4.00 p.m.	Tortola	5.00 p.m.	Sun	

It is of course possible to fly between the islands, but I don't see the point.

Accommodation: As you would expect, most accommodation is in the very expensive category. Below I list that at the lower end of the price scale:

Name	Address	Price per room in US$
Central Guest House	Central Roadtown (see map)	EP: *S* $5; *D* $7
Mayside Inn Guest House	Opposite Court House, Roadtown	EP: *D* $10/$12/$14.
Sea View Hotel	Roadtown (Tel: 42483)	EP:*S* $18; *D* $21.
Maya Cove Yacht Club	About 4 miles east of Roadtown	EP: *S* $15; *D* $20 (half price in summer)
The Last Resort	Bellamy Cay, Long Look	AP: *S* $35; *D* $50.

The *Central Guest House* is, as its name implies, centrally situated in town. Do not think from looking at its star rating that this is a comfortable habitat with all conveniences, for it isn't. In fact the rooms are very spartan, the water supply erratic and you may have to walk down to Wickham's Cay for a shower. But these prices have to represent good value for the area.

The *Wayside Inn Guest House* has double rooms only — no singles. The different prices are based on distance from a bathroom.

Roadtown: Key

1 Antilles airport
2 Central Guest House
3 Wayside Inn
4 Tourist office
5 Administration building
6 Travel agents
7 Chase Manahattan Bank

8 Barclays Bank
9 Showers, etc (50 cents)
10 Cable & Wireless
11 Police station
12 Cinema
13 The Pub
14 Fort Burt

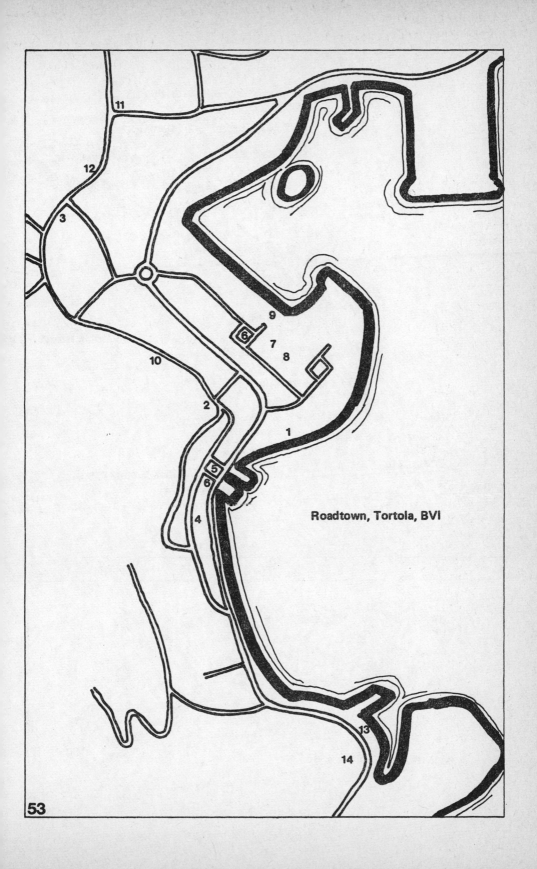

Roadtown, Tortola, BVI

53

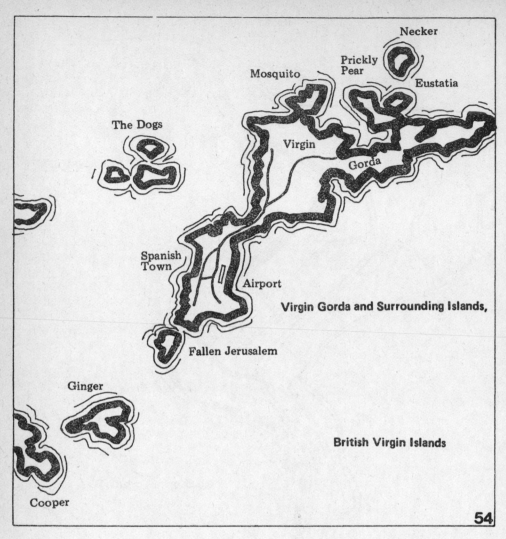

The Dogs

Mosquito

Prickly
Pear

Necker

Eustatia

Virgin

Gorda

Spanish
Town

Airport

Virgin Gorda and Surrounding Islands,

Fallen Jerusalem

Ginger

British Virgin Islands

Cooper

54

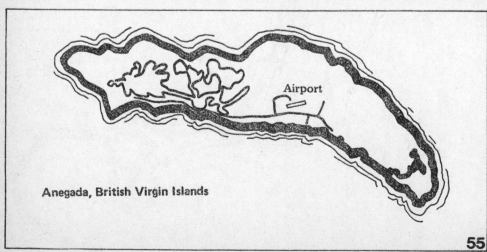

Airport

Anegada, British Virgin Islands

55

Eating: I found that *The Happy Lion* restaurant under the Central Guest House did a splendid breakfast, for about US$1. Worth investigation. Besides this there are sufficient native eating places in and around Roadtown and ample fine restaurants of varying prices around the island. *The Fort Burt Hotel* is pricey but does lunches for around US$4, whilst the nearby *Sir Francis Drake Pub* (often known as The Pub) serves snack lunches from US$1.50. The price of non-alcoholic drinks is very expensive here, largely, I guess, because this is a haunt of the yachting fraternity. This is one of the places to try if you are looking for onward transportation by yacht: getting into casual conversation with yacht owners/captains is straightforward enough. The *Seaview Club* in the same vicinity may be of greater interest as it features West Indian dishes. You can expect prices to be reasonable too. The *Harbour Lights* in the centre of Roadtown serves breakfast, lunch and dinner, and specializes in seafood, pizzas, draught beer and darts. Another place in town is *Cell 5*. Here you can get reasonably priced pizzas and sandwiches. At slightly higher prices, there is the *Poop Deck*, very close to the seaplane terminal. If you are in the region of the Deep Water Harbour (on the east road out of town) you could try *Stonehaven*, which prepares West Indian cuisine at about US$2 per meal.

Around The Islands: Tortola has the lion's share of the islands' population; some 9,000 live here. The beaches are mainly situated on the north coast, a long walk, but you may be able to hire a bicycle. The marinas are mainly along the south coast. Beef Island, joined to the mainland by Queen Elizabeth Bridge, is important as the location of the international airport.

Recent developments, both for the tourist trade and for residential requirements, are tending to favour the many other islands. So Virgin Gorda (the Fat Virgin) now has a population of 1,000 — mainly in and clustered around Spanish Town. Many of the smaller islands (Peter Island is a good example) are becoming known internationally as away-from-it-all resorts for those who like the good life. Anegada is a coral and limestone island some way from the main group.

Leaving the Virgin Islands: A plane from the BVI will not take you very far — to be precise, to Saint Thomas, Saint Croix, San Juan, Antigua or Saint Maarten. Intercontinental connections are available from the first four destinations. If you wish to continue by yacht, this is really the first country where it is a practical proposition. Details on the suggested procedure to follow are given in the *Transportation* section on page 31.

Part 4
The Eastern Caribbean

Describing these islands in order of their geographical situation
from north to south is less preferable than treating them in their
political groupings. Thus I shall deal firstly with the most northerly
of the British-affiliated islands, then the French Antilles and Sint
Maarten, then the Windward Islands, Barbados and lastly Trinidad
and Tobago. Anyone intending to visit all the islands in the Eastern
Caribbean will need to allow two or three months just for this
purpose. As I anticipate that very few, if any, readers of this book
will make such a visit, details of travel from one island to the next
are not given herein. These are irrelevant anyway, if you are
travelling by boat or ship, as you are likely to take what is available.
Instead, here are the schedules, correct at the time of writing, of
some of the principal airlines.

LEEWARD ISLANDS AIR TRANSPORT (LIAT)
Southbound — Hawker Siddeley 748 (48 seats)

Flight Number		LI 555	LI 555	LI 555	LI 503	LI 503	LI 505	LI 505
Frequency		Mon/ Sun	Tue/ Thur/ Fri	Wed/ Sat	Mon/ Wed	Sat	Tue/ Thur/ Fri	Sun
St Thomas	dep	1240		1240			1925	
St Croix	arr			1305				
St Croix	dep		1240	1335				1925
St Maarten	arr	1330	1330				2015	2015
St Maarten	dep	1345	1345		1740	1950	2030	2030
St Kitts	arr	1415	1415	1435	1810	2020	2100	2100
St Kitts	dep	1425	1425	1445	1820	2030	2110	2110
Antigua	arr	1455	1455	1515	1850	2100	2140	2140

Caribbean Island Hopping

Flight Number		LI 333	LI 333	LI 315	LI 335	LI 335	LI 355	LI 357
Frequency		Tue/Wed/Thur/Sun	Mon/Fri/Sat	Daily Ex Sat	Mon	Sat	Daily	Fri/Sat
Antigua	dep	0650	0650		1350	1305	1630	
Guadeloupe	arr	0820	0020				1800	
Guadeloupe	dep	0830	0830				1810	
Dominica	arr	0755	0755		1435	1350	1735	
Dominica	dep	0815	0815		1445	1400	1745	
Martinique	arr	0945	0945				1915	
Martinique	dep	0955	0955	1240			1930	
St Lucia	arr	0920	0920	1205		1450	1855	
St Lucia	dep	0930	0930	1215		1500	1905	2050
Barbados	arr	1015	1015	1300	1550	1545	2050	2135
Barbados	dep	1145						
Grenada	arr	1240						
Grenada	dep	1250						
Trinidad	arr	1335						

Flight Number		LI 397	LI 337	LI 301	LI 331	LI 339	LI 319	LI 312
Frequency		Daily	Daily	Daily	Daily	Daily	Daily	Fri./Sat
Barbados	dep	0545	0700	0745		1555	1645	1915
St Vincent	arr	0630	0745			1640		2000
St Vincent	dep		0755			1650		2010
St Lucia	arr							2040
Grenada	arr			0840		1720	1740	
Grenada	dep				1020	1730		
Trinidad	arr				1105	1815		

Southbound — Britten Norman Trislander/Islander (14/9 seats)

Flight Number		LI 507	LI 591	LI 161	LI 593	LI 589	LI 595	LI 597	LI 599
Frequency		Daily	Daily	Ex Mon/Wed	Daily	Ex Tue/Thur	Daily	Daily	Daily
St. Kitts	dep	0645		0805					
Nevis	arr			0815					
Nevis	dep			0820					
Montserrat	dep		0810		0930	1100	1435	1625	1825
Antigua	arr	0720	0835	0850	0955	1125	1500	1650	1850

Northbound — Hawker Siddeley 748 (48 seats)

Flight Number		LI 398	LI 302	LI 332	LI 330	LI 338	LI 318	LI 336
Frequency		Daily	Daily	Daily	Daily	Tue/Wed Thur/Sun	Daily	Daily
Trinidad	dep			0925	1135	1405		1845
Grenada	arr			1010	1220	1450		
Grenada	dep		0850		1230	1500	1750	
St Vincent	arr				1300			1945
St Vincent	dep	0640			1310			1955
Barbados	arr	0725	0945		1355	1555	1845	2040

Part 4: The Eastern Caribbean

Flight Number		LI 300	LI 314	LI 334	LI 334	LI 378	LI 312
Frequency		Daily	Ex Sat	Mon	Sat	Daily	Fri/Sat
Barbados	dep	0600	1010	1050	1010	1230	1915
St Lucia	arr	0645	1055		1055	1315	2040*
St Lucia	dep	0655	1105		1105	1325	
Martinique	arr	0820	1230				
Martinique	dep	0830					
Dominica	arr	0800		1155		1410	
Dominica	dep	0820		1205		1420	
Guadeloupe	arr	0945			1255	1545	
Guadeloupe	dep	0955			1305	1555	
Antigua	arr	0925		1250	1235	1525	

Flight Number		LI 550	LI 550	LI 500	LI 500	LI 504	LI 504
Frequency		Mon/Wed/Sat/Sun	Tue/Thur/Fri	Tue/Thur/Fri	Sun	Mon/Wed	Sat
Antigua	dep	1000	1000	1645	1645	1645	1855
St Kitts	arr	1030	1030	1715	1715		
St Kitts	dep	1040	1040	1725	1725		
St Maarten	arr	1110	1110	1755	1755	1730	1940
St Maarten	dep	1125	1125	1805	1805		
St Croix	arr		1210		1855		
St Thomas	arr	1210		1855			

* Flight LI 312 is via Saint Vincent

Northbound — Britten Norman Trislander/Islander (14/9 seats)

Flight Number		LI 506	LI 590	LI 162	LI 592	LI 162	LI 588	LI 594	LI 598
Frequency		Daily	Daily	Mon/Wed	Daily	Ex Mon/Wed	Ex Tue/Thur/	Daily	Daily
Antigua	dep	0600	0735	0740	0855	0905	1025	1400	1750
Montserrat	arr		0755		0915		1045	1420	1810
Nevis	arr			0810		0935			
Nevis	dep			0815		0940			
St Kitts	arr	0630		0825		0950			

LIAT has two airline subsidiaries, Four Island Air and Inter-Island Air Services. Both use nine seater Britten Norman Islanders. Four Island Air fly from Antigua to some of the neighbouring islands, and IAS island-hop between Saint Lucia and Grenada. Here are some specimen schedules:

Flight Number		LI 131	LI 153	LI 143	LI 163	LI 141	LI 151	LI 137	LI 165
Frequency		Tue/Sat	Ex Thu/Sun	Mon/Fri	Daily	Tue	Mon/Fri/Sun	Tue/Thur/Sat/Sun	Tue/Sun
Anguilla	dep			1045		1610			
St Kitts	arr			1120					
St Kitts	dep	0730			1230			1640	
Nevis	arr	0740			1240			1650	
Nevis	dep				1245				1655
Barbuda	dep		0755				1625		
Antigua	arr		0815		1315	1710	1645		1725

Caribbean Island Hopping

Flight Number		LI 154	LI 132	LI 142	I.I 140	LI 166	LI 152	LI 138
Frequency		Ex Thu/Sun	Tue/Sat	Mon/Fri	Tue	Daily	Mon/Fri/Sun	Thu/Sat
Antigua	dep	0730			1500	1545	1600	
Barbuda	arr	0750					1620	
Nevis	arr					1615		
Nevis	dep		0745			1620		1655
St Kitts	arr		0755			1630		1705
St Kitts	dep			1000				
Anguilla	arr			1035	1600			

Flight Number		IA 181	IA 115	IA 115	IA 115	IA 189
Frequency		Mon/Wed/Fri/Sat	Mon/Wed/Fri/Sat	Tue/Thu	Sun	Wed/Fri/Sat
St Lucia (Vigie)	dep		0925	0905	0935	
St Lucia	arr			0920		
(Hewanorra)	dep			0930		
St Vincent	arr		1000	0955	1010	
St Vincent	dep		1010	1010	1020	
Mustique	arr			1020		
Mustique	dep			1025		
Canouan	arr				1040	
Canouan	dep				1050	
Union	arr		1030	1040	1100	
Union	dep		1035	1045	1105	
Carriacou	arr		1045	1055	1115	
Carriacou	dep	0640	1050	1100	1120	1635
Grenada	arr	0655	1105	1115	1135	1650

Flight Number		IA 180	IA 108	IA 108	IA 108	IA 188
Frequency		Mon/Wed/Fri/Sat	Mon/Wed/Fri/Sat	Tue/Thur	Sun	Wed/Fri/Sat
Grenada	dep	0620	0710	0630	0710	1615
Carriacou	arr	0635	0725	0645	0725	1630
Carriacou	dep		0730	0650	0730	
Union	arr		0740	0700	0740	
Union	dep		0745	0705	0745	
Canouan	arr				0755	
Canouan	dep				0805	
Mustique	arr			0720		
Mustique	dep			0725		
St Vincent	arr		0805	0735	0825	
St Vincent	dep		0825	0755	0845	
St Lucia (Hewanorra)	arr			0820		
(Hewanorra)	dep			0830		
St Lucia (Vigie)	arr		0900	0845	0920	

Please note the LIAT schedules are notoriously subject to revision. All of the above should therefore be treated as a guide to frequency only. There are additional services at peak periods, such as December.

LIAT is often referred to in the Caribbean as 'Late If A Tall' and currently has a dreadful reputation when it comes to making reservations. As a generalisation, the counter staff are slow and unhelpful. To make a reservation, go in plenty of time and prepare for a long wait. You may be sold a confirmed seat and subsequently find yourself overbooked at the airport, or conversely you may be told a plane is full, arrive at the airport on standby, and find plenty of empty seats on the aircraft. One of the better run offices is in Barbados, and the worst is probably the one in Saint Georges, Grenada. The abysmal service provided by the Grenada office has nothing to do with the revolution there; I visited this office once before and twice after, the revolution to find the same unhelpful staff.

I had heard many people in the Eastern Caribbean complain that LIAT were very reluctant to make confirmed bookings yet continually flew with empty seats. I took this with a pinch of salt, although the plane in which I flew into Saint Vincent had 20 empty seats out of a total of 48. However, in Grenada my own experience gave credence to these allegations. I found it impossible to get a confirmed seat on any of the three flights I tried for, and noticed that many other passengers had similar problems. One man had been trying to get a confirmed seat to Trinidad for eight days! In the end I elected to go standby and set off for Pearls airport on the other side of the island. On arrival I met two other passengers on standby: we all got on the plane, which eventually took off with 12 empty seats. Thus LIAT had been refusing to take bookings on a flight that was only three-quarters full! On my second visit (in 1979, after the revolution) I found that nothing had changed. The LIAT staff was just as unhelpful, it was impossible to get a confirmed seat, I again travelled standby, and the plane left with 20 empty seats. In 1980 I made another brief visit to the office, but this time gave up, enlisted help from a local travel agent (see section on Grenada) and left for Saint Vincent on an IAS flight. In conclusion, I should add that I have had more complaints from clients and readers of the first edition of this book about LIAT, than all other airlines combined.

In addition to LIAT there are many small Caribbean airlines usually with ancient aircraft and a handful of routes. Most of these are charter airlines, such as Tropic Air, but one which has seen some expansion recently is Air Martinique. They fly Fort-de-France (Martinique)/Saint Lucia/Saint Vincent/Grenada and are certainly worth checking if you have problems with LIAT. Their designator is BT. I can however offer no guarantee that Air Martinique are better than LIAT.

It is not economic for large jet aircraft to island-hop, so the larger airlines which operate in this area tend to fly from point to point, overflying most islands: their schedules are worth noting, if you are only visiting a few of the better known islands. Eastern fly from San Juan to Guadeloupe, Martinique and Saint Lucia (Hewanorra), and from Saint Thomas to the same islands. From Saint Croix they serve Antigua and Sint Maarten. Eastern also have an ulimited mileage fare

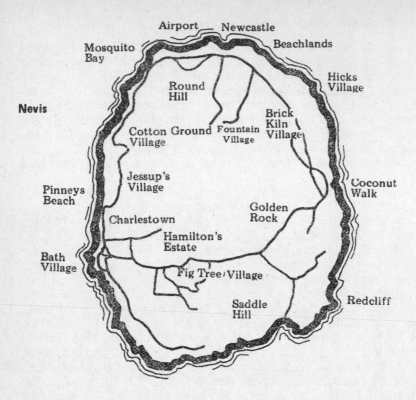

Airport — Newcastle

Mosquito Bay

Beachlands

Hicks Village

Round Hill

Nevis

Brick Kiln Village

Cotton Ground Village Fountain Village

Coconut Walk

Jessup's Village

Pinneys Beach

Golden Rock

Charlestown

Hamilton's Estate

Bath Village

Fig Tree Village

Saddle Hill

Redcliff

(valid 21 or 30 days) of US$459 which includes all their Caribbean islands. Full details of this are in Appendix 1, 'How to get there'. BWIA fly from San Juan to Antigua, Barbados, Saint Lucia (Hewanorra) and Trinidad. Prinair, the national carrier of Puerto Rico, serve Antigua, Guadeloupe, Saint Kitts, Sint Maarten and other islands near their home base. You should note that Nevis, Montserrat, Barbuda, Dominica, Saint Vincent and Grenada only have small airports not capable of handling large jet aircraft.

SAINT KITTS AND NEVIS

The government of Saint Kitts-Nevis styles the country's title as Saint Kitts-Nevis-Anguilla. This is because the territory of Saint Kitts-Nevis-Anguilla became a state in association with the United Kingdom on 27th February 1967. Within a few years however, Anguilla made a unilateral declaration of independence. Details of these events and everything relating to Anguilla are given in a later section devoted to the island (page 198). Although I am alone in dealing with Anguilla separately I feel justified in doing so as the island is 70 miles from Saint Kitts, and of a completely different character and political status (it is once again a British colony).

When C.C. spotted Saint Kitts he gave it his own name, insofar as he named it Saint Christopher. The English under the leadership of

Sir Thomas Warner arrived in 1623, when they founded what was to become the first successful British colony in the West Indies. Five years later they established a settlement on Nevis, and in succeeding years parties left here to settle other Caribbean islands. Thus to this day Saint Kitts has been described as the 'Cradle of the Caribbean'.

Within two years of Sir Thomas Warner's arrival the French landed. At first, relations between the original settlers and the newcomers were cordial, and the island was shared. However, the eighteenth century wars between England and France had their repercussions, and the islands often changed hands until the French were finally driven out in 1783.

Saint Kitts is about 20 miles long and has an area of 65 square miles and a population of 36,000. Nevis has an area of 36 square miles and is a more sensible shape, being roughly oval. The population is about 12,000.

Entry requirements: Visas are not normally required from citizens of the USA, Canada, the United Kingdom, the Commonwealth or Western European states. A return ticket and adequate funds are required. Any visitor not in possession of a return ticket may be required to deposit a sum of money sufficient to provide for his repatriation.

Climate: The highest recorded temperature this century is 92°F (33°C) and the lowest 62°F (17°C). Expect it to be in the 80s°F (27-32°C) with low humidity and the cooling effect of the Trade Winds. There is no water shortage on Saint Kitts.

Currency: The currency is the Eastern Caribbean dollar (EC$), known as EeCee dollars or BeeWee dollars (abbreviated from British West Indian dollar). The exchange rate is variable, but in approximate terms US$1 = EC$2.70. US dollars are accepted everywhere.

The cost of living: As a generalization, you can expect the Eastern Caribbean to be cheaper than those countries featured previously herein. You should find it easy to live as the natives and you can make great economies if you think in terms of EC$ instead of US$. As the islands are small, however, and dependent on imports for a large part of their needs, the cost of living is high for the natives.

Accommodation in Saint Kits

Name	Address	Price per room in US$
Guest Houses		
Park View	Basseterre (Tel: 2100)	EP: S $15; D $24
Ilan Pine	Basseterre (Tel: 2387)	MAP: S $20; D $30
Windsor	Basseterre (Tel: 3224)	EP: S $10; D $14
HOTELS		
Blakeney Hotel	Church St, Basseterre (Tel: 2222)	MAP: S $19 — $28
		MAP: D $38 — $56
Canne-a-Sucre	Basseterre (Tel: 2414)	CP: S $8; D $14

Expensive Hotels

Banana Bay Beach	Southern Saint Kitts (no phone)	MAP: *S* $60 summer, $80 winter; *D* $80 summer, $100 winter.
The Cockleshell	Southern Saint Kitts (no phone)	MAP: *S* $40 summer, $70 winter; *D* $60 summer, $90 winter.
Fairview Inn	Monkey Hill (Tel: 2472/2473)	EP: *S* $30 — $38 summer, $40 — $48 winter; *D* $40 — $48 summer, $50 — $58 winter
Golden Lemon	Dieppe Bay (Tel: 7260)	AP: *S* $50 summer, $85 winter; *D* $100 summer, $125 winter.
Ocean Terrace Inn	Basseterre (Tel: 2754/2380)	MAP: *S* $59 — $67 winter; *D* $84 — $96 winter

Beach Cottages and Apartments

Conareef Beach Cottages	Conaree Beach (Tel: 2310/2328)	EP: $110 per week summer, $150 per week winter
Coral Reef Beach Cottage	Conaree Beach (Tel: 2161)	EP: $105 per week summer, $125 per week winter.
The Cottage	Conaree Beach (Tel: 2100)	EP: $60 — $75 per week.
Southern Comfort	Conaree Beach (Tel: 3234)	EP: $100 per week summer, $120 per week winter.
Tradewinds Luxury Bungalows	Conaree Beach (Tel: 2681)	EP: $132 per week summer, $150 per week winter

Some of the cheaper establishments listed above also quote rates in EC Dollars. Where this is the case, it is usually cheaper to pay in the local currency.

Transportation: Taxis are the normal form of transportation for visitors. The taxi fare from Golden Rock International Airport to Basseterre is EC$7. Mopeds can be hired for US$12 per day, and cars cost around US$20 per day. There is a ferry to Nevis which generally leaves at 6 a.m. returning from Nevis at 6 p.m. Although the two islands are only two miles apart, the boat journey is about 12 miles. The cost is EC$5.

Food and drink: You can expect to find the usual West Indian dishes, roast suckling pig, turtle steak, chicken with rice 'n' peas, pepperpot soup, etc. In addition to the Caribbean vegetables — yam, breadfruit, sweet potato, plantain — European vegetables are grown. Fresh meat and fish are readily available. Fresh fruit is abundant. Rum and rum cocktails are the predominant alcoholic beverages. Spirits are relatively cheap.

Industry: The original industry of Sain Kitts is still the islands' most important — sugar. After emancipation the former slaves were prepared to continue working the sugar estates, and so the plantations have continued to be worked up to the present day. There is a modern sugar processing plant on Saint Kitts which can be visited and a train that encircles the island collecting the cut cane. Today, of course, there was a recession following emancipation, and Nevis in

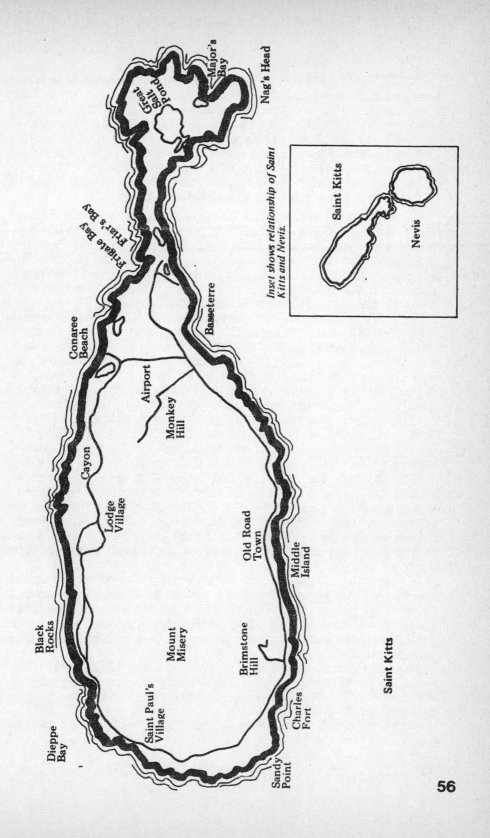

Great Salt Pond

Major's Bay

Nag's Head

Frigate Bay

Friar's Bay

Basseterre

Conaree Beach

Airport

Monkey Hill

Cayon

Lodge Village

Old Road Town

Middle Island

Black Rocks

Mount Misery

Brimstone Hill

Saint Paul's Village

Charles Fort

Dieppe Bay

Sandy Point

Inset shows relationship of Saint Kitts and Nevis.

Saint Kitts

Nevis

Saint Kitts

56

particular was soon deserted by most of the whites; both islands still have derelict and deserted plantation houses (some of which have been converted to hotels). Tourism is still in the initial stages of development (although there is a casino here, at one of the newest hotels, Royal Saint Kitts at Frigate Bay). The airport at Golden Rock has been enlarged to take big jets, but there is only one scheduled jet service at the moment (the Friday ALM service from Curacao to Miami stops here) and it will be some years before Saint Kitts-Nevis becomes one of the well-known tourist destinations.

Where to go: There are fine beaches at Conaree Beach, Frigate Bay, Friars Bay and Cockleshell Bay, all of which are a fair distance from Basseterre. This (the French equivalent of 'Leeward') is the administrative capital of St. Kitts-Nevis. It is also the largest town and main port. It is possible to take boats from here to the small islands round about (Saba, Saint Eustatius, Saint Barthelemy, Sint Maarten) as well as to other parts of St. Kitts-Nevis.

There is a road around the perimeter of the island (the interior is quite hilly with Mount Misery as its highest point), along which most of the villages stand. A jeep is needed to drive to the south-eastern part of the island. Taking the good road west from Basseterre you will come to Brimstone Hill after a drive of 8 to 10 miles. Brimstone Hill was fortified in order to repel the French and any other trouble-makers, its natural hilly aspect earning it the title of the 'Gibraltar of the West Indies'. It was badly damaged by a hurricane in 1834 and in 1852 was evacuated and partly dismantled. Parts of it, notably the Prince of Wales Bastion, have been restored and the cannon remounted.

Gibraltar has its baboons, and Saint Kitts has its monkeys. Apparently the early French colonists brought pet monkeys with them. When the French were driven from the island the monkeys escaped and ran wild, breeding to such an extent that when the French returned seven years later the monkeys had become a pest and 'periodic monkeyshoots' had to be undertaken to reduce their numbers.

If you enjoy a good climb then the prospect of ascending the volcanic cone of Mount Misery may appeal. You will need to arrange transportation from Belmont or Harris' Estate in advance. This is not a normal tourist route, so your climb will be through wild under-growth, orchids and forest. If you are fit it is possible to make a descent into the crater.

Spectacular scenery is also provided by the black rocks (lava rocks tossed down to the sea during prehistoric eruption) and the salt ponds area, which is still worked. Carib and Amerindian remains can also be viewed on the island.

Nevis: In the eighteenth century this island was known as 'The Queen of the Caribbee Islands' because of its spectacular and beautiful scenery. The capital is Charlestown, linked by a regular boat service to Basseterre, Nevis. There is a boatbuilding industry south of the town. The sugar industry is less developed and less important here, as it declined significantly after emancipation.

South of Charlestown is Bath Village, famous for its supposedly beneficial mineral springs. There are five hot baths with naturally hot water. In the past rich hypochondriacs came here to be cured.

Nevis' other claim to fame is as the birthplace of Alexander Hamilton. One of his friends, Lord Nelson, has a museum dedicated to him at Morning Star. Nelson was actually married here (at Montpelier Great House) and the records remain in the register of Saint John's Church in Fig Tree Village.

Accommodation in Nevis

Name	*Address*	*Price per room in US$*
Guest Houses		
Powell's Guesthouse	Government Road, Charlestown (Tel: 282)	US$150 per room per week
Parisville	Low Street, Charlestown	US$20 per room per day
Hotels		
Pinney's Beach Hotel	Pinney's Beach (Tel: 207)	MAP: *S* US$30 summer, US$38 winter; *D* US$58 summer, US$63 winter
Montpelier Hotel	Montpelier (Tel: 462)	MAP: *S* US$30 summer, $50 winter; *D* $50 summer, $75 winter
Expensive Hotels		
Golden Rock	Gingerland (Tel: 346)	MAP: *S* $40 summer, $70 winter; *D* $70 summer, $100 winter
Nisbet Plantation Inn	Newcastle (Tel: 325)	MAP: *S* $55 summer, $70 winter; *D* $85 summer, $100 winter
Rest Haven Inn	Old Hospital Road, Charlestown (Tel: 209)	MAP (Year round): $35 — $50; *D* $55 — $80.
Beach Cottages and Apartments		
Donna's Self Catering Apartment	Charlestown (Tel: 464/484)	EP: $20 per day, $120 per week.
White Rose Cottage	Richard Hill, Morning Star (Tel: 460)	EP: $10 per day per person
Lyndale Cottage	Charlestown (Tel: 412)	EP: $25 per day

ANGUILLA

It was in 1971 that the 6000 people of Anguilla decided that they did not wish to be governed from Basseterre, Saint Kitts. Their unilateral declaration of independence led to a British frigate being sent to the area and a commando force being landed (Anguilla is somewhat smaller than Rhodesia). As this force met no resistance it was quickly withdrawn and replaced with a number of policemen and a detachment of sappers who set about building roads, bridges, and an airstrip. These good works and a lot of talking failed to persuade the Anguillans that life would be better under the Basseterre administration, and late in 1975 the British government accepted the inevitable and bowed to the Anguillan's wishes. Which were to be re-instated as a British colony. All of this gives Anguilla a peculiar constitutional position: Saint Kitts-Nevis still claims sovereignty; the British government supports this claim, but nevertheless administers Anguilla itself.

In fact it seems to me that there is little logical reason why Anguilla should be a part of the Saint Kitts-Nevis federation. Not only is it 70 miles from Saint Kitts, but the sea in between is dotted with small Dutch and French islands. The island of Montserrat is nearer to both Saint Kitts-Nevis and Antigua than Anguilla is to Saint Kitts, yet Montserrat remains (through choice) a British Colony.

Geographically, Anguilla is a complete contrast to Saint Kitts-Nevis. There are no rugged hills covered with lush vegetation, for Anguilla is a flat, sandy coral island. The lack of industrial development is a contrast too. Most of the islanders are subsistence farmers, fishing and raising crops and chickens on smallholdings. Large-scale farming is scarcely possible as the soil is generally shallow (a normal feature of coral-formed islands).

There is great potential for the development of a tourist industry here. The beaches are superb — possibly the best in the Caribbean, and there are excellent opportunities for scuba diving, big game and other fishing. The trick is to get here before this development is put in hand.

The main beach and an important settlement is Sandy Ground on Road Bay. It has a jetty for incoming sloops and outgoing fishing boats, with boatbuilding on the beach. Behind the narrow strip of land is a salt pond. Other splendid beaches are Meads Bay (visited by Prince Philip in 1964), Long Bay (small and secluded), Maundy's Bay (perhaps the island's finest), The Cove (skin diving and sea shells) and Rendezvous Bay (where an invasion party of French met a sticky end in 1796). Please regard this list as merely a small taste of the feast in store.

Accommodation: The political difficulties outlined above mean that it is impossible to obtain current rates for hotels and guest houses in Anguilla. However, I would expect the following to be the most economical:

Anguilla

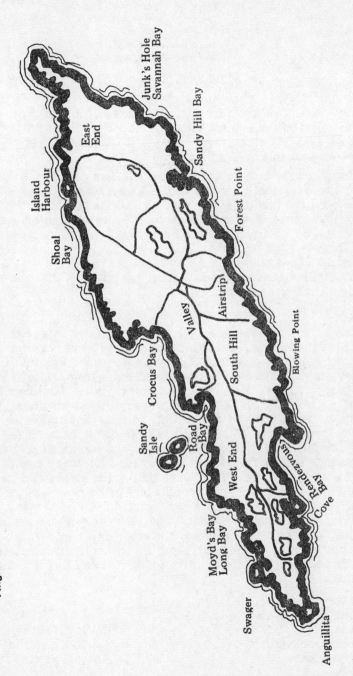

Island Harbour

East End

Junk's Hole
Savannah Bay

Sandy Hill Bay

Forest Point

Shoal Bay

Valley

Airstrip

South Hill

Blowing Point

Crocus Bay

Sandy Isle

Road Bay

West End

Rendezvous Bay

Cove Bay

Moyd's Bay
Long Bay

Swager

Anguillita

Name	*Address*
Lloyd's Hotel	The Valley, Anguilla
Florencia Guest House	The Valley, Anguilla
Hibiscus	The Valley, Anguilla
Bayview House	Sandy Ground, Anguilla
The Inter-Island Hotel	Lower South Hill, Anguilla

How to get to Anguilla: There are few international scheduled flights to Anguilla; as far as I know, these comprise the weekly flights from Antigua, bi-weekly flights from Saint Kitts (both on Four Island Air as listed earlier) and some services from Saint Barthelemy (daily) and Sint Maarten (three a day). In fact, the recently-built airstrip is only capable of handling small aircraft.

The usual method of entry is by boat from the Dutch/French island of Sint Maarten, a stone's throw to the south. There is some trade between the islands, largely due to Sint Maarten's position as a free port and source of French foods on the one hand and Anguilla's abundant supply of fish on the other. You should thus make your way to Marigot (the capital of Saint Martin, the French part) and there pick up a boat bound for Anguilla.

Details of Sint Maarten/Saint Martin are given in the section on the French Antilles (see page 213).

ANTIGUA

If you make it to the eastern Caribbean, do not miss beautiful, friendly Antigua. Perhaps its attractions for me were heightened by the contrast with San Juan and Saint Thomas, but frankly I think it would have appealed to me wherever I had come from. Here's why.

The island offers the best scenery — both landscape and seascape — I had seen anywhere: hills that plunge into the sea then change their minds and rise up again, a coastline that undulates more than a belly dancer's midriff and still finds time to unveil 365 beaches, the feeling, if not always the sight and sound, that wherever you go you are not far from the sea. But then I like small islands.

Antigua is uncrowded. You won't find here the sardine-packed buses of Jamaica, impassable sidewalks and blaring carhorns of Port-au-Prince, or the native bustle and tourist shuffle of San Juan and Saint Thomas. Leisurely walks, even downtown on Saturday afternoons, are the rule. There is always a bus seat available, or perhaps two if you are very fat. And the towns are so small that a short walk puts you into the countryside. But then I like uncrowded, small islands.

Antigua: Key

1 St John's Deep Water
   Harbour
2 Nelson's Dockyard
3 Clarence House

4 Shirley Heights
5 Falmouth Harbour
6 Antigua Sugar Factory

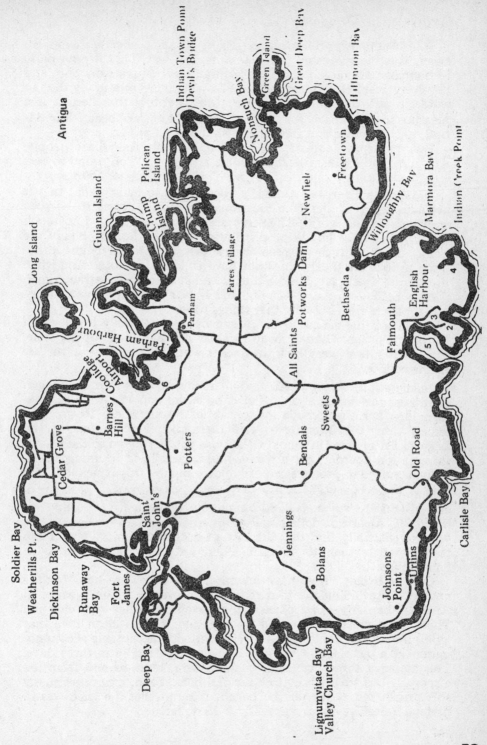

Antigua

Long Island

Guiana Island

Crump Island

Pelican Island

Indian Town Point
Devil's Bridge

Nonsuch Bay

Green Island

Great Deep Bay

Halfmoon Bay

Freetown

Newfield

Indian Creek Point

Marmora Bay

Willoughby Bay

English Harbour

Pares Village

Parham

Parham Harbour

Coolidge Airport

Barnes Hill

Cedar Grove

Soldier Bay

Weatherills Pt.

Dickinson Bay

Runaway Bay

Fort James

Saint John's

Potters

Potworks Dam

All Saints

Bethseda

Falmouth

Old Road

Sweets

Bendals

Jennings

Bolans

Johnsons Point

Urlins

Carlisle Bay

Deep Bay

Lignumvitae Bay
Valley Church Bay

59

Everywhere is so clean. True, Saint Thomas and San Juan are clean, but this is because they are American and rich; the poor parts of San Juan are not so clean. But Antigua is comparatively poor and yet everywhere cleanliness and tidiness abound. So naturally the tap water is safe to drink. More than that, I found that here it is a pleasure to drink it, as for the first time in the Caribbean I found it both unchlorinated and free from rust. Just pure water.

But perhaps most of all Antigua has the friendliest people. Antiguans are loving, friendly, honest and proud. Too proud to beg. And plenty to be proud of. They have made this a great country.

Hiding the Tourists: Antigua's coastline is so magnificent that it provides some of the best locations for tourist hotels to be seen anywhere in the world. There are so many beaches, and so much beauty, that these hotels are distributed at all far-flung points of the island. Many of them include watersports and other facilites in the price so that the tourist does not have to leave the hotel. And when the tourist does leave, besides the two main beacons to attract him — namely Saint Johns as the capital and Nelson's Dockyard as a tourist sight — there are a host of other things to see.

All in all this means that Antigua has a remarkably low level of tourist pollution. Hidden away in their enclaves most of the time, the tourists have everything they want without intruding on the life of the country.

Immigration: As you will find in many other eastern Caribbean countries, the immigration officials here like you to have a reservation for your accommodation or at least somewhere to go. The easiest thing of course is to give them the name of one of the hostelries named in this book. Otherwise you simply go to the tourist information counter, get a name, and take it back to immigration. You may need to produce onward and/or homeward air tickets.

Currency: The legal tender is the Eastern Caribbean or BeeWee dollar (EC$) which is approximately equivalent to US$1 = EC$2.70. American dollars are accepted everywhere of course, but you will generally find that the rate of exchange is more favourable to the natives than to yourself. There are three or four banks in Saint Johns.

Cost of living: Prices have increased and times are hard for the natives. By avoiding the tourist traps, however — which is easier in Antigua than any other place — the traveller can live very cheaply. There is no pressure to spend money, and it is so clean here that 'going native' is completely safe. With perfectly acceptable accommodation at a mere US$4 a night, I spent only US$25 in three days. This included three nights' accommodation, taxis to and from the airport, a bus to English Harbour and back, food, cigarettes, many soft drinks and a day on the beach. I found that the trick was to pretend a BeeWee dollar was really a US dollar!

Climate: As you will find in most of the eastern Caribbean islands, perfect. Temperatures are usually in the 80s°F (27-32°C) year round, with the cooling Trade Winds preventing the heat becoming oppressive and enough rainfall to make water shortages a rarity.

Transportation: There is no bus service between the airport and Saint John's, so you will have to take a taxi. The Tourist Board publishes a pink card with rates in US and EC dollars. Unaware of this, I was ripped off (but not by much) when coming from the airport. On my return I had my pink rate sheet handy and the correct change — EC$9 — to prevent argument. Imagine my surprise when, on arrival at the airport, the driver asked for EC$7! I was so surprised I gave him the 9.

Taxis are identified by a green registration plate prefixed by the letter 'H' for 'hire'. Below are some of the recommended taxi fares, correct at the time of writing.

Saint John's to	US$ Rate	EC$ Rate	Extra passenger over 4
Coolidge Airport	$3.50	$9	EC $1.90
Fort James	$2	$5	EC $1.10
Nelson's Dockyard	$7.50	$20	EC $4.00
Shirley Heights	$9	$24	EC $4.85
Sugar Factory	$2.50	$7	EC $1.35
Deep Water Harbour	$2	$5	

There is a limited bus service in Antigua. This is run on the private enterprise system and operates according to the rules of supply and demand. There will thus be more services in peak periods than otherwise, bringing people from the countryside into town in the early mornings and Saturday evenings, and taking passengers back out into the country in the evenings and late on Saturday nights. But there are some services during the day, and if you have to wait, well, you should be used to it by now.

Maybe because the buses are privately owned, you will find the fares reasonable and the owner-drivers friendly. The bus route will vary slightly with each trip, as the drivers like to drop their passengers (often laden with shopping) at their front doors.

There are two basic routes from Saint John's, eastward and south. Those buses destined for the east leave (believe it or not) from East Street, near the Spanish Main Inn, where the Saint Johnston Road comes into town. These buses will not normally go to or near the airport, but can be expected to visit Saint Johnston, the Sugar Factory, Pares Village and other destinations in the east.

Southbound buses for English Harbour and Nelson's Dockyard leave from the market in Saint John's (see map). The fare is EC 70/80 cents. Descending from the hills you will be treated to superlative views of the bay known as Falmouth Harbour before the bus drops you in the town or near the entrance to the Dockyard.

Accommodation

Name	Address	Price per room in US$
Guest Houses		
Main Road Guest House	Ottos Main Road, Saint Johns	EP: $4 per person
Silver Dollar Inn	Ottos Main Road, Saint Johns	EP: $9 S; $12 D;
Open View Guest House	Edward Street, Saint Johns	EP: $4.50 per person
Central Motor Inn	Ottos Main Road, Saint Johns	Unknown: approx $10 per person
Bellot's Guest House	Saint Mary.s Street, Saint Johns	EP: $12 S; $22 D
Palm View Guest House	Saint Mary's Street, Saint Johns	EP: $8 per person
Skyline Guest House	Airport Road	EP: $12 S; $21 D; $30
Cornelia's Castle	Factory Road	EP: $11 S; $19 D; $26 T / CP: $13 S; $23 D;$32 T / MAP: $18 S; $34 D; $46 T
Milis Guest House	Comacho's Avenue	EP: $10 S; $20 D / CP: $12 S; $22 D
Montgomery Guest House	Radio Range	EP: $6 S; $12 D
Montgomery Guest House	Tindale Road	EP: $6 per person. MAP: $11.50 per person.
Quiet Guest House	Villa	MAP: $8 S; $16 D; $22 T
Roslyn's Guest House	Fort Road	EP: $12 S; $22 D / CP: $15 S; $28 D
Shell Inn	Wireless Road	EP: $11 S; $18 D / CP: $14 S; $22 D / MAP: $19 S; $28 D
Hotels		
Spanish Main Inn	East Street, Saint Johns	EP: $25 S; $30 D
Stevendale Hotel	Fort Road	EP: $20 S; $30 D / CP: $23 S; $33 D / MAP: $25 S; $36 D / Add $5 for air-conditioned rooms
Piggottsville	Clare Hall	EP: $11.50 S; $19.50 D; $28T / MAP: $17 S; $31 D; $46 T
Barrymore	Fort Road	EP: $18 S; $28 D (standard rooms)
Admirals Inn	Nelson's Dockyard, English Harbour	Standard Rooms; EP: $22 S; $26 D. MAP: $39 S; $60 D. Moderate: EP: $26 S; $30 D MAP: $43 S; $64 D. Superior: EP: $30 S; $34 D. MAP: $47 S; $68 D
Atlantic Beach	Crosbies	EP: $23 S; $33 D / MAP: $35 S; $57 D
Beachcomber	Coolidge	EP: $18 S; $25 D / Self-contained units $125 per week.
Catamaran Hotel	Falmouth	EP: $20 S; $30 D; $40 T
Saint Johns Motel	Fort Road	EP: $13 S; $17 D / CP: $16 S; $20 D
Expensive Hotels		
Galley Bay	Five Island	EP: $40/$45 S; $45/$50/$60 D; $65/$70/$80 T MAP: $62/$72 S; $89/$94/$104 D; $131/$136/$145 T

Curtain Bluff	Morris Bay	MAP: *$65/$75 S*; *$90/$100 D*; *$125/$135 T*
Half Moon Bay	Half Moon Bay	MAP: *$55 S*; *$75/$90 D*; *$110/$125 T*
Halcyon Cove	Dickensen Bay	EP: *$49/$56/$62 S*; *$49/$56/$62 D* *$54/$61/$67 T* MAP Supplement *$24* per person per day.

Cottage and Apartments

Camp Runaway	Runaway Bay	EP: *$250* per week summer; *$350* per week winter. Four persons.
Clarke's Hill	Clarke's Hill (inland)	EP: *$15* per day per person (summer).

Bungalows

Seaside Bungalow	Runaway Beach	EP: *$400* per week (8 persons) all year
Falmouth Beach	Falmouth (near English Harbour)	EP: *$30 S*; *$34 D* summer

Apartments

The Copper and Lumber Store	Nelson's Dockyard, English Harbour	EP: summer: *$375* per week for 4; *$225/$300* per week for 2. winter: *$600* per week for 4; *$375/$525* for 2.

Please note that hotel and guest house rates given above were correct for summer 1980. All hotel rates and many guest house rates will be higher in the winter season.

Those making use of the cheapest accommodation available will be pleased to note that I found Antigua's cheapest guest house, the *Main Road Guest House*, very acceptable. The rooms (there are four) are very small but very clean, there is a good shower with constant (cold) water, a clean and efficiently flushing toilet and wash basin with a large mirror for shaving. Although one would think that basic facilities such as these could be provided anywhere, this was the first cheap guest house I found where they were all in good working order. Its location is good too, on Ottos Main Road, on the edge of town. It is a short walk to the bus for English Harbour, or you can wait at the gate for a taxi.

Nearby is the *Silver Dollar Inn*. If you decide to pay the extra you will find less spartan facilities here. Also very close is the *Central Motor Inn*. Still in town you could try the *Open View* in Edward Street, or one of two small places in Saint Mary's Street; *Bellot's* or *Palm View*.

For those who prefer a large place there is the Spanish Main Inn, on East Street, which has a reputation for serving the best food in Saint Johns; on Fort Road, on the way to the nearest beach, there is the Stevendale.

There are two places between the airport and Saint John's which are worthy of note. *The Skyline* in Airport Road may prove, because of its location, to be the best accommodation for anyone unwise enough merely to overnight in Antigua. The extra you spend on

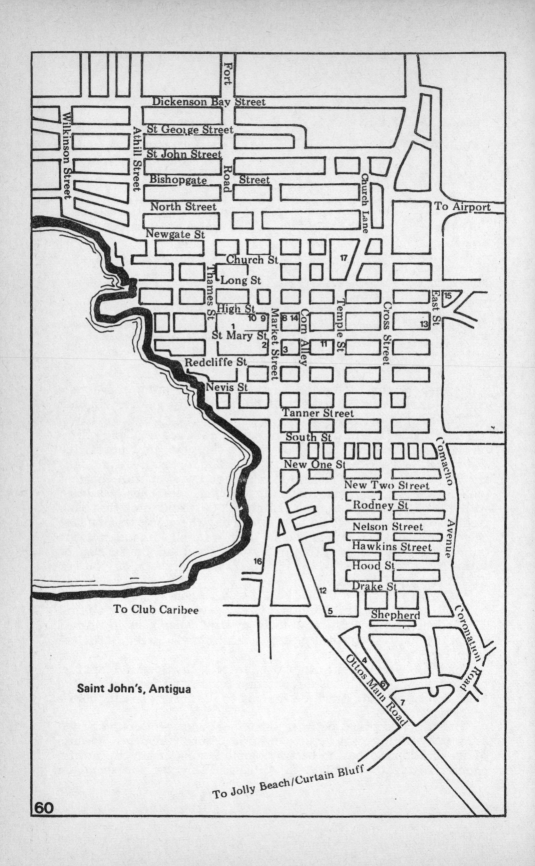

Saint John's, Antigua

60

accommodation may be cancelled out by no taxi fare. *Piggotsville* at Clare Hall could provide that country retreat. The taxi fare between the airport and Clare Hall should be about US$2.50 or EC$7, but agree this first as it is not officially listed.

Saint John's: One is immediately struck by the cleanliness and tidiness, which is unusual in a town so obviously poor. The town lacks crowds, as fortunately it possesses only one building of note, a situation that keeps most tourists away most of the time. And that one building, the cathedral, was badly damaged in the earthquake of 1974, so that its twin turrets, which dominate the town, are shored up by wooden scaffolding.

For the traveller however, the only deficiency is in native restaurants. Snack bars abound, but these are usually of the type which also offer a limited range of groceries. As often as not you stand at the counter to consume your beverage and cheese roll or hamburger. The *Cozy Nook* on Saint Mary Street offers light snacks but service can be abrupt. Very close to the suggested accommodation on Ottos Main Road is the *Soul Inn Snack Bar* run by a couple of hip guys and decorated with some neat posters. The limited menu and prices are well displayed. The clientele are young and very friendly.

Restaurants do exist however, and here are some suggestions. *Maurice's* on Market Street serves excellent lobster and native food and is centrally located. The *Spanish Main* may tend towards the touristy, but should not be obviously so; *Brother B's* is quite definitely native fare. Two Chinese restaurants are worth mention; the *China Garden* on Newgate Street and the *Sea Dragon* in Fort Road.

Market freaks should note that the best time to savour Antigua's is on Saturday mornings. You will find it — in Saint John's — at the beginning of Ottos Main Road, where the southbound buses leave from.

The rest of the island: In my view the sights worth seeing are those which are examples of Antigua's great natural beauty. I only sampled enough to whet my appetite, but you will find the tourist office eager to supply further details. You may not be able to see everything by bus, but at least you can make a start this way.

Saint John's: Key
1 Travel agent
2 Barclays Bank
3 Maurice's Bar/Restaurant
4 Main Road Guest House
5 Silver Dollar Guest House
6 Petrol (gas) station
7 Central Motel
8 Royal Bank of Canada
9 First Pennsylvania Bank
10 Bank of Nova Scotia
11 Cozy Nook
12 Soul Inn Snack Bar
13 Spanish Main Hotel
14 Tourist office
15 Eastbound buses
16 Southbound buses (market)
17 Cathedral

Nelson's Dockyard: This, Antigua's best known tourist sight, is situated in one of the world's safest natural harbours. It was used by the big names of the Royal Navy as the headquarters of the Caribbean fleet during the Napoleonic Wars. The Dockyard had fallen into disrepair but was recently rescued and restored to some of its former glory. An admission charge of EC$2 or US$1 is the main source of revenue for its upkeep.

Clarence House overlooks Nelson's Dockyard. It was built of stone for the Duke of Clarence (who was Prince William Henry at the time and King William IV later) around 1787. It is now the country home of the Governor and sometimes open to visitors.

In the same area you will find *Shirley Heights*, named after General Shirley who fortified these hills to protect English Harbour and the Dockyard.

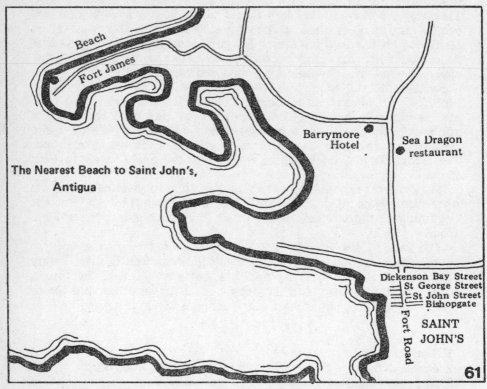

The Nearest Beach to Saint John's, Antigua

Potworks Dam is usually regarded as being one of Antigua's most beautiful inland spots. It is the island's largest man-made lake, and besides serving a most useful purpose affords beautiful views and imparts a feeling of serenity and peace. Also with a reputation for natural beauty is *Fig Tree Drive* on the southwest coast where a winding road takes you through lush tropical scenery and picturesque villages. Antigua even has megaliths. These stones, allegedly set up by human hands for the purposes of sun-worship, can be found at the end of a walk up *Green Castle Hill*. And although it is difficult to select one from the many incredibly beautiful seascapes, you will find a visit to *Indian Town Point* worth making if you have transport. This is the northeast point of the island; Devil's Bridge is one of the rugged rock formations caused by thousands of years of Atlantic surf breaking over this coast.

Barbuda: Many would say that Antigua's most beautiful scenery is 28 miles to the north. Here lies the island of Barbuda, formerly known as Dulcina, a dependency of Antigua. 62 square miles in area — about two-thirds the size of Antigua, it has a population of only 1500, all of whom live in the village of Codrington.

Like Antigua a coral island, Barbuda's beaches stretch for miles, unbroken and deserted, on both the leeward and windward coasts. The island is heavily wooded and abounds in birdlife, wild pig and deer, while the waters surrounding it are rich in seafood.

There are no customs and immigration facilities on Barbuda as

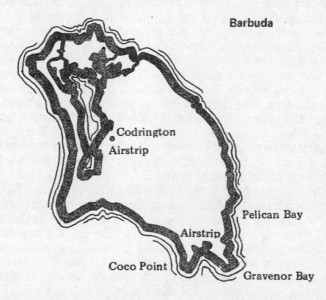

Barbuda

Codrington
Airstrip

Pelican Bay

Airstrip

Coco Point

Gravenor Bay

62

entry to the island must be made through Antigua. There are two airports: one at Coco Point, which boasts the only tourist hotel and is completely isolated from the native settlement of Codrington, where the main airport is situated. LIAT fly five times a week (Monday to Friday) early in the morning, using nine-seater Britton Norman Islander planes. The fare is US$14 (EC$38) each way. Or you may be lucky and get a passage in a fishing boat or other vessel from Saint John's.

Remarkably, there is one guest house in Codrington, run by Mr or Mrs Harris, and situated near Timbukone. It costs EC$30 per room for up to three people, and is the only place where you can eat.

Leaving Antigua: Hard but easy. Or in other words, you will hate to leave but find it simple to do so. If staying at the Main Road Guest House you need only stand at the gate until an unoccupied taxi drives past. Stop him. The fare to the airport at the time of writing is US$3.50 or EC$9; if you do not have the pink tourist office card bearing this information, agree the rate beforehand.

The airport has landing and turnaround facilities for the biggest jets, and services of a scale adequate to cope with existing levels of traffic. Thus the restaurant and departure lounge are likely to be fairly full but not overcrowded. Note that restaurant prices are very high by Antiguan standards. There is supposed to be an airport tax of EC$5, but I was not charged this, perhaps because I left on a LIAT inter-island flight.

MONTSERRAT

'The Emerald Isle in the Caribbean', Montserrat was one of the few islands in the British West Indies which chose to remain a British colony, rather than become an associated independent state, when presented with the alternatives. The choice was perhaps a wise one, as the island is small (in area 39½ square miles with a population of 12,809) and would quite possibly have otherwise been incorporated in a federation with Saint Kitts-Nevis or Antigua-Barbuda.

Montserrat was first settled in modern times around 1633 when a group of mainly Irish Roman Catholic settlers came here from Saint Kitts where they had been unable to live in harmony with their Protestant brothers. A shamrock adorning the Governor's residence and a host of Irish family names still attest to this heritage. The shamrock is the national symbol.

The capital, Plymouth, is a settlement of some 1,200 souls on the southwestern side of the island. This is the busiest part of the island, as the commercial centre, harbour and most of the limited accommodation are all here. Recently George Martin, the erstwhile Recording Manager of the Beatles, opened a recording studio in Montserrat. The complex includes watersports and other facilities for wives and girlfriends and relaxing pop stars. But do not think that there is a lot of action on the island, for there isn't: this is the ideal place for a rest cure. The rest of the population is scattered liberally over the island, which combines rugged beauty with lush vegetation and lovely beaches.

Montserrat: Key
1 Letts Guest House
2 Sea Haven Guest House
3 Hideaway Hotel
4 Coconut Hill Hotel

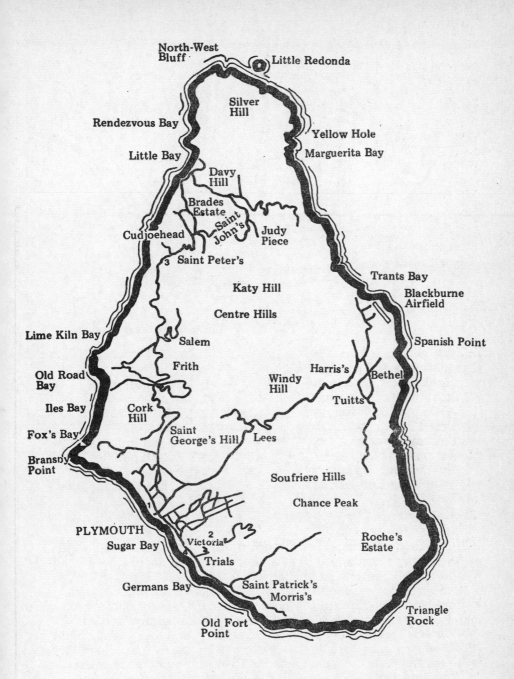

North-West Bluff

Little Redonda

Silver Hill

Rendezvous Bay

Yellow Hole

Little Bay

Marguerita Bay

Davy Hill

Brades Estate

Saint John's

Judy Piece

Cudjoehead

3 Saint Peter's

Katy Hill

Trants Bay

Blackburne Airfield

Centre Hills

Lime Kiln Bay

Salem

Spanish Point

Old Road Bay

Frith

Harris's

Bethel

Windy Hill

Iles Bay

Tuitts

Cork Hill

Fox's Bay

Saint George's Hill

Lees

Bransby Point

Soufriere Hills

Chance Peak

PLYMOUTH

Sugar Bay

Victoria

Roche's Estate

Trials

Germans Bay

Saint Patrick's
Morris's

Old Fort Point

Triangle Rock

Montserrat

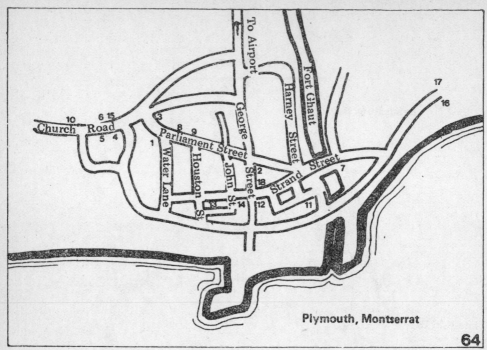

Plymouth, Montserrat

64

Plymouth: Key
1 Montserrat tourist board
2 Royal Bank of Canada
3 Wade Inn and Runaway
   Travel
4 Cable & Wireless
5 Barclays Bank
6 Government headquarters
7 Symphony Restaurant
8 Town Hall
9 Church
10 Police station
11 Markets
12 Customs
13 Post office
14 War memorial and park
15 Chase Manhattan Bank
16 Rose and Compass
17 Anchorage Restaurant
18 LIAT office

Entry requirements: Visas are not normally required and citizens of the USA, Canada and the United Kingdom do not even need passports. All visitors require adequate funds and a return ticket. You may introduce the usual personal allowances through customs.

Currency: The Eastern Caribbean dollar (EC$) which is approximately equivalent to US$0.40; US$1 = EC$2.70 approximately.

Climate: Temperatures are in the 70s° and 80s° Fahrenheit (21-32°C) as elsewhere in the eastern Caribbean. There is rather more rainfall here, due perhaps to the island's mountainous aspect.

Food and drink: Fertile soil and an industrious people produce some of the best vegetables and fruit in the Caribbean. Tomatoes, carrots and mangoes are specialities. Goat water (a kind of goat curry) is the national dish, but you will also find good Creole dishes and plenty of seafood. As this is the Caribbean, rum-based drinks are the norm.

Accommodation: There is very little accommodation on the island — seven hotels with a total of 200 beds, and a handful of guest houses. Almost all are on the west (Caribbean) coast. Blackburne Airfield is on the east coast.

Name	Address	Price per room in US$
Guest Houses		
Sea Haven . Guest House	Kinsdale	EP: *S* $15; *D* $25 (all year)
Humphrey's	Kinsale	EP: *D* $10
Hotels		
Hideaway Hotel	Rocklands (Tel: 5252)	MAP: summer: *S* $22, *D* $35 MAP: winter: *S* $26; *D* $44
Wade Inn	Plymouth (Tel: 2881)	MAP: summer: *S* $28; *D* $40 MAP: winter: *S* $30; *D* $48
Lett's Inn	Plymouth (Tel: 2396)	MAP: summer: *S* $23; *D* $42 MAP: winter: *S* $23; *D* $42
Coconut Hill Hotel	Plymouth (Tel: 2144)	MAP: summer: *S* $25; *D* $42 MAP: winter: *S* $35; *D* $52
Emerald Isle Hotel	Richmond (Tel: 2481)	MAP: summer: *S* $40; *D* $55 MAP: winter: *S* $50; *D* $72
Vue Pointe Hotel	Old Towne, Isles Bay	MAP: summer: *S* $40; *D* $56 *T* $81. winter: *S* $70; *D* $90; *T* $135

Humphrey's Guest House is, as far as I know, the cheapest accommodation in Montserrat. None of the hotels are situated on a beach in the same way as the majority of hotels in Antigua. The main tourist hotel on the island is the Vue Pointe, set above Isles Bay and with magnificent views. There are 12 rooms in the hotel and 28 hexagonally shaped cottages. There is a swimming pool, two tennis courts and the golf club is almost adjacent.

Getting to and from Montserrat: There are regular flights between Montserrat and Antigua (US$22 or EC$51 one way), Saint Kitts (US$29 or EC$69 one way) and Nevis (US$29 or EC$69 one way), operated by LIAT or its subsidiaries. There was also some talk recently that Montserrat would start its own airline (with one or two small aircraft) after independence. Alternatively, it shouldn't be too difficult to find a boat which is bound for Montserrat from either Saint Kitts-Nevis or Antigua.

THE FRENCH ANTILLES

Although geographically in the Caribbean and thousands of miles from Europe, politically the French Antilles are part of France. Administratively, Martinique forms one Department of France, and Guadeloupe (with Saint-Martin, Saint-Barthelemy, Desirade, Marie-

Galante and Les Saintes) another. The people are full citizens of France and the shops stocked with all the goods you would expect to find in Paris.

Immigration: Citizens of countries belonging to the European Economic Community do not need visas, but should carry passports. US and Canadian citizens may stay up to 21 days without a passport but will need some form of identity papers.

All travellers are officially required to possess a return air ticket, although I suspect that for EEC citizens this requirement is less stringently adhered to (I was not asked to produce any air tickets or evidence of adequate funds).

Currency: The French franc is the official currency of all the islands in the French Antilles. The US dollar is accepted, but the rate will not usually be favourable to you.

The Economy: The French Antilles must be subsidized by mainland France. Although there is some tourism, particularly French, the economy is mainly based on agriculture. The principal products are sugar cane, rum and bananas.

Supermarkets and grocery stores are as frequent and well stocked as those in France, with luxury goods for sale to the natives, not just the tourists. Prices seemed to me to be on a par with Paris. This is just one sign of the French policy which maintains that the French Antilles are part of mainland France, separated merely by 5000 miles of sea.

Any visitor can live here in the same way as the natives and find everything he wants. I do know French people who regard the islands as expensive, but they make a point of living as tourists. For me, the standard of living in the French Antilles, and particularly in Guadeloupe, was the highspot of the trip.

The people: Travel writers like to describe the people of the French Antilles as 'typically Gallic', but this just isn't true. I found them charming. Always happy to talk to you, never asking for anything. They give accurate directions and are noticeably courteous and friendly in the shops. Their warmth is more typical of the Caribbean than of France.

Language: Officially French, which everyone speaks. But in everyday conversation Creole is used, as in Haiti.

Accommodation: In general, cheap accommodation may be difficult to find in the French Antilles. The guest house system is a little different to elsewhere in the Caribbean. As in France itself, it operates on a less formal footing and it is quite normal for travellers to be put up with a local family.

Food and drink: This (and the people) is what makes the French Antilles so pleasant. So many of the Caribbean islands are without staple items of the European diet that I had begun to hunger for necessities that I take for granted at home. I had become tired of explaining what milk was — that it came from cows and not tins.

Here fresh *lait* is always available. I have already mentioned the easy availability of the world's best food and drink in supermarkets, stores and markets, and it goes without saying that there are also many superb restaurants. French and Creole dishes are featured most strongly, but you will also find touches of Africa and Asia.

Some of the best known and most representative Creole dishes are accras (cod fritters), stuffed crabs and ouassous (crawfish). But perhaps it is the use of the indigenous vegetables which most characterizes the Creole cuisine — taro (Caribbean cauliflower), sweet potato, chow-chow (potato), red bean and berengene (egg plant).

Here is a recipe for Creole punch: one-fifth sugarcane syrup, four-fifths white rum, ice cubes and lemon peel. Don't drink it all at once.

SAINT-MARTIN/SINT MAARTEN

This small island is a free port with three languages (French, Dutch and English), three currencies (French franc, Dutch guilder and American dollar) and two political affiliations. In 1648 the Dutch and French, tired of fighting over supremacy for the island, decided

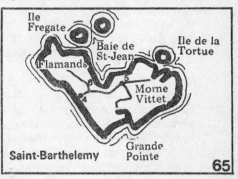

Saint Martin and Saint-Barthelemy: Key

Saint Martin/Sint Maarten	*Saint-Barthelemy*
1 Marigot	4 Gustavia
2 Philipsbourg	5 Marigot
3 Airport	6 Airport

on partition as a means of sharing control. The border was drawn in an unusual way: a Frenchman and a Dutchman set off to walk in opposite directions round the island. A line was then drawn from the point at which they met to the starting point. The Frenchman either walked faster or cheated, as the French part of the island is larger than the Dutch.

The International Airport and salt lakes are situated in the Dutch part of Sint Maarten, the capital of which is Philipsburg. There is complete freedom of movement between the Dutch and French areas, with no border controls.

Marigot on the northern coast is the most important French town. Cruising yachts and vessels from other, non-French islands call in here to stock up with French wines, cheeses, other gallic luxuries and duty-free items. There is some trade between Saint-Martin and Anguilla (a few miles to the north) and this is the normal transit point for Anguillan-bound travellers.

All the listed accommodation is expensive here. Your best bet is to stay with a local family — try asking at the airport, in Philipsburg or in Marigot.

SAINT-BARTHELEMY

The island is known as 'The Normandy of the Tropics'. The population of 2,200 is almost entirely descended from Normans who arrived in the latter part of the seventeenth century. The traditional dress of Normandy is still worn, and the customs and traditions of the homeland still adhered to. There is one town, Gustavia, which has the usual shopping facilities to be found in the French Caribbean.

Saint-Barthelemy is ten minutes away from Saint-Martin by air, and an hour's flight from Pointe-a-Pitre, Guadeloupe. There are no excise duties or taxes here.

Again, cheap accommodation may be difficult to find. Of that listed, *Le P' tit Morne* is the most reasonable at 150 French francs for a double. Staying with a local family is probably the best idea.

GUADELOUPE

The land of milk and honey. Literally.

Guadeloupe is really two islands, Grande-Terre and Basse-Terre, separated by a narrow channel, the Rivière Salée (Salt River). The Tourist Office were very anxious to point out to me that the terms Grande-Terre and Basse-Terre should not be translated literally; Grande-Terre means Windward, and Basse-Terre Leeward.

These two parts of Guadeloupe are roughly equal in area, but quite different in character and topography. Whilst Basse-Terre is quite mountainous, containing the volcano of Soufrière in the national park, Grande-Terre is flat with chalky soil and most of the agriculture.

The commercial capital of Guadeloupe is in Grande-Terre. This is Pointe-à-Pitre, the largest town (the population is either 50,000 or 82,500, depending which information source you prefer — the latter is the official figure). Its commercial importance is such that much of its Caribbean flavour has been lost. Now the town is proud of its bustling port, shopping arcades, modern buildings and important international airport. The most noticeable characteristic, clearly distinguished from the descending aircraft, is the spread of medium-rise housing developments. Ostensibly these are a benefit as they provide decent housing for the poor. Perhaps they damage the community spirit, as has proved the case in Europe and North

America; they certainly destroy any character the town may have had. Some side streets near the centre of town, and Place du Victoire, have a little character. Otherwise Pointe-à-Pitre is grey, soulless, overtly and materially French yet without the spirit of France.

Travelling southeast from Pointe-à-Pitre you quickly come to the village of Gosier. It is in this area that most of the plush hotels, restaurants and nightclubs are situated. Continuing along this coast road you pass the villages of Sainte-Anne and Saint-Francois, not to mention miles of superb, empty beaches. Unless you prefer not to pass empty beaches. If you take the road northwest from Saint-Francois you will come to Moule, now renowned for a splendid beach, but before its destruction by tidal wave in 1928 the main harbour of Guadeloupe. There is a good road across the island which connects Moule with Pointe-à-Pitre.

The mountains of Basse-Terre can be seen clearly from Pointe-à-Pitre, as the distance over the bay is not great. An iron bridge spans La Rivière Salée and the road then continues down the coast of Basse-Terre towards the capital, also called Basse-Terre. Perhaps the greatest point of interest on the way to the capital is the site of

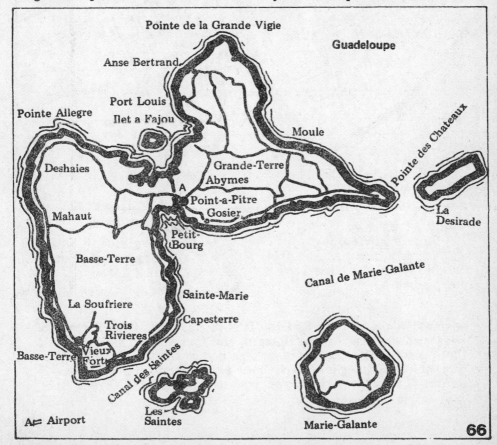

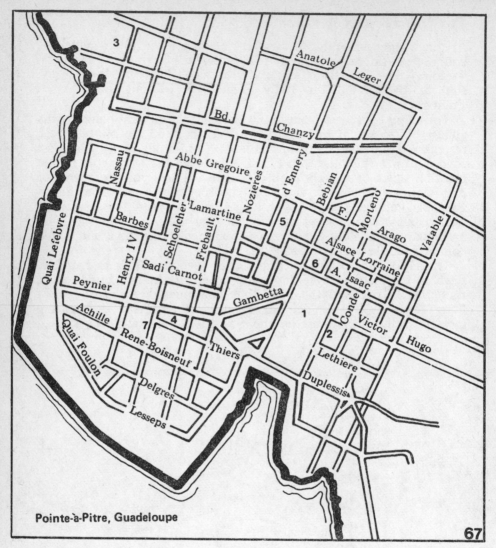

Labels on map: 3, Anatole, Leger, Bd., Chanzy, Abbe Gregoire, Nassau, Nozieres, d'Ennery, Bebian, F., Moreno, Arago, Vatable, Lamartine, Schoelcher, Frebault, 5, Barbes, Alsace Lorraine, Henry IV, Sadi Carnot, 6, A. Isaac, Peynier, Conde, Victor, Gambetta, 1, Achille, Hugo, Quai Lefebvre, Quai Foulon, Rene-Boisneuf, 7, 4, Thiers, 2, Lethiere, Delgres, Duplessis, Lesseps

Pointe-à-Pitre, Guadeloupe

67

Pointe-à-Pitre: Key
1 Place de la Victoire
2 Tourist office
3 Bus station for Basse-Terre
4 Market
5 Cathedral
6 Mogador restaurant
7 Chick Kebab

engraved rocks at Trois Rivières. It is thought that these engravings were made by the Arawak Indians, the first known inhabitants of these islands. They are set in an area rich in the foliage and vegetation which is thought to have been important to the Arawaks and Caribs. On the way there you will have passed the Carbet Falls,

218

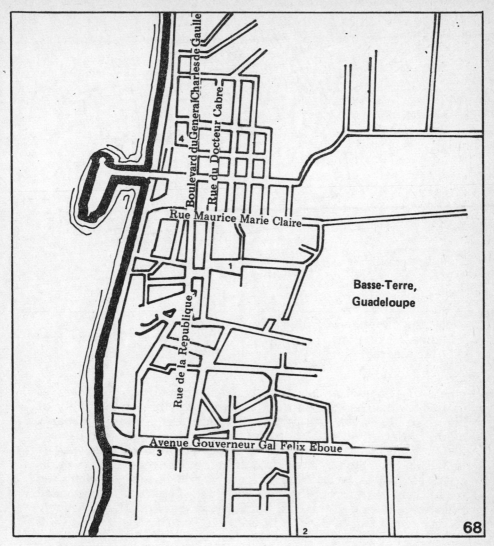

Boulevard du General Charles de Gaulle

Rue du Docteur Cabre

Rue Maurice Marie Claire

Basse-Terre,
Guadeloupe

Rue de la République

Avenue Gouverneur Gal Felix Eboue

68

Basse-Terre: Key
1 Cathedral
2 Prefecture
3 Palais de Justice (court house)
4 Hotel de Ville

waterfalls which require some walking to reach but are worth the effort.

The capital, Basse-Terre, has a population of 38,000 (official figure). It has retained much of its charm, being a small town with narrow streets lined with balconied houses. Its position at the foot of the 'dormant' volcano of Soufrière makes it susceptible to eventual catastrophe.

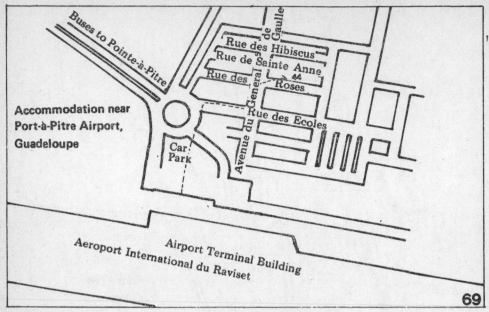

Accommodation near
Port-à-Pitre Airport,
Guadeloupe

Buses to Pointe-à-Pitre

Rue des Hibiscus
Rue de Sainte Anne
Rue des Roses
Rue des Ecoles
Avenue du Général de Gaulle

Car Park

Airport Terminal Building
Aeroport International du Raviset

69

Accommodation, near Pointe-à-Pitre Airport: Key

1 Bread/cake shop
2 Supermarket

44 Rue des Roses: Mr Renault's
    house

All of the written material I collected refers to Soufrière as 'dormant', one booklet on the National Park stressing the safety of hiking to the crater. All of this literature was obviously prepared before the eruption of 1976 which threatened to cause great damage and loss of life. In the event, no full-scale eruption developed (I understand the molten lava found an outlet elsewhere in the world's crust) so that as far as I am aware it is still possible to climb the mount and hike across the National Park. There are colour-coded trails to assist you in this end. If this is a serious intention, I strongly recommend a visit to the Tourist Office in Place du Victoire who will be pleased to give you information on how best to accomplish the hike.

Climate: Around the coast the average temperature is between 72°F and 86°F (22-30°C). It is a little lower in the mountainous interior of Basse-Terre (where the National Park is situated), at 66-81°F (19-27°C).

Transportation: There are buses into Point-à-Pitre from the airport, with a fare of francs 1.40. Pay the driver on entering. There are two routes: number 1 which is fairly direct, and number 2 which takes the 'scenic' route. From Point-à-Pitre there are buses around both islands. See map for the location of bus stations. The buses are plentiful and modern, although perhaps the most expensive in the Caribbean — sample fare: Pointe-à-Pitre to Basse-Terre, the capital,

220

10 francs.

Accommodation

Name	Address	Price per room
Monsieur Renault	44 Rue de Roses, near airport	EP: S 35 francs; D 50 francs.
Relais de la Grande Soufrière	Saint-Claude, Soufriere, Basse-terre (Tel: 81-41-27)	EP: S 65 francs; D 75 francs.
Le Flamboyant	Gosier, Grande-Terre (Tel: 84-14-41)	CP: S 50 francs, D 60 francs.
Le Barracuda	Bananier, Basse-Terre (Tel: 86-32-56)	EP: S 40 francs; D 70 francs.
Le Rejeton	Le Moule, Grande-Terre (Tel: 84-50-92)	EP: S 50 francs; D 60 francs.
Luna Park	Pointe-à-Pitre, Grande-Terre (Tel: 82-13-34)	CP: S 55 francs; D 75 francs.
Schoelcher	Pointe-à-Pitre, Grande-Terre (Tel: 82-13-12)	CP: S 56 francs; D 70 francs.
Relaxe	Basse-Terre, Basse-Terre (Tel: 81-10-00)	S 40 to 80 francs; D 50 to 90 francs.
Hotel de Basse-Terre	Basse-Terre, Basse-Terre	EP: S 35 francs; D 40 francs.

If you intend to be in Guadeloupe for a fairly short time you may as well stay in or around Pointe-à-Pitre, as it is impossible to be more central. If on a very short stay you may prefer to be near the airport. In this case, Monsieur Renault is the man and 44 Rue des Roses the address, about 500 yards from the airport. The cost should be 35 francs single, 50 francs double. If he asks for more, negotiate. Mr. Renault is a taxi driver at the airport, so he may accost you there. He is a very friendly man, especially when you are about to give him money. This location is very convenient if you are leaving on an early flight, and very good for local shopping. Superb bread and pastries are available at a patisserie, and all other foods at a small supermarket.

MARTINIQUE

About 385 square miles in area, Martinique is roughly 50 miles long by 15 wide. Mountains and tropical forest in the north become fertile plains in the centre; the south is arid, cacti being the most prominent vegetation. The population is 320,000.

Martinique has all the attributes of the French Antilles — Creole cuisine, duty-free French goods — plus more than its fair share of history. The most memorable incident was the eruption of Mount Pelée in 1902. Up to then it overlooked the town of Saint-Pierre, known as the 'Little Paris of the West Indies', the cultural and economic capital of Martinique. The eruption had been forecast, as Mount Pelée had been smouldering for several days (there had even been a two-hour-long fall of ash). This was disregarded by the inhabitants due to the reassurances of the governor. At least one ship tried to leave but was refused permission.

At this time the population of and temporary visitors to Saint-Pierre numbered some 40,000. Of this number there were only two known survivors when, on May 8th, the side of Mount Pelée split from top to bottom and a huge jet of fire poured out over the town and bay. The steamer *Roddam*, which had tried to leave that day, had dropped only one anchor. Most of the crew were immediately roasted alive on deck whilst the others jumped into what must have been the boiling sea. Only the captain survived, badly burnt, and was able to struggle with his boat to Saint Lucia. The other survivor was a convict awaiting the death penalty in a solidly built dungeon. The thick walls ensured that when he was discovered four days later he had suffered only some burns and was able to walk the four miles home. Ruins of the church, theatre and some other buildings survive, and there is a museum (the 'Musée Volcanologique') which displays relics and photographs.

Climate: Temperatures are very much the same as in Guadeloupe, or indeed as elsewhere in the Caribbean. There is more rainfall in the high north, adequate rain in the fertile centre and very little rain in the deep south.

Transportation: As in Guadeloupe, there is a good road system and a regular and comprehensive bus system.

Accommodation

Name	Address	Price per room
Le Gommier	3 Rue Bertin, Fort-de-France. (Tel: 71-88-55)	EP: *S* from 55 francs. *D* from 75 francs.
Europe	Rue de la Liberte, Fort-de-France (Tel: 71-75-90)	CP: *S* from 50 francs; *D* from 80 francs.
Le Grillardin	9 Rue Redoute de Matouba, Fort-de-France. (Tel: 71-84-23)	CP: *S* 50 francs. *D* 70 francs. MAP: *S* 80 francs; *D* 130 francs.
Un Coin de Paris	54 Rue Lazare Carnot, Fort-de-France (Tel: 71-08-52)	CP: *S* 55 francs; *D* 80 francs. MAP: *S* 80 francs, *D* 130 francs.
Gallia	3 Rue de la Liberte, Fort-de-France (Tel: 71-53-23)	EP: *S* 38/54 francs; *D* 54/97 francs.
Au Reve Bleu	50 Rue Lazare Carnot, Fort-de-France	CP: *S* 50 francs; *D* 70 francs.
Montemar	7 miles from Fort-de-France on Route de Schoelcher at 'La Colline', Schoelcher. (Tel: 71-99-19)	EP: *S* 55 francs; *D* 75 francs. CP: *S* 70 francs; *D* 90 francs. MAP: *S* 90 francs; *D* 160 francs.
Delice de la Mer	Sainte-Luce	CP: *S* 50 francs; *D* 70 francs. MAP: *S* 70 francs; *D* 110 francs.
Les Alizes	Vauclin	EP: *S* 30/40 francs, *D* 35/45 francs. AP: *S* 75/85 francs, *D* 125 francs.
Chez Julot	Vauclin	EP: *S* 50 francs; *D* 60 francs. MAP: *S* 85 francs; *D* 130 francs.
Auberge de L'Atlantique	Vauclin (Tel: 74-40-36)	EP: *S* 45 francs; *D* 60 francs. MAP: *S* 75 francs; *D* 110 francs.
Courbaril Camping	Anse-a-l'ane (Tel: 76-32-30)	Tent: 15 francs; Chalet: 25/30 francs; Room: 40/50 francs.
Au Cocotier a Deux Tetes	Fonds-Lahaye, Schoelcher (Tel: 72-27-60)	CP: *S* 50/55 francs, *D* 60/70 francs.
Mont Pele Hotel	Morne-Rouge	EP: *S* 35 francs; *D* 40 francs. MAP: *S* 63 francs; *D* 96 francs.
Le Vieux Chalet	Morne-Rouge	MAP: *S* 45/114 francs; *D* 60/168 francs.

222

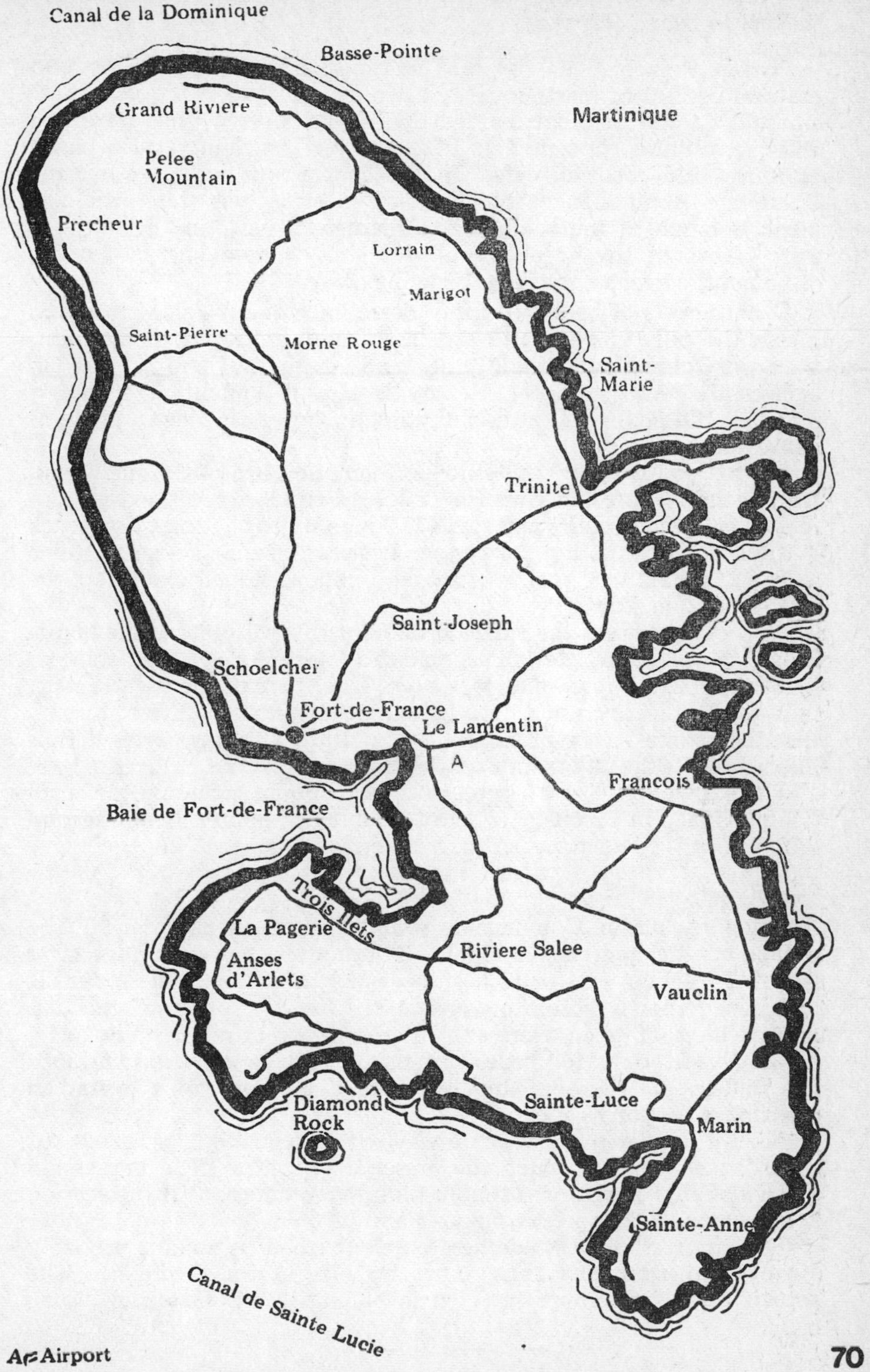

Canal de la Dominique

Basse-Pointe

Grand Riviere

Martinique

Pelee
Mountain

Precheur

Lorrain

Marigot

Saint-Pierre

Morne Rouge

Saint-
Marie

Trinite

Saint-Joseph

Schoelcher

Fort-de-France

Le Lamentin

A

Francois

Baie de Fort-de-France

Trois Ilets

La Pagerie

Riviere Salee

Anses
d'Arlets

Vauclin

Diamond
Rock

Sainte-Luce

Marin

Sainte-Anne

Canal de Sainte Lucie

A⊱Airport

70

Fort-de-France: This is the administrative, commercial and cultural capital of Martinique. A town of some 96,000 people, it is situated on the bay, surrounded by foliage-covered hills. Here you will see, on the opposite side of town to Fort Saint Louis, pastel buildings and roadside cafes. In the centre is a park, the Savane. There are a number of buildings of interest, yet the town also displays much of the soulless architecture to be found in Pointe-à-Pitre. Most of the hotels seem to be in or near Fort-de-France, although the beaches are some distance away.

Other Points of Interest: Saint-Pierre and Mount Pelée are by no means the only places worth a visit. Vauclin, on the southeast coast, is a pre-Columbian fishing port and market. There is also an eighteenth century chapel. Nearby is Mount Vauclin, the highest point in the south of the island, which affords fine views as far as Saint Lucia.

On the south coast, opposite Daimant Beach, is Diamond Rock. During the Napoleonic Wars (in 1804) a British expeditionary force loaded cannon, supplies and some 110 men on to the top of this rock and held it, obstructing the passage between it and the island, for a year and a half. The rock was actually commissioned as a sloop, the HMS *Diamond Rock*.

Also of interest is the small settlement of Trois-Ilets where Marie-Joseph Rose Tasher de la Pagerie, who later married Napoleon and became Empress Josephine, was born. The ruins of the Pagerie sugar mill and the local church have been partially restored. The Museum here has some items of interest to culture vultures. Trois-Ilets is inland, across the bay from Fort-de-France.

There is much else of interest in Martinique, including the small fishing village of Precheur, where Madame de Maintenon, the second wife of Louis XIV, spent part of her youth.

DOMINICA

Arriving by air in Dominica is something of an experience. The aspect of the approaching island is mountainous, with ridge after ridge of hills covered in lush and seemingly impenetrable forest. It had rained shortly before my arrival, so that the foliage glistened in myriad hues of green. Here and there a ruddy brown muddy track, seemingly fit only for pedestrian use, could be seen winding into the wilderness. Where, in this topography, we were going to find an airstrip was anyone's guess.

Then it appeared below, a runway with a few buildings carved out of a landscape very much the preserve of nature. The impression given was that nature was simply biding her time; a little neglect on man's part and the forest would reclaim its own.

This impression of wilderness barely curbed by man is probably stronger in Dominica than anywhere else in the Caribbean. The tourist board is perhaps justified in calling it the 'Getaway Place'.

224

Dominica

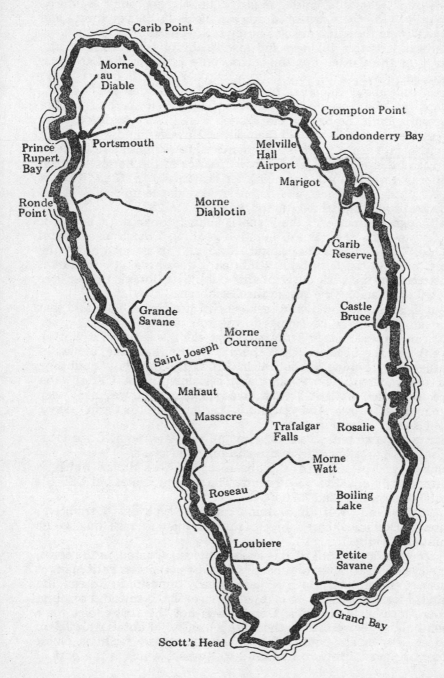

Carib Point

Morne
au
Diable

Crompton Point

Londonderry Bay

Prince
Rupert
Bay

Portsmouth

Melville
Hall
Airport

Marigot

Ronde
Point

Morne
Diablotin

Carib
Reserve

Castle
Bruce

Grande
Savane

Morne
Couronne

Saint Joseph

Mahaut

Massacre

Trafalgar
Falls

Rosalie

Morne
Watt

Roseau

Boiling
Lake

Loubiere

Petite
Savane

Grand Bay

Scott's Head

71

The island is dominated by this heavily wooded mountain range which runs along its entire length. The highest point is Morne Diablotin (4750 feet), whilst Morne au Diable in the very north and Morne Watt in the south are also noteworthy peaks.

Perhaps it is this wildness and inaccessibility which ensured the survival of the Caribs. For this is the only island in the Caribbean which has a substantial Carib population. Some 7000 have Carib blood, while about 400 are of predominantly Carib descent.

Back in the seventeenth century, and even as late as the eighteenth, both the British and French were unable to dislodge the Caribs or even gain a foothold themselves. However, midway through the eighteenth century the French managed to establish a settlement. The island then changed hands once or twice in the normal Eastern Caribbean fashion until becoming British finally in 1782. Thus it stayed until the island was given independence in 1967 as an associated state. It attained full independence in 1978.

Although the name of the island is actually Spanish (it is one of the few to keep the name Columbus gave it), French place names abound. This includes the capital, Roseau. This is not one of the finest towns in the Caribbean, although it does have a good market (illustrated on the back cover of this book). Its Botanic Gardens are reputed to be among the best in the Caribbean.

But it is that splendid wild scenery which beckons. I am told that there are 365 rivers cascading down from the mountains. In the south are the spectacular Trafalgar Falls, sulphur springs (at Wotton Waven) and the beaches. Then there is the Boiling Lake, a mass of volatile and steaming water which throws up geysers periodically. And the apparently bottomless and certainly tranquil Freshwater Lake. It is said a Carib leader dived in here and was next seen swimming out at sea. And you should certainly see the Carib reserve, which is near the airport.

Entry requirements: Passports but no visas are required for most nationalities, together with return and onward tickets.

Currency: The Eastern Caribbean or BeeWee dollar which is approximately equal to US 40 cents. The rate fluctuates but US$1 is worth between 2.50 and 2.70 EC$.

Climate: You will find temperatures 'typically Caribbean', although Dominica has a higher rainfall than average due to its mountainous aspect.

Accommodation: All of the settlements are situated on the coast, fairly evenly distributed around the island's perimeter. Petit Marigot is nearest the airport, which is diametrically opposite to Roseau, the capital. Most of the hotels take advantage of the splendid scenery, and are located in the hills. Dominica is not the first choice for a beach holiday. Nevertheless, there are a handful of hotels situated on or near beaches and equipped with the appropriate facilities. Guest houses are most likely to be found in Roseau, which is the port of call for the banana boats, and perhaps Petit Marigot. You can expect prices to be reasonable. Enquire at the airport or, if you have arrived by banana boat, down by the water-front in Roseau.

SAINT LUCIA

Saint Lucia has to be the most beautiful island. It has a natural beauty which explains why the British and French fought so long over it. Of volcanic origin, not only is it mountainous — as indeed are the other islands formed by this means — but it can truly be described as spectacular. Along the coast mountains push steeply up from the sea, yet still leave room for nearby beaches of great natural beauty. I also found most of these deserted.

The best known peaks are Les Pitons, illustrated on the cover of this book. They are two extinct volcanic cones which rise precipitously from the sea, guarding Soufrière, a dormant yet bubbling volcano. This is known as 'the drive-in volcano' due to its ease of access. Although full of bubbling sulphur springs and continually emitting steam, I was assured by everybody that it was unlikely to erupt. That's what they were saying about Soufrière in Guadeloupe until 1976.

The mountainous interior, particularly around and south of Castries is thickly covered with lush vegetation, much of which is cultivated. Saint Lucia has a great deal of rain, usually brief yet heavy showers which cascade down whilst the sun continues to shine. If it didn't have so much else to choose from, Saint Lucia's national symbol could be the rainbow!

Although Saint Lucia and her people have a distinct character which is all their own, one aspect surprised me — minor similarities with Haiti. First I noticed the houses in Castries. Many of the old ones, at the back of town on or near Brazil Street, are adorned with latticework, balconies and other points of the architecture very reminiscent of the old houses in Port-au-Prince. I attribute this to Saint Lucia's finally becoming British at about the same time that Haiti achieved independence. As both are poor countries many of the old houses of this style remain in each.

The next obvious similarity is in the form of transport. They have 'tap-taps' here! Both the small, Japanese pick-up trucks converted to a local publique service, and also the large, long-distance trucks with wooden coachwork and bench seating. The craftsmanship is much cruder here than in Haiti, and the decoration shabbier and less ornate, but the basic idea is the same.

The third similarity is in the language. English is the official language, and all but some of the old country folk speak it. But the real national language, called 'Broken French' by the people, is very close to creole.

Saint Lucia is an ideal tourist island because of its amazing and varied natural beauty, lack of large towns and relatively few tourists.

There are less hotels and guest houses here than on other island, which means that all the beaches are uncrowded. A wide range of accommodation is to be found here, normally at prices which represent good value.

The only problem is transport. The local trucks and buses mentioned above usually either operate at inconvenient times or travel short distances; and as they are intended as transport for the locals, they will not be headed for sights of natural beauty which you may wish to see. Thus on my first trip to the island I spent some time hitch-hiking, which is not recommended, as there is little traffic and, again, local traffic is not likely to be headed for tourist sights. On my second trip I hired a little 'fun bike' with a 50 c c engine for about EC\$30 a day: I had this for a week and found the mobility it afforded well worth the money. The 'fun-bike' is a particularly good investment for a couple, although those unused to motorcycling and wary of Saint Lucia's generally atrocious roads may prefer a Toyota jeep which is the only practical solution for groups of three or more. These motorbikes and cars can be hired at the reception desks of the larger hotels. Be sure to take your domestic driving licence.

Saint Lucia has one good road running from north to south. From Pigeon Point (once an island but now joined to the mainland by a causeway) to Castries the road is entirely satisfactory; coming out of the town and travelling south the road twists steeply up the Morne, then runs downhill for a little way before crossing over to the eastern side of the island; it then runs along the coast, continually ascending, descending and curving through the lush vegetation bordering the rain forest until it reaches the jet airport at Vieux Fort. On the route empty beaches pounded by the Atlantic breakers can be glimpsed. It should be noted that although Saint Lucia is only some 24 miles in length, the journey from Castries to Vieux Fort is about 40 miles. Unless you are crazy (like me) motorcycling at night is not advisable as even this good road is not without its share of potholes and roadworks.

The other road between Castries and Vieux Fort is slower, in a far worse state of repair and consequently more hazardous. You will want to use it however as many of the places worth visiting are on or near it. I rode up from Vieux Fort to Soufrière during a day of heavy showers with a local (who was acting as my guide) on the back. Many of the views are astounding, even in the rain, and Soufrière volcano itself is well interesting. Normally these Sulpher Springs emit strong smelling fumes with their steam, but I was saved the worst of this due to the heavy rain. Also there was no sign of the young people and 'guides' who usually hang around there, selling native handicrafts and leading tourists along the safe route. Just south of the Sulpher Springs are the Pitons which are breath-takingly spectacular; and along the coast are fishing villages and banana plantations which are as culturally relevant as anything in the tourist guides. Continuing north to Castries you visit Marigot Bay, certainly one of the prettiest natural harbours in the Caribbean, and where 'Doctor Doolittle' was filmed.

Customs and Immigration: Saint Lucia has two international airports, Vigie at Castries in the north, where the LIAT inter-island and other small planes are handled, and Hewanorra near Vieux Fort at the opposite end of the island. It is here that the big jets from the USA, Canada and London land.

Vigie airport is cute. From the plane you go into a small building where your onward and return air tickets and documents are checked. Then you observe your baggage being brought from the plane by methods the Wright brothers must have used. You will see one or two chaps hemmed into a corner by a low counter. You should place your luggage on this, as those chaps are customs officers.

That done, you pass an information desk with useful brochures (ask for the map, which also includes details of all the available accommodation with few exceptions. The prices are often wrong however). To take a taxi, call at the desk established for this purpose. There you will be given a ticket marked with the price you should pay — about EC$4 from the airport to Castries.

Hewanorra, the jet airport near Vieux Fort, has little traffic. Although occasional light planes are handled here (usually charters) the airport was built to receive the intercontinental jets. Compared with Barbados however, there are few of these: BWIA and Eastern fly in from Miami and other Caribbean islands, British Airways from London, the Pegasus charter from Luton and, I believe, there are charter flights from Germany. Consequently the modern terminal facilities cope well with arrivals and departures although some days you can visit the airport and find it almost deserted!

Currency: The Eastern Caribbean dollar. US$1 = EC$2.50/2.70 approximately.

Cost of living: Saint Lucia has to be one of the cheapest countries in the Caribbean. The people are not as poor as in Haiti, so it is more expensive for the natives; but it is far easier for the traveller to live as the natives do. Bottled sodas are as cheap as 30 cents BeeWee, Sandwiches from 35 cents up. Grocery stores and local 'snackettes' are not well-stocked, particularly as regards fresh food, but prices are reasonable. Of course prices will be much higher in tourist-oriented shops, restaurants and areas.

Accommodation: Please note that guest houses and other native-style hotels prefer to be paid in EC dollars, whilst tourist hotels usually prefer to receive US dollars. Prices given below are for the summer season, April 15 to December 15. Winter prices charged by the hotels will be at least 50% higher, although some of the guest houses will charge the same tarriff in the winter.

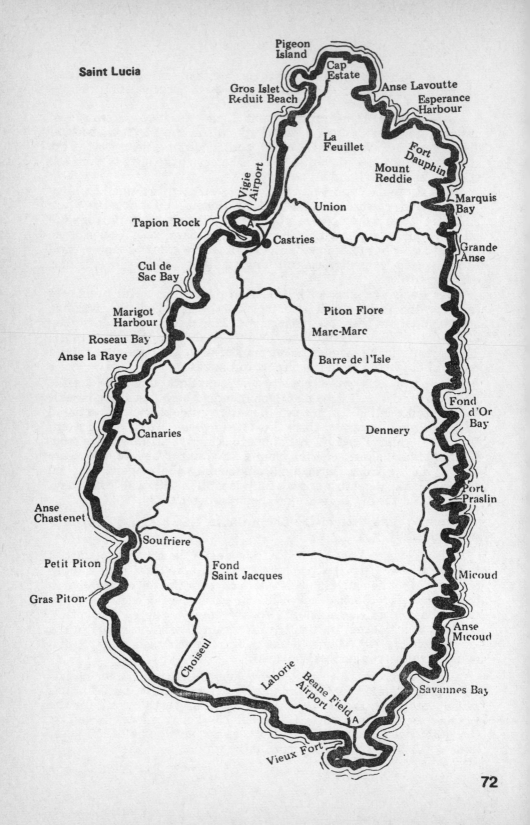

Saint Lucia

Pigeon Island

Cap Estate

Gros Islet
Reduit Beach

Anse Lavoutte

Esperance Harbour

La Feuillet

Fort Dauphin

Mount Reddie

Marquis Bay

Tapion Rock

Vigie Airport

A

Union

Castries

Grande Anse

Cul de Sac Bay

Piton Flore

Marigot Harbour

Marc-Marc

Roseau Bay

Barre de l'Isle

Anse la Raye

Fond d'Or Bay

Canaries

Dennery

Port Praslin

Anse Chastenet

Soufriere

Petit Piton

Fond Saint Jacques

Micoud

Gras Piton

Anse Micoud

Choiseul

Laborie

Beane Field Airport

A

Savannes Bay

Vieux Fort

72

Part 4: The Eastern Caribbean

Name	Address	Price per room in US$
Guest Houses		
Planters Inn	Brazil Street, Castries	EP: $8 per person; CP: $13 per person; MAP: $13 per person.
Boots Guest House	36 Micoud Street, Castries	EP: $7/$12 per person; CP: $10/$15 per person; MAP: $15/$20 per person.
La Dainty Guest House	29 Brazil Street, Castries	EP: S $9.50, D $16; CP: S $12, D $21; MAP: S $15, D $27.
Tropical Haven (mini hotel)	La Toc	EP: S $10; D $14; CP: S $12; $18; MAP: S $18; D $30.
Mathews Guest House	13 High Street, Castries	MAP: S $ 11 per person.
Elwins Guest House	Chaussee and Morne du Don Roads, Castries	EP: $7 per person; CP: $9 per person; MAP: $13 per person.
Twin Palm Inn	Victoria Road, Morne Fortune	EP: S $8, D $14; CP: S $11, D $20; MAP: S $20, D $40;
Sunset Lodge	58 Sans Soucis, Castries	EP: S $9, D $14; MAP: S $13, D $23.
Creole Inn	Vide Bouteille, Castries	EP: S $8, D $13; CP: S $10, D $16; $2 per person extra for room with bath.
Hippos Guest House	Soufrière	MAP: S $12, D $22.
Home Guest House	Soufrière	MAP: S $12.50, D $24.
Allains Guest House	Soufrière	MAP: S $12.50, D $24.
Small Hotels		
East Winds Inn	La Brolotte Bay	EP: S $28, D $35, T $43; MAP: S $44, D $67, T $91.
Edgewater Beach	Vide Bouteille, Castries	EP: D $26.
Villa Hotel	The Morne, Castries	EP: S $20, D $32
Hurricane Hole	Marigot Bay	EP: S $25, D $35
Clouds Nest	Vieux Fort	AP: $25 per person
Apartments and Villas		
Morne Fortune Apartments	Morne Fortune	EP: D $28/$36; Four persons $45.
Green Parrot Inn	The Morne	EP: S $30, D $45; MAP: S $50, D $85.
Villa Beach Cottages	Choc Beach	EP: S $22, D $28
La Toc Village	La Toc	EP: D $70/$110.
Dasheen	Soufrière	EP: D $45; Three or Four persons $65; Five or six persons $75.
Large Hotels		
Halcyon Beach Club	Choc Beach	EP: S $35, D $55. MAP: S $55, D $90.
Halcyon Sands	Vigie Beach	EP: S $23/$30, D $30/$40; MAP: S $65/$72.

| Saint Lucian | Reduit Beach, Gros Islet | EP: *S $33/$38, D $45/$50;*
MAP: *S $53/$58, D $85/$90.* |
| Halcyon Days
Hotel | Vieux Fort | EP: *S $27, D $35;*
MAP: *S $45, D $71* |

Castries, Saint Lucia

73

Castries: Key

1 LIAT office
2 Williams Guest House
3 La Dainty Guest House
4 Tourist office
5 British Airways office

6 Bank of Nova Scotia
7 Planters Inn
8 Boots Guest House
9 Police station
10 Columbus Square

All the guest houses I inspected, though quite different, are about equal in terms of value for money. Your choice may thus be influenced by their different characteristics. *Planters Inn* is small, homely and run by a British-born couple (I have had good reports back from readers of the first edition of this book); *Boots Guest House* is spick and span and tends towards the chintzy (the higher prices in the table above are for rooms with bathroom and air-conditionining); *La Dainty* is the most interesting architecturally, both outside and inside.

The problem generally with the guest houses in Saint Lucia is that few are on or near a beach. If you are not mobile this can be very inconvenient, yet even if you have transport the luxury of walking from your room to the beach without having to change is sometimes worth paying for. I was particularly impressed by *East Winds Inn*. Each 'room' is in reality a hexagonal cottage with kitchenette and a thatched umbrella on the patio. The restaurant is an open-sided pavilion at the beachside. Owner-manager Mrs Egerer, an American, is quite clearly conscientious and hardworking and the hotel efficiently run, yet an informal atmosphere prevails. *East Winds Inn* is about five miles north of Castries.

Another informal, and even smaller, beachside hotel is *Edgewater Beach*, about a mile north of Castries. Formerly apartments, *Edgewater Beach* now comprises six studios and a cottage (which is priced higher than the rates given above). Although lacking the ambience of *East Winds Inn*, it has the advantage of being closer to Castries. About halfway between *Edgewater Beach* and *East Winds Inn* are *Villa Beach Cottages*. Although in the same price range I would expect the value here to be inferior because on casual inspection the cottages looked rundown, and I was unable to find anyone to show me the interiors. However it should be noted that attached to these cottages is a Chinese restaurant which serves good lunches at truly excellent prices (there is a set menu with a wide selection available).

Under the same as *Villa Beach Cottages* is the *Villa Hotel* on the Morne. On my second visit it seemed to me somewhat tattier than the first time I had seen it. However, as a travel agent I have sent clients here who were overnighting in Saint Lucia, and they were all very happy with it. *Villa* is however a business hotel, being nowhere near a beach (although it has splendid views of Castries harbour).

The larger hotels are really for those on a package holiday. Firstly, because many of them feature sporting and leisure activities in the price (more suited to someone having a two week break than an island hopper) and secondly because they work out cheaper if booked as part of a package. In 1980 I spent a week at *Halcyon Days* as a guest of Pegasus and found that although it is 'like Butlins' it is excellent for that type of holiday. It is right on a beach with free transport to its aqua centre (on another beach), bar and restaurant service were excellent, and the food, though hardly native cuisine, quite acceptable. I found its nightlife rather a failure, but it is quite easy to visit the bar-clubs in Vieux Fort and there is a small bar-restaurant, the *Lobster Pot*, on the beach just outside the hotel gates. At the time of that visit there was also cottage accommodation at the *Lobster Pot*, but this part of Saint Lucia was badly hit by Hurricane Allen and these cottages, like the Bungalows at *Halcyon Days*, may have been badly damaged. If you want to stay in one of the larger hotels, and you are not following an extensive island hopping itinerary, you may find it better to book a Pegasus package. A good travel agent (see page 281) should be able to advise you.

Eating Out: There are a number of worthwhile restaurants in Saint Lucia, but, like the tourist sights and hotels, they are spread all round the island. Castries, of course, has the greatest concentration. *Rain* is probably the best known. A curious name, almost as though the island's relatively high rainfall is a tourist attraction in itself. *Rain* is situated in Brazil Street, in the same block as the LIAT office; so if you are experienceing LIAT trouble, and the queues are too long or the office shut, you could pop along to *Rain* for a light lunch. Besides local dishes you can get snacks such as hamburgers, and there is an interesting cocktail list with items such as 'The Reverand's Downfall' (it's a Pina Colada actually), you can sit inside or outside with water cascading by you. The restaurant with perhaps the highest reputation on the island for the excellence of its cuisine is the *Green Parrot*, up on the Morne. The *Coal Pot*, in Vigie Marina, besides being a restaurant, is the departure point for the *Rum Runner*, a facsimile of a pirate brigatine which makes day excursions down the coast.

In the Vieux Fort area *Clouds Nest Hotel* has a reputation for excellent local food with friendly fast service. There is even a restaurant out in the wilds of Soufriere — the *Still* — for those taking a day over their volcano excursion.

Travelling in Saint Lucia: It is essential that you travel around here. If you get up early enough you can make some day excursions, but for long trips you may need to overnight. The first point to remember, as already noted, is that there are two international airports. So you should plan your travel within the island according to your arrival and departure airports. If arriving by boat you will probably come to Castries or Marigot, although other marinas — such as Rodney's Harbour — are possible too.

If you arrive in Vieux Fort and travel north from there, get up early to take the truck bus. The cost is EC\$2.50 to Castries. This may take the new highway on the eastern side of the island, so take the opportunity of visiting the Pitons and Soufrière on a day trip before leaving the deep south. Alternatively you could overnight in the Soufrière area and continue north the next day.

I found the country areas and the small settlement life of Saint Lucia of very great interest. Bananas, the chief export, are more in evidence here than anywhere else in the Caribbean, and one can see the harvesting of them almost by accident. Wages are low, however, and unemployment high; the people are very poor.

SAINT VINCENT
Saint Vincent has a reputation for the friendliness of its people, although it is also rich in history, scenery and has some of the Caribbean's most fertile soil in its valleys.

The area is around 150 square miles and population in the region of 93,000. There is a volcano, Soufrière by name (surprise, surprise), which has caused trouble in the past. In 1902 it erupted one day before its namesake in Martinique, killing 2,000 people and ruining crops for some distance around. In 1971 it became active again, but although the area was evacuated there was, fortunately, no eruption. Both the activity and the evacuation were repeated in April 1979 and at the time of writing Soufrière is still simmering.

Saint Vincent shares, with Dominica, the distinction of being settled rather late by the Europeans due to the opposition of the indigenous Caribs. Thus it was not until 1773 that the British could claim to control the island, and then only because of a treaty with the Caribs. The French briefly occupied the island during the American Revolution. Then in 1795 they fostered a rebellion with the support of the slaves and Caribs.

The capital, Kingstown, is situated in a shallow bay surrounded by higher ground. Fine views of the Grenadines can be seen from here. Of some interest are the ruins of Fort Charlotte, Bay Street with its arcaded buildings and Saturday morning market, the 'Wedding Cake' Saint Mary's Church and Saint George's Cathedral. Soufrière, which is in the north, is perhaps the island's foremost attraction. A visit to the crater ridge is recommended. Looking inside you should see the cone of lava formed in 1971, surrounded by a lake of steaming water almost a mile in diameter.

Saint Vincent has not escaped the economic recession affecting the Caribbean and the rest of the world, and this has perpetuated unemployment among the young and general poverty. To articulate their resentment the more vocal young people have espoused the cult of Rastafarianism without understanding fully its meaning. Thus they talk excitedly about Jah, Ethiopia and Natty Dread as a form of protest rather than as a religion. On my first visit, I found the people less friendly than their reputation suggests, although on my second visit all signs of resentment appeared to have gone.

The economy is largely based on agriculture. Few tourists come here, largely because there is only a small airstrip served by LIAT and charter flights. The airport is thus not dissimilar to Castries in Saint Lucia, except that landing is more hazardous. The runway runs inland from the sea so that the aircraft approach low over the rocky coastline, whatever the wind direction, with the wheels a few feet above the water.

Entry Requirements: Visas are not normally required, though return air tickets and adequate funds are. Immigration and Customs officials are very courteous and there is a tourist information desk at the airport (but no bank). There is another tourist information office near the waterfront in Kingstown.

Currency: The Eastern Caribbean Dollar: US$1 = EC$2.70 approximately.

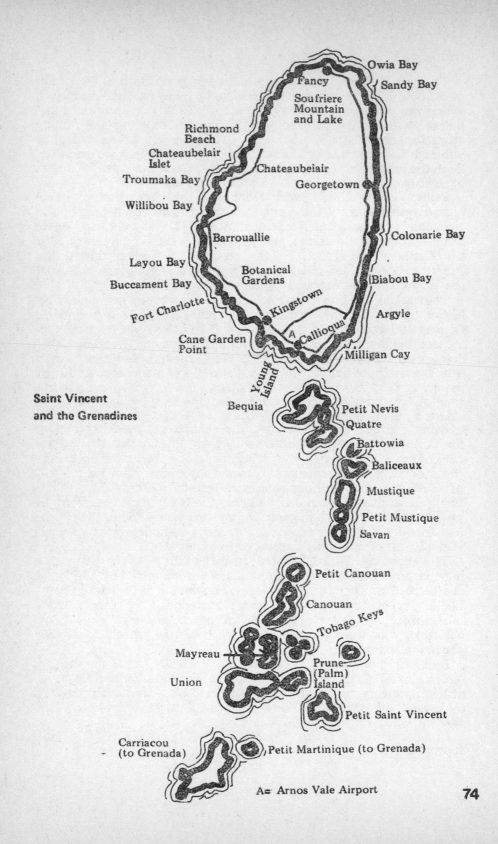

Owia Bay
Sandy Bay
Fancy
Soufriere
Mountain
and Lake
Richmond
Beach
Chateaubelair
Islet
Chateaubelair
Troumaka Bay
Georgetown
Willibou Bay
Colonarie Bay
Barrouallie
Layou Bay
Botanical
Gardens
Biabou Bay
Buccament Bay
Fort Charlotte
Kingstown
Cane Garden
Point
A
Callioqua
Argyle
Milligan Cay
Young
Island
Saint Vincent
and the Grenadines
Bequia
Petit Nevis
Quatre
Battowia
Baliceaux
Mustique
Petit Mustique
Savan
Petit Canouan
Canouan
Tobago Keys
Mayreau
Prune
(Palm)
Island
Union
Petit Saint Vincent
Carriacou
(to Grenada)
Petit Martinique (to Grenada)
A= Arnos Vale Airport

74

Accommodation

Name	Address	Price per room in US$
Coconut Beach Hotel	Indian Bay	EP: *S* $20, *D* $25, *T* $30; CP: *S* $24, *D* $33, *T* $42 MAP: *S* $32, *D* $50, *T* $66 (all year rates).
Cobblestone Inn	Kingstown	CP: *S* $20, *D* $30 (all year rates).
Haddon Hotel	Kingstown	EP: *S* $8/$11, *D* $11/$14; CP: *S* $10/$13, *D* $15/$18; MAP: *S* $14/$18, $25/$28.
Heron Hotel	Kingstown	MAP: *S* $18, *D* $33
Kingstown Park Guest House	Kingstown	MAP: *S* $10/$10/$15, *D* $20/$30
New Haven Hotel	Corner of Bay Street and Sharpe Street, Kingstown	CP: *S* $5/$10, *D* $10/$20; MAP: *S* $10/$25, *D* $20/$50.
Indian Bay Hotel	Indian Bay	EP: *S* $18, *D* $20; CP: *S* $20, *D* $28. MAP: *S* $27, *D* $44.
Olives Hotel	Saint George's Place,	CP: *S* $8, *D* $15.
Sea Breeze (Louisa Daize's)	Near Airport	EP: *S* $4, *D* $6.
Mariners Inn	Villa Beach	EP: *S* $25, *D* $35, $50; MAP: *S* $30, *D* $45, *T* $70.
Villa Lodge	Indian Bay	EP: *S* $25, *D* $30, $45; MAP: *S* $42, *D* $60, *T* $85.
Yvonette Apartments	Indian Bay	EP: *D* $18, Three or Four persons $30, Five or Six persons $45.

All of the above except for *Indian Bay Hotel, Mariners Inn, Villa Lodge* and *Yvonette Apartments*, are year round rates. Summer rates are given for these four; expect winter rates to be about 30% higher. Most of the cheaper establishments are patronised by West Indian businessmen and travellers, so there is little point in their charging seasonal rates. *Coconut Beach, Indian Bay* and *Mariners Inn* are all on the beach; *Villa Lodge* and *Yvonette Apartments* are both about 100 yards above the beach at opposite ends of Indian Bay (*Villa Lodge* has a swimming pool). *Coconut Beach* in particular offers excellent value for money. I have not stayed there, but I recently had breakfast on a whirlwind visit to Saint Vincent. The hotel is well run by Mrs Gelo, an American lady who has made her home here, and seems to attract a youngish clientele. The food is good, and the ambience provided by bamboo-clad walls and doors and an open dining area is exotic. Another spot where I managed a quick breakfast is the *Villa Lodge Hotel*. This well-run hotel, is owned and managed by Bobbie Brisbane, a native who is head of the hotels association. He has recently added a swimming pool to save his guests the hundred yard walk down to the beach. *Villa Lodge* affords superb views of Indian Bay and Young Island.

My favourite hotel is probably *Mariners Inn*, as its setting gives the best of both worlds; it is on the beach (at Villa) yet still has very pretty views of Young Island and the bay. Most of the hotel is open

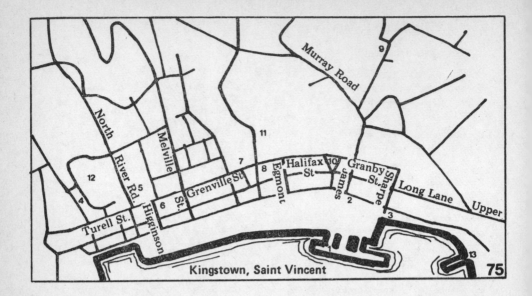

Kingstown, Saint Vincent

75

Kingstown: Key

1 Deep Water Wharf
2 Customs
3 Tourist board
4 Roman Catholic church
5 Anglican church
6 Methodist church
7 Court house
8 Police headquarters
9 Saint Vincent Craftsman Centre
10 Public library
11 Cable & Wireless
12 Victoria Park
13 Grenadine Pier

to the elements, and this, combined with the views and the trees, shrubs and flowers which thrive around it and within it, gives the feeling of being at one with nature. The *Haddon Hotel* is on the road into town from the airport. It can be seen from afar is it has its name blared in white paint across its red roof. The differences in price relate to the size of the room and whether it is air-conditioned or not. (This same yardstick should be applied to prices at the *New Haven*). The *Haddon Hotel* has twelve rooms, a good bar with large dance floor (there is sometimes a band on Saturday nights), friendly staff and a homely atmosphere.

The *Kingstown Park Guest House* is a century-old plantation house with 20 guest rooms. It is situated a little further from the airport and town. The *Heron Hotel* is a pink building of rather dilapidated appearance well situated on Bay Street. It is better inside than one would fear from first sight. The best point about the *New Haven Hotel* is its situation, near Grenadine Pier and the Tourist Office. This means only a short walk if you are taking a boat down the Grenadines. However, this same situation means that it can be noisy. It is shabby both outside and in and not well run, but if you insist on one of the cheaper rooms and have breakfast but not dinner, it must represent good value.

Transportation: Although it is theoretically possible to take a bus into town you will probably find it better to take a taxi. The fare is EC$5. There is no regular bus service, only the brightly painted truck-buses and converted pick-ups similar to those in Saint Lucia and Haiti. It is possible to take one of these buses to Georgetown for EC$3 or 4, but unfortunately it is not usually possible to return the same day.

THE GRENADINES
This string of islands running from Saint Vincent to Grenada is best visited by cruising yacht. To sail from Kingstown, Saint Vincent, to Grenada, calling in at the islands has to be one of the most visually beautiful experiences in the Caribbean. A stay on any or some of the islands will relax even the most stressed of city-dwellers' nervous systems, although landlubbers should note that the voyage can lose some of its romance if the weather is inclement.

Politically all but two of the inhabited islands are administered by Saint Vincent. Grenada looks after the interests of Carriacou and Petit Martinique. You can thus expect to leave Saint Vincent immigration at Union Island and enter Grenada's domain at the next major island, Carriacou.

Those who find themselves unable to get a ride by yacht will be pleased to note that there is a regular motor boat service, the M.V. *Seimstrand*, operating between Kingstown and Saint George's, Grenada. Here is the current schedule:

Mondays and Thursdays

Depart From	At
Kingstown, Saint Vincent	09.00
Port Elizabeth, Bequia	10.00
Mustique	11.30
Canouan	12.45
Mayreau	13.30
Union Island	14.30
Carriacou	16.00
Saint George's, Grenada	19.15 arrival

Tuesdays and Fridays

Depart From	At
Saint George's, Grenada	09.00
Carriacou	12.30
Union Island	13.30
Mayreau	13.45
Canouan	14.45
Port Elizabeth, Bequia	17.00
Kingstown, Saint Vincent	18.00 arrival

On Wednesdays and Saturdays the *Seimstrand* receives cargo in Kingstown. On Sundays there is an abbreviated service as far as Mustique via Bequia. This departs from Kingstown at 9 am and leaves Mustique for the return journey at 3.30 pm.

The above schedule is likely to alter as the government has acquired a new vessel, the *Grenadine Star* (known colloquially as the *Roll On*) which it operates in competition with the *Seimstrand*. This new vessel carries the mail.

The fare from Saint Vincent to Grenada or vice versa is EC$30. However, I boarded at Bequia and was still charged 30 dollars. There is a supplementary charge of 25 percent of the fare if you wish to travel on the lifeboat (sun) deck, and a 50 percent surcharge if you wish to travel in the Captain's saloon. Besides being a rip-off, this has the effect of segregating the tourists from the natives. The natives are thus largely confined to the stuffy main cabin, as standing on the foredeck is a very wet experience. I found the best place to be was at the stern where there is provision for perhaps eight people to sit or lie down.

In addition to the *Seimstrand*, there is a schooner service which operates daily between Kingstown and Bequia. It departs from Bequia at 6.30 am and leaves Kingstown for the return voyage at 1.30 pm every day except Saturday, when it leaves at 12.30 am. The voyage takes about 1¾ hours. *Friendship Rose* is the name of the schooner, which uses its engine to leave port but makes most of the trip under sail. The fare is EC$4 each way.

Both vessels depart from Grenadine Pier in Kingstown.

Accommodation:

Name	Address	Price per room in US$
Julie's Guest House	Port Elizabeth, Bequia	MAP: Old Building, summer: S $12, D $16; winter: S $16, D $20. New Building, summer: S $16, D $28; winter: S $20, D $32.
Frangipani Hotel	Port Elizabeth, Bequia	MAP: Old Rooms, summer: S $30, D $45; winter: S $40, D $50. New Rooms, summer: S $40, D $55; winter: S $55, D $70.
Crystal Sands	Canouan	MAP: winter: S $30, D $50 $5 per person less in summer.
Sunny Grenadines Guest House	Union Island	MAP: S $12, D $24 (year round rates)
Sunny Grenadines Beach Hotel	Union Island	CP: summer: S $17, D $28; winter: S $22, D $32; MAP: summer: S $23, D $40; winter: S $32, D $50.
Clifton Beach Hotel	Union Island	MAP: S $18, D $30 (year round rates)

The above is not a complete listing of accommodation in the Grenadines. Carriacou is excluded, because it is a dependency of Grenada and is therefore dealt with in the section on Grenada. I have also excluded two jet set paradises (Palm Island and Petit Saint Vincent) because they are not really suited to an island hopping itinerary; they are really designed for a two week get-away-from-it-all holiday. They are beautiful however, and if you are interested will cost you between $100 and $216 a day depending on the timing of your visit.

Bequia (pronounced Bekwee) is a tropical paradise of lush scenery, friendly local people and few tourists. The best word to describe it is 'charming'. Many, if not most, of the visitors come from the yachts that throng the splendid natural harbour of Port Elizabeth, particularly in the winter months. An island of perhaps some six square miles, it offers fine walks and good beaches. Here it is a pleasure, rather than an inconvenience, to walk to a beach.

My favourite place to stay here is *Julie's Guest House*. This is the best value accommodation I found anywhere in the Caribbean. There are now two buildings, the original which is tucked away behind trees and shrubs and the police station, and a new building which fronts on to the harbour about 50 yards from the jetty. The old building is exceptionally well designed to be both functional and pleasing in appearance and atmosphere. Natural wood is used throughout, and a balcony runs right around the building, preventing rain from entering the bedrooms as well as providing a nice cool place to sit. The design is such that air-conditioning is unnecessary. All of the ten rooms are well furnished with private facilities. The new building has been constructed in a completely different style. White-painted with 'antique' lamps from Barbados, the floors are tiled and here the balcony faces the sea (excellent for sunset photography). The water is heated by solar energy panels in the roof. Maybe I should mention that the owner is the island's foremost building contractor, and a man who would be a success at his trade anywhere in the world. Julie's wife, Isola, actually runs the guest house. The excellent meals are taken in the old building and standards of service cannot be faulted.

Frangipani is the other hotel in Bequia I would recommend. More of an inn than a hotel, it caters largely for the yachting fraternity who come ashore here to eat and drink and who can usually be found clustered around the bar in the evenings. The older rooms in the original wood frame building do not have private facilities, but the new stone-built rooms behind, each with balcony, are smashing.

The next island along, travelling southwards, is *Mustique*. This seems to be the favourite of Princess Margaret, but to the rest of us lacks reasonably priced accommodation, which is a pity, as from what I saw of Mustique from the Seimstrand it appeared to be the most beautiful island — gorgeous white sand beaches fringed by palms and scattered with a few brightly painted fishing boats. The sea was the most incredible shade of blue I have ever seen. There was no sign of habitation except on the rickety wooden pier. On my last trip I found that sometimes Seimstrand and Grenadine Star organise excursions (usually on Sundays) from Saint Vincent and Bequia to Mustique. So if you are in Bequia over a weekend you should have the opportunity to make a visit. Otherwise you may like to charter a yacht for a day. The going rate is generally US$150 for up to six people, and a barbecue lunch is often included.

Of some interest is the wreck of the '*Antilles*'. The waters around Mustique are shallower than those surrounding Bequia, and the '*Antilles*' was a French cruise liner which found out the hard way. Its rusting hulk can still be seen off Mustique's windward coast.

The other larger islands in Saint Vincent's sphere of influence are *Canouan*, *Union* and *Mayreau*. The first two have reasonably priced accommodation, and at the time of writing a development is currently being undertaken on Mayreau. Many of the very small islands are inhabited, and many hardly more than large rocks. Few maps have all the islands marked. *Union Island* is a major point of entry and departure for Saint Vincent. There is an airstrip (owned by the Anchorage yacht club and hotel) which handles small planes, mainly charter but also scheduled flights which stop between Saint Vincent and Grenada. Union could be quite a good base for a few days. From here you can easily visit the Tobago Cays, which is a coral reef considered to offer excellent snorkelling facilities. It is also from here that you would visit *Palm Island* and *Petit Saint Vincent*. Union itself is perhaps the driest island and not really worth a long stay alone.

Sunny Grenadines Guest House, above Mitchells hardware store, should not be confused with *Sunny Grenadines Beach Hotel*. Both are under the same ownership, but the former is primarily intended for locals travelling through the islands and the latter intended for tourists. When you leave the jetty, turn left, Mitchells store is a short walk on your right; more or less opposite, on your left, is the beach hotel. There are a small number of cottages on the (not very good) beach. The restaurant/bar is a pavilion.

GRENADA
Grenada has an area of 133 square miles and a population of 120,000. It is hilly and covered with lush vegetation, except in the south where the best beaches are. The scenery is generally described as 'unparalleled' and the state claims to be 'The Most Beautiful Island in the Caribbean'. This reputation is well founded: Grenada really is very beautiful, and the views are sometimes spectacular. The drive across the mountains from Pearls airport to the capital, Saint George's, is quite an experience. The road itself is narrow, winding and at times very steep (the buses and trucks are unable to use it) — a tar-macadamed switchback snaking through the lush greenery. Reaching the crown of a hill on the way into Saint George's you can look down and see the soft white body of Grand Anse Beach, basking in the sun. The mellowed bricks, red tiles and wrought-iron balconies of the Georgian-colonial buildings in town and around the careenage present some splendid man-made views.

242

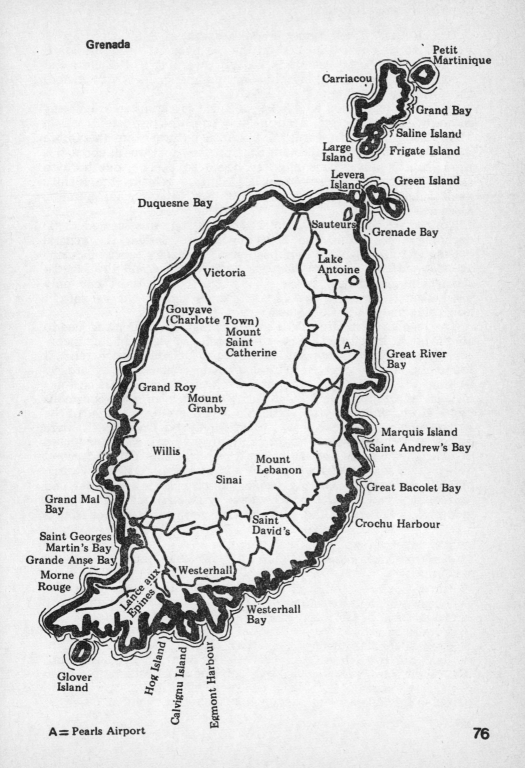

Grenada

Petit Martinique

Carriacou

Grand Bay

Saline Island

Large Island

Frigate Island

Levera Island

Green Island

Duquesne Bay

Sauteurs

Grenade Bay

Lake Antoine

Victoria

Gouyave (Charlotte Town)

Mount Saint Catherine

A

Great River Bay

Grand Roy

Mount Granby

Marquis Island

Saint Andrew's Bay

Willis

Mount Lebanon

Great Bacolet Bay

Sinai

Grand Mal Bay

Saint David's

Crochu Harbour

Saint Georges Martin's Bay

Grande Anse Bay

Morne Rouge

Westerhall

Lance aux Epines

Westerhall Bay

Glover Island

Hog Island

Calvignu Island

Egmont Harbour

A = Pearls Airport

76

Grand Anse Beach, about 4 miles south of Saint George's, is reputed to be one of the best in the Caribbean. This reputation is based largely on its size (it is broadly sweeping and shallow and excellent for swimming). It is thus very popular and less attractive to those seeking seclusion.

Grenada's reputation as the 'Isle of Spice' is attributed to its being the only spice-producing island in the western hemisphere. It was in 1843 that one Frank Gurney introduced nutmeg from the Dutch East Indies. It was an important development as it was at about this time that the sugar cane industry began to decline, due both to falling prices and emancipation. Agriculture remains the island's chief industry, the principal products now being cocoa, nutmegs, mace and bananas.

Tourism is the island's second industry, but this seemed to be declining even before the 1979 revolution. Besides the general decline of tourism in the Caribbean area, Grenada's tourist industry has also suffered as a result of its independence and the island's relative inaccessability. Pearls, the island's one airport can only handle small aircraft; a new airport, which can take bigger jets, is now being built (with Cuban assistance).

The revolution in Grenada is so recent that it is difficult for me to comment on it. Although I have heard tales of visitors being inconvenienced ("hassled" appears to be the usual descriptive term) I found that the People's Revolutionary Army behaved in an orderly fashion. On my first visit after the revolution I found that customs officials at Carriacou and Saint Georges were even more courteous than before, while the staff at the Tourist Board (on the edge of the harbour, where the road leaves town for Grand Anse Beach) were uniformly helpful. Departure formalities from Pearls were conducted in exactly the same way as before the revolution. On my second post-revolutionary visit I was closely questioned on arrival at Pearls; but this was only because my passport described me as a writer, and the country had suffered many untrue or exaggerated reports since independence. Perhaps the best view is given in this extract from a

Saint George's: Key

1	Government Handicraft Centre	11	Canadian Imperial Bank of Commerce
2	Turtle Back Restaurant	12	Post office
3	Nutmeg Bar and Restaurant	13	Barclays Bank International
4	Royal Bank of Canada	14	Rock Gardens Hotel
5	Tourist bureau	15	Hamilton Inn
6	Chase Manhattan Bank	16	Adams Guest House
7	Bank of Nova Scotia	17	To Saint Ann's Guest House
8	Botanic Gardens	18	Rudolf's Restaurant
9	Market square	19	LIAT office
10	Cable & Wireless	20	Pebbles Snack Bar

244

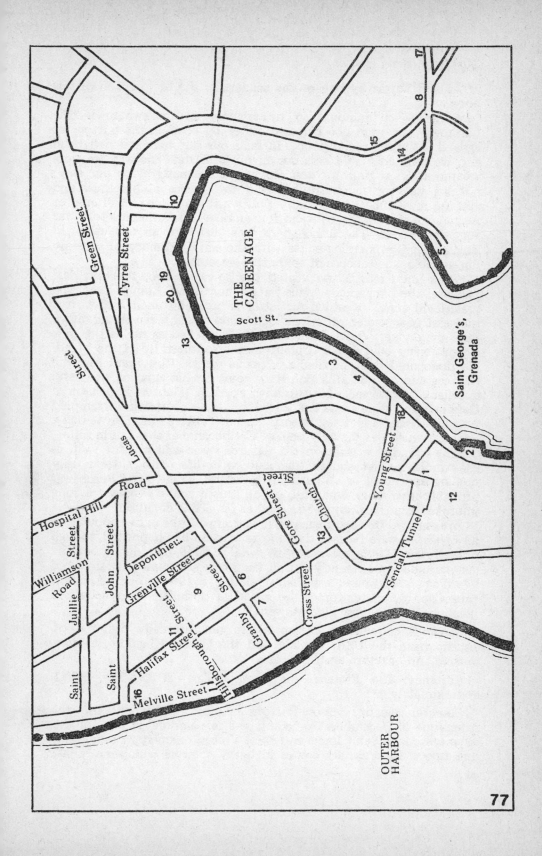

THE CAREENAGE

Saint George's, Grenada

Scott St.

Green Street

Tyrrel Street

Street

Lucas

Road

Hospital Hill

Williamson Road

Juillie Street

John Street

Deponthieu

Grenville Street

Halifax Street

Hillsborough

Granby Street

Street

Gore Street

Cross Street

Church Street

Young Street

Sendall Tunnel

Saint

Saint

Melville Street

OUTER HARBOUR

10

19
20

13

3
4

18

2

1

12

13

6

9

7

11

16

5

14
15

8

17

77

letter sent to me by one of the readers of the first edition of this book:

'Contrary to rumours in newspapers and elsewhere in the Caribbean, we were not harassed either by boats in the port as we arrived or by the island police. In fact, our stay here was delightful and we decided that it was our favourite island. The way we were treated at *Saint Anne's Guest House* set the pattern for our stay: nothing was too much trouble, and the service at breakfast and evening meal time was quaintly polite without being at all cold or formal, and mealtime conversation amongst the other visitors was very interesting. The atmosphere was just like an old-fashioned English seaside boarding-house with the warm intimacy of a family dining-table, and touches of colonial 'correctness'.

'While on Grenada, we visited the so-called zoo, the botanical gardens, the Annandale Falls, and the Grand Etang. Even the "restricted zone" in which the latter is situated was no real worry: the sight of a soldier with dreadlocks was somehow reassuring rather than unnerving! Views from the lake stretched as far as the new airport being built by the Cubans at the southern tip of the island. We discovered three particularly special places: Ross Point Inn, the Nutmeg and Pebbles Milk Bar. Ross Point Inn has amazing views and excellent food; a meal for two with aperitifs (Planters Punch and a Daiquiri) and wine costs less than £20. At the Nutmeg we sampled rum punch and a Nutmeg Special, and at Pebbles Milk Bar we had a 'Mavby' which was the only item of Caribbean diet that I didn't like.

'The crowded market on the Saturday was well worth a visit, as the whole market square throbbed with life, with buses noisily coming and going to all parts of the island. Grand Anse Beach was probably the most beautiful of all the beaches we saw: a long unbroken stretch of pure white sand as far as one could see.

'We enjoyed free and open conversation with the native population all of whom were pleased that the revolution had happened, though not all were 100% pleased with what Bishop had done; but the general mood was patently optimistic. There are banners, posters and hoardings everywhere, especially relating to the public education campaign, which reinforces the mood of optimism, buoyancy and idealism. We were very glad we went.'

Entry Requirements: Passports are not normally required of visitors from the USA, Canada and the United Kingdom, though onward and/or return air tickets are.

Currency: The Eastern Caribbean dollar. EC$2.70 = US$1 approximately.

Climate: The dry season is from January to May, and the wet from June to December. Grenada gets a fair amount of rain for the same reasons as Saint Lucia and Saint Vincent, namely its mountainous aspect. Rain usually comes in heavy showers which rarely last more than an hour or so and are usually welcome, as they relieve the heat, which can become oppressive in summer.

Temperature and Rainfall Chart

	January	February	March	April
Average Low	68°F 20°C	69°F 21°C	69°F 21°C	71°F 22°C
Average High	86°F 30°C	86°F 30°C	86°F 30°C	89°F 32°C
Average Rainfall (ins)	3	3	1	2
	May	June	July	August
Average Low	73°F 23°C	73°F 23°C	73°F 23°C	72°F 22°C
Average High	89°F 32°C	87°F 31°C	87°F 31°C	88°F 31°C
Average Rainfall (ins)	6	12	10	10
	September	October	November	December
Average Low	73°F 23°C	72°F 22°C	71°F 22°C	70°F 21°C
Average High	89°F 32°C	89°F 32°C	88°F 31°C	86°F 30°C
Average Rainfall (ins)	6	6	8	7

Food and Drink: In common with the other eastern Caribbean islands, and as you would expect, seafood is readily available. This, served with the abundant local vegetables and fruit, makes local food very good. Rum is the national drink of course; the Grenada rum punch has always been topped with nutmeg, a trend now copied throughout the islands.

I found *Rudolf's* bar and restaurant (on the corner of the Careenage and Young Street) a good place to eat. Prices are reasonable and the food very well prepared. Other local restaurants are the *Nutmeg* and the *Turtle Back* (both on the Careenage) and various *Pebbles* snack bars. Restaurants seem to be easier to find and of a higher standard than in many of the other islands.

The People: Although the people are poor, have recently been adversely affected by the economic recession, and unemployment is high, I found no trace of anti-tourist or anti-white feeling. I would go as far as to say that the people were the friendliest I had met in the Caribbean. At both points of entry to the country, Saint George's Docks and Pearls Airport, the air is filled with very good vibrations. One can walk at night through the seediest part of town knowing that one's safety is completely assured.

Accommodation: Grenada is quite well supplied with guest houses, although some have closed recently due to the reduction in the number of tourists.

Name	Address	Price per room in US$
Guest Houses		
Saint Ann's Guest House	Suburban Saint George's, on the road to Grand Anse Beach.	MAP: *S* $14, *D* $22 $1 more per person for bathroom.
Windward Sands Inn	Near Grand Anse Beach (on main road)	MAP: summer: *S* $26, *D* $35; winter: *S* $30, *D* $40.
Skyline Guest House	Near Grand Anse Beach	MAP: summer: *S* $15, *D* $28; winter: *S* $20, *D* $38.
Tita's Guest House	Overlooking the yacht lagoon	MAP: summer: *S* $14, *D* $18; winter: *S* $16, *D* $20.

Adams Guest House	Melville Street, Saint George's	EP: *S* $6, *D* $10.
Plainview Guest House	½ mile from Grenville, 2 miles from Pearls Airport	MAP: $12 per person
Sam's Inn	Close to Pearls Airport	MAP: $16 per person

Apartments and Cottages

Coral Cove Cottages	l'Anse aux Epines	EP: summer: 2 bedroom cottage $200 per week, 1 bedroom cottage $150 per week; winter: 2 bedroom $300 per week, 1 bedroom cottage $250 per week.
The Flamboyant	Grand Anse Beach	EP: summer: 2 bedroom cottage $50, 1 bedroom cottage $25; winter: 2 bedroom cottage $80, 1 bedroom cottage $40.
Riviera Beach Cottages	On Grand Anse Beach	EP: summer $25, winter $40.

Hotels

Secret Harbour	l'Anse aux Epines	MAP: summer: *S* $95, *D* $115, *T* $165; winter: *S* $155, *D* $175, *T* $240.
Horseshoe Bay	l'Anse aux Epines	MAP: summer: *S* $65, *D* $93; winter: *S* $106, *D* $144.
Ross Point Inn	Near Grand Anse Beach	MAP: summer: *S* $40, *D* $55; winter: *S* $60, *D* $75.

In the cases above where seasons are not mentioned the rates are year round.

Saint Ann's Guest House is perhaps the best place to stay in Saint George's. It is situated a little way out of town on the road to Grand Anse, about a quarter of a mile past the botanic gardens. Rooms are satisfactory, and the atmosphere and service are good. *Windward Sands Inn*, though more expensive, nevertheless represents good value, especially in the winter months. Here there are only three guest rooms, two of which are furnished with four poster beds (the other has two twin beds). All of these rooms have their own bathroom, attractively tiled and spacious. The owner-manager, Johnny Philips, has acquired a reputation as a restaurateur, and it is usual for his guests to be joined at dinner by visitors who are staying elsewhere. Wine is served with the evening meal. I have stayed here, and I am very happy to report that I found all meals delicious, service excellent, and Johnny a perfect host.

Adams Guest House offers the cheapest accommodation on the island, but it has quite obviously seen better days. Judging by the register it enjoys the patronage of a fair number of Europeans, but I am unable to recommend it, although I feel sympathetic towards the poor old lady who runs the place for she seems to have her hands full and perhaps hasn't the time or health to look after it properly. The *Plainview Guest House* is quite convenient if you are coming from or going to the airport. It is on the route from Saint George's to

Grenville so you can be dropped off at the door if you tell the driver. There are a number of interesting trips to be made in the area. It has a homely atmosphere and represents good value for money. *Sam's Inn* is the accommodation nearest to the airport, within walking distance unless you have much baggage. I stayed here one night as I had an early morning flight to catch, which meant I missed breakfast (no reduction on the MAP tariff). Evening meal had nothing particular to recommend it, and I found the place lacking in atmosphere (I think I was the only guest at the time), but the building is a fairly modern structure and all rooms have their own bathroom.

Apartments and cottages can provide a useful rest from continuously living out of a suitcase, but to make full use of them you need to stay at least a week and preferably more. Grenada is a perfect island for such a stay. If you are staying on or near Grand Anse Beach you will not need regular transport, but if you decide to stay at *Coral Cove Cottages* your own car is almost essential. *Coral Cove* is a fairly new development of two one-bedroom and two two-bedroom cottages set in isolation at l'Anse aux Epines. The cottages are set on a slight hill, thus gaining the benefit of the prevailing winds, above a white sand beach.

The off shore coral reef provides snorkelling opportunities and there is a saltwater swimming pool.

At one end of Grand Anse Beach (furthest from town), set into the hill, you will find *The Flamboyant*, which is a collection of one and two bedroom cottages scattered among flowering shrubs and trees. The walk to the beach can thus be as much as 75 yards, but the views are excellent. if you must be right on the beach then the *Riviera* is probably the best choice. The cottages here are really large studios, running back from the beach perhaps 60 yeards. *Riviera* was becoming a little dilapidated last time I saw it, but I believe money is being spent on improvements (new air-conditioning units etc) so it's certainly worth checking out.

It is very rarely that I get excited by a luxury hotel as genrally I have no need for the excellent standards of formal service one expects for the price, or the 'international cuisine', usually associated with such hotels, but Grenada has a luxury hotel which I regard as superb, namely *Secret Harbour*. Firstly the setting is exquisite: the cottages and public rooms are on the hillside overlooking a bay with two unspoilt headlands. Each suite has a very large bed-living room with two antique four poster beds, an Italian-tiled bathroom deservingly described as 'fabulous', and patio. They are designed to ensure privacy. The public lounge and bar reek with atmosphere, and there is of course a pool. a private beach, watersports, and all kinds of entertainment, I loved it.

Transportation: The basis of Grenada's transport system is the cheap truck buse, similar to that of Saint Vincent and Saint Lucia.

Slightly more expensive, and more comfortable, are the minibuses of various makes, which carry about sixteen passengers. Please note however that Sunday and evening services are few. An even greater degree of comfort can be found in shared taxis, which take up to six passengers. All the transport leaves from the market square in Saint George's (Halifax and Granby Streets — see map). The fare to Grenville by minibus or shared taxi is EC$3.50; truck bus is slightly cheaper. Normal taxi rates are EC$2 for the first mile and EC$1 thereafter.

Should you want to arrange an excursion or hire a car, you'll be pleased to know that Grenada has an excellent travel agency, Grenada Tours and Travel. They are located at Huggins Travel, on the corner of Young Street and the Careenage.

Carriacou (normally pronounced Karrykoo): Carriacou is the largest of the Grenadine islands with an area of 13 square miles. It is connected to Grenada by the boat service previously mentioned (see page 239) and by a daily Inter Island Air Services flight.

The population runs to about 7000. The people are mainly of African descent, though there is also a Scottish influence.

The 'capital' of Carriacou is the small town of Hillsborough, wherein the Parliamentary Secretary has his office. There is still a small cotton gin in the town too, though only a little cotton is grown. The main industries are boat-building, lime growing and processing, fishing and tourism. There isn't much of any of these.

Carriacou's relative inaccessibility renders it fine for studies of tropical sea birds and marine biology, both of which have remained free from pollution. And the oysters here 'grow on trees' (actually on mangrove roots).

Accommodation in Carriacou

Name	Address	Price per room in US$
Silver Beach Cottages	On the beach	EP: summer; S $18, D $25, T $32; winter: S $27, D $35, T $45.
Mermaid Inn	On the beach at Hillsborough	MAP: summer: S $28, D $45; winter: S $35, D $55.
Young Amigo Guest House	On the beach	CP: S $20, D $35; (year round rates)

Again, a 10 percent service charge and 5 percent tax will probably be added to all bills. The rates for the Efficiency Units (or House-keeping Units, as they call them) at Silver Beach include electricity, gas, linen, cutlery and crockery.

BARBADOS

I have described Trinidad and Tobago at the end of this book because of all the countries featured it is the closest to the South American mainland (in fact it is separated from Venezuela only by two narrow channels, the Dragon's Mouth and the Serpent's Mouth). But for very many of you Barbados will be the end of the trip; either you will go to Trinidad and Tobago from Grenada, and return northwards to Barbados, or you may omit Trinidad and Tobago altogether.

Barbados is a fitting end to the trip, both because of the excellent and often extremely cheap services Caribbean Airways provide from there to Britain and Luxembourg, and because the island has so much to offer in itself.

For a start, it is one of the most mature and civilized countries I have visited. Although tourism is one of its major industries (sugar, rum and sea island cotton being others) and it probably caters for more tourists each year than any other Caribbean island (except perhaps Puerto Rico and the US Virgin Islands), the level of tourist pollution is low. One area in particular — along the coast road/bus route from Maxwell to Hastings — is literally chock-a-block with hotels, guest houses, apartments, apartotels, shops restaurants, and banks. Yet the beaches are clean and uncrowded, even during peak season. And although this area and the capital, Bridgetown, see an enormous number of tourists every year, I found little of the animosity towards the tourist which can sometimes be seen in those who compare the tourist's apparent wealth with their own poverty.

This is of course due to the maturity, hospitality and easy-going nature of the people. Although I found people very friendly in most of the Caribbean countries I visited, for me the Bajans certainly lived up to their reputation as being the friendliest nation one could wish to visit.

Barbados is an ideal place to spend a week on a trip of this type. Many travellers bound for South America use Barbados as a cheap way of getting there. They often stay in Barbados longer than they intended, cutting short their South American travel plans in order to spend some more time in the Caribbean on their return.

Barbados is far larger in its reputation than in its actual size. It is 166 square miles in area, being 21 miles long by 14 wide at its broadest. One of the few Caribbean islands missed by Columbus, Barbados was actually discovered — in European terms — by a Portuguese gent by the name of Pedro a Campos who was on his way to Brazil. This was in 1536. He reputedly christened the island 'Los Barbados' after the bearded fig trees which grew there then. It was in 1627 that the first British settlers established a community at Holetown and claimed the island in the name of King James. From this date, right up to independence in 1966, Barbados remained British. British traditions are so strong (a love of cricket being perhaps the best example) that other Caribbean countries often allude to Barbados as 'Little England'. British place names abound: the hilly area is known as Scotland, whilst Barbados can also boast a Brighton, Windsor, Worthing, Hastings, Yorkshire and Whitehaven,

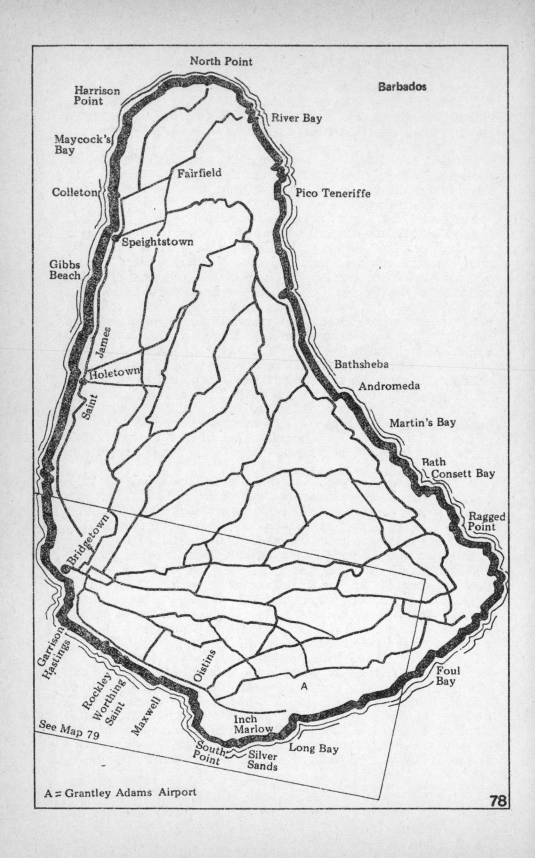

North Point

Barbados

Harrison
Point

River Bay

Maycock's
Bay

Fairfield

Pico Teneriffe

Colleton

Speightstown

Gibbs
Beach

James

Bathsheba

Holetown

Andromeda

Saint

Martin's Bay

Bath
Consett Bay

Ragged
Point

Bridgetown

Garrison
Hastings

Foul
Bay

Rockley
Worthing
Saint
Maxwell

Oistins

A

See Map 79

Inch
Marlow

Long Bay

South
Point

Silver
Sands

A = Grantley Adams Airport

78

to name just a few.

Most of the best beaches are on the leeward, Caribbean coast, while the Atlantic coast is rocky and at times marvellously rugged (Barbados is the most easterly of the Caribbean islands). Bathsheba, a part of the Atlantic coast renowned for its surfing and well worth a visit, reminded me of Cornwall in England.

The population is around 260,000 of whom some 98,000 live in the capital, Bridgetown. Barbados is one of the most densely populated countries in the world, at 1500 per square mile. This fact is quite noticeable in Bridgetown and the island's southwestern corner, but there are many uncrowded parts of the island. Bridgetown, though hectic, has much of interest. There is a Trafalgar Square which predates the one in London. Facilities for shopping, duty-free and otherwise, are comprehensive. It can be a good idea to buy your duty-frees here; they are packed and delivered to the airport where you collect them at a little customs office. You should note however that liquor and cigarettes cannot be purchased with credit cards. Bridgetown also has the careenage from where boats for Saint Lucia, Dominica and other destinations depart.

Entry Requirements: citizens of all Commonwealth countries including Canada and the United Kingdom are of course allowed to enter without visas. Most other nationalities do not require visas providing their stay does not exceed a certain limit: six months for US citizens, and 3 months for citizens of most other countries.

In recent months, Barbados immigration has become decidedly sticky. It is now *absolutely essential* that you have a return ticket to the country of which you are a resident (in the case of those resident in Common Market countries, a return ticket to Luxembourg is acceptable).

Note that the only tourist board office in Barbados (apart from the head office, which is out in the sticks) is at the airport, before you go through immigration. Therefore be sure to collect any information you think you will need on arrival. If you are flying in on Caribbean Airways you are well advised to retain a copy of their excellent inflight magazine.

Currency: Official currency is the Barbados dollar (BB$) which is approximately equal to US 50 cents; US$1 = BB$2 as near as damnit. The natives are prepared to accept the US dollar, and accommodation is usually quoted in same. As prices are sometimes quoted in either currency, you should check when making purchases. Credit cards are fairly widely accepted. BankAmericard/Barclaycard and American Express are about the best; MasterCharge/Access is not really established as yet. Although MasterCharge cardholders are able to draw cash at the First National City Bank, Access cardholders should note that this facility is not open to them.

Climate: The easiest one-word description of Barbados' climate is 'perfect'. The sun is very hot, but Barbados is ideally placed to take advantage of the cooling trade winds. This means that the heat is rarely oppressive, but also that it is very easy to become sunburnt. It is sometimes necessary to take precautions against sunburn when merely proceeding about one's business; if you start your trip in Barbados, be very careful.

Temperature

January	Max: 85°F 29°C	Min: 68°F 20°C
July	Max: 87°F 31°C	Min: 76°F 24°C
Annual Rainfall:	58 ins.	

The wettest period is July to September. Since Barbados is comparatively flat, it has less rain than some of the other islands.

Cost of living: A large population and thus a sizeable home market has enabled Barbados to become more self-sufficient than most of the other eastern Caribbean islands. While this helps to hold down prices, a thriving tourist industry and, of course, inflation have pushed up the cost of living and brought hard times for the natives. In general terms, however, prices in Barbados are only a little higher than those in the other eastern Caribbean islands, where tourism has had less effect on the cost of living.

It is quite true that Barbados can be very expensive. But — and this is not generally known — it can be very cheap. Two examples are as follows: a taxi from the airport to the Worthing/Hastings area costs BB$14, yet it is possible to take a bus for 40 cents (US 20 cents); and the cheapest accommodation I found anywhere in the Caribbean was here — the Youth Hostel at US$5 a night.

Accommodation: Barbados has a generally more sensible attitude towards its accommodation than most Caribbean islands. True, it has its fair share of luxury hotels; but it also has a greater range of cheaper accommodation than can be found anywhere else in the Caribbean. This situation is primarily caused by Barbados' situation as a convenient overnight stop for Europeans on their way to South America (as well as South Americans going home), thanks to the good offices of Caribbean Airways.

There is much accommodation available at around US$10 — US$15 per person low season (April 15 to December 15), sometimes including meals. There is so much accommodation in Barbados that

Barbados: The Deep South: Key

1 The Youth Hostel (yoga)
2 Saint Anthony's Guest House
3 Carib Guest House
4 Summer House/Place
5 Rydal Waters Guest House
6 Berwyn on Sea Guest House

7 Brigade House
8 Pegwell Inn
9 Rudy's Inn
10 La Tropical Guest House
11 The Island Inn Hotel
12 Seaview Hotel

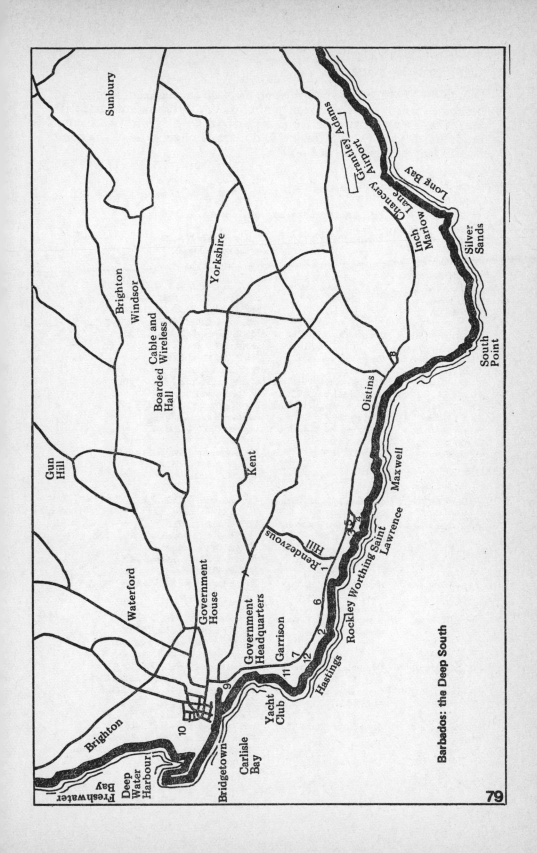

Barbados: the Deep South

it is impossible for anyone to list all of it, so this list is nowhere near complete, but it gives you plenty of choice. Establishments marked* are on the main bus route from the airport to Bridgetown. Accommodation is usually paid for in US dollars, though some of the guest houses may prefer Barbados dollars.

Name	Address	Price per room in US$
*The Youth Hostel	Behind the Vista Cinema,	MAP: Bed in dormitory $9;
(Yoga Centre)	Worthing (Tel: 87477)	Basic cottage D $22 (year round rates)

Guest Houses

Name	Address	Price per room in US$
*Summer Home on Sea Guest House	Off main road, Worthing (Tel: 86983)	CP: summer: S $13, D $24; winter: S $17, D $30. MAP: summer: S $18, D $34; winter: S $22, D $38
*Torrington Guest	Off main road, Rockley (Tel: 70141 and 70901)	MAP: summer: S $14, D $28; winter: S $20, D $40.
*Saint Anthony's Guest House	On main road, Hastings (Tel: 64756)	MAP: S $10, D $17. (year round rates)
*Carib Guest House	Off main road, Worthing (Tel: 89458 and 87304)	MAP: summer: S $15, D $30; winter: S $22, D $38.
*Rydal Waters Guest House	Off main road, Worthing (Tel: 81236)	MAP: summer: S $15, D $28; winter: S $20, D $34.
*Berwyn on Sea Guest House	On main road, Rockley (Tel: 70042)	winter: CP: S $12/$15, D $23/$28.
*Pegwell Inn	Distins (Tel: 86150)	EP: summer: S $7, D $14; winter: S $10, D $20.

Hotels

Name	Address	Price per room in US$
*Seaview Hotel	On main road at Hastings (Tel: 61450)	EP: summer: S $16, D $22, T $27, Four persons $31.
*San Remo Hotel	On main road, Maxwell (Tel: 88131)	EP: summer: S $15, D $20, T $28 winter: S $26, D $36, T $46. CP: summer: S $19, D $25, T $30; winter: S $30, D $40, T $50.
*The Island Inn	Aquatic Gap, Hastings (near Holiday Inn;) Tel: 60057)	EP: summer: S $18, D $24.
Atlantis Hotel	Bathsheba, Saint Joseph (Tel: 31526)	AP: summer: S $17, D $34, T $48; winter: S $22, D $42, T $60. $2 per person extra for balcony and sea view.
*Fairholme Hotel	Off main road, Maxwell (Tel: 89425)	EP: summer: S $15, D $21, T $27; winter: S $23, D $33, T $45.
Crane Beach Hotel	Crane Beach, Saint Philip (Tel: 36220)	EP: summer: S $40/$55, D $50/$70, T $60/$80; winter: S $65/$80, D $75/$95, T $85/$110
Cobblers Cove Hotel	Saint Peter (Tel: 2?.291)	EP: summer: S $43, D $60, T $75; MAP: summer: S $61, D $96, T $129. Higher rates are charged for beachfront rooms

Apartments

Maresol Beach Apartments	Saint Lawrence, Christchurch (Tel: 89300)	EP: summer: Studio $150 per week, 1 bedroom $180/$200 per week, 2 bedroom $175/$300 per week. winter: Studio $300 per week, 1 bedroom $400/$425 per week, 2 bedroom $375/$600 per week.
*Sheringham Beach Apartments	Maxwell, Christchurch (Tel: 89339)	EP: summer $30/$35; winter $50/$55
Coral House	Silver Sands (Tel: 87620)	EP: $8/$15 per person
Romans Apartments	Enterprise (Tel: 87635)	EP: $7/$9 per person

The Youth Hostel. For location see map of Worthing. If travelling by bus from the airport, ask to be dropped at the Vista Cinema, behind which you will find the Youth Hostel. You should note that one does not need to be a member of any Youth Hostelling organisation to stay here. This is the cheapest accommodation I found in the Caribbean (though prices have since gone up to those shown in the table above), and although spartan it is certainly not of the lowest standard. During the last four years I have made five visits to the Youth Hostel, and each time I have found facilities improved. It is

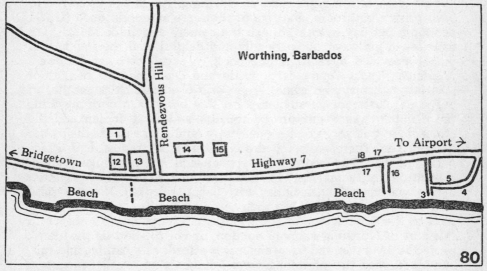

Worthing: Key

1 The Youth Hostel (yoga centre)
3 Carib Guest House
4 Summer House/Summer Place
5 Rydal Waters Guest House
12 Vista Cinema
13 Mobil petrol (gas) station
14 Supermarket and Shell petrol (gas) station
15 Ship Restaurant
16 Worthing Plaza shops
17 Banks
18 Supermarket

always spotlessly clean and tidy. To discourage campers from cooking out in the gardens and perhaps leaving refuse which would attract vermin, accommodation is now only provided with meals included.

The location is good, on the bus route, with an excellent beach over the road, shops, banks, a laundromat and entertainment nearby. Accommodation is generally in dormitories, although there are four double rooms (described as cottages) available at a higher price of US$11 per person. The prices are unbeatable, and if all you want is somewhere clean to sleep, adequate toilet facilities, the company of young travellers (mainly Europeans bound for or returning from South America), this is the place. In fact this is more than a Youth Hostel. There is also a restaurant, the *Lotus Garden*, which serves good healthy food with a vegetarian bias (sometimes they bake their own wholemeal bread). There are regular yoga classes (the establishment started life as the Yoga Centre) which are free to guests. Other courses, such as French, are sometimes run here, and they have been involved in some training of staff from hotels on the island. It is run by very nice people, namely Torrey and Phyllis Pilgrim.

Summer Home/Summer Place on Sea is one of a cluster of guest houses just off the main road in Worthing. All of the seven rooms have private bathroom, and five of them are air-conditioned (US$1 per room per day extra). Though the owner, George de Mattos, is a little set in his ways, he is friendly and helpful, and the standard of dinner provided by Selwyn, the cook, is excellent by guest house standards. *Rydal Waters* is opposite and *Diamondsville* next door (the latter displays no name). The *Carib Guest House* is another of the same cluster of guest houses on this beach. On both my visits the clientele was a mixture of tourists and West Indian and the atmosphere was very good — one happy family, exactly as the owner described it. There are six bedrooms, three bathrooms, and a nice patio and bar. The bedrooms are small and not particularly good, though on my second visit I found that the establishment was under new management and facilities were being improved. You may also find the winter rates are less than those I have listed. On the beach next to the *Carib* is one of the windsurfer companies. The beach in this part of Worthing is, in my opinion, one of the best on the island; protected by a reef and fairly shallow it affords safe bathing and this, combined with the prevailing winds, makes it an excellent location for windsurfing.

Torrington Guest House is a large attractive building about 500 yards the other side of the Youth Hostel. Rockley Beach, generally considered one of the island's finest (though crowded in July/ August) is adjacent. There is a good, friendly atmosphere inside the hotel and, being just off the main road on a side lane, it is quiet. As this is one of the best value guest houses in Barbados, with a regular clientele who return year after year, you may find it difficult to get a reservation; this situation has been recently exacerbated by its inclusion in the brochures of two British inclusive tour companies.

Saint Anthony's Guest House is recommended for those who have used and prefer native-style accommodation. Nowadays unlisted by the tourist board, with whom the proprietor does not see eye to eye, it consists of a restaurant/bar and five rooms up by the road, and four rooms at a beach house. The location is good, but I think you will find privacy somewhat lacking.

The *Pegwell Inn* is about seven miles from town, but about the closest cheap accommodation to the airport. This establishment enjoys a good reputation among overnighters. Almost all the rooms in the main building here have their own bathrooms, and there is a smaller building across the road on the beach. *Pegwell Inn* is not really intended as a holiday hotel, and the accommodation consists of overnighters, travelling West Indians, and those on their way to or from South America, with just a smattering of guests having one or two weeks holiday. There is a bar and restaurant here, and many shops nearby.

On most of my visits to Barbados I have visited the *Seaview Hotel* and I have always been impressed. This is an old building of character. Rooms are well-appointed with air-conditioning, private bathrooms and telephones. These facilities and its proximity to Bridgetown (it is near the racecourse at Garrison) make it an ideal hotel for the travelling businessman, but it would be wrong to call it a businessman's hotel: it is very much a holiday hotel, a fact emphasized by its inclusion in many UK tour operator brochures.

There is an open-air restaurant, the *Tamarind Tree Club*, which serves breakfast and lunch. Open till 5 pm, it is not cheap, but it is good value and the menu is varied. Examples of breakfast are: 'Continental' (BB$2) — fruit juice, hot french bread, jam, coffee; 'Eye Opener' (BB$5) — grapefruit segments, two eggs, bacon or sausage, toast and coffee. There are many other alternatives. The lunch menu has a good selection of tasty dishes. There is another restaurant, the *Virginian* (open for dinner only), which is patronised by many guests from the more expensive hotels. I have eaten in both restaurants and found the meals excellent. There are extensive grounds providing tree-shaded walks to the beach, which provides safe bathing, and a small swimming pool. You would be advised not to turn up without a reservation however; this hotel is almost 100% full all year so your chances of getting in 'on spec' are remote.

The *San Remo Hotel*, at Maxwell, is an excellent alternative to a guest house. One can have the facilities of a hotel and the atmosphere of the smaller hostelry. This hotel is built right on the beach, with a very good beach bar, and has an open-air restaurant shaded by palm trees. As it is also on the main road and has a bus stop outside, with three nightspots within walking (or staggering) distance, its location can be described as excellent. All rooms are air-conditioned.

all have private bathrooms, and there are some efficiency apartments at a slightly higher rate. There is also a restaurant. But what really makes the San Remo an excellent place to stay is the attitude of the management and staff, who quickly adopt one as a member of the family. *The Island Inn* has 21 good rooms, all with private facilities and air-conditioning. It is well run with a good atmosphere, and there is a fine native cabaret on Monday nights.

The ruggedly beautiful coastline of Bathsheba is not a favourite spot for foreign tourists, as the sea is generally rough and can be unsafe for swimming. But it is a favourite holiday spot for Bajans, and also very popular as a day trip for tourists staying on other parts of the island. Excursions usually include a buffet lunch, and these are the staple trade of the *Atlantis Hotel*. Its reputation is founded on Ms Enid Maxwell's Bajan home cooking, recognised even by rivals as superb. If you want a relief from the usually idyllic Caribbean beaches, tourists, hustle and bustle of the southwest coast, then a few days at the *Atlantis* may be the answer. Relative seclusion is what you will find here, and the scenery in this part of Barbados is perhaps the island's finest. The prices at the *Atlantis*, which include three meals a day, are extremely low by hotel standards (but beware of the potency of the rum punches).

Barbados has a fairly large number of luxury class hotels, and it is really a matter of taste when considering preferences. *Sandy Lane* is often considered the best, and it is certainly the most expensive, but it depends of course on what one is looking for. Almost all of them are situated in the parish of Saint James, on the west coast, north of Bridgetown. Personally I would want seclusion when staying in an expensive hotel, which is partly why I have chosen *Crane Beach* and *Cobblers Cove*. But I have also included them because their prices are a little less than those generally charged in this category.

Crane Beach is set by itself on the south of the island above a superb beach (although the sea can be dangerous for adventurous swimmers). Until recently it catered for overnighters, (tourists bound for Grenada or Saint Vincent) but the new management is developing the hotel as a resort hotel in its own right. Views from the terraces and some of the rooms are exhilarating and the rooms, as you would expect, are luxurious. There is a large swimming pool, a smaller one with its own bar at beach level, restaurant, bar, boutiques etc. Crane Beach has been described as 'the most beautiful spot in Barbados'.

Bridgetown: Key

1 Lord Nelson's statue
2 Saint Mary's church
3 Old Town Hall
4 Library
5 Synagogue
6 Freemason's temple
7 Saint Michael's church
8 The Fountain
9 Trafalgar Square
10 Careenage

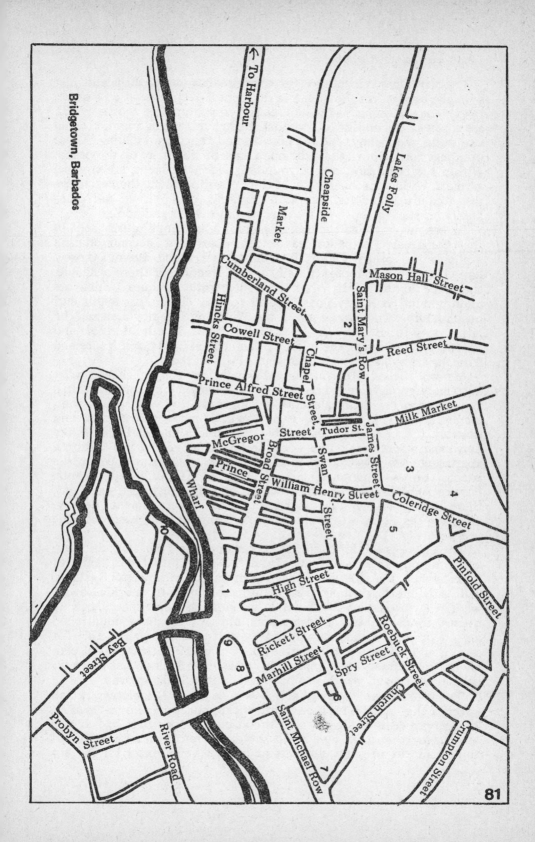

Bridgetown, Barbados

To Harbour

Cheapside

Lakes Folly

Market

Mason Hall Street

Cumberland Street

Saint Mary's Row

2

Hincks Street

Cowell Street

Reed Street

Chapel Street

Prince Alfred Street

Milk Market

McGregor

Street

Tudor St.

James Street

3

Coleridge Street

4

Broad Street

Swan Street

5

Prince

William Henry Street

Wharf

10

Pinfold Street

1

High Street

Rickett Street

Roebuck Street

9

Marhill Street

Spry Street

8

Bay Street

Church Street

Crumpton Street

Probyn Street

River Road

Saint Michael Row

7

81

Cobblers Cove is located at the opposite extreme of the island, just over the border from Saint James (in Saint Peter). It is set on a quiet, sandy cove with just a few houses for company. The rooms, which are really suites, consist of bedroom, bathroom, sitting room, kitchen and patio or balcony, and are constructed four to a building. These buildings form a horseshoe, the open ends of which are on the beach. Within the horseshoe, and surrounding each apartment, are tropical gardens. Within the open ends of the horseshoe, along the beach, are the administration and reception builidng, which is an old pink-painted castle, the open-air restaurant, and the bar and pool.

In keeping with its reputation as the number one tourist spot in the Caribbean, Barbados has more apartment accommodation available for foreign visitors than any other island. Besides those I have listed, which represent only a tiny fraction of those available, there are luxury villas, often furnished with antiques, which are mainly found in Saint James, as well on very cheap apartments and beach houses. The former are in the Worthing/Rockley area and the latter are in Bathsheba. Of those I have listed, *Maresol* and *Sheringham* represent the middle price bracket, and *Coral House* and *Romans* are at the very cheapest end of the market.

Maresol Beach Apartments, although no longer cheap, offer extremely good value for money. Over the years they have built up a strong rapport with their clientele, who regularly return. The owner-manager, Mr Peter Morgan, is a former Minister of Tourism, and possibly the man most responsible for establishing Barbados as the Caribbean's foremost holiday destination. The one and two-bedroom apartments are constructed in blocks of four and run down to the beach. Across a minor road is a block of 12 studio apartments. Service is both friendly and efficient, and the location is excellent, there being restaurants, nightspots and entertainment nearby. *Maresol* has its own minimart with competitive prices on the premises.

The above is a brief listing of accommodation, most of which are easily found on the bus route from the airport to town. Many of them are on the stretch of coast from Saint Lawrence to Hastings. This is the most developed part of Barbados (apart from Bridgetown), where the road is lined with hotels, guest houses, apartments, private homes, shops, banks and restaurants. Most of the places mentioned are on or near a good beach. Most establishments charge 10% for service and 8% government hotel tax. During 1980 there was also an energy surcharge; where applicable it has been included in the rates quoted above, and was due to be phased out in 1981 anyway.

Transportation: There is a bus service from Bridgetown to all parts of the island. This is certainly cheap, but it may not be regular. The service from Bridgetown to the airport is downright bad. If you are leaving the island by air you should therefore either take a taxi to the airport or allow yourself at least 2 hours extra for the bus journey. This is the only time, however, when waiting for a bus should prove a great inconvenience. Normally, the bus service provides a perfectly adequate means of seeing the island.

You may prefer a rented car. Mini-mokes are about the most popular. Besides being economical on gas (BB$2 per gallon here) they are open to the elements and provide nature's air-conditioning. (A note for North American readers: the mini-moke is a jeep-like vehicle built on the chassis of the original sub-compact, the mini. Although built in Britain, it was a failure there because it is always raining.) Rates are BB$40/50 a day or BB$260 a week. This includes free mileage of 50 miles a day or 300 miles a week. You can expect lower rates between April 15 and December 15. You will need to bring your driving licence with you and you should register with the police at the airport, or at a police station, for a cost of BB$10.

TRINIDAD AND TOBAGO
If we take the French territories as separate entities, Trinidad and Tobago is the largest state (in area) in the eastern Caribbean. It is also the closest to South America, being separated from Venezuela by two narrow channels.

It would be easy, for several reasons, to describe Trinidad and Tobago as 'unique'. For a start, it is the only country in what was the British West Indies to become a Republic within the Commonwealth (at the time of writing). Queen Elizabeth II is no longer the head of state, although she is still recognized as head of the Commonwealth, of which Trinidad remains a member. Secondly, Trinidad and Tobago have not shared the recent depression which has effected the Caribbean. Tourism has never been the major industry, so the recent reduction in numbers has had little if any effect; in addition Trinidad has been affected advantageously by rising oil prices, as the country is a major producer. This and other industries (for example asphalt from the pitch lake) means that Trinidad and Tobago is one of the richest countries in the Caribbean. A wealth of flora and fauna, a genuinely multiracial society, diversity and tolerance of religions, and the most spectacular carnival are all further evidence of Trinidad and Tobago's claim to be unique within the Caribbean.

Entry requirements: This is one of the very few Caribbean countries which requires all visitors to show a valid passport. On arrival you will be given an immigration card which you should complete and sign, keeping the carbon copy to surrender on your departure. You will also be required to show onward and/or return tickets. A certificate showing immunization against smallpox is advisable.

Currency: The Trinidad and Tobago dollar (TT$) which is approximately equivalent to US 45 cents. US$1 = TT$2.35 approximately. Although the US dollar is accepted, it is best to use local currency. The major credit cards are recognized. Banks are open from 8 am to 12.30 am Monday to Thursday, and 8 am to 12 noon and 3 pm to 5 pm on Fridays.

Climate: The tropical warmth is regulated by the trade winds as elsewhere. Average annual temperatures are $74^{\circ}F$ ($23^{\circ}C$) at night and $84^{\circ}F$ ($29^{\circ}C$) during the day. You can expect lower temperatures (slightly) and more rain in the highlands.

Food and drink: Most types of cuisine are popular here. The West Indian or Trinidadian dishes include callaloo soup (made from crab meat, ochroes and dasheen leaves), crab-backs, pastelles (minced meat mixed with corn flour and wrapped in banana leaves) to name a few. Creole dishes abound, as do genuine Indian curries and Chinese meals, besides 'International' food if you want it. Trinidad is as blessed with fruit and vegetables as any other Caribbean country. Rum has to be the national drink.

The people: The melting pot of Trinidad and Tobago is one of the world's few multiracial societies. After the original Amerindian inhabitants came the Spanish and their African slaves. Spain remained in possession of Trinidad until as late as 1797 when the British decided it was time for them to go. From the mid-nineteenth century until 1914 the British imported East Indians and Chinese as indentured labourers to solve the contemporary labour shortage.

Thus all racial types are evident in Trinidad and Tobago, living together, and it is just as common to see all possible mixtures of peoples. This same history has given the country a rich cultural heritage. Besides Christians, there are many Hindus and Moslems. Thus as well as the annual Christian Carnival, the Moslem festival of Eid-Ul-Fitr and the Hindu festival of Divali are officially celebrated.

Flora and Fauna: The flora, fauna and bird life of Trinidad and Tobago form a complete contrast to that found anywhere else in the Caribbean. This is because the islands were once part of South America, and are still close enough to retain the same botanical and zoological make up. The Botanic Gardens north of Port of Spain display the native flowers and shrubs, whilst the indigenous wildlife is housed in the Emperor Valley Zoo.

Trinidad's national bird is the scarlet ibis which is protected in the Caroni Bird Sanctuary. There are also 19 different species of hummingbird in Trinidad and 7 in Tobago. Frigate birds, herons, kingfishers, toucans and kiskadees are just some of the 400 species of bird life to be found on these two islands.

Language: The official language is English, but there is also some French, Spanish, Chinese and Hindi.

Galera Point

Matelot

Toco

Matura Bay

Cocos Bay

Galeota Point

Blanchisseuse

Sangre

Biche

Pierreville

Guayaguayure

Rio Clara

Maracas Bay

Tacarigua

Arima

San Rafael

Talparo

Flanagin Town

Tabaquite

Basse Terre

Arouca

Airport

Longdenville

Blue Basin Falls

Port of Spain

Tunapuna

Chaguanas

Couta

Princes Town

San Fernando

St Mary's

Siparia

Gulf of Paria

La Brea

Buenos Ayres

Pitch Lake

Guapo Bay

Moruga

Erin Bay

Fullarton

Trinidad

Icacos Point

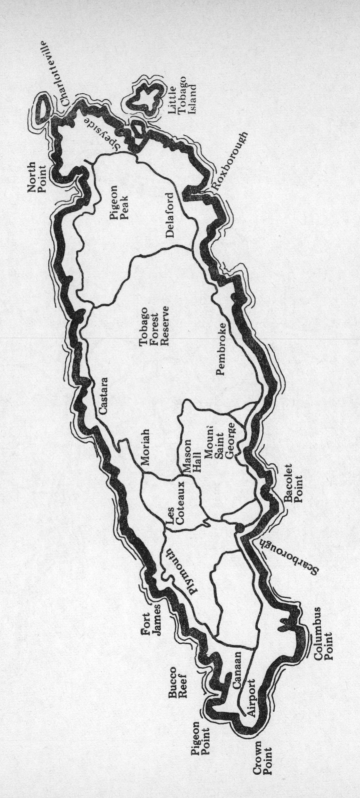

Tobago

Accommodation

Name	Address	Price per room in Trinidad dollars
Hotels		
Bagshot House	9 Saddle Road, Maraval, Port of Spain (Tel: 62-26828)	EP: *S* $36, *D* $72
Chaconia Inn	106 Saddle Road, Maraval, Port of Spain (Tel: 62-25474)	EP: *S* $69/$92, *D* $104/$120; MAP: *S* $120/$142, *D* $205/$228.
Erroll J Lau Hotel	66 Edward Street, Port of Spain (Tel: 62-54381)	EP: *S* $46, *D* $65.
Pelican Inn	2/4 Coblentz Avenue, Cascade, Port of Spain (Tel: 62-47486)	EP: *S* $18/$25, *D* $32/$45: EP: *S* $26/$33, *D* $45/$48.
Hotel Tropical	6 Rookery nook, Maraval, Port of Spain (Tel: 62-23837)	EP: *S* $50/$60, *D* $60/$70.
Scarlet Ibis Hotel	Eastern Main Road, Saint Augustine (Tel: 66-23251)	EP: *D* $45/$60
Bel Air Hotel	Piarco Airport (Tel: 66-44771)	EP: *S* $52/$66, *D* $80/$94.
Las Cuevas Beach Hotel	Las Cuevas, Maracas (Tel: 63-73798)	EP: $22; CP: $30; MAP: $45. (all rates for double)
Blue Waters Inn	Batteaux Bay, Speyside, Tobago (Tel: 639-4341)	EP: *S* $25, *D* $50 MAP: *S* $65, *D* $130
Guest Houses		
Central Guest House	45 Murray Street, Woodbrook, Port of Spain (62-27137)	CP: *S* $22, *D* $46.
Monique's Guest House	114 Saddle Road, Maraval, Port of Spain (Tel: 62-21007)	EP: *S* $35/$43, *D* $46/$52.
Success Inn Guest House	4 Sarah Street, Laventille, Port of Spain (Tel: 62-35504) (east, in hills)	EP: *S* $16/$20, *D* $31/$32; CP: *S* $22/$26, *D* $43/$44.
Fabienne's Guest House	3 Elizabeth Street, Saint Clair, Port of Spain (Tel: 62-21018)	CP: *S* $25, *D* $50.
Jardine's Guest House	8 Alcazar Street, Saint Clair, Port of Spain (Tel: 62-26920)	CP: *S* $30/$35, *D* $50/$60.
The Belle Circle Guest House	27 Belmont Circular Road, Belmont, Port of Spain (Tel: 62-35796)	CP: *S* $30, *D* $40.
Poinsettia Guest House	56 Maloney Street, San Juan (Tel: 63-83309)	CP: *S* $40/$50, *D* $80/$100
Pan American Guest House	Piarco Airport (Tel: 66-44731)	EP: *S* $54, *D* $82.50.
Della Mira Guest House	Scarborough, Tobago (Tel: 639-2531)	EP: *S* $24/$30, *D* $40/$50; CP: *S* $30/$30/$36, *D* $52/$62; MAP: *S* $45/$51, *D* $83/$92.
Glenco Guest House	Glen Road, Scarborough, Tobago	EP: *S* $14, *D* $24; MAP: *S* $26, *D* $48.
Jacob's Guest House	Carrington Street, Scarborough, Tobago (Tel: 639-2271)	EP: *S* $10, *D* $20; CP: *S* $14, *D* $28; MAP: *S* $20, *D* $40
Plaza Guest House	Milford Road, Canaan, Tobago (Tel: 639-8860)	EP: *S* $15, *D* $24; MAP: *S* $27, *D* $54.
Sun Star Haven Guest House	Cinamon Hill, Tobago (Tel: 639-2376)	EP: *S* $19, *D* $29; MAP: *S* $36, *D* $64.
Golden Thistle Guest House	Store Bay Road, Crown Point, Tobago (Tel: 639-8521)	MAP: *D* $91

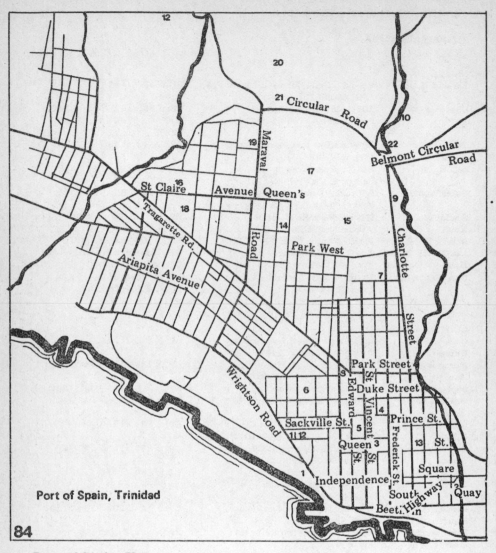

Port of Spain, Trinidad

84

Port of Spain: Key

1 Tourist bureau
2 Columbus Square
3 Holy Trinity cathedral
4 Town Hall
5 Red House
6 Victoria Square
7 Museum and art gallery
8 Errol J Lau Hotel
9 Parillon Hotel
10 Pelican Inn
11 Holiday Inn

12 BWIA offices
13 Market
14 US Embassy
15 Race course
16 King George V Park
17 Queen's Park
18 The Oval
19 Prime Minister's residence
20 Botanical Gardens
21 Zoo
22 Trinidad Hilton

Part 4: The Eastern Caribbean

These prices are valid for the summer season (April 15 to December 15) and should be treated with discretion. Most will be higher in winter, particularly in Tobago.

This listing represents a fairly small proportion of the accommodation available. For more details of guest houses you should contact Make Charbonne, Chairman Guest Houses Association, 114 Saddle Road, Maraval, Port of Spain. Telephone 622 1007. Two more economical guest houses you can try are: Mrs L. Commenlong, 7 Luis Street, Woodbrook, Port of Spain (telephone 622 5593) and Mrs Sheila Rocke, 9 Gloster Lodge Road, Belmont (telephone 623 8111).

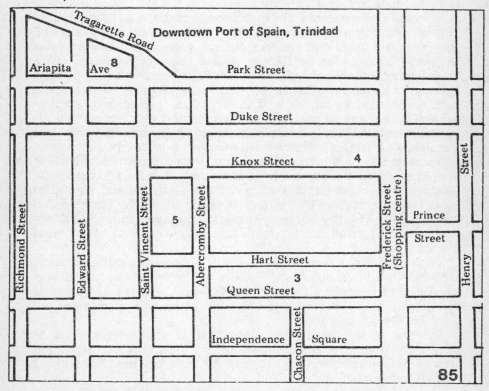

Downtown Port of Spain: Key

3 Holy Trinity church

4 Town Hall

5 Red House

8 Errol J Lau Hotel

Transportation: The fact that gas is cheap means that people are not afraid to use it. The people's comparative wealth means that there are many motor vehicles of all types. Those without their own transport tend to use publiques and taxis to a great extent. Although there are government-operated bus services, taxi fares are comparatively low. 'Publico' or point (shared) taxi rides cost about 50 cents a trip within Port of Spain. These are identified by the prefix 'H' on their licence plates and their route is displayed on the windscreen. Two useful pick-up points for taxis are Independence Square and the corner of Park Street.

Geography: Trinidad and Tobago's geography is as diverse as the other facets of her character. There are, on Trinidad, the three mountain ranges which inspired the island's name (named after the Holy Trinity). The northern range of mountains is the highest, whilst the central hills of Montserrat and southern Trinity Hills rise less spectacularly from the undulating countryside. Besides many small rivers, Trinidad has two big swamps, the Caroni, part of which is a bird sanctuary, and the Nariva.

Trinidad's oil reservoirs are in the south of the island, both underground and offshore. The pitch lake is the result of asphaltic oil seeping into a huge mud volcano. Natural gases and movement, plus the evaporation of the lighter oils, caused the deposits which are so useful today. In modern times the Pitch Lake was first found in 1595 by that well known discoverer, Sir Walter Raleigh. There are a number of mud volcanoes in Trinidad which periodically erupt — causing little if any damage, but no conventional volcanoes.

The economy: The petroleum industry comprises 80 percent of Trinidad and Tobago's exports. Nowadays this is mainly drawn from offshore wells. Refining crude oil from Venezuela, the Middle East and Africa as well as the home-produced supplies is Trinidad's main industry. The most important agricultural industry, and second in total terms, is sugar. The majority is exported, whilst Trinidad also has a thriving industry in the by-products, molasses, rum and bagasse board. Total agricultural production is only 5 percent of the gross domestic product.

Trinidad is very advanced in the field of processing crude materials supplied by other countries. Besides oil refining, an aluminium smelter to be owned by Trinidad and Tobago, Jamaica and Guyana is being built, as well as a sponge-iron plant which will process iron ore from Brazil and elsewhere.

Tourism is the third most important revenue earner. This is principally Tobago's contribution to the economy, as it is 'the Robinson Crusoe Island' which has the best beaches, history and peaceful atmosphere.

The Mas: This is short for 'Masquerade', the carnival. The Trinidadian Mas ranks with Rio's Carnival and New Orleans' Mardi Gras as one of the world's greatest carnivals. It originated as a Latin

Christian festival and is held around February/March, depending on the Christian calendar. Originally the participants dressed up (hence 'masquerade'). There are less costumes nowadays, although costume competitions are still arranged. Today the event has strong musical overtones. The various steel bands and calypso singers, amateur and professional, vie for popularity and compose songs celebrating the event. And, of course, there is still an overwhelming atmosphere of gaiety and joyful abandon — with or without the use of artificial stimulants.

THE OTHER ISLANDS

The number of islands in the Caribbean has probably never been counted. The problem when writing a book of this nature is what does one include, and what does one leave out? If we use as our yardstick the compilation of a logical, interesting and enjoyable itinerary, then there is a good argument for omitting Cuba, the Cayman Islands and those islands off the South American coast. In fact, Cuba only has to be missed for political reasons, whilst the Cayman Islands, although a little off-route, can be visited at little extra expense and inconvenience. Although Trinidad and Tobago is in many ways more a part of South America than of the eastern Caribbean chain, it is undeniably a Caribbean island state without which this book would be incomplete.

I draw the line, however, at the cluster of islands strung out along the north coast of Venezuela. Just over half of these (in area — there are about 15 in number) are part of Venezuela; three—Curacao, Aruba and Bonaire — comprise (with the Dutch half of Sint Maarten) the Netherlands Antilles. I have decided against including these mainly because of the difficulties they impose when calculating economic air fares from your home country. Though Curacao can be reached by direct flights from many different countries, the cost of doing so can be high (it is US$93 from Port of Spain and US$105 from Port-au-Prince, the two nearest points on our island-hopping itinerary). San Andres, though a very famous Caribbean possession of Colombia, is much more easily reached from Barranquilla, Miami or Central America.

Thus this book does not include every speck of land in the Caribbean Sea. But it does, I hope, give all the necessary details for anyone undertaking an island-hopping trip through the chain of Caribbean islands. And I expect this will be only the first of many trips you will make to this amazingly beautiful, colourful and peaceful corner of the world. Paradise regained.

Appendix 1
How to Get There

.

APPENDIX I: HOW TO GET THERE
The aims of this book are the same as the function of a good travel
agent: primarily to ensure that you gain the maximum benefit and
enjoyment from the trip, and secondly to make sure you spend no
more money than you wish to.

One of the greatest areas in which you can save money is that of air
fares. Although you probably intend to use ships and yachts for a
great deal of your trip, it is a fact that the immigration authorities of
most countries require you to have onward and homeward air
tickets as a condition of entry. This means that in practice you will
be advised to hold air tickets for journeys which you will make by
other means. Sometimes you will be eligible for a refund on unused
portions of your ticket(s), but this is not uniformly the case; it will
depend on the fare on which your ticket is based.

I have been actively engaged, as a travel agent, in sending travellers
to this part of the world for some years. Thus I feel able to provide
some guidelines to help you work out, with your travel agent, the
best flight arrangements for this trip.

THE BASIC RULES
First, decide your itinerary. Read this book, choose the places you
want to travel to and how long you want to stay there. As a travel
agent I always ask the client three questions: 'Where do you want to
go, when, and for how long?' The answers to these questions provide

me with a basis for calculating the best itinerary and lowest fare. Allow your travel agency some flexibility if you can, because sometimes quite a minor change can save much expense.

Obviously I cannot give here the exact answer for every need. An understanding of the fundamental factors which effect air fares will help you considerably however. Some guidelines follow:

1. The season of travel: December 15 to April 15 is high season in the Caribbean. Whilst this will not normally affect air fares in the Caribbean area itself, you will pay more for accommodation and other services if you travel during this period. You can also expect to encounter more tourists.

High and low season air fares will depend on which part of the world you are travelling from. The fares are highest at the most popular times of travel. Thus residents of Canada and the northern cities of the USA will find fares high between December 15 and April 15, because this is when everyone wants to fly to the Caribbean to escape the cold. On the other hand, residents of the United Kingdom will find fares highest in July, August, September, December and January. This is because travel has been largely ethnic — West Indians living in the United Kingdom who time their visits to the Caribbean to coincide with school holidays.

2. The duration of the trip: If you will be travelling in the Caribbean for only a matter of weeks you may be able to utilise some sort of excursion fare. The validity of these can be as little as 21 days or as long as 60. This will depend on your starting point, your destination, and sometimes even the airline. There may be certain conditions to be observed, such as an advance booking period, and there will be a limit to the number of stopovers permitted.

3. Your furthest destination: Very often it is cheaper to have a return ticket to your furthest point with numerous stopovers on the way, than to have a collection of separate tickets. As this is the most difficult point for the layman to understand, I give examples later in this section.

4. The route: Sometimes large distances can be covered at low cost, for a variety of reasons. For example, New York to San Juan, Puerto Rico is a low fare (at the time of writing it can be as low as US$110) because of Puerto Rico's association with the United States and the large number of Puerto Ricans living in New York. Similarly there are low fares available from the United Kingdom to those West Indian countries which were (or are) British colonies.

5. The airline: Most major airlines are members of an organisation known as IATA (the International Air Transport Association). One of IATA's functions is to decide fares on all routes operated by its members throughout the world. Once the fares are fixed, all IATA member airlines are required to stick to them (although there have been occasions when members have breached this regulation). These

fares are usually calculated on the basis that there will be a certain proportion of empty seats. Thus you will often find yourself paying for the empty seat beside you as well as the one you are occupying.

There are a number of airlines who do not belong to IATA. Often these airlines charge lower fares, depending on the regulations of the countries they operate between. Thus, for example, Dominicana and Aerovias Quisqueyana are able to charge lower fares between San Juan and Santo Domingo than the IATA carriers.

European readers may benefit by using the services of either Caribbean Airways or International Air Bahamas from Luxembourg. International Air Bahamas charge £144 from Luxembourg to Nassau and have a 'Budget' fare of £98 (bookable within 48 hours of departure). At certain times of the year they have a fare of US$150 from Nassau to Luxembourg. These fares compare with a London to Nassau fare of £233.50 (low season). Caribbean Airways ask £163 Luxembourg/Barbados as against £271 *on the same aeroplane* from London (which in fact flies Luxembourg/London/Barbados). They have fares from Barbados to Luxembourg starting from BB$429 (approximately US$215 or £108).

You should not presume that an airline offering a lower fare offers lower standards of service. On the contrary, in my opinion both airlines in the above paragraph offer far superior service to their IATA counterparts.

The above is a summary of the main factors which will affect the fare you pay in order to travel to and from the Caribbean. Below I give some examples as illustrations (subdivided into three sections: the USA, Canada and Europe). Please note that these are examples only: although the fares and conditions were correct at the time of writing they are notoriously subject to alteration and will have changed by the time you read this.

FROM THE USA TO THE CARIBBEAN

In this section I have given examples of possible flight arrangements from New York and Miami for each of the suggested itineraries listed at the beginning of this book (page 22). My apologies to those millions of American citizens who live elsewhere, but it would take another book to cover the entire USA.

From New York

Itinerary One: The Bahamas, Jamaica, Haiti, Republica Dominica, Puerto Rico, the Virgin Islands, Antigua, Guadeloupe, Saint Lucia and Barbados. Booking your flights as you would intend to take them, you could expect to pay $670, as follows:

New York/Nassau/Montego Bay	$188
Kingston/Port-au-Prince/Santo Domingo/San Juan	$122
Saint Thomas/Antigua/Guadeloupe/Saint Lucia/Barbados	$110
Barbados/New York	$250
Total:	$670

This sum of $670 compares badly with the normal New York/ Barbados return fare of $500. We would thus want to reduce the flight costs above while retaining some flexibility.

The normal return fare has a 'mileage allowance' of 2520 miles in each direction. The mileage on the route detailed above is 2837 on the outward journey and 2100 on the return. The permitted mileage is thus slightly more than the mileage contained in the itinerary.

It is not possible to amend the itinerary to reduce the air mileage to 2520 in each direction, but you could have a round trip ticket with a surcharge of 15 per cent on the outward journey. The cost of this would be $538, a saving of over $100.

Alternatively you could book the outbound trip with the 15 per cent surcharge ($287.50), then a Barbados/San Juan ticket ($139) and then a San Juan/New York ticket (cheapest fare $110). The total cost of this would be $536.50.

Itinerary Two: The Grand Tour, Bahamas to Trinidad. Your flights for this trip are probably best organized as in the example above: ie an outbound ticket including most stopovers (your travel agent will advise you which are possible) and a return via San Juan using the cheap fare already mentioned. Your mileage surcharge on the outbound trip could be as much as 20 per cent, and you can in any case expect the total fare to be higher than that quoted in the above example.

Itinerary Three: The Western Islands. The difficulty you will have here is in making any reservation in New York between the Turks and Caicos Islands and Haiti. I would suggest the following air ticket routing.

Your ticket should read New York/Nassau/Montego Bay/surface/ Kingston/Port-au-Prince/surface/South Caicos/Inagua (or Mayaguana/Nassau/New York. The New York/Port-au-Prince return fare is at present $344 with a permitted mileage of 1840 miles in each direction. Although you may be liable for an excess charge of 5 per cent on the outbound journey, your return journey should be shorter than the maximum allowed, and so you could expect to pay a total fare of $353. You will still have to pay the cost of your travel from Cap Haitien to the Turks and Caicos Islands, of course. You will have onward tickets from every country except Haiti, which is not likely to cause any difficulty.

If you intend to make an abridged version of this trip you should note that there is a 21-day excursion fare from New York to Port-au-Prince. You are allowed 2 stopovers. I would suggest Montego Bay or Kingston on the way out and Nassau on the homeward leg. The excursion fare varies from $238 to $297 depending on the season and day of travel.

Itinerary Four: The Bahamas to the Virgin Islands. Obviously you would use the cheap fares from San Juan to New York for the homeward leg. For the outbound journey you may find it best to use sector fares, which are as follows:

New York/Nassau:	$121
Nassau/Inagua/South Caicos:	$ 84
Port-au-Prince/Santo Domingo:	$ 30
Santo Domingo/San Juan:	$ 31
Total	$265

With the San Juan/New York cheap fare of $110, this makes a total return fare of $375, not including your travel between the Turks and Caicos Islands and Haiti and between San Juan and the Virgin Islands. But this itinerary does offer great facilities for surface travel, and as you are paying sector fares any unused tickets should be completely refundable on your return.

Itinerary Five: The Eastern Caribbean. The best and cheapest way of taking flights to connect with this itinerary will depend upon your exact routing and the current fare levels at the time of travel. One possibility is to use the New York/Port of Spain return fare (presently $496) with all your intended stopovers written into the ticket. All of the stopovers mentioned in itinerary five are possible within the permitted mileage. Note that it is important for you to advise your travel agent of all the countries you think you may vist. It is not normally possible to add extra stops without cost while travelling, whilst it is possible to miss out stops if you wish. On this fare basis it is unlikely that you will be eligible for a refund on unused sectors.

Another possibility is for you to fly to San Juan (return fare from $214) and have separate tickets from there. A San Juan/Barbados ticket allowing you the stopovers you require would cost $258 return, and there is a 1-17 day excursion fare between Barbados and Port of Spain, Trinidad, for $47. This reduces your total fare to $519 (a saving of over $50) and introduces the possibility of a refund on unused sectors, whilst ensuring that you have the correct documentation for all the immigration authorities.

If you intend abridging this trip and taking less than 21 days in total, you should consult your travel agent about the possibility of using an excursion fare.

From Miami

Itinerary One: The Bahamas, Jamaica, Haiti, Republica Dominicana, Puerto Rico, the Virgin Islands, Antigua, Guadeloupe, Saint Lucia and Barbados. Booking your flights on a point to point or 'sector' fare basis you could expect to pay $545. The normal Miami/Barbados round trip fare is $428. Following the itinerary as given in this book you could expect to pay a mileage surcharge of up to 10 percent on your outward journey. Your cost would therefore be $450. It is possible to save this 10 percent by omitting Jamaica on your outward journey and by returning home via Barbados/Kingston and Montego Bay/Miami. Your return ticket should include a Kingston/Montego Bay portion which you probably will not use.

Itinerary Two: The Grand Tour, Bahamas to Trinidad. The fare construction given in the example above is probably the best way of organizing your connecting flights, based on a $460 return flight to Port of Spain. You may find it possible to include the Cayman Islands on your return trip.

Itinerary Three: The Western Islands. I would suggest you have two main air tickets: one for an outward journey, Miami/Montego Bay/Kingston/Port-au-Prince, which should be possible at the normal fare (presently $104) with a 5 per cent mileage excess, and another from the Turks and Caicos islands via the Bahamas to Miami. You will have to vary the itinerary as published herein, but this method can simplify matters greatly. The fare from South Caicos to Nassau on Bahamasair is $73 (you should be able to stopover at Great Inagua or Mayaguana en route) and from Nassau to Miami the fare on this same airline is $32. Mackey also fly from Miami and Fort Lauderdale to the Bahamas and Turks and Caicos Islands. Information should be readily available in Miami. Consult your travel agent if you want to include the Cayman Islands on your outward journey, and ask him about excursion fares if you wish to take less than 21 days on an abridged tour.

Itinerary Four: The Bahamas to the Virgin Islands. Information on fares, routings and frequencies on your outward journey are best obtained in Miami as these are constantly changing. Current sector fares are as follows: Miami/Nassau $32, Nassau/South Caicos $73, Port-au-Prince/Santo Domingo $30, Santo Domingo/San Juan $31. A fare of $70 is available from San Juan to Miami; I do not think stopovers are possible on this, but it is worth checking.

Itinerary Five: The Eastern Caribbean. Air fares in the eastern Caribbean can be expensive. One possibility is to fly out to San Juan (from $70) and return from Saint Thomas or Saint Croix ($76). Alternatively you could fly direct to Antigua. In practice your itinerary is likely to vary as you travel. The best advice I can give you is that you should first study a map and then calculate the possible combinations of one way and excursion fares with your travel agent.

FROM CANADA TO THE CARIBBEAN

Most of the regulations and fares governing flights to the Caribbean area discussed in the previous examples are common to Canada. You can expect fare levels to be slightly higher, because you are travelling further. There may be occasions (for example if you are returning through San Juan) when you would be advised to route your journey through New York. A perusal of the foregoing section and the help of a good travel agent should provide you with the information you require.

Appendix 1: How to Get There

FROM EUROPE TO THE CARIBBEAN

The range of Transatlantic flight possibilities is staggering. Besides the obvious means of a normal ticket with all stopovers included (you will usually find that your stopovers can all be included within the mileage allowance) there are other fares available to those countries with British connections which can show substantial reductions. With the recent introduction of ultra cheap fares between London and the USA it may even be cheaper to travel via New York or Miami. First of all, here is a short explanation of the different fares available:

(1) Advance Booking Charter (ABC): A concept introduced by the British government in 1973 to stamp out illegal ticket discounting. ABCs have become a popular means of visiting the Americas, and are generally the cheapest way. Advance Booking Charter flights are operated to Barbados, Trinidad, Guyana and Jamaica. The minimum stay is two weeks. In the case of Jamaica dates are fixed, so that a four or five week stay is generally the only period possible. In the cases of Barbados and Trinidad you are allowed to stay in the Caribbean area for up to 120 days. There are a few basic rules to which you must adhere:

Your ticket must be booked (outward and return dates) and paid for at least 45 days before departure. In practice you should book before to be sure of getting a seat. Cancellation within 60 days of departure means loss of the full fare (insurance can be taken out to enable you to be refunded if you cancel for a 'genuine reason' such as sickness).

Neither outbound or return date can be altered once booked.

If you miss the plane, you've had it.

In practice all ABC operators use normal scheduled flights on which they have an allocation. This means that you can find yourself sitting next to a passenger who has paid more than twice as much as you for his ticket.

The best known ABC operators are Jetsave (Barbados, Trinidad and Guyana), Laker (Barbados), Airplan (Barbados) and Rainbow Travel (Barbados, Trinidad and Jamaica). For up to date details contact your travel agent.

(2) Earlybird (APEX) Fares: British Airways introduced these low fares in the 60s when most of the Caribbean countries were still British colonies. They are now also available from those Caribbean airlines which fly into London (Caribbean Airways, BWIA, Air Jamaica and, possibly in the near future, International Air Bahama). Available at little more than the cost of ABCs, the conditions appertaining to them are as follows:

Bookings must be made, and paid for, and tickets issued, at least two months before departure (although this has just been reduced to 45 days for some destinations). Minimum stay is 14 days and maximum either 45 or 60, depending on destination. The fares are available only to British residents and those countries to which the

fares are applicable.
There is a cancellation penalty of 25 per cent of the fare.
Reservations can not be changed.
If you miss the return flight your ticket is useless.

The advantage of these fares is that more destinations are available (Bahamas, Jamaica, Antigua, Barbados, Trinidad, Guyana, Saint Lucia). Also it is possible to have an 'open-jaw' ticket — flying into one country and returning from another.

(3) Excursion Fares: Whilst they show savings on normal fares, only a limited number of stopovers are available and excursion fares are subject to a 60 day maximum stay. 'Open-jaw' arrangements are allowed. In practice specialist travel agents can offer fares which are competitive with these.

(4) Caribbean Airways: This airline, the national carrier of Barbados, operates twice weekly flights Luxembourg/London/Barbados and also a weekly direct service London/Barbados. Flights are generally by Boeing 707 aircraft, but often wide-body DC-10 aircraft are used. Standards of service are difficult to fault; traditional Bajan hospitality includes wine with meals, complimentary rum punch and inflight movies and stereo on DC-10 flights. Laker and Airplan are the ABC operators with allocations on Caribbean Airways' services.

In additions to the low ABC and APEX fares Caribbean Airways also offer cheap one way and open return tickets from Luxembourg to Barbados. Whilst these are more expensive than the APEX fares you do have the advantage of flexibility (they are valid for up to a year and an open return is possible). They do not have to be booked in advance.

(5) International Air Bahamas: The best flight I have ever had was from Luxembourg to Nassau on this airline. It is impossible to spend money on the plane: drinks are free, wine is served with meals, and cognac after dinner. I found service of a high standard too. One way and return fares compare favourably with those of other airlines who fly to Nassau.

(6) Via New York or Miami: Sir Freddie Laker's Skytrain has revolutionized travel between the UK and the United States. From London the fare is £70 single or £160 return. However, it is also possible to buy the New York/London ticket in New York for US$159 which at the time of writing makes a fare of £82 including tax. The conditions are that you can buy a ticket only on the day of the flight, so there is a chance of last minute delay. The regulations have recently been amended to eliminate the notorious queues of summer '78: if the flight is full on the day you go to purchase a ticket, you are automatically booked on the first flight which has space available.
Skytrain's success caused the regular airlines flying to the USA to cut their fares dramatically, so that ultra low fares are now available to

many different destinations in the USA. It is not possible to list details here as the situation is constantly changing.

Even more incredibly, there are a number of ABC fares to the USA available from £89 return. For current details check with a knowledgeable travel agent.

Travel Agents: It is always better to consult a good travel agent rather than the airline direct, as the agent is in a better position to give you unbiased information and will be able to advise you of any bargains introduced subsequent to the publication of this work. The following agent specializes in this type of travel and will be able to advise you on your trip and save you money.

Transatlantic Wings Ltd.

70 Pembroke Road, Kensington, London W8 6NX.

Telephone (01) 602 4021.

This company specializes in Transatlantic travel, as its name suggests. It is an agent for Laker, Jetsave, Airplan, Caribbean Airways, International Air Bahamas, etc. and can make any transatlantic flight bookings you require. At the time of writing the author is a director and full-time travel consultant of this company.

Atlantic Crossing: Some Suggestions: You will of course treat all fares quoted below with caution.

Itinerary One: The Bahamas, Jamaica, Haiti, Republica Dominicana Puerto Rico, the Virgin Islands, Antigua, Guadeloupe, Saint Lucia and Barbados. The conventional way of calculating the fares for this journey is to 'break' the fare on a point which would allow all the stopovers within the permitted mileage. In this case it would be Kingston. This would give you, technically, an outward journey of London/Nassau/Montego Bay/Kingston and a return of Kingston/Port-au-Prince/Santo Domingo/San Juan/Saint Thomas/Antigua/Guadeloupe/Saint Lucia/Barbados/London. The low season fare is £541.

This is a case where sector fares would be advantageous. The breakdown is as follows:

London/Miami (standby)	£80 (low season)
Miami to Barbados	$206 + 10%
Barbados/Luxembourg	$215 (low season)

Total fare approximately £312. The fare between Miami and Barbados includes all stopovers: this involves a mileage excess of 10 per cent.

Itinerary Two: The Grand Tour, Bahamas to Trinidad. If the airfare is 'broken' on Kingston there would be a 10 per cent mileage excess on the return section, making a fare of £568. As this is lower than the regular Port of Spain return fare of £572 you would probably be charged the latter. Using sector fares again we would get the following:

London/Miami (standby)	£80 (low season)
Miami to Trinidad	$221 + 10%

Trinidad to Barbados				$52
Barbados/Luxembourg				$215 (low season)

Total fare approximately £349. The fare between Miami and Port of Spain (Trinidad) includes all stopovers and involves a mileage surcharge of 10 per cent.

Itinerary Three: The Western Islands. Your transatlantic flights are best based on an excursion fare to Nassau, SuperApex to Miami or a combination of Nassau and Miami fares. The following table shows current fares.

From	To	Fare Validity	Low Season	High Season
Luxembourg	Nassau	14/45 Day	£195 return	£243.50 return
Luxembourg	Nassau	Youth Fare*	£206 return	£222 return
Luxembourg	Nassau	Budget	£98 single	
Nassau	Luxembourg	Regular	$140.50 single	$162 single
London	Nassau	14/45 Day	£279 return	£357 return
London	Nassau	14/45 APEX	£226.50 return	£261.50 return
London	Miami	7/60 SuperApex	£182 return	£256 return
London	Miami	Standby+	£80 single	£90 single
Miami	London	Standby+	$184 single	$210 single

*Youth fare tickets are valid for up to one year and are available to travellers under 25 or over 55 (no, I'm not joking).

+Standby tickets are not recommended in the summer or around Christmas.

Seasons of travel vary according to the airline and fare basis, but generally high season is July, August, September, December and January.

Sector fares within the Caribbean on this itinerary are as follows: Miami/Nassau $35, Kingston/Port-au-Prince $60, South Caicos/Nassau $84 and Nassau/Montego Bay $79. A round trip is thus possible for less than £300.

Itinerary Four: The Bahamas to the Virgin Islands. The cheapest way to undertake this itinerary is to reverse it. Based on the fares given above, the following is possible.

London/Miami (standby)	£80 (low season)
Miami/San Juan	$78 (low season)
San Juan/Santo Domingo/Port-au-Prince	$61
South Caicos/Nassau	$84
Nassau/Luxembourg	$149.50 (low season)

Total fare approximately £276.

Itinerary Five: The Eastern Caribbean. If you are able to book two months in advance the best method is to take an open jaw APEX, either London/Antigua and Port of Spain/London or London/Antigua and Barbados/London. Low season fares by the first method are £235, and by the second £221. In the first instance you would take a fare Antigua/Port of Spain (including stopovers) of $105 (including estimated 15 per cent mileage excess) and in the second instance a fare Antigua/Barbados of $73 plus Barbados/Trinidad return excursion fare of $52. In both instances your fare will be around £290.

If you have been unable to book in advance, and are travelling out of season, the following is suggested:

London/Miami (standby)	£80
Miami/Antigua to Trinidad	$221
Trinidad/Barbados	$47
Barbados/Luxembourg	$215

Total around £334.

For British Residents: London to Luxembourg: The air fare from London is ridiculously high. Currently it stands at £51.50 single, £103 return, or £77 for a 6 to 30 day excursion. The fare from Luxembourg to London, for travel originating in Luxembourg, is even higher: it is currently £61 one way.

The train fare is about half this figure, around £23. Young people under 26 qualify for a greatly reduced fare of about £11 available from a company called Transalpino. This company has offices near Victoria station (71 Buckingham Palace Road, London SW1, telephone (01) 834 9656) and a kiosk on the station itself (platform 2). Ask for a ticket to 'Tout Gare Belge'. If you do not qualify purchase your ticket from Sealink, Hudsons Place, Victoria Station.

It is best to take the overnight train, the day before your flight. The train takes you to Folkestone where you immediately board the cross-channel ferry for Ostend. Here you take the Brussels train which normally leaves from Platform 6. You may be told to change at Brussels Nord for your train to Luxembourg (normally the 'Grand Ducal') but you may prefer to alight at Brussels Midi where the Grand Ducal commences its journey. You will arrive in Luxembourg around 9 to 10 am.

You will have no difficulty getting from the railway station to the airport. The Luxair terminal is about 100 yards to your right as you leave the station and well signposted. You will need 50 Luxembourg francs (about 85 pence) for the bus fare to the airport. You will find the clerk at the change desk in the airport is well used to changing £1 notes for young airport-bound travellers. There is no airport tax in Luxembourg.

PLEASE NOTE
All fares and flight information given in Appendix One are correct at the time of writing. However, air fares and regulations are notoriously fickle, and so all of the foregoing is provided as a general guide only.

Appendix 2
Useful Addresses

in the USA, p.285   in Canada, p.288   in Europe, p.289

THE UNITED STATES OF AMERICA
   Tourist boards: The following is a selection of the Caribbean countries which have representation in the USA:
The Bahamas
30 Rockefeller Plaza, New York, N.Y. 10020. Tel: (212) 757 1611.
1730 Rhode Island Avenue, N.W, Washington DC 20036.
Tel: (202) 659 9135.
255 Alhambra Circle, Suite 425, Coral Gables, Miami, Florida 33134.
Tel: (305) 442 4860.
510 West Sixth Street, Los Angeles, California 90014.
Tel: (213) 624 7543.
1950 Century Boulevard N.E, Suite 26, Atlanta, Georgia 30345.
Tel: (404) 633 1793.
1027 Statler Office Building, Boston, Massachusetts 02116.
Tel: (617) 426 3144.
875 North Michigan Avenue, Chicago, Illinois 60611.
Tel: (312) 787 8203.
211 North Ervay Street, Dallas, Texas 75201. Tel: (214) 742 1886.
26400 Lahser, Southfield, Detroit, Michigan 48076.
Tel: (313) 353 8954.
Jamaica
866 Second Avenue, New York, N.Y, 10017. Tel: (212) 688 7650.
702 Security Trust Building, 700 Bricknell Avenue, Miami, Florida
33131. Tel: (305) 358 1284.

Suite 2311, Cain Tower, 229 Peachtree Street, N.E, Atlanta, Georgia 30303. Tel: (404) 659 6048.
Suite 1210, 36 South Wabash Avenue, Chicago, Illinois 60603.
Tel: (312) 346 1546.
Suite 100, 1140 Empire Central Drive, Dallas, Texas 75247.
Tel: (214) 630 6931.
107 Northland Towers West, Southfield, Detroit, Michigan 48075.
Tel: (313) 354 4070.
Suite 705, 2 Penn Center Plaza, Philadelphia, Pennsylvania 19102.
Tel: (215) 563 5477.

Haiti
30 Rockefeller Plaza, New York, N.Y, 10020. Tel: (212) 757 3517.
4701 Connecticut Avenue, N.W, Washington DC 20008.
Tel: (202) 244 0141.
420 Lincoln Road, Suite 224, Miami Beach, Florida 33139.
Tel: (305) 531 8831.
1800 Peachtree Center, 230 Peachtree Street N.W, Atlanta, Georgia 30303. Tel: (404) 688 2546.
11 South LaSalle Street, Chicago, Illinois 60603. Tel: (312) 332 0673.

The Cayman Islands
270 Madison Avenue, New York, N.Y, 10016. Tel: (212) 689 7750.
250 Catalonia Avenue, Suite 604, Coral Gables, Florida 33134.
Tel: (305) 444 6551.
2711 West 183 Street, Homewood, Illinois 60430.
Tel: (312) 957 9750.

La Republica Dominicana
Oscar Monegro, 64 West 50th Street, Rockefeller Center, New York, N.Y. 10020.
Marta Pastoriza, 244 Biscayne Boulevard, Miami, Florida 33132.

Puerto Rico
Sperry Rand Buildings, 1290 6th Avenue, New York, N.Y. 10020.
Tel: (212) 541 6630.
1625 Massachusetts Street N.W, Suite 500, Washington DC 20036.
Tel: (202) 387 1837.
10100 Santa Monica Boulevard, Century City, Suite 1520, Los Angeles, California 90067. Tel: (213) 553 4482.
11 East Adams, Suite 902, Chicago, Illinois 60603.
Tel: (312) 922 9701.
2531 Briarcliff Road NE, Suite 215, Atlanta, Georgia 30329.
Tel: (404) 633 1473.

US Virgin Islands
10 Rockefeller Plaza, New York, N.Y. 10020. Tel: 9212) 582 4520.
1050 17th Street NW, Washington DC 20036. Tel: (202) 833 9194.
100 North Biscayne Boulevard, Suite 904, Miami, Florida 33132.
Tel: (305) 371 6382.
307 North Michigan Avenue, Suite 2012, Chicago, Illinois 60601.
Tel: (312) 329 1814.

Appendix 2: Addresses

British Virgin Islands
John Scott Fones Inc., 515 Madison Avenue, New York, N.Y. 10022.
Tel: (212) 371 6759.
Gen Bowman, 5 South Wabash Avenue, Suite 1302, Chicago, Illinois
60603. Tel: (312) 363 2919.
French Antilles
French Government Tourist Office, 610 Fifth Avenue, New York,
N.Y. 10020. Tel: (212) 757 1125.
111 North Wabash Avenue, Chicago, Illinois 60602.
9401 Wiltshire Boulevard, Beverley Hills, California 90212.
323 Geary Street, San Francisco, California 94102.
Antigua
101 Park Avenue, North, Suite 931, New York, N.Y. 10017.
Tel: (212) 683 1075.
Saint Kitts-Nevis (Anguilla)
Caribbean Tourism Association, 20 East 46th Street, New York, N.Y.
10017.
Eastern Caribbean Tourist Association, 40 East 49th Street, New
York, N.Y. 10017.
Montserrat
Eastern Caribbean Tourist Association, 220 East 42nd Street, New
York, N.Y. 10017.
Saint Lucia
220 East 42nd Street, New York, N.Y. 10017. Tel: (212) 867 2950.
Barbados
800 2nd Avenue, New York, N.Y. 10017. Tel: (212) 986 6516.
Grenada
2 Dag Hammarskjdd Plaza, 866 2nd Avenue, Suite 502, New York,
N.Y. 10017. Tel: (212) 759 9675.
Eastern Caribbean Tourist Association, 220 East 42nd Street, New
York, N.Y. 10017. Tel: (212) 986 9370.
3300 NE Expressway, Suite 4-W, Atlanta, Georgia 30341.
Tel: (404) 455 1465.
Saint Vincent and the Grenadines
c/o the Eastern Caribbean Association (see addresses above).
Trinidad and Tobago
400 Madison Avenue, New York, N.Y. 10017. Tel: (212) 838 7750.
Suite 701, 200 SE 1st Street, Miami, Florida 33131.
Suite 100, 280 Canton Avenue West, Winter Park, Florida 32789.
Tel: (305) 628 5070.
Curacao
604 Fifth Avenue, New York, N.Y. 10020. Tel: (212) 265 0230.
495 Biltmore Way, Suite 408, Coral Gables, Florida 33134.
Tel: (305) 444 1621.
   Airlines: Here are the telephone numbers of some of the
Caribbean area airlines with offices in the USA:

Air Jamaica
New York: 688 1212 (19 East 49th Street) Also 421 9750.
Miami: 866 7325 (228 71st Street). Also 358 1121.
Chicago: 782 0996 (60 East Monroe Street). Also 527 3923.
Philadelphia: 563 8844 (1725 JFK Boulevard). Also 567 7560.
Bahamasair
New York: (212) 986 3960.
Miami: (305) 379 2843 (228 SE 1st Street). Also (305) 442 8585.
Los Angeles. (213) 466 8464.
Chicago: (312) 372 9227.
Dallas: (214) 350 1641.
BWIA
New York: (212) 581 3200 (5 West 49th Street).
Miami: (305) 371 5593 (202 SE 1st Street).
Chalk's Airlines
Miami: (305) 377 8801 (Watson Island).
Eastern Airlines
New York: 986 5000. Washington DC: 393 4000. Miami: 873 3000.
Los Angeles: 380 2070. Chicago: 467 2900. Atlanta: 435 1111.
Mackey International Airlines
Miami: (305) 949 4153. Fort Lauderdale: (305) 525 2901.
West Palm Beach: (305) 833 6431.

CANADA
Tourist boards: Here is a list of those countries which have tourist board offices in Canada:
Bahamas
1255 Phillips Square, Montreal, Quebec H3B 3GI.
Tel: (514) 861 6797.
85 Richmond Street West, Toronto, Ontario M5H 2C9.
Tel: (416) 363 4441.
Jamaica
Suite 211, 1118 Saint Catherine Street West, Montreal 1, Quebec.
Tel: (514) 861 1538.
Suite 507, 2221 Yonge Street, Toronto, Ontario M4S 2B4.
Tel: (416) 482 7850.
Haiti
Place Bonaventure, Floor F, University Street, Montreal, Quebec.
Tel: (514) 871 8993.
15 Toronto Street. Suite 805, Toronto, Ontario. Tel: (416) 361 0684
Puerto Rico
10 King Street East, Suite 501, Toronto 210, Ontario.
Tel: (416) 367 0190.
French Antilles
Services Officiels Francais du Tourisme, 1840 Rue Sherbrooke Ouest, Montreal. Tel: (514) 931 3855.

Appendix 2: Addresses

Antigua
21 St. Clair Avenue East, Suite 1104, Toronto M4T 1L9, Ontario.
Tel: (416) 961 3085.
Saint Kitts-Nevis (Anguilla)
Eastern Caribbean Commission, 8 Frontenac Street, Place
Bonaventure, Montreal 114.
International Recreations Inc, 1243 Islington Avenue, Suite 713,
Toronto, Ontario M8X IIY9.
Montserrat
William Currie Esq, Montserrat Tourist Board, PO Box 494,
Station A, Toronto M5W 1E4. Tel: (416) 922 7318.

Saint Lucia
151 Bloor Street West, Toronto, Ontario. Tel: (416) 961 5606.
Barbados
11 Kings Street West, Suite 1108, Toronto, Ontario M5H 1A3.
Tel: (416) 869 0600.
Grenada
Mr Jack N Oldham, Director/Editor, Oldham Editorial Services,
Box 209, Pt Credit Postal Station, Mississauga, Ontario L5G 4L8.
Tel: (416) 278 3086.
Saint Vincent and the Grenadines
Editorial Services Ltd, 980 Yonge Street, 3rd Floor, Toronto 285.
Trinidad and Tobago
145 King Street & West University Avenue, Toronto, Ontario
M5H 1J8. Tel: (416) 863 0300.
Curacao
8 King Street East, Toronto, Ontario 201. Tel: (416) 364 7617.
    Airlines: Here are some airline telephone numbers:
Air Jamaica
Toronto: 366 3711 (Royal York Hotel, 100 Front Street West).
Also 363 0061.
Bahamasair
Toronto: (416) 923 4273.
BWIA
Toronto: (416) 863 9595 (York Centre, 145 King Street West).

EUROPE
    Tourist boards: This is a selection of Caribbean area tourist
boards in Europe:
Bahamas
23 Old Bond Street, London W1X 4PQ, England. Tel: (01) 629 5238.
Zimmerweg 10, 6000 Frankfurt am Main, West Germany
Tel: 722 123.
Jamaica
6/10 Bruton Street, London W1. Tel: (01) 493 3647.
Friedenstrasse 7, 6000 Frankfurt am Main, West Germany.
Tel: (0611) 234 741.

Caribbean Island Hopping

Haiti
17 Queens Gate, London SW7 5JE (10 am to 1 pm).
Tel: (01) 581 0577.
Cayman Islands, British Virgin Islands, Turks and Caicos Islands
18 Grosvenor Street, London W1X 0HP, England. Tel: (01) 629 6353.
Puerto Rico
United States Travel Service, 22 Sackville Street, London W1X 2EA.
Rossemarket 14, Frankfurt Main, West Germany. Tel: (0611) 291 483.
French Antilles
FRANCE, 178 Piccadilly, London W1. England. Tel: (01) 493 3171.
Commissariat a la Promotion des Investissements dans les DOM-TOM,
83 Boulevard de Montparnasse, Paris 75006, France. Tel: 325 8040.
Services Officiels Francais de Tourisme, Goetheplatz 5, Frankfurt
Main, West Germany. Tel: 28 1801.
Antigua, Saint Kitts-Nevis (Anguilla), Montserrat, Saint Lucia,
Grenada, Saint Vincent and the Grenadines.
Eastern Caribbean Tourist Association, 200 Buckingham Palace Road,
London SW1W 9TJ, England. Tel: (01) 730 6221.
Barbados
c/o Barbados High Commission, 6 Upper Belgrave Street, London,
England. Tel: (01) 235 2449.
Munchner Str. 42, 6000 Frankfurt am Main, West Germany.
Tel: (06111) 284157.
Grenada
Mr Peter Capeller, Director Grenada Tourist Office, 8 Munchen 90,
Geiselgasteigstr. 130a, West Germany.
Trinidad and Tobago
20 Lower Regent Street, London SW1Y 4PH. Tel: (01) 839 7155.
    Airlines: Here are some details of those airlines mentioned in
Appendix One:
Air Jamaica
6 Bruton Street, London W1, England. Tel: (01) 493 4455 &
499 6802.
6000 Frankfurt/Main, Friedenstrasse 7, West Germany.
Tel: (0611) 234 491 & 250 131.
BWIA
20 Lower Regent Street, London, England. Tel: (01) 839 7155.
Caribbean Airways
6/10 Bruton Street, London W1. Tel: (01) 493 6251.
Thistle Air, 129 King Street, Kilmarnock, Ayrshire KA1 1QN,
Scotland. Tel: Kilmarnock 27476 & 29259.
11 Rue Tronchet, Paris 8e. France. Tel: 265 1581.
Air Charter Market, Bleichstrasse 12, 6000 Frankfurt/Main 1.
Tel: (0611) 284 157.
Findel Airport, Luxembourg. Tel: 479 8455.
International Air Bahamas
73 Grosvenor Street, London W1X 9DD. Tel: (01) 499 9971 & 6721.

Index to Place Names

Index to Place Names

Jamaica, isl, 14, 15, 22-9 passim,
 30, 31, 32, 33, 76-109, 132,
 135, 273-284 passim
Jeremie, Hai, 116-17

Kendal, Jam, 81
Kenscoff, Hai, 126
Kingston, Jam, 30, 75, 79, 81, 83,
 97-105, 108, 137, 140, 144
Kingstown Saint Vincent, 234,
 236-38, 240

Little Cayman, isl, 135
London, GB, 20, 28, 153, 178,
 279-284 passim
Long Island, Bah, 63-4
Love Hill, Andros, Bah, 71
Luxembourg, 28, 251, 253, 273,
 279-284 passim

Manchester, Jam, 95
Mandeville, Jam, 76, 79, 81, 91-7
Mangrove Cay, Andros, Bah, 64
Marie Galante, isl F Ant, 15, 213
Marigot, Saint Martin, F Ant, 201,
 215
Martinique, isl, F Ant, 15, 22-9
 passim, 189, 221-224, 273-284
 passim
Mastic Point, Andros, Bah, 64, 66-71
Matthew Town, Great Inagua, Bah, 73
Maxwell, Bar, 251
May Pen, Jam, 81
Mayaguana, isl, Bah, 132
Mayaguez, PR, 156
Miami, USA, 26, 30, 55, 132. 135,
 137, 140, 142
Middlesex, Jam, 76
Milot, Hai, 131
Montego Bay, Jam, 30, 75, 76, 83,
 84-91, 108
Montserrat, isl, 14, 22-9 passim, 198,
 210-13, 273-284 passim
Moscow, USSR, 144
Moule, Guadeloupe, F Ant, 217
Mustique, isl, Gren, 240, 241

Nassau, New Providence, Bah 30, 36,
 39-49, 55, 57, 73, 74-5, 132, 275
Negril, Jam, 79, 83 91-4
Nevis, isl, 22-9 passim, 192-93, 195
 273-284

New Providence isl, Bah, 31, 39-49,
 75
New York, USA, 26, 178, 274,
 275-76, 277-278
Nicholls Town Andros, Bah, 64
Nueva Gerona, Cuba. 144

Ocho Rios, Jam, 81, 83, 90, 107

Paradise Island, New Providence,
 Bah, 45-6
Parrot Cay, isl, T&C, 135
Peter Island, BVI, 185
Petionville, Hai, 126
Petit Marigot, Dominica, 226
Petit Martinique, isl, Gren, 240
Philipsburg, Sint Maarten, D Ant,
 216
Pine Cay, isl, T&C, 135
Plymouth, Montserrat, 211-12
Pointe-a-Pitre, Guadeloupe, F Ant,
 216, 217-222
Ponce, PR, 156
Port Antonio, Jam, 81, 105-6, 108
Port au Prince, Hai, 30, 108, 116-17,
 118-26, 126-9, 271
Port of Spain, Trinidad, 144, 155,
 268
Port Royal, Jam, 104-5
Providence, USA, 178
Providenciales, isl, T&C, 134-5
Puerta Plata, Dom Rep, 30, 148, 152
Puerto Rico, isl, 16, 22-9 passim, 30,
 32, 142, 153-68, 273-284

Rabat Israel, 144
Reading. Jam, 91
Red Bay Village, Andros, Bah, 64
Republica Dominicana see under
 Dominican Republic
Roadtown, Tortola, BVI, 179, 181-5
Rock Sound, Eleuthera, Bah 57,
 59-60
Roseau Dominica, 226
Runaway Bay, Jam, 107

Saint Barthelemy, isl, F Ant, 15,
 216-17
Saint Croix, isl, USVI, 168, 174-6,
 185
Saint-Francois, Guadeloupe, F Ant.
 217

293

ABOUT THE AUTHOR

Since graduating from Wolverhampton College of Art in 1970, Frank Bellamy has worked in the travel business, for two 'package tour' companies, overland companies, and finally for agencies specialising in transatlantic travel. His employment has been punctuated by transatlantic visits to write and research travel books. He is currently a director of Transatlantic Wings, a company specialising in arranging inexpensive travel to the Americas and holidays to the Caribbean.

Also in the Island Hopping Series in Sphere Books:

GREEK ISLAND HOPPING by Dana Facaros
MEDITERRANEAN ISLAND HOPPING: The Spanish Islands
by Dana Facaros and Michael Pauls
MEDITERRANEAN ISLAND HOPPING: The Italian Islands,
Corsica/Malta, by Dana Facaros and Michael Pauls
SCOTTISH ISLAND HOPPING by Jemima Tindall